# Global Dynamics of Social Policy

**Series Editors**
Lorraine Frisina Doetter
University of Bremen
Bremen, Germany

Delia González de Reufels
University of Bremen
Bremen, Germany

Kerstin Martens
University of Bremen
Bremen, Germany

Marianne Sandvad Ulriksen
University of Southern Denmark
Odense, Denmark

## About the Series

The intervention of states in fields such as health, social security and work, dates back to the nineteenth century, and became more dynamic over time. Imperial Prussia, a social policy pioneer, first showcased its progress at the Paris World Fair in 1900: the Prussian exhibit drew large crowds eager to find out more about state pensions. Clearly, social policy had become a matter of great interest to states and citizens alike.

Other nations soon embarked on implementing discrete social policies, thus turning the twentieth century into a time of remarkable welfare state expansion. The end of World War II marked a new departure, as an increasing number of countries outside the Western hemisphere began to introduce social policy measures. States not only copied established forms of welfare, but often developed measures *sui-generis* to meet their specific needs. While episodes of policy retrenchment and ruptures can be observed over time, recent developments point to an expansion of social policies in low-to-upper-middle-income countries of the Global South. Social policy has thus become a global phenomenon.

It is generally accepted that the state is responsible for welfare and that domestic politics and ideas have been a primary driver of its expansion. However, in an increasingly interconnected world, social policy is implemented at the national-level but influenced by international developments and relations. It is shaped by trade, migration, war, and colonialism. Just as people travel, policy ideas follow. These factors merit scholarly attention and demand interdisciplinary collaboration to generate new insights into the global dimension of social policy.

This is what the Global Dynamics of Social Policy book series sets out to accomplish. In doing so, it also contributes to the mission of the Collaborative Research Center 1342 (CRC) "Global Dynamics of Social Policy" at the University of Bremen, Germany. Funded by the German Research Foundation, the CRC leaves behind the traditionally OECD-focused analysis of social policy to stress the transnational interconnectedness of developments.

The book series showcases scholarship by colleagues worldwide who are interested in the global dynamics of social policy. Studies can range from in-depth case studies, comparative work and large quantitative research. Moreover, the promotion of scholarship by young researchers is of great importance to the series.

The series is published in memory of Stephan Leibfried to whom our research on state and social policy at the CRC is indebted in countless ways.

Series Editors:
Lorraine Frisina Doetter, Delia González de Reufels,
Kerstin Martens, Marianne S. Ulriksen

More information about this series at
http://www.palgrave.com/gp/series/16294

Open access of this publication was made possible through funding by the Collaborative Research Center 1342: Global Dynamics of Social Policy at the University of Bremen, funded by the Deutsche Forschungsgemeinschaft (DFG, German Research Foundation) – Projektnummer 374666841 – SFB 1342 and Specialised Information Service Political Science – POLLUX.

Carina Schmitt
Editor

# From Colonialism to International Aid

External Actors and Social Protection in the Global South

*Editor*
Carina Schmitt
SOCIUM Research Center on Inequality and Social Policy
University of Bremen
Bremen, Germany

ISSN 2661-8672     ISSN 2661-8680   (electronic)
Global Dynamics of Social Policy
ISBN 978-3-030-38199-8     ISBN 978-3-030-38200-1   (eBook)
https://doi.org/10.1007/978-3-030-38200-1

© The Editor(s) (if applicable) and The Author(s) 2020. This book is an open access publication
**Open Access** This book is licensed under the terms of the Creative Commons Attribution 4.0 International License (http://creativecommons.org/licenses/by/4.0/), which permits use, sharing, adaptation, distribution and reproduction in any medium or format, as long as you give appropriate credit to the original author(s) and the source, provide a link to the Creative Commons licence and indicate if changes were made.
The images or other third party material in this book are included in the book's Creative Commons licence, unless indicated otherwise in a credit line to the material. If material is not included in the book's Creative Commons licence and your intended use is not permitted by statutory regulation or exceeds the permitted use, you will need to obtain permission directly from the copyright holder.
The use of general descriptive names, registered names, trademarks, service marks, etc. in this publication does not imply, even in the absence of a specific statement, that such names are exempt from the relevant protective laws and regulations and therefore free for general use.
The publisher, the authors and the editors are safe to assume that the advice and information in this book are believed to be true and accurate at the date of publication. Neither the publisher nor the authors or the editors give a warranty, expressed or implied, with respect to the material contained herein or for any errors or omissions that may have been made. The publisher remains neutral with regard to jurisdictional claims in published maps and institutional affiliations.

This Palgrave Macmillan imprint is published by the registered company Springer Nature Switzerland AG.
The registered company address is: Gewerbestrasse 11, 6330 Cham, Switzerland

# Acknowledgments

The book volume is based on a symposium held at the University of Bremen in June 2018. The symposium "Building Social Protection Systems in the Global South: Different Trajectories and the Influence of External Factors" brought together experts on social policy in developing countries. It aimed at improving our understanding of the role of external actors and transnational relationships for the formation, development and transformation of social protection in the Global South. I am very grateful to the symposium participants, who significantly contributed with their expertise and experience in moving the book volume forward, and to a number of people without whom the realization of this book volume would not have been possible. My special thanks go to Judith Ebeling who perfectly organized the symposium and contributed significantly to the content alignment of the workshop. I also extend my sincere appreciation to Maria Ignatova who devoted considerable energy to this book project, especially in the final stages of the editing process. Last but not least, I would like to thank Bastian Becker, Amanda Shriwise and Herbert Obinger for their comments which significantly helped to improve the coherence and substance of this book volume.

# Praise for *From Colonialism to International Aid*

"With few exceptions, social policy scholars have ignored the impact of European imperialism and colonialism on social welfare in the Global South. This book seeks to fill the gap by discussing the way social protection in many developing countries has been affected by the colonial legacy. It also examines the current role of international aid in perpetuating Western influences. It makes an important contribution and deserves to be widely read."
—James Midgley, Professor, *University of California Berkeley, USA*

"This volume opens a new frontier in global social policy research, the study of post-colonial countries. Colonizing powers structured social policy regimes in their colonies well before the formation of the World Bank or ILO. These legacies live on today in different approaches to social protection and many other areas. This book does a great service by exploring different forms and types of influence, extending the study of global social policy back in time and outwards in geographical scope."
—Mitchell A. Orenstein, Professor, *University of Pennsylvania, USA*

"This volume is a broad and comprehensive study of the drivers and outcomes of social protections in developing economies. The authors carefully explore the roles of domestic, external, transnational actors, as well as the impacts of historical legacies in the development (or not) of much needed social policies in the Global South. By providing new perspectives and focusing on countries that most scholarship has ignored, this volume is bound to make a significant impact in the literature."
—Nita Rudra, Professor, *Georgetown University, USA*

# Contents

**Part I  Introduction**     1

1   External Actors and Social Protection in the Global South: An Overview     3
*Carina Schmitt*

2   Advancing Transnational Approaches to Social Protection in the Global South     19
*Amanda Shriwise*

**Part II  The Influence of the Colonial Legacy and Cold War on Social Protection**     43

3   Cold War and Social Protection in Burma and Malaysia     45
*Michele Mioni and Klaus Petersen*

4   The Influence of Colonialism and Donors on Social Policies in Kenya and Tanzania     79
*Daniel Künzler*

x    Contents

5   The Effects of Colonialism on Social Protection in South
    Africa and Botswana                                            109
    *Jeremy Seekings*

6   The Colonial Legacy and the Rise of Social Assistance in
    the Global South                                               137
    *Carina Schmitt*

7   Colonial Legacies in International Aid: Policy Priorities
    and Actor Constellations                                       161
    *Bastian Becker*

Part III   The Influence of Donors on Social Protection           187

8   International Donors and Social Policy Diffusion in the
    Global South                                                   189
    *Marina Dodlova*

9   The World Bank and the Contentious Politics of Global
    Social Spending                                                221
    *Rahmi Çemen and Erdem Yörük*

10  The Limits of the Influence of International Donors:
    Social Protection in Botswana                                  245
    *Isaac Chinyoka and Marianne S. Ulriksen*

11  External Donors and Social Protection in Africa: A Case
    Study of Zimbabwe                                              273
    *Stephen Devereux and Samuel Kapingidza*

## Part IV   Critical Reflections and Conclusion         303

12  Transnational Actors and the Diffusion of Social Policies:
    An Ideational Approach                               305
    *Privilege Haang'andu and Daniel Béland*

13  Transnational Actors and Institutionalization of Social
    Protection in the Global South                       333
    *Armando Barrientos*

14  Critical Assessment and Outlook                      357
    *Carina Schmitt, Bastian Becker, Judith M. Ebeling, and
    Amanda Shriwise*

Index                                                    377

# Notes on Contributors

**Armando Barrientos** is Professor Emeritus of Poverty and Social Justice at the Global Development Institute, University of Manchester. He is a Mercator Fellow at CRC 1342 'Global Dynamics of Social Policy' at the University of Bremen. He was Co-Director of the International Research Initiative on Brazil and Africa. His research interests focus on the linkages existing between welfare programs and labor markets and on emerging welfare institutions in developing countries.

**Bastian Becker** is a post-doctoral researcher within the ERC Starting Grant Project "The Legacy of Colonialism: Origins and Outcomes of Social Protection" at SOCIUM Research Center on Inequality and Social Policy, University of Bremen. His research focuses on the political economy of inequality, redistribution and development. Bastian completed his PhD in political science at Central European University (Budapest). He previously taught courses at Bard College Berlin and worked for the German Development Institute, German International Cooperation and Institute of Development Studies.

**Daniel Béland** is Director of the McGill Institute for the Study of Canada and James McGill Professor in the Department of Political Science at McGill University (Montreal, Canada). A student of social and fiscal policy, he has written more than 140 articles in peer-reviewed journals such as *Governance, Journal of Social Policy, Political Studies,*

*Policy & Politics*, *Social Policy & Administration* and *Social Politics*. He has also written more than 15 books, including *An Advanced Introduction to Social Policy* (Edward Elgar, 2016; with Rianne Mahon) and *Obamacare Wars: Federalism, State Politics, and the Affordable Care Act* (University Press of Kansas, 2016; with Philip Rocco and Alex Waddan).

**Rahmi Çemen** is a PhD candidate in Comparative Politics at the University of Florida and a research assistant for the ERC Grant Project: "Emerging Welfare". His research investigates the Europeanization of immigration policies and social policy in emerging markets.

**Isaac Chinyoka** is DST-NRF South African Chair Welfare and Social Development Postdoctoral Research Fellow at the Centre for Social Development in Africa, University of Johannesburg in South Africa and a Yale University Fox International Fellowship Associate. His research interests include the political economy of comparative social protection, social policy, poverty, international development, social justice, social movements, public policy, global production networks and child well-being.

**Stephen Devereux** is a research fellow at the Institute of Development Studies at the University of Sussex, UK, where he is Co-Director of the Centre for Social Protection. He also holds the NRF–Newton Fund (SA-UK) Research Chair in Social Protection for Food Security, affiliated to the DST–NRF Centre of Excellence in Food Security and the Institute for Social Development at the University of the Western Cape, South Africa. He is currently a Mercator Fellow at the University of Bremen, Germany. His work is supported by the National Research Foundation of South Africa (Grant Number: 98411) and the Newton Fund, administered by the British Council.

**Marina Dodlova** is an assistant professor at the Chair of Development Economics of the University of Passau. Her research interests include the political economy of development, institutional and public economics. Her recent projects focus on the politics of social assistance and redistribution policies, impacts of external shocks such as natural disasters on development outcomes and the link between social policies and political participation and violence. Her work is supported by the TMENA2 project funded by the French National Research Agency (ANR) (No.ANR-17-CE39-0009-01).

**Judith M. Ebeling** is a PhD student within the ERC Starting Grant Project "The Legacy of Colonialism: Origins and Outcomes of Social Protection" at SOCIUM Research Center on Inequality and Social Policy, University of Bremen. She holds an MSc in Development Management from London School of Economics and Political Science (LSE).

**Privilege Haang'andu** works as a regional director for Development and Peace-Caritas Canada in charge of Saskatchewan and Keewatin Le-Pas in Manitoba. He holds a PhD from the Johnson-Shoyama Graduate School of Public Policy at the University of Saskatchewan, a Masters' degree in Political Science from Marquette University in Wisconsin and a Bachelor of Arts Honors degree in Political Philosophy from the University of Zimbabwe. Prior to starting his doctoral studies in Public Policy, Priva spent several years working as a governance advisor at the United States Department of State where he researched and drafted several annual Department of State Human Rights Reports on Zambia. He has also worked with several civil society organizations in Zambia, among them, the Jesuit Centre for Theological Reflection. Although Priva has published on a range of topics, his research passion is policy transnationalization with specific interest in the role of ideas in policy change.

**Samuel Kapingidza** is a post-doctoral research fellow at the Centre for Social Development in Africa (CSDA), University of Johannesburg. His research focuses on the political economy of social protection in sub-Saharan Africa. Samuel completed his PhD in 2018 at the Institute for Social Development at the University of the Western Cape in South Africa. He has several years of working experience in both the government and non-governmental sectors.

**Daniel Künzler** is a lecturer at the Department of Social Work, Social Policy and Global Development, University of Fribourg. He is working on the dynamics and politics of social policies in Kenya and colonial legacies and social policies in Middle Africa. His general research interests are social policy in sub-Saharan Africa and popular culture, with a special focus on Eastern Africa.

**Michele Mioni** is a post-doctoral researcher within the DFG-funded project "Universal Conscription, the Military, and Welfare State Development in Western Europe" at SOCIUM Research Center on Inequality and Social Policy, University of Bremen. He is also a research associate at the Centre d'histoire sociale des mondes contemporains, Paris 1 Panthéon-Sorbonne. His research interests cover the relations between social policy, international relations and domestic stabilization. His ongoing research focuses on the links between decolonization, the early Cold War and social security in South East Asia.

**Klaus Petersen** is Professor at the Centre for Welfare State Research & Department of History, University of Southern Denmark. He is also Director at the Centre for Welfare State Research. His research has focused on the historical development of welfare states with special emphasis on Denmark and on the Nordic model. He has also written widely on the relationship between warfare including the Cold War and welfare.

**Carina Schmitt** is Professor of Global Social Policy at the Institute of Political Science, University of Bremen. She is also principal investigator at the ERC Starting Grant Project "The Legacy of Colonialism: Origins and Outcomes of Social Protection" at SOCIUM Research Center on Inequality and Social Policy, University of Bremen. Besides that she is interested in Comparative Politics, Political Economy and Public Policy.

**Jeremy Seekings** is Professor of Political Studies and Sociology and Director of the Centre for Social Science Research at the University of Cape Town. He has written widely on the politics of inequality and public policy in Africa and the Caribbean, both historically and in the present.

**Amanda Shriwise** is a post-doctoral researcher within the ERC Project: "The Legacy of Colonialism: Origins and Outcomes of Social Protection", at SOCIUM Research Center on Inequality and Social Policy, University of Bremen. Her research focuses on the role that social policy plays in foreign policy, international migration and transnational social protection in conjunction with the Transnational Studies Initiative at Harvard University, with a particular focus on the relationship between social protection and health.

**Marianne S. Ulriksen** is an associate professor at the Danish Centre for Welfare Studies, University of Southern Denmark, and affiliated to the Centre for Social Development in Africa (CSDA), University of Johannesburg, as a senior research fellow. Marianne's research areas include comparative politics, political economy of welfare policy development, social protection, social justice, poverty and inequality, mineral wealth and resource mobilization and state–citizens relations. Her research work focuses primarily on Southern and Eastern Africa.

**Erdem Yörük** is an associate professor in the Department of Sociology at Koç University and an associate member in the Department of Social Policy and Intervention at University of Oxford. He is also a member of Young Academy of Europe and an associate editor of European Review. He holds a PhD from the Department of Sociology at Johns Hopkins University (2012), an MA in Sociology and a BSc in Electrical and Electronics Engineering from Boğaziçi University. His work focuses on social welfare and social policy, social movements, political sociology and comparative and historical sociology. His work has been so far supported by the National Science Foundation (NSF), Ford Foundation, European Commission Marie Curie CIG, European Research Council and the Science Academy of Turkey BAGEP. Erdem Yörük is the principle investigator of an ongoing ERC project, Emerging Welfare (emw.ku.edu.tr). He has written articles in *Politics & Society, Governance, World Development, New Left Review, Social Policy and Administration, Current Sociology, South Atlantic Quarterly, New Perspectives on Turkey* and *International Journal of Communication*.

# Abbreviations

| | |
|---|---|
| AFPFL | Anti-Fascist People's Freedom League |
| ANC | African National Congress |
| AusAID | Australian Agency for International Development |
| BBVA | Banco Bilbao Vizcaya Argentaria |
| BDP | Bechuanaland Democratic Party |
| BDP | Botswana Democratic Party |
| BIDPA | Botswana Institute for Development Policy Analysis |
| BTSCS | Binary time series cross section |
| CB-CCT | Community-based conditional cash transfer |
| CCTs | Conditional cash transfers |
| CNTS | Cross-national time series |
| CPF | Child Protection Fund |
| CRPD | Convention of the Rights of Persons with Disabilities |
| CRS | Creditor Reporting System |
| CSG | Child Support Grant |
| CT-OVC | Cash transfers for orphans and vulnerable children |
| DAC | Development Assistance Committee |
| DFID | Department for International Development (UK) |
| ECPR | Emergency Crisis Response Project (Yemen) |
| EMBI Global | Emerging Market Bond Index Global |
| EMEs | Emerging market economies |
| ETF | Education Transition Fund |
| EU | European Union |

# Abbreviations

| | |
|---|---|
| FAO | United Nations Food and Agriculture Organisation |
| FRUS | Foreign Relations of United States |
| FSG | Family Support Grant |
| GIZ | German Institute for International Cooperation |
| GLS | Generalized least squares |
| GNU | Government of National Unity |
| GoB | Government of Botswana |
| GTZ | German Technical Cooperation |
| HSCT | Harmonised social cash transfer |
| HSNP | Hunger Safety Net Programme |
| HTF | Health Transition Fund |
| ICRG | International Crisis Risk Group |
| IDPs | International Development Partners |
| IDS | Institute of Development Studies (UK) |
| IFIs | International financial institutions |
| ILO | International Labour Organization |
| IMF | International Monetary Fund |
| INGOs | International non-governmental organizations |
| IR | International relations |
| JICA | Japan International Cooperation Agency |
| KTA | Knappen Tippets Abbett |
| LMIC | Low- and middle-income countries |
| M&E | Monitoring and evaluation |
| MCA | Malayan Chinese Association |
| MCDSS | Ministry of Community Development and Social Services |
| MCP | Malaysian Communist Party |
| MDC | Movement for Democratic Change |
| MDGs | Millennium Development Goals |
| MENA | Middle East and North Africa |
| MIC | Malayan Indian Congress |
| MIS | Management Information Systems |
| MLG | Ministry of Local Government |
| MNLA | Malayan National Liberation Army |
| MoLSS | Ministry of Labour and Social Services |
| MP | Member of parliament |
| MPSLSW | Ministry of Public Service, Labour and Social Welfare |
| NACA | National AIDS Coordinatory Agency |
| NGOs | Non-governmental organizations |

| | |
|---|---|
| NHIF | National Health Insurance Fund |
| NPF | National Provident Fund |
| NSHIF | National Social Health Insurance Fund |
| NSPP | National Social Protection Policy |
| NSPPF | National Social Protection Policy Framework |
| NSPS | National Social Protection Strategy |
| NSSF | National Social Security Fund |
| NSTP | Non-contributory social transfer programs |
| OCP | Orphan Care Programme |
| ODI | Overseas Development Institute |
| OECD | Organisation for Economic Co-operation and Development |
| OVC | Orphans and vulnerable children |
| PDOs | Organizations of persons with disability |
| PEPFAR | President's Emergency Plan for AIDS Relief |
| PSNP | Productive Safety Net Programme |
| PSSN | Productive Social Safety Net |
| PWP | Public Works Project (Yemen) |
| RADP | Remote Area Development Programme |
| RCT | Randomized control trial |
| RHVP | Regional Hunger and Vulnerable Programme |
| SADC | Southern African Development Community |
| SAPI | Social Assistance, Politics and Institutions |
| SCT | Social cash transfer |
| SCTP | Social Cash Transfer Programme |
| SDC | Swiss Agency for Development and Cooperation |
| SDGs | Sustainable Development Goals |
| SEA | South East Asia |
| SFD | Social Fund for Development (Yemen) |
| SFP | School Feeding Programme |
| SIDA | Swedish International Development Cooperation Agency |
| SOCX | OECD social expenditure database |
| SSA | Sub-Saharan Africa |
| STPA | Short-Term Plan of Action |
| TAP | Technical Assistance Program |
| TASAF | Tanzania Mainland Social Action Fund |
| TNAs | Transnational actors |
| UBR | Unified Beneficiary Registries |
| UMNO | United Malays National Organization |

| | |
|---|---|
| UN | United Nations |
| UNESCO | United Nations Educational, Scientific and Cultural Organization |
| UNDP | United Nations Development Programme |
| UNHCR | United Nations High Commissioner of Refugees |
| UNICEF | United Nations International Children's Emergency Fund |
| UNSC | United Nations Security Council |
| UN-WIDER | United Nations University World Institute for Development Economics Research |
| UPE | Universal Primary Education |
| USAID | United States Agency for International Development |
| VACs | Vulnerability Assessment Committees |
| VGFP | Vulnerable Group Feeding Programme |
| WBSPR | World Bank social policy recommendations |
| WFP | World Food Programme |
| WHO | World Health Organization |
| ZANU-PF | Zimbabwe African National Union-Patriotic Front |
| ZimAsset | Zimbabwe Agenda for Sustainable Socio-Economic Transformation |

# List of Figures

| | | |
|---|---|---|
| Fig. 6.1 | The rise of social assistance | 138 |
| Fig. 6.2 | Effect of democracy by colonial sphere | 154 |
| Fig. 7.1 | Average annual aid flow by donor and colonial legacy, absolute disbursements (2007–2016) | 175 |
| Fig. 7.2 | Average annual aid flow by donor and colonial legacy, share disbursed through government channels (2007–2016) | 176 |
| Fig. 8.1 | Donor assistance and type of transfer. (Compiled by the author on the basis of the NSTP database. If a program is supported by two or more donors, then a donor with a large share of assistance is considered) | 200 |
| Fig. 8.2 | Donor assistance and targeting methods. (Compiled by the author on the basis of the NSTP database) | 202 |
| Fig. 8.3 | Targeting methods employed by different donors. (Compiled by the author on the basis of the NSTP database) | 202 |
| Fig. 9.1 | Average marginal effects of WBSPR I | 235 |
| Fig. 9.2 | Average marginal effects of WBSPR II | 236 |
| Fig. 9.3 | Average marginal effects of WBSPR III | 236 |
| Fig. 11.1 | Share of governments and donors in social assistance funding in Africa. (Source: World Bank 2018, 18. Note: Social assistance programs include "unconditional and conditional cash transfers, noncontributory social pensions, food and in-kind transfers, school feeding programs, public works, and fee waivers" (World Bank 2018, 5)) | 281 |

| | | |
|---|---|---|
| Fig. 11.2 | Sources of financing for social protection in Zimbabwe, 2010 to 2015. (Source: Government of Zimbabwe and World Bank 2016, 15) | 293 |
| Fig. 12.1 | Ideational negotiation vs. reductionist political-institutional policy diffusion. (Notes: **Option A**: Bricolage and translation (through socialization, rationalization and institutionalization); **Option B**: Political institutional approach) | 308 |
| Fig. 12.2 | Demand and supply sides of policy diffusion | 314 |

# List of Tables

| | | |
|---|---|---|
| Table 6.1 | Introduction of social assistance—cross-section analyses | 152 |
| Table 6.2 | Introduction of social assistance—binary time-series cross-section analyses | 155 |
| Table 7.1 | Descriptives of donor-recipient aid flows | 174 |
| Table 7.2 | Linear model results: Total and social aid to former colonies | 177 |
| Table 7.3 | Linear model results: Aid disbursement through governmental channels | 179 |
| Table 8.1 | Number of programs with and without donor assistance by type in the year of starting them | 199 |
| Table 8.2 | Coercion by donor | 205 |
| Table 8.3 | Coercion by donor type | 208 |
| Table 8.4 | Targeting methods promoted by donors | 210 |
| Table 9.1 | Summary statistics | 228 |
| Table 9.2 | Social expenditure and social unrest | 233 |
| Table 9.3 | Social expenditure, social unrest and the World Bank | 234 |
| Table 10.1 | Programme coverage and spending | 249 |
| Table 11.1 | Coverage of the HSCT program in Zimbabwe, 2011–2017 | 288 |

# Part I

Introduction

# 1

# External Actors and Social Protection in the Global South: An Overview

Carina Schmitt

## Introduction

In recent times, social protection has been one of the most popular instruments for promoting human development in the Global South.[1] Understanding contemporary social protection in countries of the Global South requires a deep comprehension of its historical roots and the conditions under which welfare institutions emerged. However, as most research on social protection continues to focus on the Organisation for Economic Co-operation and Development (OECD) world, our knowledge of drivers, characteristics and outcomes of social protection in the Global South is still limited. The existing narrative of welfare state emergence, developed

---

[1] Global South is not a clearly defined term in the literature. In this book volume, we follow the definition by the UN and the World Bank which use the term for low- and middle-income countries.

C. Schmitt (✉)
SOCIUM Research Center on Inequality and Social Policy,
University of Bremen, Bremen, Germany
e-mail: carina.schmitt@uni-bremen.de

for rich democracies with an emphasis on domestic structural conditions and national actors, provides only partial insight into the emergence and structure of social protection systems in other regions of the world. Several studies analyzing social protection in the Global South have emphasized the influence of external national and transnational actors for contemporary social policy-making (Kaasch and Martens 2015; Yeates 2009; Deacon 2007). International bilateral donors, multilateral agencies, international financial institutions, non-governmental organizations (NGOs) and influential nation states are assumed to influence social protection pathways in the Global South.

However, the transnational nature of social protection arrangements in the Global South is also not a new phenomenon. From the very beginning, when social protection was put on the global agenda, especially during and after World War II, social protection arrangements in the Global South have been shaped by external actors. In those days, the international landscape was still characterized by colonial empires (Abernethy 2000), and the great majority of countries in the Global South were still dependent territories. In the course of the twentieth century, colonial powers became more and more engaged in social policies in their colonies because of the pressure from inside the colonies in the form of rising demands for social protection, but also from the outside in the form of soft pressure by international organizations (Schmitt 2015). Following the end of the colonial era and the process of decolonization, the former colonies and other countries of the Global South became major battlegrounds for regime competition between the capitalist and the communist regime during the Cold War. The US, China and the Soviet Union as big global powers tried to bring the emerging nation states into their respective influential spheres. Hence, social policy-making in those days was interfered by the interests and interventions of colonial empires or the communist and Western superpowers.

The influence of external actors did not stop with the end of the Cold War. Even today, social protection in the Global South is influenced by interests and paradigms of international organizations and donors, such as the International Labour Organization (ILO) and the World Bank. Due to their financial resources and administrative capacity, these actors often support social protection programs and legislations

(Kott and Droux 2013; Surender 2013). In fact, international actors have been the "primary and most consistent advocates for expansionism [of social protection, the editor] across the developing world" (Rudra 2015, 464).

However, not all countries react to external pressure in the same way. Social policy models pushed and promoted by external actors have not been simply translated into national policies and institutions but have rather been adapted, mediated and transformed according to national and local conditions. Policy-makers in the Global South have had to find ways of managing, negotiating and asserting themselves when designing social protection systems in a context where often more powerful external actors have been present from the outset. In some countries, national policy-makers withstand the pressure exerted by external actors or even explicitly deviate from policies they were supposed to implement by external actors. Whether and how external actors shape social protection is therefore conditioned by the strength of local political parties, labor unions, but also by domestic financial, administrative and political circumstances. It is therefore important to consider the interplay between external actors and national factors when analyzing social protection pathways in countries of the Global South.

But what exactly does the influence of external actors look like? And how is the influence translated by national factors? Do external actors really shape social protection pathways in a significant way or is their influence overemphasized?

In this volume, we ask whether and how external actors and transnational relationships have influenced the formation, development and transformation of social protection in the developing world. We use a broad definition of social protection, including health and education policies, but also, for example, famine relief and food security programs. A broad definition is more suitable for covering the range of social protection programs existent in the Global South which goes beyond the classical social security programs mainly introduced in Western countries. The edited volume addresses the need to systematically integrate external actors into the narrative of social policy-making in the Global South to enhance our understanding and knowledge of welfare institutions in regions beyond the OECD.

In this book, we focus on a selective range of actors to make cross-case comparisons possible. We elucidate the influence of colonial and Cold War superpowers as examples of the long-lasting influence of external actors on social protection pathways. The book provides insights into how colonial powers and the Cold War superpowers shaped social protection arrangements, for example in order to serve their objectives such as fighting communism or maintain the imperial order. Moreover, we focus on the role of international donors and international financial institutions as the most important contemporary external actors developing and promoting social policies in the Global South. In this volume, scholars applying quantitative frameworks are brought together with others using qualitative techniques. The quantitative analyses provide broad brush pictures that are necessary for evaluating the role of external actors in the transnational social protection arrangements for a larger country sample. The qualitative case studies, in contrast, are essential for identifying how external actors have to be integrated into the social protection actor network, how they intervene in social protection-making, but also to assess the limitations of their influence. We moreover combine historical as well as social science approaches to show how social protection arrangements have ever since been shaped by external actors. This is especially important as knowledge is scarce when analyzing the influence of external actors further back in history. The edited volume furthermore contributes to the literature by explicitly analyzing the interplay between external actors and national conditions as well as by critically assessing the explanatory power of external actors for social protection pathways in the Global South. The volume shows that social policy-making in most countries of the Global South has never been a strictly national story. External actors have been part of social protection decisions from the very outset. However, the influence of external actors has always been translated by national actors and domestic circumstances into social policies and institutions. After all, the volume offers a critical assessment of the role of external actors and discusses ideational and institutional approaches to systematically integrate external actors into the domestic arena of social protection-making in the Global South.

# External Actors and Social Protection in the Global South: State of the Art

The field of social protection in the Global South has attracted growing interest of scholars since the beginning of this century. Several scholars have in the meantime outlined and discussed social protection trajectories in the Global South and provided valuable insights into different social protection pathways in different regions of the world (e.g. Haggard and Kaufman 2008; Huber and Stephens 2012; Rudra 2008; Gough and Wood 2004; Barrientos 2013; Surender and Walker 2013; Midgley and Piachaud 2011). They show that most countries in the Global South have implemented social insurance programs in the first place and demonstrate how social assistance programs have in recent decades spread across countries (Schmitt, Chap. 6, this volume). These studies, mainly stemming from Comparative social policy research, emphasize the role of national actors in social policy-making. Differences in national social protection trajectories have been mainly traced back to different national actor constellations and class coalition building processes. The power resource theory (Korpi 1983) and the closely related partisan theory (Hibbs 1977) argue that labor unions and political parties shape social policy dynamics. Strong left power resources in the executive and legislative are assumed to be key drivers of generous social protection schemes (Castles 1978). Partisan theory (Castles 1982; Schmidt 1982) additionally stresses the importance of Christian democratic parties and political Catholicism for encompassing social policies (van Kersbergen 1995; van Kersbergen and Manow 2009; Manow 2015). Furthermore, the political economy literature argues that political leaders make use of public policies in general and social policies in particular to create winning coalitions and secure regime survival (Knutsen and Rasmussen 2014). In this view, social protection is an important instrument for governments, especially in authoritarian contexts of non-liberal states, to secure elite privileges in recompense for political loyalty and to legitimate the political system (Magaloni et al. 2007; Rudra and Haggard 2005; Wibbels and Ahlquist 2011). Research on non-Western countries additionally emphasizes that substantial cross-national differences in social policy priorities are related to distinct post-war development strategies, such as import-substitution industrialization and export-oriented industrialization (Rudra 2002, 2007, 2008; Avelino et al. 2005; Barrientos and Santibáñez 2009; Wibbels and Ahlquist 2011). In the context of this tradition, external actors have not been systematically considered or only in a very general and superficial way.

Global social policy as another relevant strand of literature for this book volume, in contrast, takes external actors as the point of departure. Global social policy research has drawn our attention to a broad array of individual and corporate global social policy actors, ranging from internationally operating intergovernmental organizations, in particular the World Bank (Orenstein 2010), the ILO (Supiot 2006; Maupain 2009; Deacon 2013), the OECD (Mahon 2009; Martens and Jakobi 2010) or the EU (Walkenhorst 2008; Lamping and Steffen 2009; Natali 2009), to states formations, such as the G20, as well as South-South relations such as BRICS (Surender 2013) and to NGOs (Martens and Kruse 2015; Stubbs 2003) or business actors (Farnsworth 2012). Studies in this field elucidate the role of international, supranational and transnational organizations. They address the questions of how these organizations have shaped international standards and norms regarding social policy and how these global norms and recommendations feed into the domestic social policy arena (Orenstein 2010; Yeates 2009; Deacon 2013, 2007; Kaasch and Martens 2015). One major strong point of global social policy research is that it has brought forward scholarship on how international organizations produce and disseminate policy ideas across countries and regions. Some contributions, often based on constructivist approaches, have developed conceptualizations of how international organizations exert influence, taking into account that most international organizations, in particular in the field of social policy, are not able to apply hard governance but rather use soft governance mechanisms (Abbott and Snidal 2000). Global social policy research has advanced the understanding that social issues transcend borders, explaining why international organizations can be influential actors (Hulme and Hulme 2008; Jenson 2010). However, the interdependencies between actors at the global and national level have been neither fully grasped in a coherent conceptual manner nor comprehensively and systematically in their empirical existence. Nevertheless, global social policy research reveals the tension between the global perspective of social problem identification and the implementation of social policies at the national level, which we take up in this paper.

In sum, the existing literature offers valuable insights to understand social protection in contexts where powerful external actors have been present from the very outset. However, in each individual case and isolated from each other these approaches are not sufficient for capturing and appropriately situating all actors that are relevant for social protection arrangements. Comparative social policy research mainly focuses on national actors and their preferences and, if at all, only very roughly integrates external economic and political influences. In contrast, global social policy research rather focuses on transnational and international actors relevant for social protection without elucidating domestic politics at the national level. It mainly analyzes the influence of external actors from the perspective of the international organizations, but not from the perspective of the developing countries themselves. What is missing are studies linking both strands of research. Moreover, most of the studies focus on contemporary external actors and social protection, while the historical dimension of external influences on social protection, such as colonialism and Cold War, is almost completely left out of the equation in both strands of literature (e.g. Deacon 2007; Brooks 2015; Rudra 2008) Hence, even though scholars across a range of disciplines have acknowledged and demonstrated the inherently transnational nature of social protection arrangements, our knowledge of the potential and limits of external national and transnational actors as explanatory factors and drivers of social policy-making in the Global South is scarce. This especially applies when going further back in history, to the mid-twentieth century when social protection was put on the global agenda. This volume contributes to existing scholarship by addressing the mentioned shortcomings. In contrast to the existing work, it explicitly focuses on the role of external actors in different periods of time and in relationship to each national context. The book integrates external actors and their interplay with national conditions into the narrative of social policy-making in the Global South to understand the conditions under which social protection has emerged historically and is expanding in the developing world today.

# External Actors from Colonialism to International Aid: Types, Strategies and Objectives

In the literature, different external actors are assumed to influence social protection pathways in the Global South. In this volume we apply a broad notion of what an external actor is. External actors in a broad sense can be understood as collectives of individuals who share an interest in and ability to act together toward a common end. Moreover, they are mainly based outside the territory which they aim to influence (Pontusson 1995; Huber and Stephens 2010). Even though there is no systematic classification of external actors, there are several possible dimensions along which they can be categorized. For example, external actors can be separated according to whether they are governmental or intergovernmental, public or private, or whether they provide technical expertise or financial leverage.

Most of the recent literature within global social policy research, but also within comparative welfare state research, focuses on the role of international donors, international governmental and NGOs. Most of these actors, however, were not always as widely spread as they are today. Especially intergovernmental organizations have been established only in recent decades. When going back further in history, to the colonial and the Cold War era, external actors were very often powerful individual nation states which made use of the power asymmetries to influence policy-making in dependent territories or in their spheres of influence.

Not only the types of actors might have changed over time but also the mechanisms or strategies through which external actors have tried to influence and shape national social protection pathways. Many studies focusing on the role of contemporary international financial institutions, international organizations and governmental donors emphasize the production and spread of knowledge and the provision of technical and financial support (Orenstein 2010; Deacon 2013; Kott and Droux 2013). These strategies can rather be classified as "soft" than as "hard" power instruments, as at least on the surface they do not force domestic actors to implement specific social protection policies against their will. However, during colonial and Cold War times, other strategies might have been important. France, for example, imposed the *Code du Travail* in all its African colonies in 1952. This labor code, strongly related to the social insurance principle, was the basis for initial social security systems in all French African colonies. This strategy can be regarded as a hard form of exerting influence on social protection pathways.

Changes and continuities are not only observable with regard to the type of relevant external actors and their strategies but also with regard to the objectives and preferences connected to social protection. For example, in the aftermath of World War II, the ILO mainly pushed social security legislations strongly related to waged labor. At that time, social security was supposed to protect the worker against risks of unemployment, work accidents, old age or sickness. The colonial powers at least after World War II also emphasized social protection being strongly linked to the workforce. For the superpowers during the Cold War period, however, social reforms often constituted part of anti-communism strategies (Obinger and Schmitt 2011). Nowadays the ILO supports a more social rights-based approach to social protection as it finds expression by the ILO Social Protection Floors Recommendation. The World Bank, in contrast, rather pushes means-tested social assistance. This exemplifies how external actors differ with regard to the specific social protection policies they prefer and with regard to the objectives to be realized by way of social protection.

However, social policy models supported by external actors have almost never been directly translated into national policies and institutions but have rather been adapted, mediated and transformed by national and local conditions. For example, the influence of colonial powers might depend on the domestic factors of the dependent territories, such as economic structure, geographic position and strength of political leaders. In the case of the Cold War superpowers, some political leaders resisted the influence of the Cold War superpowers; others played off both sides against one another, or explicitly deviated from what they were supposed to do. In present times, especially countries that are politically weak or financially dependent might be receptive to the influence of external actors. Tracing this interplay between national conditions and external actors should elucidate some of the domestic framework conditions for the influence of external actors.

In sum, in this book volume we aim at elucidating changes and continuities with regard to types of external actors, their strategies, objectives and social policy preferences as well as their interplay with national factors, from colonialism to international aid.

## Structure of the Book

This volume contains four parts addressing the long-lasting and contemporary role of external actors for social protection-making in the Global South from the post-war period until today.

Part I provides a systematic introduction to the analysis of external actors of social policy-making in the Global South. Apart from this introduction, then following Chap. 2 by *Shriwise* addresses existing theoretical approaches to the analysis of external actors and outlines the theoretical implications of understanding social protection in transnational relief.

Part II addresses the long-lasting influence of colonial and Cold War superpowers on early and contemporary social protection-making in developing countries. Part II consists of five chapters. The first three contributions pursue a qualitative approach, while the final two provide statistical analyses. In Chap. 3 Michele *Mioni* and Klaus *Petersen* shed light on how social reforms were used as an instrument to fight against the respective competing regime in the early Cold War period. To address this question, the authors historically analyze two Asian countries, that is, Burma and Malaysia. They show how debates on the concepts of welfare and social protection in both countries were influenced and challenged by the Cold War logic. In the subsequent Chap. 4 Daniel *Künzler* assesses the influence of colonial powers and donors on social protection arrangements, comparing Kenya and Tanzania. Even though both were British colonies, colonial Kenya was considered a labor reserve, whereas Tanzania was rather a cash crop economy for the British officials. Künzler comes to the conclusion that even though both countries follow similar social protection pathways at the first glance, the scope and extent of social policy instruments differ between both countries. In Chap. 5 Jeremy *Seekings* addresses the role of the British welfare model for social policy-making in colonial and post-colonial times in Botswana and South Africa in the past

70 years. He demonstrates that in neither South Africa nor Botswana foreign models have been imposed but rather considerably adapted to local norms and conditions. External influences entailed primarily the diffusion of ideas which were combined with local ideas to shape policy outcomes. In Chap. 6 *Schmitt* addresses the long-lasting influence of the colonial legacy on contemporary social policy-making for a large country sample including around 100 low- and middle-income countries. Applying a quantitative framework, she shows how the recent rise of social assistance in the Global South depends on the colonial heritage of a country. Social assistance programs are by far more frequent in British colonies than elsewhere, while in former French colonies social assistance is almost completely absent. This is traced back to different notions of both colonial powers regarding social protection. In Chap. 7 *Becker* in his contribution investigates how colonial legacies shape contemporary international aid patterns. He also uses a quantitative framework to answer whether former colonial ties affected aid priorities and whether aid priorities differ between former colonial powers. He demonstrates that former colonial ties become manifest by increased efforts toward supporting social policy projects. Moreover, he shows that these institutional patterns are most visible with regard to the French aid system.

Part III elucidates international donors and international financial institutions as important players in the transnational social policy arena of today. In Chap. 8, by Marina *Dodlova*, the question of how the World Bank and international donors have influenced the spread of non-contributory social transfer programs throughout the countries of the Global South is addressed. She applies a quantitative framework to analyze how donors drive the diffusion of social policy and how they influence the design of social transfer programs, particularly the targeting method used to determine the beneficiary base. Rahmi *Çemen* and Erdem *Yörük* investigate in Chap. 9 whether transnational actors such as the World Bank influence the way in which domestic social unrest is translated into social policy. Their empirical analysis contains a sample of 42 countries from 1989 until 2015. Their results show that efforts on social assistance are larger in countries with high levels of social unrest. In contrast, the influence of the World Bank is limited and only visible in countries with high levels of social unrest. In Chap. 10 Isaac *Chinyoka* and Marianne *Ulriksen* analyze how international donors have attempted to influence child welfare policies in

Botswana. Their analysis highlights that although transnational actors have succeeded with persuading the government in Botswana to change certain policy aspects, they have been unable to fundamentally sway the government to pursue an individual, rights-focused welfare policy paradigm. In Chap. 11 Stephen *Devereux* and Samuel *Kapingidza* analyze whether social protection-making is nationally owned or donor-driven. The international development community has invested heavily in propagating social protection policies and programs throughout Africa in the past 20 years. The authors use the case of Zimbabwe to investigate whether donor agendas on social protection are aligned or in conflict with national priorities. They offer several indicators that allow for evaluating whether a social policy process is nationally defined or donor-driven. All contributions in Parts II and III discuss not only the role of external actors for social policy-making but also their interplay with domestic factors.

Part IV critically evaluates the potential and limits of institutionalist and ideational approaches to the influence of transnational actors. It starts with Chap. 12, by Daniel *Béland* and Priva *Haang'andu*, who propose an ideational approach for elucidating the influence of transnational actors on social policies. Their proposed framework determines the circumstances under which external actors succeed and/or fail to diffuse transnational norms in an ideationally charged socio-political environment. In Chap. 13 Armando *Barrientos* critically assesses the influence of external actors and donors in low and middle-income countries. He asks whether donor agencies are actually shaping social assistance institutions in the Global South or whether their influence has been overrated. The dominance of donor organizations and their global policy agendas as opposed to domestic policy has delayed the theorization of the rapid development of welfare institutions in developing countries. The volume is completed by Chap. 14, by Carina *Schmitt*, Bastian *Becker*, Judith *Ebeling* and Amanda *Shriwise* who summarize the main insights presented by the book. This chapter critically evaluates all contributions of this book volume researching the role of external actors for social protection-making and their interplay with domestic influences. It provides a balanced summary of the relative contributions of external actors and domestic factors to the explanation of social policy-making in the Global South. It also formulates an agenda to inspire future avenues for further research.

# References

Abbott, Kenneth W., and Duncan Snidal. 2000. Hard and Soft Law in International Governance. *International Organization* 54 (3): 421–456. https://doi.org/10.1162/002081800551280.

Abernethy, David B. 2000. *The Dynamics of Global Dominance: European Overseas Empires, 1415–1980*. New Haven, CT: Yale University Press.

Avelino, George, David S. Brown, and Wendy Hunter. 2005. The Effects of Capital Mobility, Trade Openness, and Democracy on Social Spending in Latin America, 1980–1999. *American Journal of Political Science* 49 (3): 625–641. https://doi.org/10.1111/j.1540-5907.2005.00146.x.

Barrientos, Armando. 2013. *Social Assistance in Developing Countries*. Cambridge: Cambridge University Press.

Barrientos, Armando, and Claudio Santibáñez. 2009. New Forms of Social Assistance and the Evolution of Social Protection in Latin America. *Journal of Latin American Studies* 41 (1): 1–26. https://doi.org/10.1017/S0022216X08005099.

Brooks, Sarah M. 2015. Social Protection for the Poorest: The Adoption of Antipoverty Cash Transfer Programs in the Global South. *Politics & Society* 43 (4): 551–582.

Castles, Francis G. 1978. *The Social Democratic Image of Society: A Study of the Achievements and Origins of Scandinavian Social Democracy in Comparative Perspective*. London, Boston: Routledge & K. Paul.

———., ed. 1982. *The Impact of Parties: Politics and Policies in Democratic Capitalist States*. London, Beverly Hills, CA: Sage Publications.

Deacon, Bob. 2007. *Global Social Policy and Governance*. London: SAGE.

———. 2013. *Global Social Policy in the Making: The Foundations of the Social Protection Floor*. Bristol: Policy Press.

Farnsworth, Kevin. 2012. *Social versus Corporate Welfare: Competing Needs and Interests within the Welfare State*. Basingstoke: Palgrave Macmillan.

Gough, Ian, and Geof Wood, eds. 2004. *Insecurity and Welfare Regimes in Asia, Africa and Latin America*. Cambridge: Cambridge University Press.

Haggard, Stephan, and Robert R. Kaufman. 2008. *Development, Democracy, and Welfare States: Latin America, East Asia, and Eastern Europe*. Princeton: Princeton University Press.

Hibbs, Douglas A. 1977. Political Parties and Macroeconomic Policy. *American Political Science Review* 71 (04): 1467–1487. https://doi.org/10.1017/S0003055400269712.

Huber, Evelyne, and John D. Stephens. 2010. *Development and Crisis of the Welfare State: Parties and Policies in Global Markets*. Chicago: University of Chicago Press.

———. 2012. *Democracy and the Left: Social Policy and Inequality in Latin America*. Chicago, IL: University of Chicago Press.

Hulme, Moira, and Rob Hulme. 2008. The International Transfer of Global Social Policy. In *Understanding Global Social Policy*, ed. N. Yeates. Bristol: Policy Press and The Social Policy Association.

Jenson, Jane. 2010. Diffusing Ideas for After Neoliberalism: The Social Investment Perspective in Europe and Latin America. *Global Social Policy: An Interdisciplinary Journal of Public Policy and Social Development* 10 (1): 59–84. https://doi.org/10.1177/1468018109354813.

Kaasch, Alexandra, and Kerstin Martens, eds. 2015. *Actors and Agency in Global Social Governance*. Oxford: Oxford University Press.

Knutsen, Carl Henrik, and Magnus Rasmussen. 2014. The Autocratic Welfare State Resource Distribution, Credible Commitments and Political Survival. *SSRN Electronic Journal*. https://doi.org/10.2139/ssrn.2482593.

Korpi, Walter. 1983. *The Democratic Class Struggle*. London: Routledge.

Kott, Sandrine, and Joëlle Droux, eds. 2013. *Globalizing Social Rights: The Internationalization Labour Organization and Beyond*. Edited by ILO, ILO Century Series. Basingstoke: Palgrave Macmillan.

Lamping, Wolfram, and Monika Steffen. 2009. European Union and Health Policy: The "Chaordic" Dynamics of Integration. *Social Science Quarterly* 90 (5): 1361–1379. https://doi.org/10.1111/j.1540-6237.2009.00659.x.

Magaloni, Beatriz, Alberto Diaz-Cayeros, and Federico Estévez. 2007. Clientelism and Portfolio Diversification: A Model of Electoral Investment with Applications to Mexico. In *Patrons, Clients, and Policies: Patterns of Democratic Accountability and Political Competition*, ed. Herbert Kitschelt and Steven I. Wilkinson. Cambridge, UK, New York: Cambridge University Press.

Mahon, Rianne. 2009. The OECD's Discourse on the Reconciliation of Work and Family Life. *Global Social Policy* 9 (2): 183–204.

Manow, Philip. 2015. Workers, Farmers and Catholicism: A History of Political Class Coalitions and the South-European Welfare State Regime. *Journal of European Social Policy* 25 (1): 32–49. https://doi.org/10.1177/0958928714556969.

Martens, Kerstin, and Anja P. Jakobi. 2010. *Mechanisms of OECD Governance*. Oxford: Oxford University Press. https://doi.org/10.1093/acprof:oso/9780199591145.001.0001.

Martens, Kerstin, and Johannes Kruse. 2015. NGOs as Actors in Global Social Governance. In *Actors and Agency in Global Social Governance*, ed. A. Kaasch and K. Martens, 1st ed. Oxford, UK: Oxford University Press.

Maupain, Francis. 2009. New Foundation or New Facade? The ILO and the 2008 Declaration on Social Justice for a Fair Globalization. *European Journal of International Law* 20 (3): 823–852. https://doi.org/10.1093/ejil/chp070.

Midgley, James, and David Piachaud, eds. 2011. *Colonialism and Welfare. Social Policy and the British Imperial Legacy*. Cheltenham: Edward Elgar.

Natali, David. 2009. *Pensions in Europe, European Pensions: The Evolution of Pension Policy at National and Supranational Level*. New York: P.I.E. Peter Lang.

Obinger, Herbert, and Carina Schmitt. 2011. Guns and Butter? Regime Competition and the Welfare State during the Cold War. *World Politics* 63 (2): 246–270.

Orenstein, Mitchell A. 2010. *Privatizing Pensions: The Transnational Campaign for Social Security Reform*. Princeton: Princeton University Press.

Pontusson, Jonas. 1995. From Comparative Public Policy to Political Economy: Putting Political Institutions in Their Place and Taking Interests Seriously. *Comparative Political Studies* 28 (1): 117–147.

Rudra, Nita. 2002. Globalization and the Decline of the Welfare State in Less-Developed Countries. *International Organization* 56 (2): 411–445. https://doi.org/10.1162/002081802320005522.

———. 2007. Welfare States in Developing Countries: Unique or Universal? *The Journal of Politics* 69 (2): 378–396. https://doi.org/10.1111/j.1468-2508.2007.00538.x.

———. 2008. *Globalization and the Race to the Bottom in Developing Countries: Who Really Gets Hurt?* Cambridge, UK, New York: Cambridge University Press.

———. 2015. Social Protection in the Developing World: Challenges, Continuity, and Change. *Politics & Society* 43: 463–470.

Rudra, Nita, and Stephan Haggard. 2005. Globalization, Democracy, and Effective Welfare Spending in the Developing World. *Comparative Political Studies* 38 (9): 1015–1049. https://doi.org/10.1177/0010414005279258.

Schmidt, Manfred G. 1982. *Wohlfahrtsstaatliche Politik unter bürgerlichen und sozialdemokratischen Regierungen: ein internationaler Vergleich*. Frankfurt/Main, New York: Campus.

Schmitt, Carina. 2015. Social Security Development and the Colonial Legacy. *World Development* 70: 332–342. https://doi.org/10.1016/j.worlddev.2015.02.006.

Stubbs, Paul. 2003. International Non-State Actors and Social Development Policy. *Global Social Policy: An Interdisciplinary Journal of Public Policy and Social Development* 3 (3): 319–348. https://doi.org/10.1177/14680181030033003.

Supiot, Alain. 2006. The Position of Social Security in the System of International Labor Standards. *Comparative Labor Law and Policy Journal* 27 (2): 113–121.

Surender, Rebecca. 2013. The Role of Historical Contexts in Shaping Social Policy in the Global South. In *Social Policy in a Developing World*, ed. R. Surender and R. Walker, 14–36. Cheltenham: Edward Elgar Publishing.

Surender, Rebecca, and Robert Walker, eds. 2013. *Social Policy in a Developing World*. Cheltenham: Edward Elgar.

van Kersbergen, Kees. 1995. *Social Capitalism: A Study of Christian Democracy and the Welfare State*. London, New York: Routledge.

van Kersbergen, Kees, and Philip Manow. 2009. Religion and the Western Welfare State. In *Religion, Class Coalitions, and Welfare States*, ed. Kees van Kersbergen and Philip Manow. Cambridge, New York: Cambridge University Press.

Walkenhorst, Heiko. 2008. Explaining Change in EU Education Policy. *Journal of European Public Policy* 15 (4): 567–587. https://doi.org/10.1080/13501760801996741.

Wibbels, Erik, and John S. Ahlquist. 2011. Development, Trade, and Social Insurance. *International Studies Quarterly* 55 (1): 125–149.

Yeates, Nicola. 2009. *Globalizing Care Economies and Migrant Workers: Explorations in Global Care Chains*. Basingstoke: Palgrave Macmillan.

**Open Access** This chapter is licensed under the terms of the Creative Commons Attribution 4.0 International License (http://creativecommons.org/licenses/by/4.0/), which permits use, sharing, adaptation, distribution and reproduction in any medium or format, as long as you give appropriate credit to the original author(s) and the source, provide a link to the Creative Commons licence and indicate if changes were made.

The images or other third party material in this chapter are included in the chapter's Creative Commons licence, unless indicated otherwise in a credit line to the material. If material is not included in the chapter's Creative Commons licence and your intended use is not permitted by statutory regulation or exceeds the permitted use, you will need to obtain permission directly from the copyright holder.

# 2

# Advancing Transnational Approaches to Social Protection in the Global South

Amanda Shriwise

## Introduction

The suggestion that social protection arrangements have transnational underpinnings is not new (e.g. Yeates 2001). An increasing number of social scientists have recognized the extent to which transnational dynamics, including those surrounding colonialism and conflicts (Obinger et al. 2018; Schmitt 2015; Obinger and Schmitt 2011), have affected the emergence of social protection systems and welfare regimes (Wood and Gough 2006). Transnational actors, such as international non-governmental organizations, multi- and transnational corporations, trade unions and Churches, continue to impact social protection arrangements in the Global South as they have since colonial times, and indeed much of the literature on social protection has focused on the role of these actors (Deacon 2007, 2013a, b). Furthermore, both national (Slaughter

---

A. Shriwise (✉)
SOCIUM Research Center on Inequality and Social Policy,
University of Bremen, Bremen, Germany
e-mail: shriwise@uni-bremen.de

2004) and intergovernmental (Cronin 2002) actors have been recognized as having the ability to act transnationally, despite their respective national and international governance arrangements.

Transnational perspectives are not meant to replace a focus on national actors and domestic conditions but rather to complement them and to promote a more comprehensive understanding of social policymaking, particularly in cases where external actors may be pivotal. While recognizing the transnational nature of a number of social problems, intergovernmental efforts to address them rightly acknowledge the continued salience of the nation state and national actors. Both the International Labour Organization's emphasis on establishing social protection floors and the World Health Organization's push to achieve universal health coverage focus on working with countries to achieve these goals in the context of the United Nations (UN) 2030 Agenda for Sustainable Development. Equally, the 2030 Agenda stresses the need to build strong partnerships and institutions to support implementation efforts in countries by working transnationally, including through the promotion of effective public-private partnerships as well as through partnerships with international non-governmental and civil society organizations (United Nations General Assembly 2017).

This chapter examines how transnational approaches to social protection can advance our understanding of welfare arrangements in the Global South in a way that maximizes contributions to theory-building. Using a transnational lens to examine the key actors and institutions affecting social protection arrangements can help to illuminate the origins, asymmetries and ideas that have impacted these arrangements in the Global South. The chapter argues that transnational approaches must move beyond a recognition that context matters in policymaking to identifying causal patterns that can inform social policymaking on a global scale. While transnational perspectives are not a panacea for problems within the social policy literature, they are a necessary first step toward advancing theoretical development in ways that are empirically grounded and relevant for policymaking in the present.

The chapter proceeds as follows. First, it reviews understandings of the transnational across relevant disciplines to find common ground. Then, in the third section, the chapter defines transnational actors and their relationship to global institutions with respect to social protection. The fourth section examines how analyzing the dynamics of transnational actor constellations might contribute to theory-building by identifying causal patterns across country cases in relation to recent advances in social protection in the Global South. The final section concludes by summarizing these interdisciplinary insights and reflecting on how they can best support theory and practice in the area of social protection.

## Understandings of the Transnational: Finding Common Ground

Transnational approaches to social policy have been described as a "means of revealing the constructed parameters of the 'national'" (Yeates and Irving 2005, 403). As argued by Clarke (2005, 414), "The idea of the transnational draws our attention to processes that *work in and across* nations". As an inherently interdisciplinary area of study, viewing social policy through a transnational lens can mean different things to scholars from different disciplines. This section explores the range of definitions of the transnational employed by sociologists, political scientists and international relations (IR) as well as legal scholars that are relevant for understanding the emergence of social protection in the Global South.

Sociologists take a broad approach to the transnational, understanding it as the study of social structures and processes that transcend or go beyond the national, often with a focus on the way in which the global and the national are constituent parts of each other. For example, as described by Sassen (2006, 2010, 1–2), "the global—whether an institution, a process, a discursive practice, an imaginary—both transcends the elusive framing of national states and also partly emerges and operates within that framing. … Further, if the global gets partly structured inside the national, then the methodological and theoretical challenges to state-centric social sciences will be different from those posed by the common binary of global vs. national."

Sociologists also make strong distinctions between state and society, which opens up space for considering: (1) societal relationships beyond national borders, (2) how national actors impact social protection beyond their geo-political boundaries and (3) how transnational actors and transnational social movements affect policymaking. The need to view social protection through a transnational lens has been emphasized by migration scholars in particular, whose work stems largely from a recognition that a growing number of individuals and families are socially embedded in multiple societies across national boundaries (Levitt and Jaworsky 2007; Levitt and Nyberg-Sørensen 2004; Levitt 2001). This research illuminates how the production and acquisition of social protection is distinct for individuals and families living transnational lives in ways that concepts such as social citizenship and the study of national welfare regimes does not fully capture and may even occlude (Faist et al. 2015; Levitt et al. 2017).

When examining transnational dynamics, political scientists and IR scholars focus on governance and have increasingly taken an actor-centric approach. Global social governance has been defined as "a multi-actored process of shaping global and national social policies" (Kaasch and Martens 2015, 7). Here, the global and national are distinguished by both the level at which such policymaking processes take place and the scale on which they seek to make an impact. In a global governance context, policymaking occurs within "political arrangements which rely primarily on non-hierarchical forms of steering. … In other words, governance beyond the nation-state means creating political order in the absence of a state with a legitimate monopoly over the use of force and the capacity to enforce the law and other rules authoritatively" (Risse 2006, 180).

The IR literature distinguishes between two types of global governance arrangements affecting global and national policymaking, depending on the actors involved: intergovernmental and transnational. Intergovernmental governance refers to processes in which states seek to move behavior toward a shared public goal; transnational governance refers to the same process but for non-state actors (Roger and Dauvergne 2016). Similar to the way in which the welfare mix recognizes both the public and private dimensions of national social policies, the umbrella of global social governance includes both intergovernmental and transnational governance arrangements with respect to social policy. The strong affinity between what is considered to be private and transnational within the

IR literature has three key effects. First, it narrows understandings of the transnational compared to sociological understandings. Second, the notion of transnational as private can imply that what is transnational is not public and is therefore separate, beyond and/or exempt from governmental intervention. Third, it siloes discussions of intergovernmental and transnational governance mechanisms and obscures links between them. This makes it more difficult to discern the transnational dynamics underpinning social protection arrangements, particularly in developing country contexts.

Like social policy, legal scholarship is inherently interdisciplinary, and broad and narrow understandings of the transnational exist within this literature as well. Similar to the way in which migration scholars shed light on the unique nature of social protection arrangements for individuals and families living transnational lives, a recognition of transnational law has arisen in part because of the emergence of legal problems that are not solely national, international, public or private. Some legal scholars treat transnational law as pertaining predominantly to private actors, but in ways that transcend national understandings of both the "state" and "market" (Calliess 2007; Calliess and Zumbansen 2010; Zumbansen 2011). Alternatively, Jessup (2006, 45) defines transnational law broadly as "all law which regulates actions or events that transcend national frontiers" (Cotterrell 2012, 501). Under this definition, transnational law can address a range of public and private actors, including states, intergovernmental organizations, international and national nongovernmental organizations, civil society organizations and families.

In a fashion somewhat akin to distinctions between social policies and social policymaking, transnational legal scholars recognize transnational law as substantive, part of an ongoing process and inherently normative. Substantive understandings of transnational law "emphasize the way regulatory regimes seek uniformity across limited (usually functionally defined) transnational operational spheres" (Cotterrell 2012, 501). This can be achieved either by harmonizing unique sets of national, international, public and private laws that pertain to transnational activities in a way that promotes legal pluralism (Zumbansen 2011) or in a way that promotes convergence and universal approaches toward transactions that "move[s] toward a 'world law'" (Cotterrell 2012, 501). Process-based understandings of transnational law tend to be broader and have been defined as "the theory and practice of how public and private actors—nation-states, international organizations, multinational enterprises, non-governmental organizations, and private individuals—interact in a variety of public and private, domestic and international fora to make, interpret, enforce, and ultimately, internalize rules of transnational law" (Koh 1996, 183). Finally, both substantive and process-based understandings of transnational law stress the importance of norms for bringing actors into compliance. While an actor may choose not to comply with transnational rules and standards at a given point in time, norms may affect the degree to which an actor will deviate from established norms, and most actors will align with dominant norms over time—a testament both to the durability of the substance of the law and to the legitimacy of the process through which laws have been created. In the case of social protection, this perspective suggests that just because every country does not yet have a social protection floor does not mean that they will never have one, nor does it mean that the Social Protection Floors Recommendation, 2012 (No. 202) is without teeth.

Understanding social policy from a transnational perspective can mean many different things to different scholars, depending largely on one's disciplinary vantage point. Sociologists are likely to focus on the ways in which the social transcends the national, as in the case of transnational migration, and also on the ways in which global social policies, such as social protection floors, are both constitutive of, and constituted by, national actors and interests. For political scientists and IR scholars, there is a close affinity between the private and the transnational, which makes it difficult to discern how transnational governance arrangements impact social protection. While some legal scholars also view transnational law as pertaining predominantly to private actors, there is broad agreement that transnational law pertains to cross-border activities for which there is no singular approach by the state. From a process view, transnational law recognizes that national, international, public and private actors all play a role in its emergence and realization. Building on Koh (1996, 184), understanding social policy from a transnational perspective suggests that social protection arrangements in the Global South may be: (1) pluralistic; (2) non-statist, but may include state actors; (3) dynamic and mutually constitutive; and (4) normative.

## Transnational Actors and Social Protection

It is important to distinguish between viewing social protection through a transnational lens and understanding the role of transnational actors in social protection arrangements throughout the Global South. As discussed later in this volume by Barrientos (Chap. 13), transnational actors have received a great deal, arguably a disproportionate amount, of attention within the literature on social protection. Here, the focus on transnational actors is not meant to suggest that both domestic and indigenous actors and domestically driven, state-oriented processes have not played a critical or even determining role in social protection in the Global South, because indeed they have. Furthermore, while there are many transnational underpinnings of social protection in the Global South, it is important to acknowledge that social protection continues to be framed predominantly as a national policy issue, not least because the nation state remains the political unit of the international system. These trends are stated explicitly in the 2030 Agenda, which encourages the implementation of "nationally appropriate social protection systems and measures for all, including floors" (United Nations General Assembly 2017, 1).

The application of a transnational lens to policymaking processes and more detailed understandings of the inner workings of intergovernmental organizations have challenged traditional definitions of transnational actors as private, non-state actors affecting global politics. Under traditional definitions, key transnational actors in relation to social protection in the Global South include firms, Churches and missionaries, trade unions and other non-governmental organizations. However, scholars such as Cronin (2002) illustrate how attention to the way in which UN agencies approach policy implementation across countries swiftly blurs the boundaries IR scholars have established between intergovernmentalism and transnationalism. Whether through contracting non-governmental organizations or consultants, creating expert advisory groups, facilitating trainings and capacity building or accepting funding from large philanthropic foundations, these activities regularly involve parties beyond governments alone. The need to work with and through non-governmental agencies is even emphasized in the current 2030 Agenda which aims to "encourage and promote effective public, public-private and civil society partnerships" arrangements (United Nations General Assembly 2017, 21), including in the implementation of social protection arrangements. In sum, while the governance mechanisms underpinning intergovernmental and private transnational actors may differ, the way in which these entities act and approach social policy implementation across borders may be much more similar than different. For this reason, it is important to recognize transnational actors as a group that is broader than and distinct from the governance arrangements that underpin them.

Second, the behavior of transnational actors is often difficult to characterize and predict. As illustrated above, transnational actors are autonomous entities capable of exercising agency and taking purposive action (Barnett and Finnemore 2004). This enables transnational actors to act not only in the interest of their members states as recognized by political scientists but also according to their own interests. It also enables them to play a particularly influential role in establishing global norms and fixing meanings (Barnett and Finnemore 2004). As a result of their dual political character, transnational actors may begin to decouple what they say and do about a given policy problem, resulting in incoherence (Bromley and Powell 2012; Meyer and Rowan 1977). Decoupling may happen unintentionally, particularly in situations where there is a lack of clarity or internal disagreement on the interests of a given transnational actor. Alternatively, transnational actors, such as the World Bank (Weaver 2008), may engage in organized hypocrisy (Brunsson 2002, 2007), or the utilization of decoupling as part of a strategy for managing a diverse range of interests. This can make it difficult to discern whether changes in the discourse on social protection among transnational actors bear a relation to substantive policy changes (Shriwise et al. forthcoming).

The dualistic nature of transnational actors, which are mutually constituted on the one hand and yet able to act autonomously on the other, is explained differently by sociologists, political scientists and IR scholars. Sociologists tend to view transnational actors as embedded within systems of global cultural production (Meyer et al. 1997; Boli and Thomas 1997), or a mutually constitutive process where "actors are treated not as unanalyzed 'givens' but as entities constructed and motivated by enveloping frames (Jepperson 1992)" (Boli and Thomas 1997, 172). From this view, transnational actors are defined by their unique blend of constituent frames; by extension, this literature places "the institutional character of transnational development front and center" (Boli and Thomas 1997, 172). The institutions at the heart of global cultural production are presumed to be universally valid and applicable across nation states, and the transnational actors embedded within this mutually constitutive system are considered impervious to vested interests, or more simply put, as "objective disinterested others" (Meyer et al. 1997, 160).

Systems of global cultural production also result in the emergence and institutionalization of global norms through an iterative process of inter-organizational exchange predominantly between states, intergovernmental organizations and international non-governmental organizations (Kentikelenis and Seabrooke 2017; Babb 2013; Babb and Chorev 2016; Chorev 2012; Halliday and Carruthers 2007). Global social policy scholars have long recognized the politics inherent in these exchanges (e.g. Deacon et al. 1997 and more recently Kaasch 2013), with a recent focus on how international organizations construct social policy proposals (Berten and Leisering 2016). In the case of social protection, the exchange of policy ideas between international organizations has resulted in the emergence of models, or micro-paradigms, of social cash transfers, representing what von Gliszczynski and Leisering (2016, 325) refer to as a "fragmented and incomplete universalism". In other cases, transnational actors produce policy scripts for countries to follow in order to achieve nationally and internationally agreed aims, goals and targets; in the case of the International Monetary Fund, evidence suggests that the implementation of scripts focused on various aspects of economic policy have had substantial and long-lasting effects on social protection systems in the Global South (Kentikelenis and Seabrooke 2017; Kentikelenis et al. 2014, 2016; Kentikelenis 2017; Kentikelenis and Papanicolas 2011). The global diffusion of these policies is thought to take place through a number of mechanisms (Dobbin et al. 2007), and in the case of social protection in the Global South, to be driven by a unique set of factors, including jobless agrarianization, heterogeneous political paths amid a range of democratic and autocratic regimes, and shifts in the global ideational context (Böger and Leisering 2018).

While sociologists examining systems of global cultural production view nation states as simply another actor defined by its unique set of constituent frames, political scientists and IR scholars recognize that national and transnational actors have different resource bases, interests, capabilities, histories and governance structures that result in power asymmetries. The key insight here is that some actors have played a more influential role than others in shaping the institutional context in which strategic interactions take place. For instance, many national actors in the Global North played an active role in shaping the UN system after World War II, while formerly dependent territories throughout the Global South were instead strongly shaped by notions of sovereignty practiced and perpetuated by this system. Further still, the asymmetries that persist within the international system enable some actors to influence the shape of global institutions themselves—or to change the rules of the game—more than others, resulting in distinct advantages in situations where cooperation is desired (Axelrod and Keohane 1985).

For political scientists and IR scholars, transnational actors are constituent parts of global institutions, defined as "persistent and connected sets of rules that prescribe behavioral roles, constrain activity, and shape expectations" (Keohane 1988, 386). They can be understood in multiple ways. Realist view transnational actors as epiphenomena or as representations of the current balance of power (Strange 1982). This view suggests that powerful, self-interested, rational actors dictate the structure of global institutions and the transnational actors within them, not the other way round. Simply put, many realists see transnational actors as "merely instruments of governments, and therefore unimportant in their own right" (Keohane and Nye 1974). A slightly modified realist perspective is that transnational actors may matter in their own right and prove to be more robust over time when they facilitate and support coordination of an issue area in a way that aligns with the interests of powerful states (Krasner 1982). Finally, transnational actors may be viewed as embedded within a socio-political environment where repeated patterns of behavior result in the emergence of norms that shape and constrain the behavior of actors (Ruggie 1982). While much more aligned with sociological understandings of global institutions, these scholars recognize the extent to which global norms both constitute and are constituted by powerful actors, but with a greater stress on the influence of national actors. In other words, the international order itself is an institutional formation in which transnational actors serve as key pillars that uphold asymmetries and guarantee key functions in line with the interests of powerful nation states over time (Ikenberry 2018; Huntington 1973).

Within this context, the set of global institutions in a particular issue area have been referred to across disciplines as regimes, or "sets of implicit or explicit principles, norms, rules, and decision-making procedures around which actors' expectations converge in a given area of international relations" (Krasner 1982, 186). This approach has been applied to welfare as an issue area, both by Esping-Andersen (1990) in his seminal classification of welfare state regimes in the Global North and by Wood and Gough (2006) who extended this work on a global scale. Wood and Gough (2006, 1708) argue that countries can be classified as belonging predominantly to one of three types of welfare regimes: welfare state regimes, informal security regimes or insecurity regimes depending on their degree of de-clientelization, or "the process of de-linking client dependents from their personalized, arbitrary and discretionary entrapment to persons with intimate power over them". While this work recognizes that welfare regimes may "spill over national boundaries" (Wood and Gough 2006, 1707) and that multiple welfare regimes may be layered within one country, it falls short of applying a transnational lens to the historical emergence of welfare institutions from the perspective of countries in the Global South, giving this typology more descriptive than explanatory power. Furthermore, the way in which this work extends an institutional approach to welfare devised for rich countries on a global scale divorces an understanding of welfare regimes in the Global South from their micro-foundations. This runs the risk of obscuring rather than clarifying the nature of social policy dynamics in these countries, particularly from the perspective of the domestic and indigenous actors within them.

Finally, political scientists recognize the role of ideas in relation to global institutions and policymaking beyond the establishment of norms alone (Béland 2005). As illustrated by Lavers and Hickey (2016, 391), "comparative analysis of social protection interventions in developing countries suggests that ideology has played a significant role, including popular attitudes on who deserves assistance (Graham 2002) and ideas around the responsibility of the state towards its citizens (Hickey 2012)". Furthermore, ideas are inextricably linked to policy implementation preferences and approaches (Devereux and Sabates-Wheeler 2007), with implications for the kinds of policy change the introduction of social protection arrangements represents (Hall 1993). Within the realm of social protection, these debates have centered largely on whether conditional or unconditional cash transfers are most appropriate, which member of the household should receive such transfers and whether health, education and broader forces such as climate change should be considered as integral to social protection arrangements.

In sum, transnational actors appear to be chameleons. Their behavior may be neither coherent nor unitary. They may act independently in line with their own interests or as instruments of powerful nation states, and they may also act in line with broader institutional norms and practices over time. While being influential and present across countries, their presence is not enough to assume that they cause or determine social policy or welfare outcomes in any one country case. Furthermore, the dynamic relationship between transnational actors and global institutions has led both to an interdisciplinary consensus that institutions and norms matter (e.g. Hall and Taylor 1996) and also to varying interpretations of the relationship between transnational actors and global institutions among sociologists on the one hand and political scientists and IR scholars on the other.

However, the consensus that global institutions and norms matter has obscured two key issues: (1) the way in which transnational actors, including intergovernmental organizations, are embedded in national and sub-national structures in ways that can affect social protection (Tarrow 2001); and (2) the impact of domestic actors and conditions on the emergence of social protection arrangements. These problems are representative of the way in which methodological nationalism has affected the examination of social protection across disciplines, where nation states were reified as equal containers and reduced to unitary actors in the international order. This is particularly problematic when it comes to understanding policymaking in the Global South, where asymmetries between external and domestic as well as indigenous actors have had critical, at times detrimental, and potentially long-lasting effects on the state of social protection dating back to colonialism. There are exceptions to the rule, such as research examining the domestic politics of social protection arrangements in emerging economies in Latin American (Huber and Stephens 2012). However, substantial gaps remain in properly joining up the micro-foundations of policymaking at the level of actors within countries in the Global South with what is known about transnational actors and global institutions across disciplines. The question then remains: How can transnational approaches help scholarship move beyond methodological nationalism and strengthen its micro-foundations so as not to perpetuate global institutional and ideational determinism when seeking to explain social protection arrangements in the Global South?

## From Context to Causation: Analyzing Transnational Actor Constellations

To better understand the transnational policymaking dynamics underpinning social protection arrangements, one useful tactic is to move one level below institutions, both global and national, and to focus instead on the transnational actor constellations affecting social protection from the perspective of countries in the Global South. A transnational actor constellation can be defined as a group or network of actors involved in policy interactions that either includes transnational actors or is impacted substantially by transnational relationships, with the assumption that "a thorough understanding of the underlying constellation is an essential precondition for the explanation and prediction of interaction outcomes" (Scharpf 1997, 16). While every actor or relational element that constitutes an actor constellation need not be transnational, the presence of transnational actors and relations that affect the dynamic of these constellations is what identifies them as transnational. Equally, it should be noted that a transnational approach is defined by consideration of the possibility of transnational actors and relationships being substantial elements of a policy process; if neither of these criteria proves to be true empirically, the relevant actor constellation might best be described as national or global or urban, depending on definitions and empirics. In these cases, the consideration that actor constellations may be transnational amounts to necessary due diligence in line with what is expected from working hypotheses and the possibilities suggested by existing literature.

At least two analytical challenges appear when using transnational actor constellations as a unit of analysis: identifying the actors and determining causation. Developing strong criteria for actor identification is critical, not least because it shapes the data and information considered when describing transnational actor constellations from the outset and subsequently the findings and conclusions that can be drawn concerning their dynamics. Current literature on global social policy provides actor matrices that can be used as deductive frames for identifying key actors involved in social policymaking to avoid biasing analyses based on data availability and available literature. Building on the work of Esping-Andersen (1990), both Wood and Gough (2006, 1701) as well as Yeates (2001) recognize the importance of considering both domestic and transnational actors and institutions central to the operation of states, markets, communities and families in order to understand the social policy dynamics within countries across the Global South. For the purpose of identifying actors relevant for social protection, these deductive frames should be as inclusive as possible, and when key actors and institutions not previously considered are found to have causal effects on social protection arrangements, these new elements should be incorporated into future deductive frames.

Determining how to understand causation within these constellations is a much more difficult matter. While the study of transnational phenomena has been largely interdisciplinary, it has also been described as "'undisciplined' in its use of diverse concepts, theories and literature. … Besides a few exceptions … shared theoretical frameworks or concepts on transnational processes across the subfields are comparably lacking" (Go and Krause 2016, 6). Indeed, understandings of the dynamics of these constellations are likely to differ according to disciplinary understandings of the relationship between transnational actors and global institutions as discussed above. Furthermore, as highlighted by Obinger et al. (2013, 121), "comparative welfare state research has only recently begun to systematically study relational policy processes". In this area, transnational legal scholarship has parallels with social policy in the way it is conceptualizing transnational processes. Koh (2006, 745–746) suggests that law is either downloaded from international to domestic law, uploaded from domestic law to international law or horizontally transferred from one national system to another. This aligns closely with the concluding observation from Obinger et al. (2013, 124) that "the systematic combination of processes of horizontal spatial interdependencies with vertical relationships between international and supranational institutions and their member states … is perhaps the biggest challenge for future research". As a unit of analysis, transnational actor constellations bring these processes and their component parts into focus in order to better understand their dynamics.

There is a plethora of information on country experiences in relation to social protection in the Global South from intergovernmental organizations, international non-governmental organizations, think tanks, consultancies, country reports and academic literature. However, all too frequently, case studies attribute their unique or distinguishing features to differences in country context, without a serious and detailed exploration of what this means and what, if any, theoretical implications these claims have. To break through this impasse, it will be necessary for global social policy scholarship: (1) to continue to develop a coherent and pluralistic discourse on the theoretical and conceptual frameworks being used to support the analysis of transnational actor constellations with respect to social policy in the Global South; and (2) for case studies to be both better harnessed and more specifically designed to contribute to theoretical and conceptual development.

Process tracing supports the discovery and re-construction of how policy dynamics play out in practice. Within the context of transnational actor constellations, tracing the development and implementation of social protection arrangements can contribute both to theory-building and, in carefully selected cases, to theory testing (Beach 2016). Ulriksen and Dadalauri (2016, 223) illustrate how well-designed single case studies can "contribute to the testing and modification of solid theoretical frameworks undertaken through a rigorous research design that ensures substantial empirical leverage and constructive conclusions". The use of case studies in this way is both possible and important for at least two related reasons. First, using process tracing in a single, most crucial case (Gerring 2007) provides a means of evaluating "theoretically specified causal mechanisms that link variables in a comprehensive and temporal explanation of interesting societal phenomena" (Ulriksen and Dadalauri 2016, 225). While this use of case studies should complement and cannot replace testing focused on explaining variance between an independent and dependent variable, confirming and specifying the causal mechanisms at play has implications for policy practice. Uncovering causal mechanisms within a transnational actor constellation with regard to social protection provides policymakers with critical information and perspective about the context in which they are operating and can, at best, enable them to respond with agility and ingenuity to challenges and barriers. Moreover, if policymakers are better informed and able to act on the best available knowledge, their experiences are also better able to inform theoretical development, creating a much more productive and mutually beneficial relationship between academic research and policy practice with respect to social protection.

## Conclusion

Across disciplines, scholars have focused increasingly on the ways in which transnational dynamics have affected social protection in the Global South. Together, research across disciplines suggests that social protection arrangements in the Global South will be: pluralistic; non-statist, but may include state actors; dynamic and mutually constitutive; and normative. While a transnational approach is not a substitute or replacement for a focus on national actors and domestic conditions, it draws attention to the role of transnational actors in social policymaking, encouraging critical engagement and examination of their behavior and activities. Literature from across disciplines reveals that these actors appear to be chameleons. Their behavior may not be coherent or unitary, and they may behave in line with their own interests or as instruments of powerful nation states that govern them. Examination of these actors and the ways in which they impact and are impacted by global institutions has resulted in an interdisciplinary consensus that global institutions and norms matter. However, the methodological nationalism inherent in much of this work has masked the relationship between global institutions and norms and national and sub-national environments and structures as well as the impact of domestic actors and conditions on the emergence of social protection arrangements.

Identifying and analyzing transnational actor constellations is one way of encouraging the development of stronger micro-foundations in global social policy research in order to gain a much more specific understanding of the interplay between external actors and domestic conditions when it comes to social protection. As policies have proven to 'work' in some country contexts and not in others, policymakers and academics alike continue to espouse the need to tailor and adapt policies to their particular political and institutional contexts, and this rightly remains a hallmark of global policymaking to date. However, this leaves a critical theoretical and practical gap, as attention to context does not help to determine causality. Given the inherently interdisciplinary nature of global social policy research, it is critical that scholars continue to develop a coherent and pluralistic discourse on the theoretical and conceptual frameworks being used to analyze transnational actor constellations and social protection arrangements in the Global South. Within this frame, the plethora of information on country cases and social protection can be better harnessed, and carefully designed case studies and process tracing can be conducted in ways that can help to build, revise and test theories. This is a necessary complement to cross-country quantitative research, as thorough and more specific understandings of the dynamics of transnational actor constellations are critical to informing policy practice, and ideally by extension, to enhancing social protection. From a theoretical standpoint, the study of transnational actor constellations in relation to social protection can promote a better understanding of the relational elements underpinning social protection arrangements in the Global South, which has been identified as "perhaps the biggest challenge for future research" (Obinger et al. 2013, 124).

Understanding social policy from a transnational perspective is becoming increasingly important in the context of the 2030 Agenda. The ways in which social protection is affected by cross-border social problems, ranging from disease to migration to environmental degradation, is demonstrated on an almost daily basis. Broader understandings of the transnational could advance global social governance and policymaking by illuminating the relationships and divisions between intergovernmental and transnational governance mechanisms. Looking at how both of these sets of governance mechanisms impact each other with regard to social rights, redistribution and regulation may lead to particularly insightful findings related to social protection. Also, the chameleon-like behavior of transnational actors makes them an intriguing focal point for interdisciplinary researchers, as they present conceptual and analytical challenges that appear to defy explanation from the dispositions of sociologists as well as political scientists and IR scholars alone. Such work is of critical and timely importance. Theory-driven research, in addition to being important in its own right, has the potential to better inform policy practice and to support efforts to ensure that no one is left behind when it comes to social protection.

# References

Axelrod, Robert, and Robert O. Keohane. 1985. Achieving Cooperation under Anarchy: Strategies and Institutions. *World Politics* 38 (1): 226–254.

Babb, Sarah. 2013. The Washington Consensus as Transnational Policy Paradigm: Its Origins, Trajectory and Likely Successor. *Review of International Political Economy* 20 (2): 268–297.

Babb, Sarah, and Nitsan Chorev. 2016. International Organizations: Loose and Tight Coupling in the Development Regime. *Studies in Comparative International Development* 51 (1): 81–102.

Barnett, Michael, and Martha Finnemore. 2004. *Rules for the World: International Organizations in Global Politics*. Ithaca: Cornell University Press.

Beach, Derek. 2016. It's All About Mechanisms—What Process-Tracing Case Studies Should Be Tracing. *New Political Economy* 21 (5): 463–472.

Béland, Daniel. 2005. Ideas and Social Policy: An Institutionalist Perspective. *Social Policy and Administration* 39 (1): 1–18.

Berten, John, and Lutz Leisering. 2016. Social Policy by Numbers. How International Organisations Construct Global Policy Proposals. *International Journal of Social Welfare* 26 (2): 156–167.

Böger, Tobias, and Lutz Leisering. 2018. A New Pathway to Universalism? Explaining the Spread of 'Social' Pensions in the Global South, 1967–2011. *Journal of International Relations and Development*: 1–31. https://doi.org/10.1057/s41268-018-0152-2.

Boli, John, and George M. Thomas. 1997. World Culture in the World Polity: A Century of International Non-Governmental Organization. *American Sociological Review* 62 (2): 171–190.

Bromley, Patricia, and Walter W. Powell. 2012. From Smoke and Mirrors to Walking the Talk: Decoupling in the Contemporary World. *Academy of Management Annals* 6 (1): 483–530.

Brunsson, Nils. 2002. *The Organization of Hypocrisy: Talk, Decisions and Actions in Organizations*. Herndon, VA: Copenhagen Business School Press.

———. 2007. *The Consequences of Decision-Making*. Oxford: Oxford University Press.

Calliess, Graf-Peter. 2007. The Making of Transnational Contract Law. *Indiana Journal of Global Legal Studies* 14 (2): 469–483.

Calliess, Graf-Peter, and Peer Zumbansen. 2010. *Rough Consensus and Running Code: A Theory of Transnational Private Law*. Oxford: Hart Publishing.

Chorev, Nitsan. 2012. Changing Global Norms through Reactive Diffusion: The Case of Intellectual Property Protection of AIDS Drugs. *American Sociological Review* 77 (5): 831–853.

Clarke, John. 2005. Welfare States as Nation States: Some Conceptual Reflections. *Social Policy and Society* 4 (4): 407–415.

Cotterrell, Roger. 2012. What Is Transnational Law? *Law & Social Inquiry* 37 (2): 500–524.

Cronin, Bruce. 2002. The Two Faces of the United Nations: The Tension Between Intergovernmentalism and Transnationalism. *Global Governance* 8: 53–71.

Deacon, Bob. 2007. *Global Social Policy and Governance*. London: Sage Publications.

———. 2013a. *Global Social Policy in the Making: The Foundations of the Social Protection Floor*. Bristol: Policy Press.

———. 2013b. The Social Protection Floor and Global Social Governance: Towards Policy Synergy and Cooperation between International Organizations. *International Social Security Review* 66 (3–4): 45–67.

Deacon, Bob, Michelle Hulse, and Paul Stubbs. 1997. *Global Social Policy. International Organizations and the Future of Welfare*. London: SAGE.

Devereux, Stephen, and Rachel Sabates-Wheeler. 2007. Editorial Introduction: Debating Social Protection. *IDS Bulletin* 38 (3): 1–7.

Dobbin, Frank, Beth Simmons, and Geoffrey Garret. 2007. The Global Diffusion of Public Policies: Social Construction, Coercion, Competition, or Learning? *Annual Review of Sociology* 33: 449–472.

Esping-Andersen, Gøsta. 1990. *Three Worlds of Welfare Capitalism*. Cambridge: Polity Press.

Faist, Thomas, Başak Bilecen, Karolina Barglowski, and Joanna Jadwiga Sienkiewicz. 2015. Transnational Social Protection: Migrants' Strategies and Patterns of Inequalities. *Population, Space and Place* 21: 193–202.

Gerring, John. 2007. *Case Study Research: Principles and Practices*. Cambridge: Cambridge University Press.

Go, Julian, and Monika Krause. 2016. Fielding Transnationalism: An Introduction. *The Sociological Review Monographs* 64 (2): 6–30.

Graham, Carol. 2002. *Public Attitudes Matter: A Conceptual Frame for Accounting for Political Economy in Safety Nets and Social Assistance Policies*. Social Protection Discussion Paper Series, No. 0233. Washington, DC: World Bank Social Protection Advisory Service.

Hall, Peter A. 1993. Policy Paradigms, Social Learning, and the State: The Case of Economic Policymaking in Britain. *Comparative Politics* 25 (3): 275–296.

Hall, Peter A., and Rosemary C.R. Taylor. 1996. Political Science and the Three New Institutionalisms. *Political Studies* 44: 936–957.

Halliday, Terence C., and Bruce G. Carruthers. 2007. The Recursivity of Law: Global Norm Making and National Lawmaking in the Globalization of Corporate Insolvency Regimes. *American Journal of Sociology* 112 (4): 1135–1202.

Hickey, Sam. 2012. Turning Governance Thinking Upside-Down? Insights from the Politics of What Works. *Third World Quarterly* 33 (7): 1231–1247.

Huber, Evelyne, and John D. Stephens. 2012. *Democracy and the Left: Social Policy and Inequality in Latin America*. Chicago: University of Chicago Press.

Huntington, Samuel P. 1973. Transnational Organizations in World Politics. *World Politics* 25 (3): 333–368.

Ikenberry, G. John. 2018. The End of the Liberal International Order? *International Affairs* 94 (1): 7–23.

Jepperson, Ronald L. 1992. *National Scripts: The Varying Construction of Individualism and Opinion across Modern Nation-States*. PhD Dissertation, Department of Sociology, Yale University, New Haven, CT.

Jessup, Philip C. 2006. Transnational Law (Extracts). In *Philip C. Jessup's Transnational Law Revisited—On the Occasion of the 50th Anniversary of Its Publication, Essays in Transnational Economic Law, No. 50*, ed. Christian Tietje, Alan Brouder, and Karsten Nowrot. Accessed 29 September 2019. http://www.wirtschaftsrecht.uni-halle.de/sites/default/files/altbestand/Heft50.pdf.

Kaasch, Alexandra. 2013. Contesting Contestation: Global Social Policy Prescriptions on Pensions and Health Systems. *Global Social Policy* 13 (1): 45–65.

Kaasch, Alexandra, and Kerstin Martens. 2015. *Actors and Agency in Global Social Governance*. Oxford: Oxford University Press.

Kentikelenis, Alexander E. 2017. Structural Adjustment and Health: A Conceptual Framework and Evidence on Pathways. *Social Science & Medicine* 187: 296–305.

Kentikelenis, Alexander, and Irene Papanicolas. 2011. Economic Crisis, Austerity and the Greek Public Health System. *European Journal of Public Health* 22 (1): 4–5.

Kentikelenis, Alexander E., and Leonard Seabrooke. 2017. The Politics of World Polity: Script-Writing in International Organizations. *American Sociological Review* 82 (5): 1065–1092.

Kentikelenis, Alexander, Lawrence King, Martin McKee, and David Stuckler. 2014. The International Monetary Fund and the Ebola Outbreak. *The Lancet Global Health* 3 (2): PE69–PE70.

Kentikelenis, Alexander E., Thomas H. Stubbs, and Lawrence P. King. 2016. IMF Conditionality and Development Policy Space, 1985–2014. *Review of International Political Economy* 23 (4): 543–582.

Keohane, Robert O. 1988. International Institutions: Two Approaches. *International Studies Quarterly* 32 (4): 379–396.

Keohane, Robert O., and Joseph S. Nye. 1974. Transgovernmental Relations and International Organizations. *World Politics* 27: 39–62.

Koh, Harold Hongju. 1996. *Transnational Legal Process.* Faculty Scholarship Series 2096.

———. 2006. Why Transnational Law Matters. *Penn State International Law Review* 24: 745–753.

Krasner, Stephen D. 1982. Structural Causes and Regime Consequences: Regimes as Intervening Variables. *International Organization* 36 (2): 185–205.

Lavers, Tom, and Sam Hickey. 2016. Conceptualizing the Politics of Social Protection Expansion in Low Income Countries: The Intersection of Transnational Ideas and Domestic Politics. *International Journal of Social Welfare* 25: 388–398.

Levitt, Peggy. 2001. *The Transnational Villagers.* Berkeley: University of California Press.

Levitt, Peggy, and B. Nadya Jaworsky. 2007. Transnational Migration Studies: Past Developments and Future Trends. *Annual Review of Sociology* 33: 129–156.

Levitt, Peggy, and Ninna Nyberg-Sørensen. 2004. *The Transnational Turn in Migration Studies.* Global Commission on International Migration (GCIM), Global Migration Perspectives, No. 6, Geneva.

Levitt, Peggy, Jocelyn Viterna, Armin Mueller, and Charlotte Lloyd. 2017. Transnational Social Protection: Setting the Agenda. *Oxford Development Studies* 45 (1): 2–19.

Meyer, John W., and Brian Rowan. 1977. Institutionalized Organizations: Formal Structure as Myth and Ceremony. *American Journal of Sociology* 83 (2): 340–363.

Meyer, John W., John Boli, George M. Thomas, and Francisco O. Ramirez. 1997. World Society and the Nation-State. *American Journal of Sociology* 103 (1): 144–181.

Obinger, Herbert, and Carina Schmitt. 2011. Guns and Butter? Regime Competition and the Welfare State during the Cold War. *World Politics* 63 (2): 246–207.

Obinger, Herbert, Carina Schmitt, and Peter Starke. 2013. Policy Diffusion and Policy Transfer in Comparative Welfare State Research. *Social Policy and Administration* 47 (1): 111–129.

Obinger, Herbert, Klaus Petersen, and Peter Starke. 2018. *Warfare and Welfare. Military Conflict and Welfare State Development in Western Countries.* Oxford: Oxford University Press.

Risse, Thomas. 2006. Transnational Governance and Legitimacy. In *Governance and Democracy. Comparing National, European and International Experiences*, ed. Arthur Benz and Yannis Papadopoulos, 179–199. London: Routledge.
Roger, Charles, and Peter Dauvergne. 2016. The Rise of Transnational Governance as a Field of Study. *International Studies Review* 18: 415–437.
Ruggie, John Gerard. 1982. International Regimes, Transactions, and Change: Embedded Liberalism in the Postwar Economic Order. *International Organization* 36 (2): 379–415.
Sassen, Saskia. 2006. *Territory, Authority, Rights: From Medieval to Global Assemblages*. Princeton: Princeton University Press.
———. 2010. The Global Inside the National: A Research Agenda for Sociology. *Sociopedia.isa*. Accessed 19 December 2018. http://saskiasassen.com/PDFs/publications/the-global-inside-the-national.pdf.
Scharpf, Fritz W. 1997. *Games Real Actors Play: Actor-Centered Institutionalism in Policy Research*. New York: Routledge.
Schmitt, Carina. 2015. Social Security Development and the Colonial Legacy. *World Development* 70: 332–342.
Shriwise, Amanda, Alexander Kentikelenis, and David Stuckler. forthcoming. Universal Social Protection: Is It Just Talk? *Sociology of Development*.
Slaughter, Anne-Marie. 2004. *A New World Order*. Princeton, NJ: Princeton University Press.
Strange, Susan. 1982. Cave! Hic Dragones: A Critique of Regime Analysis. *International Organization* 36 (2): 479–196.
Tarrow, Sidney. 2001. Transnational Politics: Contention and Institutions in International Politics. *Annual Review of Political Science* 4: 1–20.
Ulriksen, Marianne S., and Nina Dadalauri. 2016. Single Case Studies and Theory-Testing: The Knots and Dots of the Process-Tracing Method. *International Journal of Social Research Methodology* 19 (2): 223–239.
United Nations General Assembly. 2017. Global Indicator Framework for the Sustainable Development Goals and Targets of the 2030 Agenda for Sustainable Development, A/RES/71/313. Accessed 29 September 2019. https://unstats.un.org/sdgs/indicators/Global%20Indicator%20Framework%20after%202019%20refinement_Eng.pdf.
von Gliszczynski, Moritz, and Lutz Leisering. 2016. Constructing New Global Models of Social Security: How International Organizations Defined the Field of Social Cash Transfers in the 2000s. *Journal of Social Policy* 45 (2): 325–343.

Weaver, Catherine. 2008. *Hypocrisy Trap: The World Bank and the Poverty of Reform*. Princeton, NJ: Princeton University Press.

Wood, Geof, and Ian Gough. 2006. A Comparative Welfare Regime Approach to Global Social Policy. *World Development* 34 (10): 1696–1712.

Yeates, Nicola. 2001. *Understanding Global Social Policy*. Bristol: Policy Press.

Yeates, Nicola, and Zoë Irving. 2005. Introduction: Transnational Social Policy. *Social Policy & Society* 4 (4): 403–405.

Zumbansen, Peer. 2011. Neither 'Public' nor 'Private', 'National' nor 'International': Transnational Corporate Governance from a Legal Pluralist Perspective. *Journal of Law and Society* 38 (1): 50–75.

**Open Access** This chapter is licensed under the terms of the Creative Commons Attribution 4.0 International License (http://creativecommons.org/licenses/by/4.0/), which permits use, sharing, adaptation, distribution and reproduction in any medium or format, as long as you give appropriate credit to the original author(s) and the source, provide a link to the Creative Commons licence and indicate if changes were made.

The images or other third party material in this chapter are included in the chapter's Creative Commons licence, unless indicated otherwise in a credit line to the material. If material is not included in the chapter's Creative Commons licence and your intended use is not permitted by statutory regulation or exceeds the permitted use, you will need to obtain permission directly from the copyright holder.

# Part II

## The Influence of the Colonial Legacy and Cold War on Social Protection

# 3

# Cold War and Social Protection in Burma and Malaysia

Michele Mioni and Klaus Petersen

## Introduction

It is often said that the Cold War was a battle of hearts and minds—a conflict between two rival models for society battling to become the legitimate and preferred horizon of the future for people. Whereas the Iron Curtain during the early Cold War remained a stable line of division through Europe, for emerging countries outside Europe the battle was more intense and open. This was not least the case in formerly colonized countries. Following the Communist victory in China in 1949, US policy-makers certainly considered South East Asia (SEA) a Cold War

---

M. Mioni (✉)
SOCIUM Research Center on Inequality and Social Policy, University of Bremen, Bremen, Germany
e-mail: michele.mioni@uni-bremen.de

K. Petersen
Centre for Welfare State Research & Department of History, University of Southern Denmark, Odense, Denmark
e-mail: klaus.petersen@sdu.dk

© The Author(s) 2020
C. Schmitt (ed.), *From Colonialism to International Aid*, Global Dynamics of Social Policy, https://doi.org/10.1007/978-3-030-38200-1_3

hotspot and a pivotal case for containing the spread of Communism (Westad 2017).

Cold War studies have focused mainly on military aspects, foreign policies and various forms of cultural diplomacy. Less attention has been directed toward the links between the Cold War and welfare state development. Obinger and Schmitt (2011) showed that systemic competition is one important explanatory factor for the growth in social spending in the Organisation for Economic Co-operation and Development (OECD)-world since 1945. However, we still know very little about the mechanisms behind this (for a discussion, see Petersen 2013). In this chapter, we scrutinize the ways in which Western actors integrated social reforms as part of an anti-Communist strategy in SEA and how this was reflected in the domestic context. We will notably consider the actions of Britain, the US and the International Labour Office.

One of the classical explanations of the origins of the welfare state considers social reforms as a bulwark against social unrest and revolutionary movements. Social policy mitigated the socio-political effects of economic and industrial changes and ensured political consensus and legitimation (Spitzer 1962). This anti-revolutionary strategy triggered reforms even in the colonies (Seekings 2011; see Schmitt, Chap. 6, this volume), playing an important role also in the Cold War. Social reforms were an effective way to hamper Communism and other revolutionary movements, legitimizing the existing power relations and building state structures. IR-scholar Klaus Knorr picked up this point already in 1950; speaking mainly to an US audience, Knorr presented the European welfare state and ended up arguing for it as a domestic defense strategy:

> it is plausible that the democratic welfare state is the most constructive defense of the free world against Communist expansion, for it offers to many societies, rightly or wrongly dissatisfied with the free-enterprise economy they had, an alternative to the attractions of Communism. (Knorr 1950, 448)

As we will argue, the early social security and welfare reforms in SEA were no stranger to these considerations. This line of argumentation does not exclude competing explanations on welfare state growth, such as modernization and democratization. On the contrary, in the 1950s modernization discourses provided the theoretical and political tools for Western interventions and state-building (Gilman 2003). Modernization, social security and political stabilization complemented the struggle against Communism in the area. Cold War was a crosscutting moment of competition, which affected or triggered social reforms. The Cold War led to reconsidering social reforms as part of modernization strategies, state-building and the anti-Communist struggle. Domestic policy-makers either agreed upon or made use of reform agendas, to carry on their own political agendas which often had a nationalistic and Socialist bend that did not necessarily fit with the goals and economic paradigms of the Western powers.

Recent trends in Cold War historiography have focused on the interplay of the two superpowers with other international and regional actors (Westad 2005, 2017; Bradley 2010). Similarly, we consider the interaction of Western interests and the emerging non-Communist ruling classes in the two former Southeast Asian colonies of Burma and Malaysia. Both countries shared a common British colonial heritage and there, according to some observers of the time, "labor movements were comparatively well delineated before the war and [where] subsequent conditions have combined to further their growth. […] At the present time Malaya and Burma have the only labor movements in the area worthy of the name" (Thompson 1947, 14). While the decolonization was the historical context of these reforms, the local and international policy-makers operated within two different institutional frameworks, as Burma was independent since 1947, while Malaya gained independence only ten years later. The common ground of social security reforms was rather geopolitical concerns connected to the Cold War.

The chapter looks at how the new international paradigms of "social security" were introduced in SEA and inspired both Western experts and local policy-makers to projects of state-building. During and immediately after the war, indeed, the Western powers, the newly born United Nations and the ILO contributed to put "social security" at the very foundations of reconstruction policies (ILO 1944). Welfare state development in Burma and Malaysia was structured by a number of factors, of which anti-Communism was only one (others being ethnic cleavages, religion, political parties, economic growth or state capacity). Yet, the idea of social welfare reforms became integrated into the Cold War struggle for hearts and minds.[1] Our study connects to the ongoing debate about colonial legacies in social policy development (see Cooper 1996; Eckert 2006). However, whereas this strand of literature emphasizes the variations among former Western colonies, we argue that the Cold War was a crosscutting factor that put social reforms on the agenda and influenced the timing of reform.

However, this is not meant to say that the Western powers spoke with one voice or acted in unison in this respect. Especially in the US the "welfare state" did not have a good press, labeled as "Socialism", and in 1951 President Truman declared it a "scare word" (Petersen 2013, 231). Even among the advocates of a socio-economic soft-power strategy we find a conflict between those, like the US State Department, favoring economic growth and modernization, and others (like the ILO) with a broader reform agenda, including social security. The social reforms in Malaysia were still promoted by the British under the paradigms and rules of colonial development. On the contrary, the US—and to a certain extent the ILO—already framed their aid and assistance to Burma in a post-colonial understanding of socio-economic development. SEA was therefore also the ground for a competition between the various Western actors; the ILO's assistance programs were in line with US President Truman's doctrine on foreign aid, whereas Britain did not look favorably at the interferences of the international organizations in its dependent territories. These perspectives were not necessarily mutually exclusive; often the rhetoric of development complemented the promotion of social security schemes and other social services.

The chapter starts with a comparative overview of the geopolitical conditions under which Burma and Malaysia gained independence and with the importance of the perceived Communist threat in shaping their institutional and political settings. In the following section, we discuss how

---

[1] In this chapter, we decided to consider exclusively the former British colonies, except for the Indian case, which should be dealt separately. In order to stress the Anglo-American strategy with regard to the nexus Cold War/welfare state during decolonization, we also left out the case of French colonies. Anyway we intend to deal more systematically with this subject with further studies on the field.

Western anti-Communist strategies in SEA entailed different approaches, including economic aid, industrialization and social reform. These eventually came to define a Western way of promoting a model of development to counter the spread of Communism in the area. In the third section, we briefly look at the major social reforms introduced in both countries, to assess the way in which they might be framed as anti-Communist policies. Finally, we draw some conclusions on how welfare social policies became part of a strategy allowing for a progressive non-Communist strategy that signaled an anti-colonialist third-way position between Communism and US capitalism. We base our analysis on a mixed bag of sources: archival documents and published sources, such as academic articles and studies by contemporary observers and scholars. We will use this literature as a primary source to account for the Western takes on the "e base question" in SEA, which was interwoven with the rise of Communism in the context of decolonization.[2]

## Burma and Malaysia: From British Colonies to Independent States

World War II (WWII) signaled a watershed for the process of decolonization. The war fueled nationalism in the colonies and weakened the colonial powers. In the Atlantic Charter (1941, §3), Churchill and Roosevelt promised "to respect the right of all people to choose the form of government under which they will live", and these ideas were echoed by De Gaulle at the Brazzaville Conference of 1944. In the following years, the United Nations became a platform for decolonization debates; the UN Charter (Chapter IX, articles 73–74) defended the right to self-determination, and served as a platform for national liberation movements, denouncing colonial powers (see Jensen 2016). The process of decolonization varied from country to country. In most cases, the Cold

---

[2] For interpretive and practical reasons, we focus on Anglo-American views and strategies concerning the use of social security in Burma and Malaysia, rather than on the systematic tracing of the policy process behind reforms within the two countries.

War framed and influenced the path to independence, and the two countries under scrutiny make no exception.

Burma had been a British colony since 1886; the British made Burma an Indian province that experienced a period of economic growth and modernization. However, as this was mainly to the benefit of British companies and migrant communities from India or Britain, it triggered a nationalist movement in Burma, resulting in growing social and political unrest. In 1937, Burma again separated from India and was granted a constitution with a fully elected assembly. However, this did neither end the nationalist striving for independence nor the conflicts with the British. One of the driving forces of the protest was the strong Burmese Communist movement whose ranks were swollen during the Japanese occupation. Granting independence to Burma in 1947 was mainly the result of British problems with controlling the situation in the colony, and, as the country did not join the Commonwealth, direct British influence in Burma was limited.

The 1947 constitution included a Western-style liberal democratic parliament and political system, with a welfare-statist outlook including ideas of economic planning, state ownership of public utilities, while still guaranteeing private business (Trager 1958, 4–5). In the British House of Lords the new constitution was labeled as a blueprint for the development of a welfare state:

> The new Constitution of Burma [...] proclaims a more varied list of individual rights, both male and female, than the Declaration of the Rights of Man or the Constitution of the United States of America and its acceptance of the duties of the State to secure the fulfilment of these rights is in complete accordance with the modern view of the functions of a welfare state.[3]

However, the realization of these promises of a welfare state future was not easily achieved, due to internal political conflicts, lack of resources and a weak state (Taylor 1987, Chap. 4). Burma witnessed political

---

[3] HMSO, *Burma Independence Bill*, 25 November 1947, vol. 152 cc. 846–924, London, 1947. http://hansard.millbanksystems.com/lords/1947/nov/25/burma-independence-bill#S5LV0152P0_19471125_HOL_58.

### 3 Cold War and Social Protection in Burma and Malaysia

turmoil and domestic rebellions by Communist and ethnic groups that threatened the basic functions of the state—and at the same time called for a positive political reform agenda to strengthen the legitimacy of the politically dominant Anti-Fascist People's Freedom League (AFPFL)—a Socialist coalition of anti-colonial movements. Aung San, the leader of the Burmese independence movement, was a former Communist who had turned increasingly nationalistic and cooperated with the Japanese during the war. In the spring of 1945 he founded the AFPFL together with the Burmese Communist Party.

Burmese non-alignment was driven more by domestic factors than idealism. Anti-colonialism was widespread in Burma, something also clearly stated by numerous reports by British and US intelligence agencies, and neutralism allowed the government to demonstrate its independence of Western powers (Than 2013). This emphasis on Burmese independence appealed to Socialists within the government, workers and the rural population, and defended the government against Communist accusations of being Anglo-American puppets. The Burmese governments were thus in a difficult situation, as foreign aid was very much needed but almost impossible to accept. A Commonwealth loan of 1950 was never used, and in 1954 Burma declined assistance through the Colombo-Plan (Adeleke 2004).

Things turned out differently in Malaysia. From the late nineteenth century on the country had gradually become part of the British Empire. Growing exports of rubber and tin supported the economy but also fueled nationalist protests, as the economic development benefitted mainly British and immigrant groups. During WWII Malaya was occupied by Japan. The defeat of the British Empire contributed to the growing anti-colonial sentiments, and the occupation had strong negative effects on rubber and tin production, leaving the Malaysian economy in a bad shape.

Malaysian independence was more troublesome, and divorce from the colonizers took a long time. After the defeat of Japan in 1945, colonial rule was restored. British initiatives for democratic reform triggered widespread protest from the Malay population, as the reform granted citizenship and equal rights also to Chinese and Indian residents. Consequently, in 1948, the idea of universal citizenship was given up, and political turmoil turned into open insurrection; from 1948 to 1960 the British and the Commonwealth armies were engaged in guerrilla warfare against the Communist insurgency triggered by the Malayan National Liberation Army (MNLA), the military arm of the Malaysian Communist Party (MCP).

The timing of the social legislation reforms in Malaysia followed this change of the British strategy against the MNLA, opening up to political and social enhancement to win both the "hearts" (the emotional support of the people) and the "minds" (the consensus of the people motivated by "rational self-interest"). Even though the threat of Communism (and Communist China) remained a factor in the country, the British succeeded with establishing an inter-ethnic and mildly reformist "Alliance", built around the dominating party, United Malays National Organization (UMNO), with the non-Communist Malayan Chinese Association (MCA) and the Malayan Indian Congress (MIC) participating. They won the national elections of 1955 and formed the first government after independence in 1957. Immediately after independence, though, revolts by MNLA insurgents went on until 1989, but mostly these were local outbreaks, increasingly characterized by ethnical claims (Boon Kheng 2009).

Burma and Malaysia differed in size and economic capacity but also shared many characteristics. Being former British colonies close to China and following a non-alignment policy in international affairs (more pronounced in Burma than in Malaysia), the countries were dominated by agriculture and had limited state capacity. Politically, both countries became dominated by party-alliances growing out of the struggle for independence and uniting both nationalist and Socialist groups. Both countries engaged in strategies for economic modernization and the development of industrial production.

In the 1940s and 1950s they also developed ambitious social reform agendas. Even if not fully realized, they included the gradual expansion of social protection schemes inspired by social security as well as land reforms, educational reforms and developing industrial relations. In the long run, the goal was to start a genuine process of modernization; in the short run, these plans and the promises they made served to limit the Communist appeal to the national publics. As argued by Dean (1950,

200), the military security outlook of the US and British policy-makers aligned well with these domestic goals: "For if the Asian nations, still as a low level of development, are now to devote their meager resources to the building up of a war machine, will this not mean the indefinite postponement of the economic and social improvements which, in their opinion, would prove the only effective bulwark against Communism?" (see also Chancellor 1951 for a similar argument).

In both countries, the Communists had played important roles in the struggle for independence, and the parties participated in democratic elections and had regional influence. Likewise, the local ruling parties had a clearly—but not always outspoken—anti-Communist profile. This was also recognized by American and British observers. The foreign policy doctrine of non-alignment (especially in Burma) left the door open for cooperation with both China and the USSR, while both AFPFL in Burma and the "Alliance" in Malaysia had moderate Socialist platforms at home. Yet, Communism was generally considered a threat in terms of the stability and legitimacy of the state by both parties. It was considered a possible competitor for the support of the industrial working class, small-scale farmers and intellectuals.

In Burma, the first years of independence were characterized by strong political and military conflicts between rivaling Communist and ethnic groups (Taylor 1987). Following the Communist victory in China in 1949, the northern areas of Burma were controlled by Kuomintang troops and consequently attracted the attention of both China and the US. Until the early 1950s, rebelling Communist groups controlled northern parts of the country, resulting in direct military conflicts with government troops. However, the Communists also appeared as a legal party, as competitors to AFPFL on the domestic parliamentary scene. The Burmese governments thus had the triple task of controlling the state, modernizing the country, ensuring the unity of the Burmese territory. Political turmoil in Burma led to the establishment of a military regime in 1962, led by Ne Win and his Burma Socialist Program Party, advocating the "Burmese way to Socialism". With the introduction of a one-party regime Burma was lost for democracy for the coming decades.

The "Malaysian Emergency" was instead a major anti-colonial guerilla warfare, where Communist stances mixed with ethnic rivalries; the

MNLA was mainly mobilizing the ethnic and unassimilated Chinese minority (almost 38% of the population) but also some ethnic Malayans. However, the insurgency did not ground on merely ethnic bases, as the MNLA proselytized among the rural lower classes and the dispossessed. The rebellion spread outside the great cities and had in the countryside and jungle the material bases where to develop. The MNLA mainly attacked infrastructure, rubber plantations and tin industries, which constituted the framework of Malaysian economy, also directly affecting British economic interests. Albeit the insurgency never stepped up into a mass uprising, it turned out as an escalade of insurgent incidents that reached their peak in 1951–1952, when the rebellion lost momentum (Komer 1972).

The British stick-and-carrot response aimed at separating the rebels from their social basis. The British operated coercive measures such as resettlement and food control, while launching programs for improving social services and living standards in the most underdeveloped areas, which were implemented from 1950 onward. These included the support of inter-ethnic national trade unions, educational reform and a thorough plan of social security, comprehensive of social insurances, healthcare, regulation of working hours and public housing (Mackenzie 1952). Alongside social reform the government passed, under the supervision of the British colonial offices, several projects of economic development and planning, such as the *Rural Industrial Development Authority* and the *Draft Development Plan*, which introduced elements of Keynesian planning and favored the growth of public social services through a policy of investments (Rudner 1972).

# The Western Actors and the Anti-Communist Strategies in South East Asia: Economic Development and Social Security

SEA quickly became a hotspot of the Cold War. Communist China, the US-led rebuilding of Japan and the Korean War (1950–1953) signaled the importance of the region for the superpowers. US analysts particularly saw in the Communist seizure of power the beginning of a Communist offensive in the region to be countered through "the necessary combination of political and military means" (Sacks 1950, 247). The American government kept the position acquired in the Pacific during WWII in order to control the spread of Communism. According to the "domino theory", the collapse of non-Communist regimes in Burma and Malaysia and their turning toward the Socialist bloc would cause a serious threat to US security interests: "If Burma or Indochina can be held against communism, we can probably hold all of Southeast Asia. If either Burma or Indochina falls, Siam would probably follow, and Southeast Asia would be practically defenseless against the onrush of communism."[4] Consequently, the Western powers closely monitored domestic developments in SEA countries. The major powers shared an interest in stabilizing the new democracies and in fighting the threat of Communism, leading to a high level of coordination and sharing of information.[5]

The American experts were aware of the relevancy of the "social question" to understand the spread of Communism in the area and the multifaceted quests for social enhancement and higher standards of living among the local population (Thompson and Adloff 1950). For this reason, the Western policy advisors stressed the importance to carry on a state-building process through circumscribed social services (mostly healthcare and limited measures of social protection) and an assisted program of development and industrialization. This was supposed to ensure the creation of the financial bases for the development of sounder welfare states along the Western lines (Mills 1949; Buss 1949).

British ILO civil servant Wilfrid Benson recommended the stabilization of the whole area through an incremental social policy including social services and healthcare, labor legislations, the creation and support of reformist workers' organizations. By the help of Western aid, these policies were supposed to accompany economic development and industrialization

---

[4] FRUS, 1950, Vol. 6, document 115, 'Policy Statement prepared in the Department of State, 16 June 1950'.
[5] TNA, Cabinet Papers, CAB 129/29, 'Survey of Communism in Countries outside the Soviet Orbit, 13 September 1948'.

(see Becker, Chap. 7, this volume). They were of capital importance for geopolitical considerations, as "the countries of SEA will be unable to play their part in the peace of prosperity of the world without drastic improvements in the economic and social life of their peoples. [...] The change is that the countries will need economic and social assistance which can aid their political evolution" (Benson 1947, VIII). He also suggested to gradually implement public policies that met the workers' specific social needs and universal social welfare:

> an improved standard of living is one of the essentials for stability in Southeast Asia. [...] The change would help to close the gap between the employed and the rest of the population, and, with that pride which newly won self-government can often inspire, the assumption by national governments of the direction of social services may lead to an unexpected response in the desire of the peoples for higher standards of living. (Benson 1947, X–XI)

However, the implementation of this strategy had to be deployed on a case-by-case basis. In Burma, numerous reports underlined the strong skepticism against foreign aid and support from the Western powers, even though material welfare and social development were needed. As stated in a report from the US consul in Rangoon in September 1946 on the Burmese government, "they cannot produce rabbits from an empty hat".[6] In November 1947, the US chargé in Rangoon pointed out that, taking the strong anti-US opinion in Burma into account, the best counteroffensive might be "concrete US assistance maternal and infant welfare as the most efficient means of winning the masses".[7] In the following months a bilateral agreement between Burma and the US on educational exchange was established, while also technical equipment (for civil purposes) was made available.[8] In a policy statement by the Department of State of June 1950 it was explained that "if this present cabinet can, with the help of American technical experts, initiate and successfully carry out

---

[6] FRUS, 1946, Vol. 8, document 5, 'Telegram from the Consul General at Rangoon (Packer) to Department of State, 28 September 1946'. See also document 8, 'Telegram from the Acting Secretary of State to the Chargé in United Kingdom (Gallman), 8 November 1946'.
[7] FRUS, 1947, Vol. 6, document 54, 'Telegram from the Acting Secretary of State to the Consul General at Rangoon, 21 August 1947'.
[8] FRUS, 1947, Vol. 6, document 55, 'Telegram from the Acting Secretary of State to the Embassy in Burma, 19 December 1947'.

a few economic development and public welfare schemes, its policy of looking to the US and the Commonwealth for aid might gain popular acceptance".[9]

The use of technical and material assistance while enhancing national traditions in the fight against Communism aligned with the political strategy of the Burmese government after the military defeat of the Communist rebels in 1950–1951. From the late 1940s on and into the 1950s there was a growing awareness that the weak Burmese state depended on external help, even though, for domestic political reasons, Burmese leaders were very reluctant with receiving it.[10] On top of this, the US (covert) support to the Kuomintang troops in the northern regions of Burma did not go down well with the political elite in Rangoon.[11]

The US crusade against Communism in SEA included soft policies such as cultural diplomacy and financial aid to covert operations, cooperation with authoritarian local leaders and even direct military involvement. The need of social reform was framed within a dominant anti-Communist paradigm, and this favored short-term policies typically focusing on power relations. This created a trade-off, where the fight for security in the short run threatened the long-term goal of stabilizing SEA societies. This was acknowledged even by US observers in the early 1960s, asking the question: "How effectively has the United States employed its power and influence to promote meaningful, economic, and social reform in the region?" (Henderson 1963, 260; see also Fifield 1963). The rhetoric of "development" stepped up the US strategy of accompanying social security with anti-Communism in the area. President Truman, in his inaugural message, stated that: "We must embark upon a bold new program for making the benefits of our scientific advances and industrial progress available for the improvement and growth of underdeveloped areas. [...] Democracy alone can supply the vitalizing force to stir the

---

[9] FRUS, 1950. Vol. 6, document 115, 'Policy Statement prepared in the Department of State, 16 June 1950'.

[10] See for example FRUS, 1951, Vol. 8, document 131, 'Memorandum by the Central Intelligence Agency, 1 August 1951'.

[11] In the US reports this is a frequent topic: The Burmese leadership points out to this as a fact, the US officials deny any support and the debate goes on, creating frustration especially in Rangoon.

peoples of the world into triumphant action, not only against their human oppressors, but also against their ancient enemies—hunger, misery, and despair" (Truman 1949, 2).

For Britain, "development" became a key concept in its strategies for maintaining the British Empire, now in the form of the Commonwealth, and for checking the spread of Communism. The British parliament debated Burma and Malaysia on several occasions, including the *Colonial Development and Welfare Act* of 1950.[12] There was a shared understanding that modernization and "a higher standard of life there will do more to combat Communism than militarism".[13] However, there was some disagreement on the question if British support for colonies (including former territories such as Burma) should aim at economic development or social welfare (see Schmitt, Chap. 6, this volume). The proponents of the former argued that economic growth would lead to growing social stability and warned that throwing in social reforms would include an economic burden the countries could not bear. This strategy had also the advantage of serving British economic interests in these countries as well. On the other hand, the advocates of a more welfarist strategy did not deny the need for economic development but emphasized the virtues of also including social reform:

> Let us strengthen our friendship with these people by developing social schemes, and at the same time ensuring a more equitable distribution of the wealth that is being won in the Colonies. A higher standard of life there will do more to combat Communism than militarism. We cannot destroy Communism by militarism any more than we can destroy a plague by power; it knows no frontiers. But we can destroy an ideology by a better and a nobler one.[14]

Whereas the British came to terms with Burma's independence and sensibility toward outside interference, they could pursue a more active strategy in Malaysia where several welfare reforms had been introduced

---

[12] HMSO, *Colonial Development and Welfare Bill, 1950*, vol. 480 cc 1135–251. http://hansard.millbanksystems.com/commons/1950/nov/09/colonial-development-and-welfare-bill.
[13] Ivi. § 1176.
[14] Ibidem.

prior to independence in 1957. Britain also acted through the Commonwealth, as exemplified by the Colombo-Plan of 1950 (Oakman 2010). This Australian initiative created a lasting regional organization with the purpose of strengthening economic and social development in the Asia-Pacific region. The idea of the plans was, according to Adeleke (2004, 594), to "resolve the correlation between poverty and communism". It allowed the UK (and the US) to assist indirectly through a regional organization and served as an element of the regional containment of Communism (Lowe 2009).

It is important to note, however, that also for Britain military and social spending were two competing strategies in securing Asia against Communism. In his *Security in the Colonies* report to the British government, General Sir Gerald Templer—the most important advocate of the "hearts and minds" strategy in Malaysia—pointed out that:

> Apart from the problem of raising money from the Treasury, there is the problem of seeing that Colonial territories spend their own money to the best effect. Here of course one comes up at once against the old constitutional snag; they can spend it as they please. But there is one aspect of public finance in the Colonies which is directly relevant to this Report, and that is the conflict between the claims of "welfare" and "law and order". There are two main ways of tackling Communism—economic action, to prevent or check it at the source, and police action, to contain or suppress it. In the Colonies the emphasis has hitherto been on the first approach, which is obviously the only constructive one. But if Malaya had spent on law and order a fair proportion of the large sums she was devoting to welfare, the present emergency, with the attendant colossal expenses, might well have been avoided. I submit, therefore, that the state of the cold war to-day and of our defences against it, may call for a temporary change of emphasis. Improving economic conditions do not always mean political tranquility; on the contrary, the desire to see improvement accelerated is a potent source of unrest. In the process of evolution, the development of welfare must not allow the preserving of public order—a primary function of the government—to go neglected. The Romans put communications and policing first; and it is still true that, unless these are sound, social and political development cannot be given full rein. This truth should be driven

home, in whatever ways are most appropriate, to Colonial administrations.[15]

The US and Britain were not the only international players advocating social reform as a way of achieving socio-political stability. France, the other major colonial power in the region, played the Cold War card to internationalize its own conflict with the Viet Minh, at the time when the Communist Party was seizing power in China. While the British and French approaches regarding decolonization changed on a case-by-case basis, in the years 1947–1948 both identified the struggle against the national liberation movements with the international conflict with Communism. This strategy was meant to justify military commitment in the area toward the international public opinion and to ensure US support.

The contacts between the three Western powers resulted in the attempt to establish informal tripartite consultation bodies. They were meant to share information and coordinate actions in the area to secure the "freedom" of the region, by military assistance and by "favoring the economic development and standards of living of the Southern Asian countries. [*The powers*] will jointly carry on the implementation of measures that could ensure economic balance and social progress."[16] Eventually, also for France the issue of "development", meant both in its economic (infrastructures, industry, trade) and social (assistance, social insurances, healthcare) aspects, became fundamental for containing Communism. In divided Viet Nam, both the French and the Americans promoted economic assistance in the 1950s to counter the Communist influence coming from the North. In the words of an analyst of the time, indeed, "with the achievement of independence, political stability and the beginnings of economic development in the south, there is every reason to believe that unity, when it comes, will be established on nationalist and not on Communist terms" (Hammer 1957, 235).

---

[15] TNA, Cabinet Papers, CAB/129/76, '*Security in the Colonies*, Report by general Templer to Government Committee, July 1955', p. 11.
[16] MAE, E/170/5, 'Défense de l'Indochine. Stratégie Commune, Janvier 1952–Juin 1952'.

International organizations, regional institutions and non-governmental organizations (NGOs) (such as the Rockefeller and Ford Foundations from the US) were equally involved in social reform in SEA. After WWII the ILO accompanied its traditional action of promoting tripartism and social collaboration, with a greater emphasis on modernization and social security. From the end of the war on, the ILO also focused more on SEA. This was due to the persistence of structural backwardness in the region: a huge mass of seasonal agricultural workers and seasonal unemployment; slow industrialization and poor levels of protection for workers (including women and children); generally low standards of living, low wages and low productivity, and demographic pressure. All these factors represented a threat as well as an opportunity to lead the integration of SEA in the world economy, as also the local modernizing elites recognized:

> Not only the prosperity of Asia but abiding world prosperity is bound up with rapid economic development in Asia and an appreciable rise in "the standards of living and the purchasing power of the Asian peoples". [...] Many Asian countries have in hands, or propose to take up shortly, the preparation and execution of far-reaching programmes of economic development and social reform. Their task will be considerably facilitated and world economic development on sound lines effectively ensured if they were able to secure assistance from such international agencies as the Social and Economic Council of the United Nations, the International Bank for Reconstruction and Development and the I.L.O. (ICWA 1947, 16)

The organization of the 1947 Asiatic Regional Conference, two years after WWII, was more important in the eyes of the ILO experts, who were confident that local governments wanted to take advantage of their expertise to set up national programs for social and economic development. The Conference brought together Western and local policy-makers to discuss ways of raising the living standards of the people, by introducing guidelines for social security, healthcare, social services and employment policy reforms. At the same time the Conference highlighted the emergence of the Asian countries as independent actors on the international stage. SEA was a pivotal region in determining domestic and international stabilization through freedom and social justice. Indian Prime Minister Jawaharlal Nehru stressed that greater social inclusion and the progress of the newly independent or still colonial territories would grant international stability and economic growth. Recalling the 1944 Philadelphia Declaration, he stated that this would assure a new world order based on common social outlooks: "the well-being of the people living in those regions was exceedingly important. It was not a question of rich and powerful countries being generous. It was in their own interest to prevent infectious disease and poverty. Poverty anywhere was a danger to prosperity anywhere."[17]

The recommendations of the Conference moved in this direction. Social security was set as the first item on the agenda. Its implementation was conditional to measures "providing for an adequate growth and supply of essential foodstuffs sufficient to meet the accepted standards of subsistence and nutrition, a living wage, decent housing and a healthy environment and free and compulsory education" (ILO 1947, 273). The general guidance on social security reform was modeled on general principles and administrative arrangements that recalled common European standards: "security for all" and "income maintenance", to be achieved through an integral and long-term plan of tripartite-funded social insurances, employment injury benefits (both industrial and agricultural), maternity benefits, old-age pensions and medical care services. The Director-General's report to the Conference, however, recommended proceeding with a gradual approach, attentive to regional differences in the social and occupational stratifications (Phelan 1947).

The Technical Assistance Programmes (TAP) started in SEA soon thereafter. They were meant to provide ILO's technical expertise in the drafting of comprehensive socio-economic reform to the governments that formally requested it. They were full-fledged state-building programs in "the Western way", which included social security, employment policies, vocational training, manpower organization and so forth. The ILO put in place a sequence of TAP in almost all the countries of the region at least until the early 1960s. Newly independent Burma was the first

---

[17] ILOA, RC/158-1, 'The Indian Information Service, Conference of Historic Significance in New Delhi, 31/10/1947', p. 1.

government that joined the extended programs in 1952 and for the whole decade (ILO 1952, 1958), and the Burmese TAP became the pilot program for the others, those for Viet Nam (ILO 1956, 1959) and Malaysia (ILO 1960) probably being the most extended and long lasting of all.

The TAP did not have ideological goals in the stricter sense; individual ILO officials might have had different views on the goals of social reform, but the archival documentation does not reveal any direct political involvement in the elaboration of social security programs. According to historian Daniel Maul, however, such programs were far from providing merely neutral technical assistance. On the contrary, created by American ILO Director-General David Morse, the TAP were "motivated by the looming Cold War and the nation-building imperatives generated by decolonization in Asia" and they were designed to be "an effective means of shaping the domestic policies of the 'developing countries' in such a way—basically by raising the productivity of their economies—as to render them immune to the rise of Communism" (Maul 2016, 110–111).

The assistance programs for social enhancement contributed to the Western rhetorical arsenal of human rights and development, which was also used in the 1960s in the competition against Soviet Russia during decolonization in Africa (Maul 2012; Hilger 2017; Lorenzini 2017). In the harshest years of the Cold War, ILO stood on the side of the Western powers. The active promotion of social security in SEA since 1945 was functional to the strategy of the Western powers to counter Communist influence. It offered attractive prospects for newly independent countries to maintain democratic institutions while supporting social enhancement. And, by doing so, to stay in the Western orbit.

There was a shared concern among the major Western powers and agencies of the possible spread of Communism in SEA in the late 1940s and 1950s. As we have shown, there was also a recognition that the battle against Communism could not be won only with military means. Social reform and economic modernization thus became a key element of the strategies for state-building and keeping SEA safe against Communism. The multiple actors, of course, had slightly different views on this. For the US, it was mainly geo-strategical concerns related to the global Cold War, with some variations between State Department and other groups of experts. For the British, it was also a matter of colonial power and legacies within the framework of the Commonwealth. The ILO generally had a more specific and technical agenda, reflecting the narrower purpose of the organization. However, as we will see in the next section, such ideas also drew from the domestic level. Domestic actors and the interaction between the international Cold War and domestic policy-making have to be included in the shaping of early welfare state in SEA.

## The Local Actors and the Welfare Legislation: Hampering Communism and Building State Policies

The state-building of newly independent political elites (Burma) or by gatekeeper colonial governments (Federation of Malaysia) required political legitimization through social inclusiveness. Local elites sought for it regardless of the great powers' international political considerations. In both countries, some policy areas enforced the "hearths and minds" asset of the struggle against Communism: public schemes to bolster the loyalty of civil servants and public sector as well as social insurances for farm and industrial workers; programs that favored socio-economic development (e.g. land reforms); health policy and medical care; and education. These actions were expected to bring political stability through economic modernization and social security.

Already since the late 1940s, the concept of "welfare state" was linked to the new Burmese state. As we have seen, British politicians and newspapers labeled the new Burmese constitution a welfare state constitution. The concept gained more political leverage as it became the key concept for the modernization strategies of the early 1950s. Several books and articles by international observers described Burma as an emerging welfare state (Trager 1958, 1959; Lockwood 1958; H.T. 1955). The first Burmese "two-year plan" (the "Sorrento Villa Plan", 1947–1948) had only limited effect because of the many Communist and ethnic insurgencies. The plan included a land reform and fostered the growth of the public sector within the field of infrastructure and public utilities; employment in the public sector rose from just above 50,000 in the

1940s to 250,000 in the 1950s (Taylor 1987). The background was the intense struggle against the Communists, amplified by the influence of Communist China on the Chinese minority, to such an extent that "winning the hearts and minds of the rural poor meant winning the then ongoing battle against the communist" (Than 2013, 639). However, day-to-day war on Communist insurgents prevented long-term strategic considerations and the steady strengthening of Burmese state's structures (Taylor 1987).

In 1951–1952, with the stabilization of domestic security, the Nu government started more consistent social and economic development programs (Lockwood 1958, 391; Trager 1958). The government cooperated with UN agencies and, despite stern skepticism toward the US, it also invited, in 1951, the American consulting firm Knappen Tippetts Abbett McCarthy (KTA) to work out a comprehensive analysis of the challenges and potentials of economic modernization in Burma. The report was financed by the US Technical Cooperation Administration and produced a detailed (more than 800 pages) analysis that was submitted to the government in 1953.[18] Based on the drafts of the report, the Nu government launched the development plan, called *New Burma Program* in 1954, which spelled out the so-called *Pyidawtha*-plan, which was presented to thousands of AFPFL delegates from all over the country in 1952. The preamble declared that "Burma can become one of the most prosperous nations of all Asia. In this New Burma we can enjoy a high standard of living, health and security for our people, social justice for all."[19] The plan included ten overarching policy areas: regional development, health, education, economy, nationalization (of arable lands), transportation, welfare, democratic local councils, development of frontier areas and rebuilding. Public welfare and utilities were at the heart of the plan, even

---

[18] *Economic and Engineering Development of Burma*. Prepared for the Government of the Union of Burma by Knappen, Tippetts, Abbett, McCarthy in Association with Pierce Management and Robert R. Nathan Associates, Aylesbury 1953. Online version see: https://www.nathaninc.com/insight/economic-and-engineering-development-of-burma-1953/.

[19] See Manual Instructions for Executions of Pyidawtha Plans (Rangoon 1952). Online version see: https://digital.soas.ac.uk/content/LO/AC/00/00/74/00001/PDF.pdf. See also *PYIDAWTA. The new Burma*. A report from the Government to the People of the Union of Burma on our long-term program for Economic and Social Development (1954). For an online version see: https://www.nathaninc.com/insight/economic-and-engineering-development-of-burma-1953/.

though it also had an undertone of economic modernization as a precondition for welfare reform. The project covered rural health centers, new hospitals, more and better buildings for schools, high schools and vocational schools, public housing program, nurseries and child guidance clinics, training of social workers and so forth.

The comparison between the English and the Burmese version of the documents testifies to the domestic political use made of the plan. The semantic strategy made modernization safe for the Burmese, limiting the room for Communist criticism at home, while appealing to foreign capital (Than 2013, 650). Whereas the English version speaks the language of modernization theory and social engineering, the Burmese version, meant for domestic use and addressing the population, featured a much more delicate use of local references. The main challenge for Nu was not to give the impression of importing Anglo-American ideas of development, which would fuel accusations of dependence and imperialism by the public opinion at home. Especially as the plan included ideas of opening Burma toward foreign capital, this could be negatively interpreted as inviting new colonizers. Words such as "aid" or "foreign aid" were left out for the Burmese audience; even the title *Pyidawtha*, often translated as "welfare state" (Trager 1958), is, according to Than (2013, 647) "a unique Burmanization of the word development" that included references to the country's national traditions and underpinned an idea of prosperity. In this way it linked Burma's glorious history with a modernization strategy and promises of a brighter future. The link between the past and the future was also emphasized in public speeches and campaigns for the program and included references to history and Buddhism, anticipating the Buddhist revival of the early 1950s, also fostered by US observers.[20]

The English-language version of the plan was more aligned with the technical language used in the KTA-report and by international experts. The *Pyidawtha*-plan had a threefold effect. First, it provided a strategy for Burmese modernization that allowed the country to receive aid and support from the outside: financial support from the US and the

---

[20] FRUS, 1951, Vol. 8, document 167, 'Memorandum by Acting Assistant Secretary of State for Far eastern Affairs (Allison) to Acting Secretary of State, 27 December 1951'. See also Trager (1958, 10).

Commonwealth; technical advice from US, American foundations, the ILO; aid from both regional powers such as India and the Eastern Bloc (Lockwood 1958, 397). Second, by portraying this as a national strategy it promised an avenue of reform that confronted the Communists and could strengthen loyalty to the state. Third, the plan was consistent with the Burmese policy of non-alignment.

In line with the new party-slogan "Towards the welfare state" (Trager 1958, 26) and the indicators set in the *Pyidawtha*-plan, the Burmese government in the following years presented a number of social reforms (see Lockwood 1958 for more details). The 1956 social security program was designed with the assistance of the above-mentioned TAP. It required very low contributions by industrial workers (1% of salary), offering short-term insurance for medical and disability cases. Following ILO recommendations, it was first introduced in Rangoon and only gradually spread to the rest of the country. Still with the support of international agencies, the government undertook public health initiatives including anti-malaria programs and the establishment of the Burma Pharmaceutical Industry in 1954, securing the supply of vaccines and medication. By 1958, the Burmese Secretary to the Social Security Board assessed positively the outcomes of the governmental actions, as "the pilot scheme of social security in Burma has proved a most satisfactory beginning to the setting up of a Welfare State" (Sein 1957, 60). The report also recognized that the scheme also enjoyed positive publicity among the population and, most importantly, ensured the collaboration of workers and employers, with a few exceptions.

The strategy of the Burmese governments in the late 1940s and 1950s attired to take an autonomous path from both Western and Chinese influences, a "third way" between liberal capitalism and Communism. Most of the promises of the *Pyidawtha*-plan were only partially realized; Burma lacked the resources, the administrative capacity and the political stability needed. As noted by an international observer, "the road to Pyidawtha lies through a maze" (Lockwood 1958, 440). In 1956 a new, revised plan was presented, with a less ambitious and more pragmatic approach to the modernization of the country, while in 1962 the whole process was halted, as a direct result of the military coup and regime change in Burma (Maung 1964, 1187–1189; Taylor 1987, Chap. 5).

In Malaysia, the early welfare development started under British rule. The understanding of the British was that the key to legitimacy for the UMNO and the Alliance coalition was that "a successful effort is made to relieve the very serious state of poverty and distress among the peasants" (quoted from Stockwell 1977, 511), and control of the industrial workers through trade unions which, as seen above, covered the workers of all the three main ethnicities of the country.

The reforms were a comprehensive package of social security measures that complemented the effort to boost economic growth and modernize the industrial structures of the country. Between 1950 and 1960, two plans were implemented. The above-mentioned *Draft Development Plan* (1950–1955) was elaborated in coordination with the British in the framework of the Colombo-Plan. It focused on social services, social security, development of infrastructures and trade. From 1956 to 1960, instead, the *First Malayan Plan* focused more on rural and industrial development, as well as national security (Lee and Chew-Ging 2017). During the same period, the government invited the ILO to carry out a more detailed survey on social security reform proposals. Only the subsequent Five-Years Plan, in the mid-1960s, gave new impetus for social legislation enhancement. In the industrial relations, the role of trade unions was highly regulated through the 1950 *Trade Union Act*, leaving their recognition to a centralized authority. Designed as a way of preventing trade unions from becoming a stronghold of Communist partisans, the act defused industrial conflict for the years to come.[21] The Malaysian trade unions indeed remained relatively small, without much influence, and did not push forward expanded social rights, but on the contrary regimented industrial conflict and centralized the workers' movement (Zin et al. 2002, 128).

The core of the first wave of social reform took place in 1951–1952, simultaneously with the change of tides of guerrilla warfare against the MNLA. In 1951, a program of public pensions covered specific working categories. The *Civil Service Pension* was a generous non-contributory scheme for civil servants funded by the state (through taxes), also

---

[21] See also: TNA, Cabinet Papers, CAB 129/76, '*Security in the Colonies*, Report by General Templer to Government Committee, July 1955', p. 64.

including benefits for work injuries, disability and dependent's pensions. The *Employee Provident Fund* covered workers not included in the former scheme. Until 1970, the contribution was 5% of the salary, paid by both employer and employee; 60% of savings to be withdrawn at the age of 55 (as a lump sum), and the remaining can be withdrawn for housing, education or (10% of savings) for medical expenses. In 1952 the *Employer's Liability Scheme*, covering employment injuries, required employers to insure their companies against accidents. This scheme did not become fully developed or significant, as it was still based on employer's liability, while many other countries had already shifted to a form of state insurance (it was replaced by *the Employees Social Security Act* only in 1969). Three years later, the sickness and maternity benefits (as part of the *Employment Act*) allocated a paid sick leave of 14–22 days, depending on length of employment. Maternity leave was 60 days (for a maximum of five children), including a benefit similar to wage.

A relevant field of social reform in Malaysia was education. As noticed by the experts of the time, "since the war the British have been pursuing a more 'enlightened' social policy than formerly. This especially notable in social welfare activities, for which a new welfare department has been founded, and primary education, which within a ten-year period is to be free to children of all races" (Thompson and Adloff 1947, 112). The British government regarded a comprehensive and compulsory basic education for all children as part of a "war of ideas" which supplemented the "war of arms".[22] In 1951 these ideas turned into more detailed policy actions, marking the beginning of a decade of re-organizing the educational system which, however, did not originally move on the ethnically universalist lines advocated by the British. The colonial government's report recommended a national system with six years of primary education in Malay or English; only after protests by the Chinese community, the largest ethnic group, Chinese tracks were introduced. In 1955, a new plan for a school system with Malay as the national language was presented and enacted in 1957, after independence.

---

[22] TNA, Cabinet Papers, CAB 129/48, 'Memorandum by the secretary of state for the colonies, 21 December 1951'.

In the first years since independence, the Malaysian development strategy was about economic growth leading to increasing inequality and poverty problems, particularly with regard to the living conditions in the rural areas (Zin et al. 2002, 127). The early social security system adopted some elements of universalism (the state pensions) while covering other risks in a piecemeal fashion. It aimed at winning the loyalty of specific sectors of the population through welfare policies; this was notably the case with the public sector and the growing industrial working class. At the same time social policy complied with ethnic cleavages, as demonstrated by the educational reform.

By the first half of the 1960s the Communist threat had greatly diminished; with the end of British colonial rule, the external aid for social reforms in Malaysia became primarily a matter of international organizations (see Schmitt, Chap. 1, this volume). In 1958, after full independence, the government required ILO assistance for an expanded program of social security; the expert in charge, a former civil servant of the British Ministry of Pension and National Insurance, recommended gradually strengthening the existing schemes set up in the beginning of the 1950s. The immediate amendments should enlarge the sickness and maternity benefits, by extending the provisions to the whole of the wage earners (slightly more than 50% of the active population) and, at a later stage, including specific categories of self-employed as well. It was also suggested to turn the Employer's Liability Scheme into a true state insurance and to launch pilot schemes for the improvement of medical care. The report was more cautious on unemployment benefits, due to the relative backwardness of the employment exchange service that made it impossible to collect data to plan a national unemployment scheme (ILO 1960).

The use of social reform as a key element of anti-Communist strategies also existed in the local context. Western policy-makers and technical advisors pushing for social reform as part of the state-building of stable democratic socio-political institutions heavily influenced the political elites in the two countries. This was not only a transfer of ideas fostered in Washington, London or Geneva into the domestic context. Domestic politics also played an important role for understanding of the actual timing and content of the reform agenda. In both countries it was part of party politics, and it reflected both domestic ideological considerations (for instance the Burmese non-alignment policy) and the existing ethnic cleavages and conflicts. In other words, Western Cold War concerns cannot alone explain specifics such as why Burma, in 1952, launched its *Pyidawtha*-plan or the Malaysian educational reforms of the late 1950s. We must analyze it as a complex interplay between the international Cold War and domestic politics.

## Conclusions

This chapter reconsiders the relevancy of the Cold War context when explaining welfare development in the developing world (especially in the first decades after 1945). Albeit other elements such as economic development, state capacity, political actors or colonial legacies are clearly relevant factors in explaining both social policy development and outcomes, the Cold War clearly influenced (directly or indirectly) these standard explanations and provided a wider historical framework to explain the development in the area.

We argue that the timing of welfare reforms in Burma and Malaysia can be explained by looking at the larger context of the Cold War in SEA. The concerns of the Western powers about the spread of Communism in the region were even more important than those related to the decolonization process. The two cases account for similar strategies implemented by the Western powers and by non-Communist local elites, in the presence of two different juridical statuses: Burma was formally independent, while the Federation of Malaysia was still a colony of Britain. The chapter focused on the multiple levels of making use of social security and welfare policies to counter Communism. Different institutions and political actors were involved in the remolding of social policies: international organizations such as the ILO, the Western powers (the US and the UK and—with a slightly different approach—France) and the domestic non-Communist establishments.

For the Western actors (including the ILO), social security was a plank in the process of state-building and in anchoring SEA in the Western political and economic institutions: providing economic development and social progress was deemed essential to prevent social unrest or a

Communist seizure of power in a strategically relevant area. While the colonial powers kept acting in a colonial development manner, the US and ILO rationale already underpinned a post-colonial approach to development and modernization (Gilman 2003; Maul 2016). The ILO's less important role in outlining social reform in Malaysia than in newly independent Burma might be evidence of the competition between colonial rulers and other external actors. Social security reforms were part of the Western "hearts and minds" approach that was expected to hamper the spread of Communism in SEA. There was a broad consensus on implementing social security among Western policy-makers and policy advisors in governmental bodies as well as in international organizations.

On the other hand, the local ruling classes used social reform rhetoric and policy for their own political legitimization through economic growth, development and social inclusiveness. Social welfare reforms also resulted from the interplay between Western and local political considerations. In Burma, for the AFPFL and U Nu, social security complemented rapid industrialization, land reform, healthcare improvements and free education. The national way to Socialism combined elements of social progress and a pronounced nationalism (Aung-Thwin and Myint-U 1992). In Malaysia, the political goal was rather to lay the foundations of a more Unitarian national policy that could weaken ethnic cleavages and social discrimination. Urban and land development in the countryside, planning and social security reforms pointed at legitimizing the state in the transition from colonial rule to full independence.

As the chapter is exploratory and based on two case studies, we need to be careful when generalizing our interpretative hypotheses. However, it is not unlikely that the Cold War also served as an important frame for the social security development in other countries in SEA. Furthermore, we centered our analysis on the early Cold War, from 1945 to 1960. However, the 1960s were also a period of intense decolonization, and our analytical frame may also apply to case studies in the 1970s and 1980s. Finally, SEA attracted very strong concerns from the major Western powers during the early Cold War. More explorations on this subject may reveal that similar concerns drove policies in the African region. We need more systematic and comparative research on the links between the Cold War and the welfare state in former colonial spaces.

# References

Adeleke, Ademola. 2004. The Strings of Neutralism: Burma and the Colombo Plan. *Pacific Affairs* 76 (4): 593–610.

Aung-Thwin, Maureen, and Thant Myint-U. 1992. The Burmese Ways to Socialism. *Third World Quarterly* 13 (1): 67–75.

Benson, Wilfred. 1947. Preface. In *Labor Problems in Southeast Asia*, ed. Virginia Thompson. New Haven: Yale University Press.

Boon Kheng, Cheah. 2009. The Communist Insurgency in Malaysia, 1948–1990: Contesting the Nation-State and Social Change. *New Zealand Journal of Asian Studies* 11 (1): 132–152.

Bradley, Mark. 2010. Decolonization, Revolutionary Nationalism, and the Cold War, 1919–1962. In *The Cambridge History of the War*, ed. Melvyn P. Leffler and Odd Arne Westad, 1st ed., 464–485. Cambridge: Cambridge University Press.

Buss, Claude. 1949. International Relations in Southeast Asia. In *The New World of Southeast Asia*, ed. Lennox Mills, 371–433. Minneapolis: The University of Minnesota Press.

Chancellor, C.J. 1951. Nationalism in Asia: The Eleventh Conference of the Institute of Pacific Relations. *International Affairs* 27 (2): 184–191.

Cooper, Frederick. 1996. *Decolonization and African Society. The Labor Question in French and British Africa*. Cambridge: Cambridge University Press.

Dean, Vera Micheles. 1950. Impressions of Lucknow. *Far Eastern Survey* IXI (19): 197–201.

Eckert, Andreas. 2006. Exportschlager Wohlfahrtsstaat? Europäische Sozialstaatlichkeit und Kolobialismus in Afrika nach dem Zweiten Weltkrieg. *Geschichte und Gesellschaft* 32: 467–488.

Fifield, Russel H., ed. 1963. *Southeast Asia in United States Policy*. New York: Praeger.

Gilman, Nils. 2003. *Mandarins of the Future*. Baltimore: The Johns Hopkins University Press.

H.T. 1955. Awaiting the Welfare State. *The World Today* 11 (7): 309–318.

Hammer, Ellen. 1957. Progress Report on Southern Viet Nam. *Pacific Affairs* 30 (3): 221–235.

Henderson, William. 1963. *Southeast Asia: Problems of United States Policy*. Cambridge, MA: MIT Press.

Hilger, Andreas. 2017. Communism, Decolonization and the Third World. In *The Cambridge History of Communism. Vol. 2. The Socialist Camp and World Power, 1941–1960s*, ed. Norman Naimark, Silvio Pons, and Sophie Quinn-Judge, 317–340. Cambridge: Cambridge University Press.

India Council of World Affairs. 1947. *Asia and the I.L.O.* New Delhi: Indian Council of World Affairs.

International Labour Office. 1944. *Declaration Concerning the Aims and Purposes of the International Labour Organization*. Adopted by the Conference at Its 26th Session. Philadelphia, 10 May 1944.

———. 1947. *Preparatory Asiatic Regional Conference of the International Labour Organization*. Appendix VII. Resolutions adopted by the Conference. New Delhi: International Labour Office.

———. 1952. *Expanded Programme of Technical Assistance*. Report to the Government of the Union of Burma on Social Security. Geneva: International Labour Office.

———. 1956. *Programme ordinaire d'assistance technique. Rapport au Gouvernement du Viet-Nam sur la sécurité sociale*. Genève: Bureau Internationale du Travail.

———. 1958. *Expanded Programme of Technical Assistance*. Report to the Government of the Union of Burma on Social Security. Geneva: International Labour Office.

———. 1959. *Programme élargi d'assistance technique. Rapport au Gouvernement du Viet-Nam sur la sécurité sociale*. Genève: Bureau Internationale du Travail.

———. 1960. *Expanded Programme of Technical Assistance*. Report to the Government of the Federation of Malaya on Social Security. Geneva: International Labour Office.

Jensen, Steven. 2016. *Decolonization—Not Western Liberal-Established Human Rights on the Global Agenda*. September 29. https://www.openglobalrights.org/decolonization-not-western-liberals-established-human-rights-on-g/.

Knorr, Klaus. 1950. The European Welfare State in the Atlantic System. *World Politics* 3 (4): 417–449.

Komer, Robert. 1972. *The Malayan Emergency in Retrospect: Organization of a Successful Counterinsurgency Effort*. A Report Prepared for Advanced Research Projects Agency. Santa Monica: Rand.

Lee, Cassey, and Lee Chew-Ging. 2017. The Evolution of Development Planning in Malaysia. *Journal of Southeast Asian Economies* 34 (3): 436–461.

Lockwood, Agnese Nelms. 1958. The Burma Road to Pyidawtha. *International Conciliation* 518: 383–450.
Lorenzini, Sara. 2017. The Socialist Camp and the Challenge of Economic Modernization in the Third World. In *The Cambridge History of Communism. Vol. 2. The Socialist Camp and World Power, 1941–1960s*, ed. Norman Naimark, Silvio Pons, and Sophie Quinn-Judge, 341–363. Cambridge: Cambridge University Press.
Lowe, Peter. 2009. *Contending with Nationalism and Communism: British Policy Towards South-East Asia, 1945–1965*. New York: Palgrave Macmillan.
Mackenzie, K.E. 1952. *Malaya: Economic and Commercial Conditions in the Federation of Malaya and Singapore*. London: HMSO.
Maul, Daniel. 2012. *Human Rights, Development and Decolonization: The International Labour Organization, 1940–70*. London: Palgrave Macmillan.
———. 2016. The ILO, Asia and the Beginning of Technical Assistance, 1945–1960. In *The ILO from Geneva to the Pacific Rim: West Meets East*, ed. Nelson Lichtenstein and Jill Jense. London: Palgrave Macmillan.
Maung, Mya. 1964. Socialism and Economic Development of Burma. *Asian Survey* 4 (12): 1182–1190.
Mills, Lennox. 1949. Problems of Self-Government. In *The New World of Southeast Asia*, ed. Lennox Mills, 288–342. Minneapolis: The University of Minnesota Press.
Oakman, Daniel. 2010. *Facing Asia: A History of the Colombo Plan*. Canberra: ANU Press.
Obinger, Herbert, and Carina Schmitt. 2011. Guns and Butter? Regime Competition and the Welfare State during the Cold War. *World Politics* 63 (2): 246–270.
Petersen, Klaus. 2013. The Early Cold War and the Western Welfare State. *Journal of International and Comparative Social Policy* 29 (3): 226–240.
Phelan, Edward. 1947. *Preparatory Asiatic Regional Conference of the International Labour Organization*. Report of the Director-General. New Delhi: International Labour Office.
Rudner, Martin. 1972. The Draft Development Plan of Malaya 1950–55. *Journal of Southeast Asian Studies* 3 (1): 63–96.
Sacks, Milton. 1950. The Strategy of Communism in Southeast Asia. *Pacific Affairs* 23 (3): 227–247.
Seekings, Jeremy. 2011. British Colonial Policy, Local Politics, and the Origins of the Mauritanian Welfare State, 1936–50. *Journal of African History* 52 (2): 157–177.

Sein, Maung. 1957. The Development of Social Security in Burma, 1954–57. *International Labour Review* 76: 47–60.
Spitzer, Alan. 1962. The Good Napoleon II. *French Historical Studies* 2 (3): 308–329.
Stockwell, A.J. 1977. The Formation and First Years of the United Malays National Organization (U.M.N.O.), 1946–1948. *Modern Asian Studies* 11 (4): 481–513.
Taylor, Robert. 1987. *The State in Burma*. London: C. Hurst & Co.
Than, Tharapi. 2013. The Languages of Pydawtha and the Burmese Approach to National Development. *South East Asia Research* 21 (4): 639–654.
Thompson, Virginia. 1947. *Labor Problems in Southeast Asia*. New Haven: Yale University Press.
Thompson, Virginia, and Richard Adloff. 1947. Britain's Policy in Malaya. *Far Eastern Survey* 16 (10): 112.
———. 1950. *The Left Wing in Southeast Asia*. New York: William Sloane Associates.
Trager, Frank N. 1958. *Building a Welfare State in Burma, 1948–1956*. New York: Institute of Pacific Relations.
———. 1959. The Propaganda Battle in India and Burma. *The Annals of the American Academy of Political and Social Sciences* 324: 55–65.
Truman, Henry. 1949. Inaugural Address, January 20, 1949. In *World Economic Progress through Cooperative Technical Assistance. The Point Four Program*. The Department of State, Washington: US Government Printers Office.
Westad, Odd Arnet. 2005. *The Global Cold War: Third World Interventions and the Making of Our Times*. Cambridge: Cambridge University Press.
Westad, Odd Arne. 2017. *The Cold War: A World History*. New York: Basic Books.
Zin, Ragaya Haji Mat, Hwok Aun Lee, and Saaidah Abdul-Rahman. 2002. Social Protection in Malaysia. In *Social Protection in Southeast and East Asia: Towards a Comprehensive Picture*, ed. Erfried Adam, Michael von Hauff, and Marei John, 119–169. Singapore: Frederich Ebert Stiftung.

**Open Access** This chapter is licensed under the terms of the Creative Commons Attribution 4.0 International License (http://creativecommons.org/licenses/by/4.0/), which permits use, sharing, adaptation, distribution and reproduction in any medium or format, as long as you give appropriate credit to the original author(s) and the source, provide a link to the Creative Commons licence and indicate if changes were made.

The images or other third party material in this chapter are included in the chapter's Creative Commons licence, unless indicated otherwise in a credit line to the material. If material is not included in the chapter's Creative Commons licence and your intended use is not permitted by statutory regulation or exceeds the permitted use, you will need to obtain permission directly from the copyright holder.

# 4

# The Influence of Colonialism and Donors on Social Policies in Kenya and Tanzania

Daniel Künzler

## Introduction

Kenya and Tanzania are two neighboring countries in East Africa that inspired a number of paired comparisons in the 1970s and 1980s (e.g. Cliffe 1973; Barkan 1984).[1] These mainly investigated the effects of different economic and political systems but neglected social policies. The comparisons were based on the assumption that the two countries are quite similar in terms of cultural heritage and natural setting: both are located on the East African coast, have a British colonial legacy and house significant pre-colonial Muslim populations. According to the literature, these similarities should produce a similar colonial tax income (Frankema

---

[1] Tanganyika is used for the colonial period and Tanzania for the period after independence, although Tanganyika gained independence under this name and was renamed United Republic of Tanzania three years later, with the unification of Tanganyika and Zanzibar.

---

D. Künzler (✉)
Department of Social Work, Social Policy and Global Development, University of Fribourg, Fribourg, Switzerland
e-mail: daniel.kuenzler@unifr.ch

© The Author(s) 2020
C. Schmitt (ed.), *From Colonialism to International Aid*, Global Dynamics of Social Policy, https://doi.org/10.1007/978-3-030-38200-1_4

and van Waijenburg 2014). A similar colonial tax income ought, in turn, to be linked to a similar post-colonial tax income and post-colonial social policy development (Mkandawire 2010, 2016).

However, a look at human development indicators reveals considerable differences between the two countries. In 2015, a Kenyan baby had a life expectancy of 62.2 years at birth and could expect to receive 11.1 years of schooling (UNDP 2018). In neighboring Tanzania, a baby had a longer life expectancy (65.5 years) but could expect considerably less schooling (8.9 years). On average, each of the Kenyan baby's parents had an income of US $2881 (purchasing power parity of 2011), while the Tanzanian baby's parents were somewhat poorer, with an income of US $2467 each. The Kenyan parents are less likely to be poor, as 36% of the Kenyan population lives in poverty, compared to 66% in Tanzania.[2]

Thus, Kenya and Tanzania do not really fit the theory. This makes the longer-term social policy trajectories of Kenya and Tanzania a promising research gap for a comparative study. Such a study will help especially with achieving a better understanding of differences *within* British colonialism and its legacies, assuming that the comparatively brief period of German colonialism in Tanganyika (1885–1918) is hardly formative for later social policies.[3] However, colonialism was not the only form of external influence, and it is important to also look at key post-colonial periods. This paired comparison thus tackles the following research question: What is the influence of external actors on social policies in Kenya and Tanzania?

Initially, the literature on colonial social policies and the empirical evidence for Kenya and Tanganyika are presented. The following sections then deal with the influence of donors in post-colonial Kenya and Tanzania in the following key periods. The first key period especially relevant for health care was during structural adjustment around the 1980s. The second key period begins with the turn of the millennium. It concerns the fields of health care and education and finally also the fields of pension policies and cash transfers. Lastly, the interplay between external

---

[2] This comparison is based on the indicator "Population in multidimension poverty, headcount (%)".
[3] The umbrella term "colonialism" is used here also for mandates, trusteeships and protectorates.

actors and national factors and differences between Kenya and Tanzania are discussed in the section preceding the conclusion.

## Colonial Influences on Social Policies

### Theorizing International Influences on Domestic Social Policies: Differences Within British Colonial Social Policies

The first section looks at one key external influence: colonialism. Before presenting empirical evidence on colonial social policies in Kenya and Tanganyika, it starts by picking up some threads of the introduction and discussing the literature on colonial social policies more generally. In contrast to Frankema and van Waijenburg (2014), Mkandawire (2010, 1652) claims colonial Kenya to have a higher per capita tax income than Tanganyika. The theoretical explanation for this claim is based on the literature and especially on Amin (1972) and points to the different ways these colonies were incorporated in the colonial economy. It is thus able to explain differences within British colonialism.

According to Mkandawire (2016), Kenya was a *labor reserve economy*. Concentrated in Southern and Eastern Africa, this type depended on cheap African waged labor. The education of Africans and independent forms of income were minimized; levels of land alienation and direct taxation were high, to push Africans toward waged labor. With the growth of the export industry, trade taxes became increasingly important but never completely substituted for direct taxation. High taxation was also necessary to finance the racially exclusive welfare regimes established for the white (male) population. As Künzler and Nollert (2017, 8) summarize this theoretical argument: "The exploitation of labour was based on burdening its reproduction on rural communities kept at subsistence level. Social policy was dependent on employment in the formal sector of the economy. The poor non-employed urban population was kept to a minimum and social policies based on the English Poor Laws were targeted at this group" (see also Schmitt, Chap. 6, this volume). In labor reserve economies, the colonial state was strong. The post-colonial legacy of labor reserves includes high inequality, a higher HIV prevalence rate and racialized social policies, but also a broader tax base that can potentially finance the extension of social policies.

In contrast, again according to Mkandawire (2016), Tanganyika was one of the few East African *cash crop economies*.[4] This type is mainly located in West Africa and is characterized by smallholder peasant access to land. African peasants could control their agricultural production and participated directly in international commodity markets. This allowed them to invest in the education of their children. Mkandawire (2016) assumes that cash crop economies thus had higher school enrolment rates during colonial times and that social protection was informally provided and community-based. The final assumption is a post-colonial legacy of a weak tax base linked with lower social expenditures.

To summarize the theoretical argument, Tanzania was incorporated into the colonial economy as a cash crop economy. Theoretically, this should mean mainly informal or community-based forms of social protection in colonial times and low post-colonial social expenditures. In contrast, Kenya is classified as a labor reserve and expected to have a more elaborated system of social welfare for the white settlers. While social policies for Africans during colonial times were supposedly focused on formal employment and, in a very limited capacity, the urban poor, post-colonial social expenditures are expected to be higher. What is the empirical evidence for these theoretical assumptions?

## Colonial Social Policies in Kenya and Tanganyika

This subsection will demonstrate that Kenya differs from the theoretical labor reserve model in two key aspects. First, it will demonstrate that agricultural production could support the rural poor and, second, that there was no significant welfare system for white settlers. It will then

---

[4] Amin (1972), on whose work Mkandawire (2016) builds, classified what he called German Tanganyika as a labor reserve, or more precisely as settler agriculture driving rural communities into reserves. However, in the subsequent literature colonial Tanganyika is described, in line with Mkandawire (2016), as a cash-crop economy (e.g. Cliffe 1973).

## 4 The Influence of Colonialism and Donors on Social Policies...

show how the general orientation of colonial social policies in Kenya and Tanganyika was quite similar and also that some selected policy fields (old-age pensions, minimum wages) differed less than the theory assumes. It then looks at another policy field (education), where the empirical data do not really fit to the theoretical differences. Finally, this subsection points to the extent to which the responsibility of the central colonial state differed in Kenya and Tanganyika, a key difference that is in line with the theory.

The labor reserve model was developed with classic examples such as South Africa in mind. While colonial Kenya did indeed have a substantial settler population and large-scale farms, it differed from the model in two key respects. First, the areas that supplied labor were also the centers of the production of cash crops by African farmers. This production went beyond what was needed for the reproduction of waged labor. It was oriented toward domestic and international markets and continually expanded, not least during the Second World War, when both the settler farming sector and African farmers could capitalize upon the circumstances (Anderson and Throup 1985). Agricultural production could support the rural poor. While Mkandawire (2010, 6) acknowledges that "various forms of market incorporation took place within the same economy", he did not name Kenya as an example. To a certain extent, Tanganyika too combined cash crop production with the supply of labor for plantations (see also Amin 1972). Second, while there was a dual policy of segregation in Kenya, there was no significant welfare system for white settlers, "presumably because there had never been a strong white working-class or a white urban poor demanding public welfare schemes" (Seekings 2005, 27).

In line with Mkandawire's (2010, 2016) claim, colonial Kenya had a higher extractive capacity and a higher per capita tax income than Tanganyika (Frankema and van Waijenburg 2014, 383).[5] The two colonies had different financial resources. This should theoretically result in differences in colonial social policies. However, as agricultural production in both colonies could support the rural poor, the general orientation of colonial social policies was surprisingly similar. In colonial Kenya,

---

[5] Mkandawire (2010, 1652) himself uses post-colonial data to substantiate his argument.

officials attempted to preserve rural family and communal ties and revive them when economic changes put the idealized agrarian society under pressure (Lewis 2000; Seekings 2005). Increasing urbanization led to some urban welfare initiatives. Only with the return of African soldiers after the Second World War did the Colonial Office in London and colonial officers in Nairobi see the need for intervention, but they "diverged in their visions" (Lewis 2000, 244) and met resistance from the white settlers. Finally, as in the rural areas, a logic focusing on family and communal ties was applied and urban community development was promoted. As part of the demobilization program, ex-servicemen were used as community development workers. The idea of offering gendered education and literacy training in community centers had a short boom and was followed by a productivist turn, leaving social welfare to community initiatives.

What happened in the neighboring cash crop colony of Tanganyika was broadly similar, despite differences in detail. There were isolated colonial welfare initiatives in urban areas before the Second World War. The engagement of the colonial state in the field of urban welfare in Tanganyika also increased in the context of returning African soldiers, when short-lived welfare centers were established with the aim of integrating ex-servicemen and offering gendered education and literacy training (Eckert 2004). There were differences between London and colonial officials in Tanganyika concerning their respective visions. However, generally the policy of the colonial administration "attempted to strengthen the efficiency and influence of traditional institutions in the field of social security" (Eckert 2004, 475).

Within the scope of this chapter it is not possible to look in detail at all social policy fields. In the following, old-age pensions and minimum wages are discussed to show that these policy fields were less different than theory would assume. The picture would be similar for other policy fields, such as health care or social protection against employment injury. Concerning old-age pensions, workers in Kenyan government service had a certain coverage, but there was a fairly distinct racial divide on the formal labor market. There was a common agreement that a more comprehensive pension coverage was needed, but there were long debates about what the exact nature of such a pension scheme would be. A

## 4 The Influence of Colonialism and Donors on Social Policies... 85

committee appointed in 1953 to study social insurance (Clayton and Savage 1974) recommended a contributory pension fund. However, independence was imminent, and the matter was left. In Tanganyika, the colonial administration was also not supportive of a compulsory provident fund for non-governmental formal sector workers (Eckert 2004, 475). Lower ranks of government service were covered by the provident fund of 1942 (Bossert 1985).[6] Both Tanganyika and Kenya fit in the general pattern of British colonies, as more comprehensive social protection for old age was introduced only after independence (Schmitt 2015).

Old-age pensions were among the demands of Kenyan labor movements in their frequent strikes (Singh 1969).[7] However, the emphasis was more on the acceptance of unions, political participation of Africans and especially minimum wages, housing and working conditions (Singh 1969; Clayton and Savage 1974). Especially after the Second World War there was a significant policy change: As a means of stabilizing the workforce, the minimum wage was no longer deemed to be intended to provide for a bachelor but for an urban family and was raised considerably (Neubert 1986, 90–91). However, this minimum wage was based on a very narrow conception of a nuclear family and was also supposed to solve housing problems. Family allowances were not common in colonial Kenya, as they were considered to impede the competitivity of male workers with children on the labor market (Neubert 1986, 91). Tanganyika had a Minimum Wage Ordinance from 1939 on, but there was no mechanism for wage fixing and thus, in contrast to Kenya, de facto no minimum wage during the colonial period (Bryceson 1990).

Looking at another policy field, education, there are differences between Kenya and Tanganyika, but not in the way claimed by theory. According to Mkandawire (2016), enrolment should be higher in Tanganyika. This is not the case: At the end of the colonial period Kenya had higher primary and secondary education enrolment rates (Künzler 2007, 75). But Kenyan enrolment was highly unequal, and a substantial

---

[6] In principle, higher ranks could expect pensions from 1932 on, but there were no Africans in such positions (Bossert 1985, 102).
[7] Labor movements also referred to the ILO to back this claim.

part of the education budget went to a small number of children of European settlers.

However, focusing too narrowly on colonial social policies might miss a more indirect effect linked to the lower extractive capacity of Tanganyika. The late colonial state in Tanganyika was more modest in spending and placed greater emphasis on engagement at the local level. In contrast, the colonial state in Kenya had a more top-down, interventionist manner and spent more. In line with other labor reserves (Mkandawire 2016), colonial Kenya introduced, in 1919, strong racially exclusive policy measures to manage labor migration by way of registration. "The registration system brought virtually the entire adult male African population under much more direct administrative control, and made it possible to trace back to the reserves and arrest deserters and other violators who failed to be properly signed off by an employer" (Berman and Lonsdale 1992, 112–113). This registration system was a tool to raise African taxes, but proof of employment also exempted Africans from compulsory labor. The hated system was abolished in 1947, but a somewhat similar passbook system was introduced among ethnic groups mostly linked to the *Mau Mau* insurgency that officially lasted from 1952 to 1960. Also this insurgency contributed to the top-down interventionist nature of the colonial state.

In many ways, the legacy of the colonial period is not linked to different social policies but rather to the differing extent to which the central colonial states were responsible for social policies. One example of this is famine relief. Colonial Kenya introduced measures such as free famine relief, free school meals, work-for-food programs or the provision of foodstuffs for markets on subnational levels. However, as early as 1918, reactions to food shortages were centrally coordinated by the colonial government (Maxon 1980). During the famine of 1960, too, the central administration became involved, and food for famine relief was imported in the context of a coordinated operation. By contrast, in Tanganyika famine relief was initially an ethical imperative for district-level administrators rather than a government obligation (Bryceson 1990). It was quite elementary and never a national task or a right.

Thus, contrary to the theoretical expectation, the general orientation of colonial social policies was surprisingly similar in Kenya and

Tanganyika. However, the central colonial state was less directly responsible for social policies in Tanganyika. These differences in responsibility continued in the years following independence, and the emphasis on local-level engagement and questions of affordability were more important in Tanzania than in Kenya.[8] Within the scope of this chapter it is not possible to describe the 1960s and 1970s in detail, and these decades are skipped to have enough space for the following decades when the influence of international actors in the field of social policies is more pertinent. Indeed, the dominant models of social policies championed by international actors during the 1960s and 1970s were quite in line with domestic priorities, based on both a modernization framework that emphasized formal sector-based social security and government planning of social services. Thus, the next section picks up the thread starting in the 1980s, because this is a key period to discuss the influence of international donors.

## The Influence of Donors During Structural Adjustments Around the 1980s

The second key influence after colonialism discussed in this chapter is international donors. Again, literature assumes them to be important drivers of social policy-making in the Global South (e.g. Niño-Zarazúa et al. 2012). There is ample empirical evidence that suggests that this was the case around the 1980s, for example when donors such as the World Bank and the International Monetary Fund (IMF) pushed national governments to implement structural adjustment programs. They generally included the cutting of budgets for the civil service or for social expenditures and were accompanied by the introduction of official user fees in the health care and/or education sectors (e.g. Künzler 2007, 2016c). Lacking viable alternatives, many sub-Saharan African countries were dependent on the financial backing of these international financial

---

[8] The focus on the informal social welfare system of the community, described above for British colonies, continued after independence: The Kenyan *Harambee* movement asked communities to support social services with labor, building materials and money. In Tanzania the situation was different, as community participation in development was partly enforced top-down.

institutions and introduced such policies, sometimes backed by internal actors. However, there is also evidence of national governments only paying lip service to international obligations. There seem to be limits to donor influence.

Unfortunately, the observation by Boyle, Songora and Foss (2001, 524) is still quite correct: "No comprehensive sociological theory explains this variation in the adoption of policies promoted through the international system." The World Polity Theory acknowledges differences in the adoption of global policy models under the label of "de-coupling" and points to the influence of two factors: relevance and leverage (Boyle et al. 2001). A necessary condition for de-coupling to occur is adverse relevance of a policy proposal for domestic key constituencies. However, de-coupling is more likely and greater in countries with more leverage in the international system.[9] Richer countries have more leverage than poorer (e.g. post-conflict) countries, but geo-strategic importance also matters.

The empirical evidence for donor influence in Kenya and Tanzania after the late 1970s shows that Kenya indeed had more room for manoeuver than Tanzania. After the death of President Kenyatta in 1978, the new president Moi pledged to follow the footsteps of his predecessor. Some of his early decisions were indeed reminiscent of earlier policies (increase of minimum wages, systematic hiring of graduates, national famine relief). However, Kenya had increasing financial problems and became more dependent on international financial institutions. Kenya became one of the first countries to receive a structural adjustment loan after it had devaluated its currency and slowed down government hiring.

The Kenyan government announced user charges in two subsequent development plans (1979–1983 and 1983–1988), however, without introducing them. In the next development plan (1989–1993) this commitment to introduce user charges was replicated, and finally user charges were announced. After a public outcry the government used the more acceptable term of "introduction of cost-sharing" to communicate the same thing: the end of free health care (Mwabu 1995, 248). A cost-sharing scheme was hastily introduced in 1989, under "considerable pressure from donors" (Mwabu 1995, 248). After only nine months of

---

[9] Niño-Zarazúa et al. (2012, 165) mention such a difference without much discussion.

implementation, the suspension of outpatient fees was abruptly communicated in the mass media. The reason was that media reported the disastrous effects of the fees on the poor and vulnerable and that the government came under pressure. It is unclear if the imminence of the first multiparty elections, of December 1992, also played a role. However, in April 1992, shortly after the suspension, the Kenyan government announced the reintroduction of facility-dependent outpatient fees, again through mass media (Mwabu 1995, 248). In reaction to earlier criticism, the new fees were to be charged after the patient was treated, and there were unclear exemptions. There were no protests anymore (Mwabu 1995, 252).

Tanzania also came under economic pressure and was confronted with international financial institutions and their technocratic structural adjustment demands. Like Kenya, Tanzania tried to manoeuver in the space available. In 1981, a domestically crafted program was launched. However, donors doubted the sincerity of the government and reduced aid. This pushed government, in 1982, to a structural adjustment program that included the partial removal of maize price subsidies, cushioned by a rise of the minimum wage. In contrast to the country's first president Nyerere, his successor Mwinyi was less reluctant to introduce economic reforms (D'Arcy 2013, 233). In 1986, the donor-backed economic recovery program introduced user fees for education. Other donor-backed programs followed and included the formal introduction of health care user fees in 1993, strongly pushed by donors and complemented by an exemption and waiver policy. Politicians were hesitant, but there was some domestic support from bureaucrats (Pedersen and Jacob 2018, 7). Multiparty elections were introduced only after this policy change, and the opposition unsuccessfully promised to abolish the user fees.

Thus, while both countries support the theoretical assumption that the influence of international donors was quite high during the period of structural adjustment, there were differences in terms of room for manoeuver. Tanzania has less leverage in the international system and was quickly sanctioned (see Devereux and Kapingidza, Chap. 11, this volume). The introduction of multiparty elections is another crucial effect of donor influence that had important consequences for later social policies (D'Arcy 2013). This will become evident in the discussion of the influence of donors after 2000 in the fields of health care and education (next section) as well as pensions and cash transfers (following section).

## The Influence of Donors After 2000: The "Millennium Development Goals" (MDGs)

After 2000, the MDGs received a great deal of attention from international donors. Especially goals 2 to 5 became important for the domestic political agenda in Kenya and Tanzania. Goals 2 and 3 concerned education and called for an expansion of enrolment to achieve universal primary education and gender equality in primary, secondary and later also tertiary education. Goals 4 and 5 focused on the reduction of child and maternal mortality rates. In contrast to the remaining goals, Goals 2–5 are in line with two potential domestic priorities: they can be framed as being productivist and have a broad electoral appeal. However, there is an important difference between health care and educational goals. There are no clear models in global health care policies (Kaasch 2013), and countries therefore can choose different policies in the name of attaining global goals. This subsection will show that donors are somewhat influential, but the resulting national politics in the health care sector are quite varied and inconsistent. In the domain of education there was a wide international consensus that user fees had to be abolished in order to raise enrolment. Even the World Bank, deviating from its earlier cost-sharing policies, argued against user fees in primary education. As discussed below, both countries abolished user fees and followed the international prescription.

In Kenya, school fees were an important topic of the electoral campaign in the run-up to the contested Kenyan presidential election of 2002. The governing party wanted to reduce fees, while the oppositional coalition promised to abolish them. Shortly after winning the election, the new president, Kibaki, from the oppositional coalition summarily declared free primary education. This policy was financially supported by the World Bank and the UK Department for International Development (DFID) and other donors. The government proposed a new "National

Social Health Insurance Fund" (NSHIF) to replace the "National Health Insurance Fund" (NHIF), with advice by the World Health Organization (WHO) and the then Deutsche Gesellschaft für Technische Zusammenarbeit (GTZ) (Künzler 2016a, 10). Parliament passed a highly controversial bill in December 2004, but President Kibaki declined to sign it into law, and the unsigned bill later lapsed. In parallel, government also partly removed health care user fees. Another significant reform was again summarily introduced shortly after the 2013 presidential election. The winner, Uhuru Kenyatta, represented a new coalition and shortly after the election declared that public maternity services would henceforth be for free (Künzler 2016a, 6–8). While there was no direct donor support for this policy, donors are generally quite important for the financing of the Kenyan health system. An important campaign issue of both the governing party and the main opposition coalition in the 2017 election was free secondary education. After his re-election, Uhuru Kenyatta introduced this policy with effect from January 2018, until now without any known major donor support.

In Tanzania, in the run-up to the second multiparty presidential elections of 2000, several candidates, including the incumbent successor of Mwinyi, Mkapa, "promised to reduce or abolish primary school fees, which they perceived to be a widespread concern among voters" (Kjær and Therkildsen 2013, 597). D'Arcy (2013, 235) cites a civil society observer who described the promise as "definitely a vote winner" and concludes that the abolition of school fees would "yield a particularly high political return for the government". After being elected for his second term, Mkapa fulfilled his promise and re-introduced free primary education. While the political return of such a policy change was surely quite high for the government, there was also "public pressure during the Poverty Reduction Strategy Paper process and (…) active lobbying of the president by the World Bank Country Director, who was keen to repeat Uganda's UPE [Universal Primary Education, dk] success in Tanzania" (Kjær and Therkildsen 2013, 597). However, pressure was associated with financial support through a World Bank loan in the form of debt relief for the social sectors. According to D'Arcy (2013, 236), "the removal of fees would not have been feasible without the help of donors".

Secondary education was also a topic in the 2005 presidential elections, as a result of which Kikwete succeeded Mkapa. However, the electoral promise was an expansion of the lower secondary education infrastructure, pushed less by Kikwete than by Prime Minister Lowassa, who later became an oppositional presidential candidate (Languille 2015). This policy choice does not follow the preference of international donors for the abolition of school fees but is still in line with the MDGs.[10] However, free secondary education was declared shortly after the election of the new president, Magufuli, in 2015 without major donor support.

As D'Arcy (2013) emphasizes, the government of Tanzania remained committed to cost-sharing in the health care sector. She explains this by the lack of significant donor funding for a fee-removal policy. While a few donors such as DFID and UNICEF were supportive of the removal of health care fees, others, including the World Bank, were more ambiguous. The switch of DFID to General Budgetary Support in 2002 weakened the fee abolition position. Yet other donors supported community (e.g. Swiss Agency for Development and Cooperation) or national (GTZ) health insurance schemes. Consequently, the NHIF was introduced in 1999, focusing on public sector employees and their dependents. In 2001, the "Community Health Fund" was introduced for the informal sector. The term "community" refers to local involvement in the management of the fund. From 2007 on the NHIF mandatory also covered formal sector workers in the private sector. There are discussions to make the NHIF compulsory for all Tanzanians. There are also patchwork attempts at reforms in the health sector without donor support, for example, by providing free health insurance cards to poor pregnant women and their households or by plans to make NHIF membership mandatory for all citizens.

In a nutshell, while national governments followed the clear international prescriptions in the domain of education, this was not the case in the domain of health care, where there was more room for manoeuver.

---

[10] It represented a rupture with the educational policy of Nyerere which strongly emphasized primary education and limited secondary education to a meritocratic elite (Languille 2015).

## Pension Policies and Cash Transfers Since the Turn of the Millennium

### Pension Policies

There is also some room for manoeuver for national governments in the field of global pension policy, but for different reasons. In this field there is contestation between policy models (Kaasch 2013). The historically older model, social insurance, is pushed by an epistemic community around the International Labour Organization (ILO). The second model emerged around the World Bank and promoted a three-pillar pension system with a strong emphasis on privately funded and managed pension schemes. While the second model was for some years highly influential in Central and Eastern Europe, it was less influential in sub-Saharan Africa (Kpessa and Béland 2012). The World Bank later adapted its policy model and included social pensions. More recent publications are more cautious and no longer recommend a clear policy model (Künzler 2016c). The field of pension policies shows quite clearly that the prescriptions of international donors are not static but constantly revised and adapted. Different donors might favor contradictory policies at certain moments. Donor influence is higher when this is not the case (see Shriwise, Chap. 2, this volume).

Both countries sought and followed ILO advice for pension reforms. In Kenya, the "National Social Security Fund" (NSSF) was in 2013 turned from a lump-sum provision scheme into a pension scheme with monthly payments (Künzler 2016b). Early 2020, contributions to be deducted from civil servants' pay were announced. In Tanzania, the transformation of the "National Provident Fund" (NPF) into the NSSF was decided in 1996. Monthly payments were introduced and coverage was extended to former non-pensionable employees of the central government, the formal private sector and the self-employed. In 1999, the previous non-contributory pay-as-you-go pension system for employees of the central government was changed to a contributory scheme offering a monthly pension. However, in recent years the focus switched—as it did in Kenya—to cash transfers, the topic of the next subsection.

## Cash Transfers

Cash transfers are used in several policy fields, and different donors support different varieties of cash transfers. Empirical evidence shows that African countries with more financial resources (leverage) and also some poorer countries used their room of manoeuver and adopted unconditional cash transfer programs with the support of various donors (Simpson 2018). In contrast, poorer countries more frequently adopted conditional cash transfer programs with support from the World Bank. Indeed, Kenya adopted unconditional cash transfers supported by the World Bank and other donors, while Tanzania introduced a conditional cash transfer with support of the World Bank and other donors.

In Kenya, UNICEF used the run-up to the 2002 elections to campaign for orphans and vulnerable children and made parliamentary candidates sign a call to action (Alviar and Pearson 2009). More than 100 of them later became Members of Parliament, including the new president, Kibaki, and many ministers of his cabinet. After the elections, a pre-pilot and then a pilot for a "Cash Transfer for Orphans and Vulnerable Children" (CT-OVC) were started, both financed by donors such as the Swedish International Development Cooperation Agency (SIDA), DFID, UNICEF, the United States Agency for International Development and World Bank. UNICEF also provided three technical advisors to the Kenyan government (Ouma and Adésínà 2019, 385). However, the influence of this kind of external actors is very difficult to assess. UNICEF continued lobbying, not least by financing study trips to Colombia and Jamaica where cash transfer programs existed. These trips made some key officials change their critical attitude toward cash transfer programs, including fears of dependency (Ikiara 2009, 21). Among the early key supporters was former Vice-President Awori. Conditionality was initially considered but then dropped. The Ministry of Finance considerably multiplied the initial budget allocation in subsequent years. This continued after the 2007 election, when opposition politicians were included in a Government of National Unity. The new Prime Minister Raila Odinga, who had narrowly lost the presidential elections to Kibaki, also became supportive after a study trip to India (Ikiara 2009, 21). Donors such as the World Bank, DFID, UNICEF and SIDA contributed. However, the World Bank contribution is a credit facility that has to be repaid. In this sense, the notion of donor support is misleading. Cautious domestic voices warned against rising debts (Ikiara 2009, 17). The second major cash transfer program is the "Hunger Safety Net Programme" (HSNP) in 2008, conceived and funded by DFID without much consultation with the Kenyan government (Ouma and Adésínà 2019, 386). Smaller programs include the "Older Persons Cash Transfer", the "Disability Grant" and the "Urban Food Subsidy" (Künzler 2016b).

After the election of the new president, Uhuru Kenyatta, in 2013 the "Urban Food Subsidy", advocated by NGOs Concern and Oxfam, was suspended in 2016. However, in February 2014 the "Disability Grant", the pensions-tested "Older Persons Cash Transfer" and the CT-OVC were expanded and consolidated under the name of "Inua Jamii Cash Programme". Remarkably, the HSNP, which was rather imposed on the Kenyan government, was not included. The "Inua Jamii Cash Programme" was again supported by a loan from the World Bank. In a speech on the occasion of its introduction, President Kenyatta presented this program as a responsibility of the government toward the population (RoK 2014). There were no references to questions of affordability or dependency of recipients. In recent years the program has been further expanded and an additional 500,000 Kenyans aged 70 years and above have been included by a top-down decision. The cash transfer program also includes NHIF cover for the elderly and aims at universal coverage of this age group. Finance Minister Rotich was cited by media in favor of this inclusion and without concerns regarding affordability or dependency (Nyataya 2017). Indeed, this quite remarkable expansion of social policies in Kenya did not trigger any significant public discussions about affordability and sustainability. This is not to say that there are no discussions about the growth of government expenditures. However, cash transfer programs are generally not blamed for this. President Kenyatta even legitimized the proposed levy of value added tax on petroleum products with references to free education and cash transfers to the elderly.

Donor support clearly worked in favor of the introduction of the orphans and vulnerable children (OVC) and HSNP cash transfers. While several donors were involved, they pushed in the same direction.

However, there are important domestic co-drivers. It is hardly a coincidence that cash transfers were introduced in the context of growing political competition. Since 2003, the country has been governed by presidents and vice-presidents from different, highly personality-driven and thus constantly changing political parties. They have a short-term focus on their (re)election. In 2013, decentralization was introduced and political competition on the subnational level intensified. The expansion of cash transfers gave national-level politicians important leverage at the local level, as the local Member of Parliament is involved in the selection of beneficiaries. In the context of term limits and personality-driven political parties, politicians have incentives to incur debts, as neither they nor their parties will necessarily be in power when the debts have to be repaid. Domestic priorities are thus important intermediary factors that shape the way global goals and donor priorities are translated into national policies.

In contrast to this Kenyan experience, concerns of affordability and long-term sustainability are more important in Tanzania. By way of illustration, President Mkapa (2005, 61) called debts dangerous for the freedom of the country. This concern stems from the colonial past but is also reinforced by a political system where a dominant party has been in power since independence and has a self-conceived notion of its perpetual responsibility for the country. In line with this is a preference for more restricted social policies.[11] In 2008, donors such as the World Bank, Japan, the USA and Norway supported a pilot project of the "Tanzania Mainland Social Action Fund" (TASAF) that paid a cash transfer on condition of regular school attendance by children or regular health checks for elderly ("Community-Based Conditional Cash Transfer", CB-CCT). This pilot followed a World Bank-funded workshop in 2005 (Ulriksen 2016a). Interestingly, the World Bank took officials on study trips to Ethiopia, Kenya and Jamaica, resulting in a different kind of policy learning than the Jamaica trip mentioned for the CT-OVC in Kenya. In Tanzania, key domestic players (politicians of the ruling party, Ministry

---

[11] One example is the program for most vulnerable children which, in contrast to Kenya, does not include a cash transfer but rather small in-kind transfers (Ulriksen 2016b, 5).

of Finance, TASAF), the government and the World Bank alike favored conditional transfers and opted for scaling them up.

Concerning cash transfers, not much happened in the run-up to the 2010 elections, when the image of the ruling party was marred by high-level corruption scandals. The focus of the ruling party was on fertilizer subsidies, whose coverage was expanded prior to the elections to include rice- and maize-growing districts (Kjær and Therkildsen 2013, 600). Members of the ruling party dominate the councils that choose the beneficiaries of the subsidies. This is an interesting case of policy learning: "Interviews with (...) party officials show that the role of subsidies in the Malawi elections inspired the (...) leadership" (Kjær and Therkildsen 2013, 601). The World Bank, previously against fertilizer subsidies, changed its stance and supported this expansion.

In 2012, the government approved the "Productive Social Safety Net" (PSSN) program that included a conditional cash transfer targeting the extremely poor population and a public work component (Ulriksen 2016a). The cash transfer component is rooted in the CB-CCT mentioned above and supported by the World Bank and other donors such as DFID and SIDA. In contrast to Kenya, in Tanzania the World Bank has a strong preference for a restricted cash transfer program that is in line with domestic political priorities. The PSSN has a strong productivist touch (Ulriksen 2016b, 17). According to Ulriksen (2016a), the idea of productivity and co-responsibility was an important argument for an upscaling of the conditional cash transfer (CCT) program. This does not mean that the government did not toy with the idea of a universal social pension, at certain moments favored by DFID and other donors as well as the Ministry of Labour. Announced ahead of the 2015 election, it has yet to be introduced. Instead, the government supported conditional cash transfers, which helped to convince donors to support the PSSN (Ulriksen 2016a). From a donor perspective, an additional advantage of the PSSN as opposed to the social pension was that the PSSN was already operational. For the government, the timing of the identification of additional beneficiaries of the scaled-up PSSN just ahead of the 2015 elections was politically advantageous. Nevertheless, there is lacking financial commitment with the CCT component of the PSSN (Jacob and Pedersen 2018, 21). Indeed, under the new president, Magufuli, the CCT component of the PSSN seems to have become less important than the public works element, in contrast to opposing donor preferences (Jacob and Pedersen 2018).

# The Interplay Between External Actors and National Factors

## The Interplay Between External Actors and Domestic Factors in the Colonial Period

This subsection attempts not only to compare the influence of colonialism with regard to similarities and differences between social policies in Kenya and Tanzania but also to discuss the role of domestic actors. Neither colonial Kenya's nor Tanganyika's social policies fit very well to Mkandawire's (2016) descriptions of labor reserve and cash crop economies. In Kenya there was a dual policy of segregation, imposed by particular colonial officials against the resistance of parts of the white settler population (Maxon 1980). However, there was no significant welfare system for white settlers. These settlers were in general often in conflict with colonial officers in Nairobi and the Colonial Office in London (Anderson and Throup 1985). However, they were less influential than their counterparts in classic examples of labor reserves such as South Africa. Against their interests, the colonial state intervened and encouraged African cash crop production alongside settler production. Thus, agricultural production could support the rural poor in colonial Kenya, as was the case in Tanganyika.

Consequently, the general orientation of colonial social policies was surprisingly similar, in contradiction to the theoretically expected differences. In both colonies there were isolated and short-lived colonial welfare initiatives in urban centers. This was in line with the vision of the Colonial Office in London that favored educated and urban working-class Africans (see Seekings, Chap. 5, this volume). However, it was in conflict with the rural focus of colonial officers in Kenya and Tanganyika.[12] Local colonial officers impeded or even boycotted the initiatives of the disconnected Colonial Office (Lewis 2000; Eckert 2004). Concerned with the political legitimacy of colonial rule in rural areas, local colonial officers focused on efficient rural institutions that were able to provide social welfare.

The policy fields discussed were also less different than theory (Mkandawire 2016) assumes: Neither colony focused much on family allowances, and there were no comprehensive colonial pension schemes for formal sector workers outside the civil service. In these policy fields, local colonial officers and the Colonial Office in London shared quite similar positions. More in line with Mkandawire (2016), Kenya has a stronger focus on formal sector workers insofar as minimum wages were actually introduced. Also in support of Mkandawire's (2010, 2016) claim, colonial Kenya had a higher extractive capacity and a higher per capita tax income. A more indirect effect linked to the lower extractive capacity of Tanganyika is that the late colonial state spent less and placed more emphasis on local-level engagement than Kenya. Exemplary in this respect was famine relief: While famine relief involved the central colonial government in Kenya, it was not a government obligation but rather an ethical imperative at the district level in Tanganyika. This also shows that it is too simplistic to equate colonial influences with external influences, as in this policy field colonial officers based in Kenya and Tanganyika clearly mattered. Local actors are also important for other forms of external influence, as the next subsection will show.

## International Donors and Their Interplay with National Factors

Concerning the influence of international donors, both countries support the theoretical assumption that the influence of international donors was quite high during the period of structural adjustment. Both countries were in serious financial troubles, and there were no alternatives

---

[12] In Kenya, their opposition to urban welfare initiatives was strongly supported by white settlers (Lewis 2000, 244).

available to avoid the introduction of user fees. However, there were differences in terms of room for manoeuver. Tanzania was quite quickly sanctioned with a reduction in aid and pushed to introduce structural adjustment measures. Kenya had more leverage in the international system, being an important ally of Western powers in a region with socialist governments and civil wars (see Mioni and Petersen, Chap. 3, this volume). While the introduction of user fees has been on the domestic agenda for several years, it took World Bank pressure to introduce them swiftly. However, Kenya could sway policies with regard to domestic concerns without being sanctioned. Finally, another crucial effect of donor influence in both countries is the introduction of multiparty elections.

The empirical observations in the fields of health care and education after the turn of the millennium point to a number of conclusions. First, where donor policies were clear and significant support available (free primary education), countries were quick to follow the international prescription. These prescriptions were important in electoral campaigns, as they have a universal electoral appeal. Where there was no significant donor support, countries nevertheless introduced policies in line with the international prescriptions (free secondary education), but with quite a significant time lag. No clear picture emerges where donor prescriptions are not clear and support is indirect or fragmented (health care). In both cases, domestic politics are important for the timing of social policy changes: They cluster around elections. Different social policy fields might be substitutes. There were never two major social policy changes around one election. However, there were also elections without major social policy reform. This concerned the second terms of Kibaki (2007) and Kikwete (2010), but not the second term of Kenyatta (2017). A final observation is that there is commitment to cost-sharing in the health sector in Tanzania, while Kenya introduced a policy of fee exemption policies.

The influence of international donors seems to be more limited in another social policy field that has also become more important since the turn of the millennium. Concerns with affordability shaped the way in which Tanzania made use of a World Bank credit for the introduction of a partly conditional cash transfer program. In Kenya, such concerns are quite absent, and unconditional cash transfers have been expanded in recent years. This difference is also reinforced by the differences in the countries' respective contemporary political systems. While there is electoral pressure in Tanzania and the implementation of the PSSN was sped up before the 2015 elections, the ruling party has been in power since independence, and long-term financial sustainability is embedded in its self-conception. In contrast, since 2003 Kenya has been governed by presidents and vice-presidents from different, highly personality-driven and thus constantly changing political parties with short-term policies focused on the next elections. Kenya spends more on social assistance.[13] Consequently, the debt level is much higher in Kenya, where social policies are continuously expanded without much concern for affordability.[14] In addition to differences in the contemporary political systems and resulting different kinds of electoral pressure, this key difference between Kenya and Tanzania is rooted in the colonial past. In line with the expectations of Mkandawire (2016), former colonial labor reserve Kenya has indeed got broader tax-financed social policies and is less concerned with affordability.

## Conclusion

This conclusion starts by discussing the influence of external actors in Kenya and Tanzania. In the colonial period, the Colonial Office in London tried to shape the general outline of social policies and developed a focus on educated and urban working-class Africans. Colonial officers in Kenya and Tanganyika subverted this vision with their rural focus. Consequently, colonial welfare initiatives in urban centers in Kenya and

---

[13] World Bank (2018b) data show that the total spending on social assistance as a percentage of GDP is clearly higher in Kenya (2.52% in 2010) compared to Tanzania (0.29% in 2009). More recent data will be higher in both countries, but the effects of the new cash transfer programs still have to be researched. Interestingly, again according to older data, Kenya's social assistance spending is more pro-poor than Tanzania's: 8% of the benefits went to the poorest quintile in Kenya, compared to 1% in Tanzania (World Bank 2018b). In both countries, a considerable part of government expenditure goes to civil service pensions.

[14] Debt was at US $41.91 billion in June 2017, compared to US $23.69 billion in Tanzania (East African 2017). Looking at time series data from the World Development Indicators (World Bank 2018a), debt services have been higher in Kenya than in Tanzania throughout the period from 1971 to 2016. Of course, this level of debt is not only caused by social policies.

Tanganyika were surprisingly similar but isolated and short-lived. While white settlers and African actors also tried to shape social policies, local colonial officers were key. Concerning the absence of family allowances and of a comprehensive pension scheme for formal sector workers outside the civil service, there was no conflict of interests between local colonial officers and the Colonial Office. In these policy fields, Kenya and Tanganyika fit very well into the general pattern of British colonies. Finally in another policy field, famine relief, local colonial actors acted without reference to the Colonial Office.

Concerning the influence of external actors in the post-colonial period, there is no systematic theory explaining how successful international donors are with influencing domestic social policies. The empirical evidence for the room for manoeuver available to national governments is ambiguous. Donor influence varies between policy fields and is bigger if donor leverage is big and if donors support the same policies (e.g. during structural adjustment programs). Poorer countries have less leverage to resist policy recommendations of key international donors. The influence of international donors is limited if their policy proposals adversely affect the priorities of key domestic policy actors and especially if a country has leverage in the international system. Domestic political elites might have other priorities than international donors and might be reluctant to scale up pilot projects or assume financial responsibilities after donor funding has come to an end. Empirical evidence of domestic elite priorities includes a focus on economic growth and productivity and worries about dependency. In addition, domestic political elites might choose social policies because of their electoral appeal, without the support of international donors. This underlines the importance of domestic factors for social policies.

In both the colonial and the post-colonial periods, certain local actors matter as mediators of external influences. In the colonial period, key colonial officers subverted the visions of the Colonial Office if they deemed them inappropriate. They also had scope for their own initiatives. In both cases, concerns with the legitimacy of colonial rule in rural areas were important motivations. White settlers and African actors are less able to shape colonial social policies. In the post-colonial period, domestic political elites (especially presidents and influential ministers) are key. They resist and sometimes subvert donor initiatives if their priorities are affected and donor leverage is limited. With or without donor support, domestic political elites have a certain preference for social policies that fit their priorities (focus on economic growth and productivity) and have an electoral appeal. These policies are not necessarily supported by the bureaucrats that have to implement them. Bureaucrats as well as other domestic actors, such as NGOs, seem to matter more for the technical aspects of social policies than landmark decisions.

An important result that indicates some research gaps is the more indirect but lasting effect linked to the lower extractive capacity of Tanganyika. In line with the expectations of Mkandawire (2016), former colonial labor reserve Kenya does indeed have broader tax-financed social policies. It is less concerned with affordability. Zanzibar, another colonial labor reserve, shows a similar pattern. In 2016 it introduced a universal, tax-financed old-age pension (Seekings 2016). As in Kenya, the discourse centers more on government responsibility than on fears of dependence. Further research could focus on other countries of similar type that are less researched and might offer contrasting evidence, for example Burundi, Madagascar or Eswatini. Also worth analyzing are the countries belonging to what Amin (1972, 504) called the "Africa of the concession-owning companies". Also Mkandawire (2016, 2) uses this term, without saying much about these countries concentrated in Central Africa. Indeed, as this group consists of Francophone and some Iberophone countries, they constitute an astonishing gap in the social policy literature.

## References

Alviar, Carlos, and Roger Pearson. 2009. *Cash Transfer for Vulnerable Children in Kenya: From Political Choice to Scale-Up*. Social and Economic Policy Working Paper. New York: UNICEF.

Amin, Samir. 1972. Underdevelopment and Dependence in Black Africa—Origins and Contemporary Forms. *Journal of Modern African Studies* 10 (4): 503–524.

Anderson, David, and David Throup. 1985. Africans and Agricultural Production in Colonial Kenya: The Myth of the War as a Watershed. *Journal of African History* 26 (4): 327–345.

Barkan, Joel D. 1984. Comparing Politics and Public Policy in Kenya and Tanzania. In *Politics and Public Policy in Kenya and Tanzania*, ed. Joel D. Barkan, Revised ed., 3–42. New York: Praeger Publishers.

Berman, Bruce, and John Lonsdale. 1992. Crises of Accumulation, Coercion & The Colonial State: The Development of the Labour Control System, 1919–29. In *Unhappy Valley. Conflict in Kenya & Africa. Book One: State & Class*, ed. Bruce Berman and John Lonsdale, 101–126. Oxford: James Currey.

Bossert, Albrecht. 1985. *Traditionelle und modern Formen sozialer Sicherung in Tanzania: Eine Untersuchung ihrer Entwicklungsbedingungen*. Berlin: Duncker & Humblot.

Boyle, Elizabeth Heger, Fortunata Songora, and Gail Foss. 2001. International Discourse and Local Politics: Anti-Female-Genital-Cutting Laws in Egypt, Tanzania, and the United States. *Social Problems* 48 (4): 524–544.

Bryceson, Deborah Fahy. 1990. *Food Insecurity and the Social Division of Labour in Tanzania, 1919–85*. New York: St. Martin's Press.

Clayton, Anthony, and Donald C. Savage. 1974. *Government and Labour in Kenya, 1895–1963*. London: Frank Cass.

Cliffe, Lionel. 1973. *Underdevelopment or Socialism? A Comparative Analysis of Kenya and Tanzania*. Discussion Paper. Brighton: IDS.

D'Arcy, Michelle. 2013. Non-State Actors and Universal Services in Tanzania and Lesotho: State-Building by Alliance. *Journal of Modern African Studies* 51 (2): 219–247.

*East African*. 2017. Looming Risks as Kenya, Tanzania Debt Levels on the Rise. October 24. Accessed 15 May 2018. http://www.theeastafrican.co.ke/business/Looming-risks-as-Tanzania%2D%2DKenya-debt-levels-on-the-rise/2560-4153072-hwx7egz/index.html.

Eckert, Andreas. 2004. Regulating the Social: Social Security, Social Welfare and the State in Late Colonial Africa. *Journal of African History* 45 (3): 467–489.

Frankema, Ewout, and Marlous van Waijenburg. 2014. Metropolitan Blueprints of Colonial Taxation? Lessons from Fiscal Capacity Building in British and French Africa, c. 1880–1940. *Journal of African History* 55: 371–400.

Ikiara, Gerrishon K. 2009. *Political Economy of Cash Transfers in Kenya*. A Report Prepared for the Overseas Development Institute. London: ODI.

Jacob, Thabit, and Rasmus Hundsbæk Pedersen. 2018. Social Protection in an Electorally Competitive Environment (1): The Politics of Productive Social Safety

*Nets (PSSN) in Tanzania.* ESID Working Paper No. 110. Manchester: University of Manchester.
Kaasch, Alexandra. 2013. Contesting Contestation: Global Social Policy Prescriptions on Pensions and Health Systems. *Global Social Policy* 13 (1): 45–65.
Kjær, Anne Mette, and Ole Therkildsen. 2013. Elections and Landmark Policies in Tanzania and Uganda. *Democratization* 20 (4): 592–614.
Kpessa, Michael, and Daniel Béland. 2012. Transnational Actors and the Politics of Pension Reform in Sub-Saharan Africa. *Review of International Political Economy* 19 (2): 267–291.
Künzler, Daniel. 2007. *L'éducation pour quelques-uns? Enseignement et mobilité sociale en Afrique au temps de la privatisation: le cas du Bénin.* Paris: L'Harmattan.
———. 2016a. The Politics of Health Care Reforms in Kenya and Their Failure. *socialpolicy.ch* 2016/1, article 1.4.
———. 2016b. Social Security Reforms in Kenya: Towards a Workerist or a Citizenship-Based System? *International Social Security Review* 69 (1): 67–86.
———. 2016c. Health Care and Old Age Pensions in Latin America and Africa: Introduction to the Issue. *socialpolicy.ch* 2016/1, article 1.1.
Künzler, Daniel, and Michael Nollert. 2017. Varieties and Drivers of Social Welfare in Sub-Saharan Africa: A Critical Assessment of Current Research. *socialpolicy.ch* 2017/2, article 2.1.
Languille, Sonia. 2015. Ward Secondary Schools, Elite Narratives and Nyerere's Legacy. In *Remembering Nyerere in Tanzania. History, Memory, Legacy,* ed. Marie-Aude Fouéré, 305–337. Dar es Salaam: Mkuki na Nyota.
Lewis, Joanna. 2000. *Empire State Building. War & Welfare in Kenya, 1925–52.* Oxford: James Currey, Nairobi: EAEP and Athens: Ohio University Press.
Maxon, Robert M. 1980. *John Ainsworth and the Making of Kenya.* Washington: University Press of America.
Mkandawire, Thandika. 2010. On Tax Efforts and Colonial Heritage in Africa. *Journal of Development Studies* 46 (10): 1647–1669.
———. 2016. *Colonial Legacies and Social Welfare Regimes in Africa: An Empirical Exercise.* Working Paper 2016-4. Geneva: UNRISD.
Mkapa, Benjamin W. 2005. *Uwazi na Ukweli. Rais wa watu azungumza na Wananchi. Kitabu cha nne.* Dar es Salaam: Mkuki na Nyota Publisher.
Mwabu, Germano. 1995. Health Care Reform in Kenya: A Review of the Process. *Health Policy* 32: 245–255.
Neubert, Dieter. 1986. *Sozialpolitik in Kenya.* Münster: LIT.

Niño-Zarazúa, Miguel, Armando Barrientos, Samuel Hickey, and David Hulme. 2012. Social Protection in Sub-Saharan Africa: Getting the Politics Right. *World Development* 40 (1): 163–176.
Nyataya, Jared. 2017. Sh24bn Needed for Medicare, Elderly. *Daily Nation*. https://www.nation.co.ke/news/Plan-to-protect-elderly-to-cost-country-Sh24bn/1056-3872780-41pnir/index.html.
Ouma, Marion, and Jimi Adésínà. 2019. Solutions, Exclusion and Influence: Exploring Power Relations in the Adoption of Social Protection Policies in Kenya. *Critical Social Policy* 39 (3): 376–395.
Pedersen, Rasmus Hundsbæk, and Thabit Jacob. 2018. *Social Protection in an Electorally Competitive Environment (2): The Politics of Health Insurance in Tanzania*. ESID Working Paper 110. Manchester: University of Manchester.
Republic of Kenya (RoK). 2014. President's Speech During the Official Launch of Inua Jamii Cash Programme at Ihura Stadium in Murang'a County on Tuesday February 4, 2014. No longer available on http://www.president.go.ke.
Schmitt, Carina. 2015. Social Security Development and the Colonial Legacy. *World Development* 70: 332–342.
Seekings, Jeremy. 2005. *Prospects for Basic Income in Developing Countries: A Comparative Analysis of Welfare Regimes in the South*. CSSR Working Paper 104. Rondebosch: Centre for Social Science Research.
———. 2016. *The Introduction of Old Age Pensions in Zanzibar*. CSSR Working Paper 393. Cape Town: Centre for Social Science Research.
Simpson, Joshua P. 2018. Do Donors Matter Most? An Analysis of Conditional Cash Transfer Adoption in Sub-Saharan Africa. *Global Social Policy* 18 (2): 143–168.
Singh, Makhan. 1969. *History of Kenya's Trade Union Movement to 1952*. Nairobi: East African Publishing House.
Ulriksen, Marianne S. 2016a. *Ideational and Institutional Drivers of Social Protection in Tanzania*. UNU-WIDER Working Paper 2016/142. Helsinki: UNU-WIDER.
———. 2016b. *The Development of Social Protection Policies in Tanzania, 2000–2015*. CSSR Working Paper No. 377. Cape Town: University of Cape Town.
UNDP. 2018. *Human Development Indicators*. Dataset. Accessed 4 May 2018. http://hdr.undp.org/en.

## 4 The Influence of Colonialism and Donors on Social Policies...

World Bank. 2018a. *World Development Indicators*. Dataset. Accessed 4 May 2018. https://datacatalog.worldbank.org/dataset/world-development-indicators.

———. 2018b. *The Atlas of Social Protection: Indicators of Resilience and Equity*. Dataset. Accessed 4 May 2018. https://datacatalog.worldbank.org/dataset/atlas-social-protection-indicators-resilience-and-equity.

**Open Access** This chapter is licensed under the terms of the Creative Commons Attribution 4.0 International License (http://creativecommons.org/licenses/by/4.0/), which permits use, sharing, adaptation, distribution and reproduction in any medium or format, as long as you give appropriate credit to the original author(s) and the source, provide a link to the Creative Commons licence and indicate if changes were made.

The images or other third party material in this chapter are included in the chapter's Creative Commons licence, unless indicated otherwise in a credit line to the material. If material is not included in the chapter's Creative Commons licence and your intended use is not permitted by statutory regulation or exceeds the permitted use, you will need to obtain permission directly from the copyright holder.

# 5

# The Effects of Colonialism on Social Protection in South Africa and Botswana

Jeremy Seekings

## Introduction: The Legacy of Colonialism on Social Protection

The boundaries of empire appear to have had a profound and lasting effect on social protection policy, even into the 2000s. Whether a territory was colonized by the Spanish, French, Germans, Portuguese, Italians or British—or the Russians, Japanese or Americans—seems to correlate with both the onset and the subsequent direction and pace of policy reforms. In 2011, Midgley and Piachaud asserted that "social policy in the developing world cannot be understood without examining the way welfare policies and programmes introduced during the imperial era have continued to influence current policy-making" (2011, 10). Their edited collection included suggestive case studies of colonial influence within the British Empire. Schmitt (2015) demonstrates that the timing of the adoption of different kinds of social security programs differed

J. Seekings (✉)
Department of Sociology, University of Cape Town, Cape Town, South Africa
e-mail: Jeremy.Seekings@uct.ac.za

systematically between French, British and Spanish colonies (and former colonies). French colonies were quick to introduce social insurance in the form of family allowances but rarely (even long after independence) introduced any old-age pensions. Spanish colonies were the first to introduce old-age pensions. British colonies varied, but some of them at least were quick to provide for old age (often through non-contributory social assistance), and almost none introduced family allowances. In her chapter in this volume, Schmitt (2019) shows that the probability of a former French colony having introduced *any* social assistance program is massively lower and the probability of a former British colony having done so is very much higher than in other countries across the Global South. In previous work, I also found that a history of British colonization was closely correlated with high expenditure on social assistance relative to expenditure on social insurance, that is, a characteristic of the British welfare regime (Seekings 2014). The apparently random geography of imperial conquest—that is, which imperial power colonized any particular territory—appears to have had an enduring effect on public policy.

There are three possible explanations for these enduring differences between social protection in different parts of the world. First, the imperial power might have directly influenced policy during either the colonial or post-colonial periods, and there was some form of path dependence thereafter. Second, the imperial power might have indirectly influenced policy, perhaps through shaping the institutional environment. Third, imperial conquest might not have been entirely random, in that local conditions differed between the imperial empires. There are reasons for taking seriously all three possible explanations.

The easy explanation for inter-imperial variation in policy legacies is that different imperial powers simply imposed their own models on their colonies and these models then persisted over time through some process of path dependency. For example, the French imposed their 1952 *Code du Travail* across the whole of their empire (Cooper 1996), which certainly helps to explain the enduring prevalence of child allowances in former French colonies (Schmitt 2015). The British, however, did not impose any similarly centralized, monolithic model on their colonies. As Schmitt (2015) emphasizes, Britain's policy was to decentralize policy-making (and financial responsibility) to colonial governments.

Unsurprisingly, Schmitt shows, there was more variation for decades after independence between former British colonies than among former French colonies. Nonetheless, post-imperial aid flows—and the influence that accompanies these—track the former boundaries of empire (see Becker, Chap. 7, this volume). British aid and influence, through its Department for International Development (DFID), is thus concentrated in former British colonies. It would not be surprising if DFID's policy preferences were most influential in former British colonies.

Imperial legacies might also reflect indirect influences. This appears to have been the case with respect to schooling. Most British colonies in Africa had much higher enrolment rates in the 1950s than either French or Portuguese colonies, and this had both direct and indirect effects long after independence. Close analysis reveals that this inter-imperial variation was due not so much to direct differences in expenditure on education by colonial governments but rather to the indirect effects of colonial policies toward Christian missions. Crucially, it seems, British colonial governments allowed Christian missionaries to compete for converts, which they did in large part through expanding education through mission schools (Frankema 2012). Indirect influences might inform path dependence also. Lange (2009) suggests that variation—perhaps inter-imperial in origin—between direct and indirect rules had enduring consequences on the character of the state, politics and public policy. Schmitt also suggests that colonialism "shaped the institutional arrangements of the state and the power and preferences of actors" (2015, 332).

Differences between former British, Spanish and French colonies might reflect exogenous differences in local conditions. The samples of territories analyzed by Schmitt (2015) comprised Spanish colonies in Latin America or the Caribbean, French colonies that were mostly in Africa and British colonies that were much more widely dispersed across the world. The more pronounced heterogeneity in the date of adoption of welfare programs in British colonies might reflect the greater variation in local conditions as well as the British policy of decentralizing policy-making. The challenges facing post-colonial states in Latin America were very different to those facing their peers in Eastern Europe and East Asia (Haggard and Kaufman 2008). Conditions across most of Africa (and parts of South Asia) were very different to those in these three regions.

Africa as a whole differed from large parts of Latin America in terms of the relative sizes of indigenous, slave and settler/immigrant populations. Across most of Africa, but only in some parts of Latin America, for example, indigenous, peasant-based agrarian societies survived colonization. Even within Africa, conditions may have differed between those areas colonized by France and those colonized by Britain. The former had larger Islamic populations and contained a smaller proportion of fertile areas than the latter (which might help explain why there was weaker demand for education in French colonies than in British ones—see Frankema 2012; Cogneau and Moradi 2014; Dupraz 2017). Mkandawire (2015) found that taxation and social expenditure in Africa reflected the economic character of a colony, not the colonial power per se. The crucial difference was between cash crop economies, mostly in West Africa, and the "labor reserve" economies, mostly in East and Southern Africa. The kind of economy was clearly affected by colonial policies of settlement and development but also reflected natural and other differences that were exogenous to colonial policy. In Mkandawire's analysis, the British cash-cropping colonial economies of West Africa resembled their French colonial neighbors, while Rwanda and Burundi resembled British labor reserve economies. The implication of this is that the evolution of a distinct model or models of social protection in Anglophone East and Southern Africa might reflect similarities in local conditions as much as or more than the fact that these territories were colonized by Britain.

This chapter examines these three categories of explanation—and hence when, how and why external actors have been influential—through two case studies of welfare policy-making over time. Both cases were part of the British Empire through the early and mid-twentieth century, and both were in labor reserves rather than cash-cropping territories. Both ended up, by the end of the twentieth century, with variants of the same kind of welfare regime, with a strong focus on means-tested social assistance relative to social insurance (as well as largely tax-financed public health systems alongside large private health sectors). Yet the two cases reveal two very different routes to these outcomes, with external actors playing quite different roles.

First, I consider the case of South Africa which institutionalized a system combining social assistance with "semi-social" insurance (explained below) between the 1920s and 1940s and retains this basic system today, in the 2010s. The South African case is characterized by significant imperial influence in the formative period, followed by strong path dependence, such that the system survived hostility from both the governing National Party under apartheid (from 1948 to 1994) and the governing African National Congress (ANC) following democratic elections in 1994. Second, the chapter examines the case of Botswana, whose welfare state originated in drought relief programs in the 1960s and later evolved into social assistance programs.

The cases of South Africa and Botswana illustrate two very different pathways toward welfare states, with some common characteristics (although the welfare state in Botswana remains more conservative than the South African one, in important respects). While both pathways were shaped by ideas circulating in primarily English-speaking networks, the mechanisms of influence were far more complex than any simple imposition of a British model. Both the initial design of public policies and their subsequent path-dependent expansion reflected the resonance of specific models to local conditions and ideas.

South Africa and Botswana ended up with social protection systems with important similarities—although the South African system is far more generous—and some common features with British models not because they copied British models, but because the basic ideas informing British public policy were shared by political elites in parts of Southern Africa. Crucially, in both South Africa and Botswana social protection policies evolved on the basis of a dominant elite ideology that states should leave activities to the market except if the market fails to provide adequately for deserving groups of poor people. This was "liberal" in the sense that the state's role in social welfare (defined narrowly as transfers in cash or kind, but excluding public education) was conceived as being *residual*, provided only for people deemed deserving in that they were unable to provide for themselves (and lacked kin who could provide for them; see Chinyoka and Ulriksen, Chap. 10, this volume). In practice, this meant an emphasis on programmatic support for the specific categories of destitute people considered deserving (especially the elderly and disabled, and less often children, pregnant and breastfeeding mothers and single mothers) as well as (when necessary, especially during episodes of drought) workfare for working-age, able-bodied adults. Local political imperatives drove these initially "residual" programs to expand into universal or quasi-universal ones.

This chapter suggests that all three explanations of the enduring differences in social protection have some relevance in Southern Africa. The case of South Africa suggests that foreign ideas shaped local policy debates, both prior to 1948 (when the most influential ideas came from the UK, Australia and New Zealand) and after 1948 (i.e. under apartheid, when neo-Calvinist theology from the Netherlands exerted significant influence). The design of Botswana's welfare state was also shaped by external ideas, through the World Food Programme (WFP). Institutional design mattered, indirectly, in that both elements of indirect rule and representative democracy ensured that elites were incentivized to introduce and then conserve pro-poor programs. Both the first and second explanations contribute to understanding path dependency in these Southern African cases. Third, local conditions mattered in both South Africa and Botswana, as they posed specific challenges to the large number of small-scale farmers: climate and ecology (compounded by government policy in the South African case) mattered, framing the expansion of social assistance programs in both cases.

## Imperial Influence in the Making of the South African Welfare State

South Africa has long been at the fore of welfare state-building in Africa. As early as 1937, the new Professor of Sociology at the University of the Witwatersrand proclaimed in his inaugural lecture that "Today the provision for [the] European population … is scarcely less complete than that of Great Britain" (Gray 1937, 270). He exaggerated somewhat, even with respect to the "European" minority. The African majority of the population was almost entirely excluded. Nonetheless, the state paid means-tested pensions to elderly white men and women, pensions to white and colored people who were blind or otherwise disabled and cash grants-in-aid to poor people caring for children (as well as to institutions or associations caring for children). During recessions, the state operated workfare programs for otherwise unemployed, mostly white men. Public education and hospital care for white people was financed almost entirely from taxes. In addition, nascent contributory pension schemes were beginning to provide for select groups of workers in formal employment.

While the Union of South Africa was self-governing (as a British "Dominion"), its political and bureaucratic elites were heavily influenced by the ideas and models concerning welfare policy that circulated through the British Empire during the first half of the twentieth century. Government commissions of inquiry and civil servants collected detailed information on the social insurance and social assistance programs in place across much of the world at the time, but they borrowed most from policies in Britain, as well as in the settler societies of Australia and New Zealand. The tax-financed, means-tested social pensions, introduced for white and colored people in 1928–1929, resembled the pensions introduced in Britain itself in 1908 (see Schmitt, Chap. 6, this volume). Subsequent social assistance programs for the disabled and for single mothers and proposals for social insurance, first for pensions and later for unemployment and health also, drew on imperial precedents. Debate in Britain during the Second World War—including around the Beveridge Report, published in 1942—provided a strong impetus to the expansion of social assistance. In the early 1940s, ideas and models from New Zealand were also highly influential. In 1942, a member of parliament (MP) tabled a motion on social security, asking, "Can our government do what New Zealand has done?"[1] One of the leading activists in civil society in the early 1940s was from New Zealand (Seekings 2005).

The South African system was idiosyncratic, however, reflecting the adaptation of foreign models to local conditions and values. Policymakers borrowed but did not copy. First, South Africa never implemented a national system of social insurance ("national insurance"). The British model—providing for insurance against health and unemployment from 1911, and contributory pensions from 1925 (Boyer 2019)—was rejected. The only social insurance was a very modest unemployment insurance program. Instead, successive governments required most white

---

[1] *Hansard*, 6 January 1942, col. 3304.

workers to join government-regulated but privately operated, mostly sector-specific pension funds (i.e. "semi-social" insurance). Second, the South African social assistance programs were deeply racialized. African and Indian people were excluded entirely from social pensions until 1944. When pensions were extended to them, they were discriminated against in terms of benefits. Social assistance programs were introduced originally by political parties representing white and "colored" voters with the goal of protecting white and colored South Africans from destitution. For some Members of Parliament, this was motivated explicitly by the perceived need to preserve the racial income hierarchy. As one (white) Member of Parliament put it, "not a single white person should be allowed to go under" because the "small number of whites" had to stand together against the "uncivilised hoards"[2] (Seekings 2007). Racialized solidarity entailed providing for white men, women and children but excluding or discriminating deeply against the African majority of the population.

Social assistance was preferred to social insurance, in part because the leading (white) politicians, bureaucrats, academics, businessmen, trade unionists and other civil society activists were more firmly rooted in English-language circuits of ideas than in continental European models (although they were certainly aware of the latter, in part through the work of the International Labour Organization [ILO]). More strongly even than in Britain, Australia and New Zealand, the modernist ambitions of socialist and "new liberal" welfare state-builders were reined in by the more classically liberal views of much of the white elite, with their preference for the market and a residual state. Modernist ambitions were also framed and contained by the overt or implicit racism of most white South Africans. "National" (i.e. social) insurance was supported by many technocrats, but the political leadership did not deem it necessary. Privately run pension funds provided sufficiently well for white workers who enjoyed privileged access to better-paid formal employment. As in Australia (Castles 1985), white workers were incorporated politically through the regulation of wages in the private sector as well as through public sector and parastatal employment, and through public services,

---

[2] Dr. Stals, *Hansard*, House of Assembly, 12 August 1924, col. 429–32.

rather than through corporatist or Bismarckian models (Seekings and Nattrass 2005). This combination of wage regulation, "semi-social" insurance and social assistance made sense given that benefits were largely limited to the white minority.

"Poor whites" were politically important not only because elites sought to bolster a racialized solidarity among Afrikaners or white South Africans more broadly, but also because they had the vote in a highly competitive party system. Few black South Africans had any vote. Nonetheless, local conditions pushed the government to extend social pensions to black men and women in 1944. Just as "poor whites" were often the victims of deagrarianization, so the constraints on peasant agriculture in the 1940s were a major factor pushing local officials and even industrial employers to endorse the expansion of social pensions (Seekings 2005).

Policies were never imposed or simply transferred from Britain to South Africa. Officials in London had no direct influence in South Africa. But (white) reformers in the South African state, political parties and civil society officials were embedded in imperial networks through which both norms and policy models were diffused from both Britain and its other settler Dominions to South Africa. Models were adapted, however, to reflect the norms—including racialized and often racist norms—that were prevalent within the South African elite, as well as the political and economic conditions on the ground.

## Path Dependency and the Expansion of South Africa's Welfare State

As of 2018/19, 90 years after the introduction of old-age pensions, South Africa's welfare state remains a distinctive outlier in Africa. Monthly grants are paid to or for about 18 million elderly people, disabled people and children, or to one in three South Africans. These are paid for out of general taxation at a cost of about 3.5% of GDP. The state also operates by far the largest school feeding program in Africa, reaching 9 million children, as well as large workfare programs. Public education and health care are free for the poor. Contributory pension and medical aid schemes cover many (but not all) people in formal employment (Seekings and Nattrass 2015). The ILO identifies South Africa as the "front runner" in Africa in terms of the coverage of social protection, with an "effective coverage" of 48% of the population (ILO 2017, 123).

While racial discrimination in eligibility and benefits has been abolished, the basic design of the welfare state in the 2010s remains much the same as it did in the 1930s: the state supported the same categories of deserving poor through tax-financed, means-tested grants and able-bodied, working-age adults through workfare programs. Moreover, no social insurance had yet been introduced for either retirement or health care, and the unemployment insurance system covered very few of the unemployed. On the face of it, the post-apartheid welfare state in South Africa retained its original colonial-era design, with essentially parametric reforms that have allowed for the expansion of coverage of existing programs but not the introduction of new programs.

This apparent path dependence is especially striking given that the governing parties both under and after apartheid were ambivalent if not hostile toward the welfare state. In 1948, the more extreme wing of the National Party was elected into office. Not only was the National Party committed to the deepening of racial discrimination and segregation (i.e. apartheid), but its views on the welfare state were also deeply influenced by reformed Protestantism articulated by Dutch neo-Calvinist theologian and politician Abraham Kuyper. This foreign ideology was adapted to the local context in that the National Party rejected entirely the idea of a welfare state for the African population. On the basis of a variety of arguments—including that old-age pensions would encourage "the native to degenerate",[3] that they were culturally and socially inappropriate and that they were paid for by white taxpayers—provision for African people was severely restricted. Even with respect to its white citizens, however, the National Party government was ambivalent about its welfare programs. Shaped by Kuyper's ideas, the party's leaders argued that families should take responsibility for providing for family members: working people should save for their old age, adult children should take responsibility for their aged parents and adult husbands and fathers should take

---

[3] Van Niekerk, *Hansard*, House of Assembly, 6 September 1948, col. 1593.

responsibility for their wives and children. In this deeply conservative view, excessive public provision—that is, the "welfare state"—was "socialistic", undermined independence and responsibility and fostered instead dependency and delinquency. "Our State is a social welfare State as opposed to a socialist State", one MP explained; "We must take care of the paupers, the indigents who need assistance. But do not let us give everyone the right to be taken care of, because we deprive our people of their sense of responsibility."[4] The National Party's values were rooted in a neo-Calvinist conception of individual and familial responsibility, combined with an emphasis on a racialized *volk*. This was much more conservative than the kind of concern with social harmony that characterized social Catholicism and Christian Democracy at the same time in postwar Europe. Even the (white) opposition United Party retreated into a more conservative stance, advocating a residual welfare regime along American lines (Seekings 2020).

Despite their repeated declarations (influenced by religious ideas from Europe) that they were opposed to a welfare state, National Party governments for the most part expanded both social assistance and the semi-social insurance system, especially as they began to retreat from their grand apartheid project in the 1980s. While they sought to strengthen white families, they were unable to ensure that white families accommodated and supported elderly parents. Expenditure grew rapidly on residential institutions for the elderly. Similarly, despite their enthusiasm to abolish social pensions for elderly African men and women, the importance of pensions to most African people created a very large vested interest, while the apartheid-style devolution of responsibility to compliant African leaders gave an effective veto power to players whose modest legitimacy would vanish if they were complicit in the abolition of the pensions. As international and domestic pressure intensified on the apartheid state, persistent racial discrimination in benefits became less and less defensible. In the 1980s the National Party presided over major increases in the real value of the social pension paid to African people as it moved toward parity in benefits. Racial discrimination in benefits was finally ended in 1993, on the eve of the country's first democratic elections

---

[4] De Wet, *Hansard*, House of Assembly, 22 February 1955, col. 1494–5.

(although racial discrimination remained with respect to public expenditure on education and health care). The semi-social insurance system expanded to accommodate most skilled and semi-skilled African workers in provident funds managed by newly legal trade unions. The existing programs thus not only created directly vested interests but also provided both symbolic and material incentives to groups of African people to demand their inclusion in the welfare state, creating even stronger vested interests.

When an ANC government was elected in South Africa's first democratic elections, in 1994, it therefore inherited a welfare state designed more than 50 years earlier. While committed to the reduction of poverty among its mostly African support base, the ANC was ideologically ill-disposed to the idea of a welfare state. Without unmanageable debts and independent of foreign aid, the new government was not beholden to any international organizations or aid donors. It was, however, influenced by the developmentalist ideology that had been hegemonic across much of Africa since the 1950s. In his inaugural speech as newly elected President in May 1994, Nelson Mandela himself made it clear that the ANC would implement a developmental approach rather than distribute "handouts". Repeatedly over the following 20-plus years, ANC leaders reiterated that South Africa needed a "developmental state" rather than a "welfare state", valued the family over excessive individualism and worried about "dependency". ANC governments did rein in expenditure on residential institutions for the elderly, considered abolishing grants for poor, single mothers and rejected calls for a basic income grant. They also proposed shifting the emphasis of social protection from social assistance and provident funds to social insurance, through national pension and health insurance programs. Civil society activists pushed for programmatic expansion. Faced with electoral competition, the ANC did expand massively grants for poor mothers (and other caregivers), but they rejected a series of other proposed reforms and (as of 2018) failed to implement their promised national insurance systems (Lund 2008; Proudlock 2011; Patel 2015; Seekings and Nattrass 2015; Button et al. 2018).

The ANC after 1994 found it as difficult as the National Party before 1994 to resist the expansion of the welfare state. The dominant norms within the ruling party might be ambivalent or hostile to welfare statism,

## 5 The Effects of Colonialism on Social Protection in South Africa... 121

but institutions, interests and popular ideas all contributed to path dependency. Institutionally, the consolidation of social assistance programs within the Department of Welfare (later renamed Social Development) created an institutional vested interest. ANC party structures (and MPs), fearing a popular backlash against programmatic retrenchment, wielded a potential veto. Faced with persistent poverty, the ANC expanded programs to maintain its electoral support. The existing programs created a massive vested interest in their continuation—except for residential institutions for elderly white people who comprised a politically weak constituency. Every suggestion that the trade union-run provident funds would be incorporated into a national pension fund system was met with blanket opposition from the politically powerful trade unions. The promised national health insurance system was welcomed by the public sector unions but was resisted by the black as well as white middle classes, who had migrated to private health care after 1994, and prompted ambivalence even among sections of the working class who were covered by sector-specific or other medical aid schemes. Perhaps most importantly of all, the priority attached to deracialization generally meant that programs that had benefitted white South Africans primarily should be extended to all South Africans. The very idea of social assistance had become so taken for granted that grants could be extended to African single mothers and even a basic income grant could be put on the agenda, despite widespread concern over the payment of grants to undeserving individuals.

At no point between the 1920s and 2010s did reforms to South Africa's welfare state entail simple policy transfer from elsewhere. South African policy-makers were consistently determined to adapt foreign ideas and models to suit local circumstances. While foreign actors never had the power to impose their preferred policies, South African policy-makers were deeply influenced by foreign ideas. Between the 1920s and 1940s, policy-makers drew on some of the ideas and models in Britain (and other British Dominions) in introducing programs to provide primarily for South Africans of European descent. In the South African context, however, these programs served, inter alia, the racialized objective of securing white supremacy. In the early 1940s, debates in Britain and elsewhere influenced some policy-makers to extend some programs to African people, albeit on a discriminatory basis. From 1948, the National Party tried to reverse these reforms, in part because of the influence of a new set of foreign ideas, that is, deeply conservative neo-Calvinist ideas from the Netherlands. In the 1980s and 1990s global opprobrium over racial discrimination contributed to the National Party's slow deracialization of welfare programs. After 1994, ANC leaders drew on global developmental ideology (as well as their own conservative views about family) to resist the expansion of so-called handouts. Despite the ebbs and flows of ideas about welfare, the welfare programs introduced in the second quarter of the twentieth century were not only never retrenched to any significant extent but tended to expand through parametric reforms that extended the reach of existing programs. South Africa's welfare state was reformed down a path that depended on its origins.

## External Actors, Drought Relief and State-Building in Botswana

The British colony (or, more precisely, Protectorate) of Bechuanaland (renamed Botswana at independence in 1966) was a very different context to its neighbor South Africa. The territory was extremely poor and heavily dependent on remittances sent by migrant mineworkers in South Africa. There were very few European settlers or immigrants. Moreover, British colonial officials enjoyed considerable power until independence, although they chose to devolve considerable authority to Tswana chiefs under indirect rule. At the same time as South Africa was introducing and expanding welfare programs, the British colonial government in Bechuanaland made almost no provision for their subjects.

The absence of welfare programs in Bechuanaland was typical of British colonies in Africa. Britain might have devolved responsibility for policy-making to colonial officials on the ground, but it, nonetheless, generally provided those officials with clear guidance as to what policies they should make. When, during the Second World War, the Beveridge Report had prompted global interest in welfare state-building, Britain's Colonial Office insisted that Beveridge's proposals were inappropriate in societies in "early stages of development" where the poor were provided for by kin or community and the priority was to increase agricultural output so as to raise the general standard of living. Even in some industrializing societies—such as the Copperbelt in Northern Rhodesia (later Zambia)—the fact that most industrial workers retired to rural villages obviated the need for "more sophisticated" social welfare programs. Only in societies where there was little or no peasant agriculture, as on islands such as Mauritius, might old-age pensions or other such programs be considered appropriate. In societies without large white settler or immigrant populations, the Colonial Office actively discouraged the kinds of reform already introduced in South Africa (and in some Caribbean colonies). The challenge of poverty among black people would be addressed primarily through agricultural and other economic development, which would generate the resources needed to expand the "social services", that is, especially education and health care (Seekings 2013).

Colonial states were under pressure to protect colonial subjects against one specific risk: famine, which in Africa usually arose from drought and, more occasionally and locally, from pests (such as locusts) or flooding. The British Empire had a long experience with drought and famine in India. Official Famine Codes set out how colonial officials should respond to famine. Informed by nineteenth-century liberal thought in Britain, the Codes stipulated that free food should be distributed only to the truly "destitute" (including the elderly), while the able-bodied poor should earn minimal rations of food through food-for-work programs. The Famine Codes were sometimes catastrophically inadequate (as evident in the Bengal Famine of 1942) but were generally regarded as useful enough that they (and subsequent operational manuals) were embraced by Indian governments after independence. Colonial officials in Africa faced regular famines and sometimes responded with limited relief programs, although only in the Sudan did officials draft a Famine Code (De Waal 1989; Iliffe 1990). British colonial officials replicated the kind of approach developed in India: wherever possible, drought should be addressed through the market, in that members of poor rural families could work for wages as migrant laborers, remit their earnings and their rural families could then buy food that had been supplied to rural areas by merchants; if this was insufficient, local authorities (typically chiefs) should intervene;

colonial governments themselves should intervene only in dire emergency. In the mid-twentieth century this approach proved broadly effective in some territories (including Southern Rhodesia: see Iliffe 1990) but not in others (most notably Nyasaland/Malawi in 1949: see Vaughan 1987).

Bechuanaland, although especially vulnerable to drought, experienced no major droughts in the 1940s or 1950s. In the early 1960s, however, several years of drought threatened mass famine. The colonial government—in the process of transferring power to local leaders—reacted very slowly. In 1965, the Bechuanaland (later Botswana) Democratic Party (BDP) headed by Seretse Khama and Quett Masire was elected as the territory's new government, and the following year Botswana achieved independence. The BDP seized control of drought relief, securing massive food supplies from the WFP, a then newly established United Nations agency. Food aid was distributed to between one-third and one-half of the population through feeding schemes. The scale of these emergency programs was unprecedented in the territory.

It quickly became apparent that continued food aid from the WFP required a shift in approach. While the WFP could provide emergency assistance for only a limited period, it could support longer-lasting "developmental" programs that helped to increase production as well as keep people alive. The WFP was happy to support school and other feeding schemes for "vulnerable" groups (school and pre-school children, pregnant and breastfeeding mothers) and destitute rations for the elderly and disabled. It was unwilling to provide food to able-bodied adults. The new government of Botswana therefore introduced workfare programs, providing food for work to men and women, with the intention of supporting whole families. By the end of the 1960s, the Botswana government had put in place the key features of the Indian Famine Codes, although there is no evidence that it was even aware of them. Insofar as the design of the programs was influenced from elsewhere, it appears to have been the WFP rather than the Colonial Office in London (Seekings 2016a). While the WFP remains one of the least researched international organizations (but see Shaw 2001), it appears that its approach was framed by the developmentalist ideology that was hegemonic at the time: food might be handed out in short-term emergencies, but the medium- and long-term priority was "development" to improve long-term food security.

Seretse Khama, the first president of Botswana, was steeped in broadly liberal British values. He had been educated at a mission school, then at South African and British universities, had been living (in exile) in Britain for several years, married a British woman and employed British advisors and speech writers (Tlou et al. 1995). His ideology was, however, rooted in Tswana norms. In the late 1960s and 1970s (before his death in 1980), he articulated a benign conservative ideology of responsibility for the poor. He and his successor, Quett Masire, were respectful of the private sector and wary of enlarging the state. But they saw the new state as assuming the responsibilities for the deserving poor that chiefs, communities and kin had shouldered hitherto. In this ideology, the deserving poor were those poor people who were unable to support themselves: the destitute elderly and infirm, children and mothers. Expectations of reciprocity underlay public responsibility. Anyone who could—that is, able-bodied adults—had a responsibility to work, to support their dependents and to contribute to the common good, hence the emphasis on workfare. This ideology of welfare was rooted in agrarian conditions. Historically, the availability of land meant that people's welfare depended primarily on work, such that relief was required only when people could not work (and could not be supported by working kin) or when natural disasters such as drought meant that, in effect, there was no work. While the ideology has some similarities to more liberal versions of conservatism in Britain (specifically, "one nation" conservatism), its roots lay in a society very different to British society (Seekings 2016b).

While most of the 1970s were years of good rains, Botswana persisted with the programs introduced in the previous decade: school and other feeding schemes (supported by the WFP), destitute rations and (when necessary) workfare. These welfare programs were integral not only to resilient support for the BDP among voters but also to the construction of a modern state. When drought recurred in 1978–1979, the government and WFP together provided drought relief for about 80% of the population. The government formalized its public works program (as the Labour-Intensive Public Works Programme) and introduced a new National Policy on Destitute Persons.

The construction of a welfare state in Botswana was driven forward by further drought in the 1980s. Although cattle died on a massive scale, not a single person died, as huge volumes of WFP food aid were brought into and distributed within Botswana. In 1985, in the middle of the drought, a study of drought relief programs concluded that:

> Drought relief is coming to assume a role in Botswana politics comparable to education and welfare in the industrialised countries. Indeed, it is already so popular that the leaders of the BDP have resisted pressures for cuts from bureaucrats. It will be difficult for the Ministry of Finance and Development Planning, which quite naturally concerns itself with balancing the budget, to find a politically acceptable way of reducing the various relief programmes, once the drought is over. (Holm and Morgan 1985, 476)

When the drought finally broke, in the late 1980s, the WFP resumed discussions with the government of Botswana about withdrawing from the country. By then, as Holm and Morgan had already recognized, it had become difficult for the government of Botswana to reverse or to step away from the path it had followed hitherto.

External resources and ideas were thus central to the origins of the welfare state in Botswana. WFP food aid and accompanying ideas shaped what the new state provided, for whom and with what conditions. This was a very different set of origins to those in neighboring South Africa. Programs in Botswana were not aimed at European immigrants or settlers. They did not draw on legislation from Britain (or other settler societies). They were not linked to any racialized political project, but rather to indigenous African norms and values. Their relevance was rooted in local conditions: specifically, the risks of drought in an agrarian society comprising mostly small farmers. As in South Africa, however, they were associated with a modernist project of state-building, they were residual in that poverty reduction should be achieved primarily through economic growth (or "development") and they were focused on deserving categories of people who could not support themselves (especially the elderly, disabled and children) and only on working-age adults through workfare.

## Path Dependency and the Institutionalization of Social Assistance in Botswana

Since the mid-2000s, foreign actors have played a key role in putting ideas about social assistance onto the agenda in many African countries. Scholars and activists have argued for "just giving money to the poor", on the grounds that it reduces poverty, is "developmental" (or at least redistributes resources in a sustainable way) and is politically "transformative" (Devereux and Sabates-Wheeler 2004; Hanlon et al. 2010; Ferguson 2015). International organizations and aid donors have funded consultants to assist with writing policy documents, spent large sums on study tours, seminars and other events to build coalitions of reform-friendly politicians and officials and embedded advisors in government departments (see Devereux and Kapingindza, Chap. 11, this volume). They have funded programs and sometimes established parallel, quasi-state bureaucracies. Reform has often appeared to be driven by donors (Devereux 2010). While international organizations and aid donors have shared a common enthusiasm for social assistance, their priorities have varied. The World Bank has favored targeted (i.e. means-tested) and conditional cash transfers. The ILO calls for "social protection floors". UNICEF promotes support for children, while HelpAge International promotes pensions for the elderly (von Gliszczynski and Leisering 2016). In many former British colonies, DFID became a powerful player in promoting the social protection agenda, providing advice, financial aid and technical support. Its preferred model was the unconditional cash transfer with broad reach, not unlike the social pensions and other social assistance introduced in Britain itself in the first half of the twentieth century (Hickey and Seekings 2019).

The institutionalization of social assistance in Botswana did not, however, reflect the influence of DFID or any other international organization or aid donor. It resulted from domestic factors, although it was precipitated in part by the decision of the WFP to withdraw from Botswana (see Chinyoka and Ulriksen, Chap. 10, this volume). The WFP's withdrawal was a reaction to the mining-fuelled rapid economic growth in Botswana that lifted the country out of the ranks of "low-income" countries. The withdrawal compelled the government of Botswana to choose between assuming full responsibility for welfare programs and retrenching them. Not only did the government take over the programs, but it expanded and institutionalized them further over the following decade.

The first clear statement of the government's position was in its 7th National Development Plan of 1991, which recognized that Botswana suffered from "a structural poverty problem" in that poverty persisted even in years of good rain (Botswana 1991, 17). Social justice and the decline of extended family support required government action: "Government food aid, its drought relief and recovery programmes, and other aid measures targeted for the destitute are intended to supplement the incomes of the very poor in order to ensure that their disposable incomes, both cash and in kind, provide them with a minimum standard of living" (ibid., 33). The Plan institutionalized funding for drought relief and welfare.

The government assumed full responsibility for massive school and other feeding programs, introduced universal old-age pensions (in 1996) and then provision for orphans and reformed its policy on (other) "destitutes". These reforms preceded the embrace of social protection among international organizations and aid donors. In the 2000s, international organizations did lobby the government of Botswana to expand its cash transfer programs. The government resisted, although it did expand its workfare programs.

By the 2000s, Botswana was providing modest support, in cash or in kind, to half or more of the country's population. The country's elite worries endlessly about "dependency", but the persistence of poverty—despite economic growth—raises the political costs of retrenching programs. Social change resulted in pressure to expand provision. The introduction of old-age pensions in 1996 was in part a technical response to the challenge of poverty among the elderly, modernizing the existing and clearly insufficient provision of destitute relief in the face of diminishing familial support. It was also a political response to the BDP's electoral vulnerability. Having won elections comfortably hitherto, the BDP was shocked in 1994 when it won barely 53% of the vote. The expansion of workfare in the late 2000s also reflected electoral anxiety (Seekings 2019; Hamer 2016).

In other parts of Africa, reforms of social protection have generally been *negotiated* between external organizations and local political actors. External organizations rarely get far, unless their ideas appeal to—or fit with the existing ideas of—at least some important local actors (Hickey et al. 2019). In Botswana, the WFP's withdrawal was an important factor pushing the government to institutionalize drought relief programs into a welfare state, but there is no evidence that the WFP or any other international organization shaped significantly this process of policy reform. The process in Botswana following the WFP's withdrawal was an entirely domestic one. Indeed, when the World Bank and UNICEF did (later) propose the introduction in Botswana of a general child grant, the government of Botswana declined to do so (Chinyoka 2019).

Both the expansion of the welfare state in the 1990s and early 2000s and the subsequent rejection of a proposed child grant reflected domestic factors: the BDP government had expanded the welfare state in line with its conservative ideology of responsibility and in response of its perceived political interests, but its norms of responsibility did not entail usurping the responsibility of the family to provide for non-orphaned children nor did it perceive its political interests lying in such a reform (perhaps because it assessed that many voters shared these conservative views). The domestic politics of policy reform was, however, path dependent. The introduction of old-age pensions, most notably, was imaginable only because the idea of poor relief was deeply entrenched through the provision for destitutes and other, originally drought-driven programs.

## Conclusion

The cases of South Africa and Botswana entail two different but parallel paths to welfare states built primarily around social assistance programs. While the welfare state in Botswana is more conservative than the South African one in some respects—including the generosity of benefits, the role accorded to family and the preference for paying benefits in kind rather than cash—the basic design is common to both. Social assistance programs provide for the elderly, disabled and some children, with workfare for able-bodied adults. Social insurance remains limited. It is tempting to assume that these neighboring countries have similar systems because of a shared history, including common external influences.

In neither South Africa nor Botswana, however, were foreign models imposed. Insofar as there was policy transfer, it was with considerable adaptation to local norms and conditions. External influences entailed primarily the diffusion of ideas which were combined with local ideas to shape policy outcomes. At different times in both cases, foreign ideas meshed with local factors to drive reform. In the South African case, at other times powerful external ideas served to constrain welfare state-building. In the case of Botswana, external actors in the 2000s proposed expansionary reforms that were resisted by the government.

Diffusion is less surprising in the South African case, where the welfare state originated in initiatives to provide for South Africans of European origin in ways comparable to provision in Europe itself. Even in this case, however, foreign models and ideas were adapted. Adaptation was required because the kinds of risks that were most pressing in the Southern African context were not the same risks that faced workers as a result of industrialization and urbanization in the more industrialized countries of Europe or Latin America. Welfare states in East and Southern Africa, including South Africa, were framed by changes in the countryside. This was most obvious in Botswana, where the welfare state originated in programs of drought relief, to tide rural households through periods in which they could not feed themselves. In South Africa, also, many of the "poor whites" of the 1920s and 1930s—and poor African people in the 1940s— were in or from rural areas, and their poverty stemmed more from changes in rural areas (deagrarianization) than from industrialization and urbanization (see Künzler, Chap. 4, this volume). In both countries, local conditions encouraged policy-makers to prioritize economic growth or "development" and to see welfare programs as providing a residual safety net. The similarities between public policies in South Africa and Botswana thus reflect, in part, similar local conditions.

Policies in South Africa and Botswana developed along paths that led to a common focus on social assistance not primarily because they were exposed to the kinds of ideas associated with British public policy (and the similar developmentalism underpinning the WFP) but because those ideas could easily be adapted to fit local conditions and norms. In both cases, targeted social assistance allowed not only for the provision of support to selected deserving categories but also for the exclusion of other categories of people deemed not to be deserving on the basis of need, custom or capacity. Insofar as we can identify a common model of social protection in Southern Africa, this resulted not from the imposition of any specific foreign model but rather from a process of contestation over ideas and models and the adaptation of these to local conditions.

All three possible explanations of the policy outcomes in these two countries have some relevance. Foreign ideas about the state, welfare and "development", rooted in or linked to Britain or its empire, were influential. The experiences of welfare reform (and wage regulation) in Australia and New Zealand and of drought relief in India and elsewhere, as well as British models, shaped reforms in Southern Africa. Institutional design was also consequential. The legacy of colonial institutions of indirect rule in Botswana meant that the post-independence state sought to legitimate itself through institutionalizing drought relief. Apartheid-style indirect rule in South Africa meant that the state was unable in the 1950s and 1960s to retrench its social pension program. Finally, local conditions were of crucial importance. Botswana remained an agrarian society of small farmers for most of the twentieth century. Deagrarianization transformed South Africa much earlier, but racialized policies and incomplete industrialization under apartheid meant that the market failed to replace the former agrarian safety net. In both Botswana and South Africa in the late twentieth century, high dependency rates resulted in strong pressures for the continued expansion of social assistance. British imperial influences on policy itself and on political institutions therefore combined with local conditions to steer apparently dissimilar territories down quite different paths to similar outcomes.

## References

Botswana. 1991. *National Development Plan 1991–1992*. Gaborone: Ministry of Finance and Development Planning.
Boyer, George. 2019. *The Winding Road to the Welfare State: Economic Insecurity and Social Welfare Policy in Britain*. Princeton: Princeton University Press.
Button, Kirsty, Elena Moore, and Jeremy Seekings. 2018. South Africa's Hybrid Care Regime: The Changing and Contested Roles of Individuals, Families and the State after Apartheid. *Current Sociology* 66 (4): 602–616.
Castles, Francis. 1985. *The Working Class and Welfare*. Sydney: Allen and Unwin.
Chinyoka, Isaac. 2019. *Familial Child Welfare Regimes: The Case of Botswana*. CSSR Working Paper 430, Centre for Social Science Research, University of Cape Town, Cape Town.
Cogneau, Denis, and Alexander Moradi. 2014. Borders That Divide: Education and Religion in Ghana and Togo since Colonial Times. *Journal of Economic History* 74 (3): 694–729.
Cooper, Frederick. 1996. *Decolonisation and African Society*. Cambridge: Cambridge University Press.
de Waal, Alexander. 1989. *Famine That Kills: Darfur, Sudan, 1984–85*. Oxford: Clarendon Press.
Devereux, Stephen. 2010. *Building Social Protection Systems in Southern Africa*. Paper Prepared in the Framework of the European Report on Development 2010.
Devereux, Stephen, and Rachel Sabates-Wheeler. 2004. *Transformative Social Protection*. IDS Working Paper 232, Institute for Development Studies, Brighton.
Dupraz, Yannick. 2017. *French and British Colonial Legacies in Education: Evidence from the Partition of Cameroon*. Working Paper 333, Centre for Competitive Advantage in the Global Economy, University of Warwick, Coventry.
Ferguson, James. 2015. *Give a Man a Fish: Reflections on the New Politics of Distribution*. Durham: Duke University Press.
Frankema, Ewout. 2012. The Origins of Formal Education in Sub-Saharan Africa: Was British Rule More Benign? *European Review of Economic History* 16 (4): 335–355.
Gray, John L. 1937. The Comparative Sociology of South Africa. *South African Journal of Economics* 5: 269–284.
Haggard, Stephan, and Robert R. Kaufman. 2008. *Development, Democracy, and Welfare States: Latin America, East Asia, and Eastern Europe*. Princeton: Princeton University Press.

Hamer, Sam. 2016. *Our Father's Programmes: Political Branding and the Social Protection Agenda in Botswana, 2008–2014*. CSSR Working Paper 363, Centre for Social Science Research, University of Cape Town, Cape Town.

Hanlon, Joseph, Armando Barrientos, and David Hulme. 2010. *Just Give Money to the Poor: The Development Revolution from the Global South*. Sterling, VA: Kumarian Press.

Hickey, Sam, and Jeremy Seekings. 2019. Who Should Get What, How and Why? DFID and the Transnational Politics of Social Cash Transfers in Sub-Saharan Africa. In *The Politics of Social Protection in East and Southern Africa*, ed. Sam Hickey, Tom Lavers, Miguel Niño-Zarazúa, and Jeremy Seekings. Oxford: Oxford University Press.

Hickey, Sam, Tom Lavers, Miguel Niño-Zarazúa, and Jeremy Seekings. 2019. The Negotiated Politics of Social Protection in Sub-Saharan Africa. In *The Politics of Social Protection in East and Southern Africa*, ed. Sam Hickey, Tom Lavers, Miguel Niño-Zarazúa, and Jeremy Seekings. Oxford: Oxford University Press.

Holm, John, and Richard G. Morgan. 1985. Coping with Drought in Botswana: An African Success. *Journal of Modern African Studies* 23 (3): 463–482.

Iliffe, John. 1990. *Famine in Zimbabwe, 1890–1960*. Gweru: Mambo.

International Labour Organisation. 2017. *World Social Protection Report 2017–19*. Geneva: International Labour Organisation.

Lange, Matthew. 2009. *Lineages of Despotism and Development: British Colonialism and State Power*. Chicago: University of Chicago Press.

Lund, Francie. 2008. *Changing Social Policy*. Cape Town: HSRC Press.

Midgley, James. 2011. Imperialism, Colonialism and Social Welfare. In *Colonialism and Welfare: Social Policy and the British Imperial Legacy*, ed. James Midgley and David Piachaud. Cheltenham: Edward Elgar.

Mkandawire, Thandika. 2015. *Colonial Legacies and Social Welfare Regimes in Africa: An Empirical Exercise*. UNRISD Working Papers on The Politics of Domestic Resource Mobilization for Social Development No. 2016-4, UNRISD, Geneva.

Patel, Leila. 2015. *Social Welfare and Social Development*. 2nd ed. Cape Town: Oxford University Press.

Proudlock, Paula. 2011. Lessons Learned from the Campaigns to Expand the Child Support Grant in South Africa. In *Social Protection for Africa's Children*, ed. Sudhanshu Handa, Stephen Devereux, and Douglas Webb. London: Routledge.

Schmitt, Carina. 2015. Social Security Development and the Colonial Legacy. *World Development* 70: 332–342.

Seekings, Jeremy. 2005. Visions and Hopes and Views about the Future: The Radical Moment of South African Welfare Reform. In *Worlds of Possibility: South Africa in the 1940s*, ed. Saul Dubow and Alan Jeeves, 44–84. Cape Town: Double Storey.

———. 2007. Not a Single White Person Should Be Allowed to Go Under: *Swartgevaar* and the Origins of South Africa's Welfare State, 1924–1929. *Journal of African History* 48 (3): 375–394.

———. 2013. *The Beveridge Report, the Colonial Office and Welfare Reform in British Colonies*. Unpublished Paper, University of Cape Town, Cape Town.

———. 2014. Are African Welfare States Different? *Welfare State-Building in (Anglophone) Africa in Comparative Perspective.* Paper Presented at Workshop on "Social Policy and Regimes of Social Welfare in Africa," University of Fribourg, Switzerland.

———. 2016a. *Drought Relief and the Origins of a Conservative Welfare State in Botswana, 1965–1980*. CSSR Working Paper 378, Centre for Social Science Research, University of Cape Town, Cape Town.

———. 2016b. *A Lean Cow Cannot Climb Out of the Mud, but a Good Cattleman Does Not Leave It to Perish: The Origins of a Conservative Welfare Doctrine in Botswana under Seretse Khama, 1966–1980*. CSSR Working Paper 387, Centre for Social Science Research, University of Cape Town, Cape Town.

———. 2019. Building a Conservative Welfare State in Botswana. In *The Politics of Social Protection in Eastern and Southern Africa*, ed. Sam Hickey, Tom Lavers, Miguel Niño-Zarazúa, and Jeremy Seekings. Oxford: Oxford University Press.

———. 2020. *The Ideology of the Welfare State in South Africa under the National Party, 1948–1990*. CSSR Working Paper, Centre for Social Science Research, University of Cape Town, Cape Town.

Seekings, Jeremy, and Nicoli Nattrass. 2005. *Class, Race and Inequality in South Africa*. New Haven: Yale University Press.

———. 2015. *Policy, Politics and Poverty in South Africa*. London: Palgrave Macmillan.

Shaw, D. John. 2001. *The UN World Food Programme and the Development of Food Aid*. Basingstoke: Palgrave.

Tlou, Thomas, Neil Parsons, and Willie Henderson. 1995. *Seretse Khama, 1921–80*. Gaberone and London: Macmillan.

Vaughan, Megan. 1987. *The Story of an African Famine: Gender and Famine in Twentieth-Century Malawi*. Cambridge: Cambridge University Press.

von Gliszczynski, M., and Lutz Leisering. 2016. Constructing New Global Models of Social Security: How International Organizations Defined the Field of Social Cash Transfers in the 2000s. *Journal of Social Policy* 45 (2): 325–343.

**Open Access** This chapter is licensed under the terms of the Creative Commons Attribution 4.0 International License (http://creativecommons.org/licenses/by/4.0/), which permits use, sharing, adaptation, distribution and reproduction in any medium or format, as long as you give appropriate credit to the original author(s) and the source, provide a link to the Creative Commons licence and indicate if changes were made.

The images or other third party material in this chapter are included in the chapter's Creative Commons licence, unless indicated otherwise in a credit line to the material. If material is not included in the chapter's Creative Commons licence and your intended use is not permitted by statutory regulation or exceeds the permitted use, you will need to obtain permission directly from the copyright holder.

# 6

# The Colonial Legacy and the Rise of Social Assistance in the Global South

Carina Schmitt

## Introduction

Since the beginning of the twenty-first century there has been a rapid rise in social protection initiatives in many low- and middle-income countries (LMIC) that can be mainly attributed to a growing number of social assistance programs. Nowadays, around 70% of all developing countries have at least one social assistance program in place (Dodlova et al. 2016, 8). Social assistance programs are public and noncontributory schemes funded from general tax revenues to guarantee access to essential health care and basic income security to individuals and families in need (Leisering and Barrientos 2013; Midgley 1984a). The recent spread and expansion of social assistance reflects a shift away from contributory-based social insurances implemented in the early days of social protection in the Global South, providing benefits for workers in

---

C. Schmitt (✉)
SOCIUM Research Center on Inequality and Social Policy,
University of Bremen, Bremen, Germany
e-mail: carina.schmitt@uni-bremen.de

the formal labor market. Social insurance, which still is the predominant form of social protection, typically covers only a very small, privileged group of society. The majority of the people are often excluded because of working in the informal labor market or of not being able to pay contributions. Social assistance as noncontributory social protection is assumed to be better able than social insurances to expand coverage to the more vulnerable groups of the society and to face poverty and inequality (Dodlova and Giolbas 2015, 4; Overbye 2005; Eckert 2004, 472; Barrientos 2011). Figure 6.1 shows the spread of two main social assistance programs across LMIC, namely social pensions (left) and unconditional family support programs (right) over the last decades.

The International Labour Organization (ILO) and the World Bank have also acknowledged the need for social assistance schemes and started to promote these programs. However, the active promotion

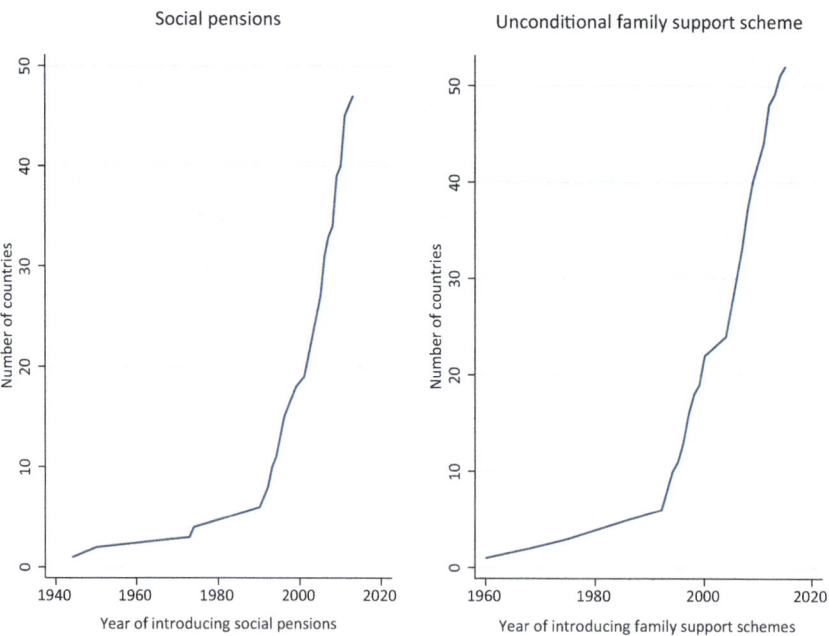

**Fig. 6.1** The rise of social assistance

of social assistance[1] requires a profound understanding of what is driving its introduction and why some countries follow the recent trend and adopt social assistance programs and others do not. Studies analyzing the spread of social assistance emphasize the importance of democratic institutions. Unlike autocratic settings, democratic institutions exert pressure on politicians to implement policies from which the majority of the population benefits. Since social insurance systems typically include only a small segment of society, democratic leaders have an incentive to expand social protection via noncontributory social assistance programs. However, I argue that this narrative only holds in the case of certain institutional preconditions. Whether a country has a social assistance program or not also depends on its colonial legacy. The colonial legacy has defined and still shapes the opportunities of governments for social policy reforms. Colonial empires differed in their imperial strategies and in their notions on the role of the state regarding social protection. These differences influenced early social protection legislation and still have consequences for today's social policy-making.

Surprisingly, the colonial heritage of social protection has been almost completely left out of the equation in comparative social policy research (Kpessa and Béland 2013; Overbye 2005; Schmitt et al. 2015). This is astonishing considering the fact that most developing countries have a colonial history and a great majority of early social protection programs in former colonies were introduced before those countries gained independence (Schmitt 2015). Literature that discussed the effect of the colonial legacy mainly focused on political (Lange 2004) and economic development (Acemoglu et al. 2001; Grier 1999; Englebert 2000). However, the omission of the colonial legacy in the analysis of determinants and consequences of early and post-independent social protection precludes a systematic grasp of contemporary social problems.

To analyze the influence of the colonial legacy on the contemporary spread of social assistance, this chapter uses a sample of ca. 100 LMIC and estimates cross-section and binary time-series cross-section logit models. I focus on two of the most important social assistance programs,

---

[1] Social assistance and noncontributory social protection are interchangeably used in this chapter.

that is, social pensions and unconditional family support schemes.[2] Moreover, I limit the discussion of the colonial influence to the British and French colonial powers. Both were the two main colonizers in the twentieth century—when social protection was put on the global agenda[3] and became actively introduced into the debate on social affairs after World War II.

The empirical findings show that the French and British colonial powers influenced the social policy configurations of their former colonies in each specific way. The French imperial power enforced a strong social insurance principle during colonial times which still today decreases the likelihood of introducing social assistance programs in former French colonies. The effect of the French colonial legacy even outweighs the positive influence of democratic political institutions. On the other hand, former British colonies very early introduced social assistance programs, due to the poor law tradition and the compatibility to the British Beveridgean notion of the welfare state, which highly inspired the whole British Empire. The findings show that the colonial heritage of a country has to be taken into account when explaining different pathways of social protection in most LMIC. That does not imply that national factors are unimportant for social policy-making but rather that the colonial legacy influences the effects of domestic conditions. The colonial heritage is one factor shaping the possibilities of policy-making and the institutional choices a government has nowadays.

The chapter is structured as follows. The next section elucidates the arguments why the colonial legacy should still have an influence on the recent spread of social assistance. The subsequent section presents details on the data and method applied. The then following section analyzes the

---

[2] CCTs (conditional cash transfers) are not considered, as—unlike unconditional programs—they are conditional to investments in education or health. Additionally, they are more heterogeneous for example, regarding the specific target they aim at and the policy field they belong to. They therefore follow a slightly different logic and are not easily comparable with the two other programs analyzed in this contribution.

[3] Other central colonizers such as Spain abandoned their imperial projects already in the first half of the nineteenth century, and therefore before social protection was put on the global agenda and the labor question became urgent in the dependent territories. Further imperial nations such as Belgium, Portugal, Italy or Germany had only a few colonies or maintained their colonies for a much shorter duration, which is why a statistical analysis on their influence would be less informative.

influence of the colonial legacy on the expansion of social pensions and unconditional family support programs across the sample of LMIC. A final section presents a conclusion.

## The Colonial Legacy of Social Assistance

Many studies focusing on the emergence and rise of noncontributory social assistance emphasize the role of democratic institutions (Brooks 2007, 2015; Dodlova et al. 2016). Democratic leaders aiming at extending social protection to groups that have been excluded from contributory social insurance are assumed to opt for social assistance. Noncontributory social protection is often the only available option toward more inclusive social protection because of being independent from formal wage employment, previous contributions and individual financial capabilities (Leisering and Barrientos 2013). Besides studies elucidating the favorable consequences of democracy, the diffusion literature emphasizes the importance of spill-over effects between neighboring countries. Countries are more likely to introduce social assistance if neighboring countries have done so before. However, spill-over effects and the influence of democracy are only part of the story. I argue that the colonial legacy has to be taken into account to obtain a more comprehensive picture of the expansion of social assistance and to explain why some LMIC have introduced social assistance and others have not. In the following, I first briefly address why colonial powers became engaged into social policy-making at all and afterward elucidate why and how the French and British colonial Empires with their general colonial policies and welfare state principles do influence contemporary trends in social protection in LMIC.

### Colonialism and Social Policy

In the late nineteenth and in the first half of the twentieth century, the question of how to deal with social risks in the case of income loss was mainly restricted to the Western world. During much of this period, colonial powers typically aimed at exploiting labor in their colonies and did not pay much attention to how workers in the colonies were protected in the case of work accidents and illness. Hence, colonial powers were not involved in the provision of social services in their colonies until the first decades of the twentieth century (Midgley and Piachaud 2011). From the 1930s and 1940s onward, the labor question in dependent territories became increasingly relevant (Eckert 2004). Labor movements gained importance in many of the colonies, and a number of colonies experienced massive strikes, particularly during World War II and the immediate post-war period (Orr 1966). Moreover, social protection in the dependent territories increasingly became a topic of debate for international organizations, particularly the ILO. In 1944, the ILO member states agreed that the basic standards of labor policy defined by the ILO should also be applied to non-metropolitan areas (Maul 2012; Plant 1994; Kott and Droux 2013). In addition, the human rights declarations of the victorious allies of World War II were an implicit challenge to the imperial systems of European states. The colonial powers could no longer ignore increasing demands for social protection and aimed at a moral upgrade after World War II (Eckert 2004, 479–480). In sum, by midway through the twentieth century, not only was there pressure on the colonial powers from inside the colonies, in the form of rising demands for social protection, but also from the outside, for example in the form of soft pressure by international organizations. As a consequence, colonial powers became more and more engaged in social policies in their colonies.

Two colonial powers highly involved in the debate around social affairs after World War II were France and Britain. However, both differed widely with respect to their notions and concepts of the state, the labor question and social protection (Mahoney 2010). I argue that these differences still have consequences for today's social policy-making and help to explain why some countries have introduced social assistance schemes and others not, independently, for example, of the economic prosperity and quality of democratic institutions.

## British Colonization Strategy and Poor Law Tradition

In the 1940s, questions around social protection and the welfare of workers in dependent territories were also discussed in Great Britain. The debate in the British Empire was characterized by two main peculiarities which not only shaped the post-war debate on social protection in former British colonies but also are still relevant for contemporary social policy-making.

First, Great Britain practiced a decentralized colonization strategy and was committed to a passive view on the role of the state with regard to social protection in their colonies. It often incorporated the local elite and maintained traditional structures of social service provision, for example, for the elderly and other needy groups (Williamson and Pampel 1991, 23). As a consequence, early social protection legislation in former British colonies was more heterogeneous than in many other empires, since colonies had a comparably large maneuvering room. For example, in the case of retirement schemes, countries and territories such as India, Nigeria and Tanzania introduced provident funds, Botswana, the Seychelles and Jamaica flat rate pensions, and Zambia and Yemen wage-related schemes (Schmitt 2015). Against the background of this decentralized colonial administrative structure, British officials did not force encompassing changes. Legislation was implemented by local political leaders in their colonies. The British officials were rather reluctant to actively push the implementation of specific social policies, and the colonial office often only emphasized the urgency of specific legislations (Eckert 2004).

Second, the debate on social protection in the dependent territories was influenced by the poor law tradition in Britain. The British Poor Law tradition dates back to the Elizabethan Poor Law Act of 1601 (Overbye 2005). It was the first nation-wide poor relief regulation in modern times, which aimed at bringing the able-bodied poor to work. In 1834, a new poor law was enacted which tightened the old poor law that had become too expensive in the course of industrialization. The British poor laws resemble very much the current trend of social assistance in the Global South. Both are noncontributory in nature, and in both cases social policy is considered an instrument of poor relief rather than of income maintenance. Already in the early twentieth century the British poor laws served as a role model and inspired some progressive colonies which adopted these ideas and introduced poor relief programs and social assistance schemes in line with the British model (see Künzler, Chap. 4, this volume). For example, Mauritius adopted a poor relief ordinance in 1902, South Africa introduced a noncontributory and means-tested old age pension in 1928 (Seekings 2013, 311), and a poor relief ordinance was passed by Trinidad and Tobago in 1931 (Seekings 2013, 312; Midgley 1984b, 22). These social assistance schemes often remained in place after decolonization or were even extended by the new governments and administrations, for example to colored people (Midgley 1984b, 27).

These two British specifics also shaped the debate on social protection in overseas territories in the 1940s. This debate was intensified by the Beveridge Report from 1942 which led to the formation of commissions on social affairs in several dependent territories across the entire British Empire (Surender 2013; Seekings 2008). After World War II, it was controversially discussed whether tax-financed social assistance schemes could be introduced throughout the British Empire. Some British officials, for example, in the Economic Department, favored noncontributory over contributory schemes (Seekings 2011, 167), while others considered an implementation of comprehensive social assistance too expensive and therefore impossible to implement. Although the discussions in the British Empire did not result in any systematic or uniform handling of social affairs in overseas territories and finally the British officials considered it unrealistic to adopt large scale social assistance schemes in all dependent territories, they brought the introduction of such schemes into the debate at a very early stage. This highly influenced the discourse about the labor question in British overseas territories. As a consequence, the implementation of social assistance programs was discussed much earlier within the entire British Empire than anywhere else. This early presence of ideas about social assistance and the early existence of social assistance schemes in the motherland, but also in some colonies, were to increase the likelihood of following the recent policy trend of introducing social assistance programs in former British colonies.

When looking at the specific risks covered within the British Empire and in Great Britain itself, social assistance traditionally focused on elderly people. For example, in Great Britain the Old Age Pensions Act of 1908, as the beginning of the system of modern state pension, stipulated the entitlement to a tax-funded old age pension for elderly people lacking sufficient income (see Seekings, Chap. 5, this volume). This retirement scheme is very similar to the current trend of social pensions. But also the early social assistance programs in Mauritius, South Africa and Namibia addressed the needs of the elderly. In contrast, family allowances remain "a contested part of a welfare system" (Pedersen 1993, 415). Especially in colonial societies during colonial times, Britain favored male breadwinner wages. Family allowances were regarded as inefficient in African societies by British officials because allowances would not only finance children but often many other dependent relatives as well (Lindsay 1999, 802).

In sum, the poor law tradition with its focus on poor relief rather than on income maintenance for industrial workers and the early discussion of social assistance in the former British Empire were to enhance the probability that former British colonies implemented noncontributory social assistance programs (Seekings 2013). Moreover, the positive influence of the British colonial footprint on the introduction of social assistance was to especially apply to social pensions but less to family support schemes.

## French Social Insurance Tradition

In France, as the second major colonial power of the twentieth century, the debate regarding social protection also accelerated in the 1940s. Two main characteristics relevant for contemporary social protection made the debate within the French colonial empire different from that in other empires.

First, France followed a pro-active colonial policy, emphasizing the decisive role of the state in enhancing social and economic prosperity (Cooper 1996; Iliffe 1987). French officials held the view that the colonies could not develop themselves but rather needed the initiative of the French Administrative Authority (MacLean 2002). The French colonial power regarded "the colonies simply as a prolongation of the mother-country beyond the seas" (Fieldhouse 1967, 308). The French imperial mission was characterized by the view that the Republic was one and indivisible. As a consequence, the French imperial system aimed at reproducing the French model in its colonies in all areas (see Becker, Chap. 7, this volume). In contrast to Britain, France centralized its power and, at least theoretically, made all basic and important decisions in Paris, where after 1894 colonial officials were trained in the École Coloniales (Fieldhouse 1967, 310). The consequence was an autocratic system of colonial government (Grier 1999, 319; Fieldhouse 1967, 308). Even though the French appointed Africans in order to fulfill administrative functions, these administrative elite owed their positions to France. The French aimed at producing an elite population in the colonies that was completely committed to the French culture, with a status comparable to that of French citizens. However, only a small portion of the native population achieved this status and became citizens (Fieldhouse 1967, 315). The great majority kept their status as colonial subjects liable to the *Code de L'Indigénat* which determines the inferiority of colonial people.

Second, one basic characteristic of the French welfare state is the strong social insurance tradition (Kaufmann 2013, 155). It is largely based on the principle of occupational solidarity. This means that social protection is linked to the occupational status of the insured person, his or her earnings and in consequence the contribution record (Béland and Hansen 2000, 512). Earning-related benefits based upon individual contributions are only provided to workers and their family in formal wage employment. Each risk is separately administered and managed within different social insurance schemes and often separated by different occupational groups (Palier 2000, 116). For example, each profession has its own pension scheme, leading to a very fragmented pension system which is highly resistant to change. France itself did not have any comprehensive social assistance system for people in need (Béland and Hansen 2000, 52). The only exception was family allowances. France implemented the *Code de la Famille* in 1939, as the first "comprehensive legislation on family policy anywhere in the world which pays universal benefits to all French citizens and residents for the second child and subsequent children" (Béland and Hansen 2000, 52). One main reason for this exceptional character of family policy was France's fear of a power imbalance and a military advantage for the German army due to the depopulation of France itself (Echenberg 1975, 179).

These two features characterized the debate on the introduction of social protection for workers in overseas territories in the 1940s. After a series of strike waves in French West Africa the French officials came to the view that conditions for workers had to be improved. From 1946 onward, after formally abolishing the *Code de L'Indigénat*, that is, the inferiority of the native population, a committee at the Ministry of Overseas Territories was working on a plan to extend social protection to workers in the colonial states. However, officials had to define who a worker was and which rights were associated with this status. After six years of debate, the French *Code du Travail* for overseas territories was passed in 1952, as the key milestone of social protection legislation in the French colonies. The Code contained many specific regulations regarding social protection programs, and it strongly reflected France's social insurance tradition. For example, it stated that family allowances and systems to protect workers from illness and accidents should be introduced in the colonies. However, according to the *Code du Travail* only those workers were included who were part of the formal labor market or were citizens (Fieldhouse 1967, 312; Eckert 2004, 481). The *Code du Travail* therefore excluded customary workers, workers on the informal labor market or people "compensated by land or crops" (Cooper 1989, 754). Due to the centralized approach of France, the *Code du Travail* applied for all colonies at the same time. After gaining independence, the former French colonies "all maintained the basic text and structure of the Code du Travail in 1952" and therefore the strong social insurance tradition of the welfare state (Cooper 1996, 464).

Regarding scheme specific differences, also family allowances played an exceptional role in the colonies (Eckert 2004, 482). As family allowances were much more important in the French welfare system (Lindsay 1999, 810), the *Code du Travail* also reflects the importance of supporting the nuclear family as part of the social protection of workers.

In sum, France had a very strong social insurance tradition, and the French administration clearly pushed for the establishment of social security systems similar to the French social insurance model. As a consequence, all former French colonies introduced social protection schemes which first of all followed heavily social insurance principles. This strong social insurance setting was to make it much more difficult for former French colonies still today to implement noncontributory social assistance. A complete shift from one system to another, with the abolishment of the old one, is highly unlikely and would come along with high transaction costs. This is illustrated by the fact that almost no country has abolished a social insurance scheme once it has been established (ILO 2017). Therefore I assume that under otherwise equal conditions former French colonies are less likely to have social assistance programs. Furthermore and against the background of the importance of family allowances and its exceptional character in France itself, French colonies are more likely to have introduced noncontributory family support schemes than social pensions.

## Summary

The main argument is that different imperial powers with different notions of the welfare state adopted different colonization strategies. For example, the French welfare state is characterized by the principle of social insurance and income maintenance rather than by poverty alleviation as it is the case with the British welfare state. In France, the social question was considered a worker's question, while in Great Britain it was more a poverty question (Kaufmann 2013, 100). These differences result in different logics of contemporary social policy-making. After having gained their independence, all French colonies maintained the social insurance nature of social protection that has been characteristic for the French notion of the welfare state. The strong social insurance tradition in former French colonies, reflecting the principles of the French welfare state, would require a complete modification of existing institutions, practices and power structures if social assistance schemes were supposed to be introduced. The costs of implementing the recent trend of social assistance are therefore disproportionally high, as the policy trend does not fit to the existing institutional setting. A strong social insurance tradition may therefore be supposed to tremendously decrease the likelihood of having a social assistance. In contrast, in former British colonies the poor law tradition and the early debate on noncontributory social protection make social assistance a concrete, available policy option, as early bird countries such as South Africa have shown. Moreover, British colonies are more likely to have social pensions than family support schemes, since poor laws and early social assistance typically have focused on protecting the elderly. Family policy has not been a central issue of the British welfare state.

## The Rise of Social Assistance in the Global South: Data and Methods

The empirical analysis proceeds by two steps. First, I estimate cross-section logit models to explain which countries have a noncontributory social pension or a family support scheme for the most recent period of time, since this allows for integrating a broader set of control variables. In a second step, I estimate binary time-series cross-section (BTSCS) models which additionally allow for an analysis of the time dimension.

The dependent variable is the introduction of two of the most important and most frequent noncontributory social assistance schemes, namely social pensions and unconditional family support schemes. Social pensions are noncontributory cash transfers paid regularly to elderly people (HelpAge International 2017). They are widely acknowledged to be one of the most effective tools to reduce old age poverty and invest in human capital development. Data on social pensions are taken from HelpAge International which provides a large database on social pensions in 107 countries. The information coming from HelpAge International is cross-validated with information provided by the ILO (2017) and Dodlova et al. (2016). Unconditional family support schemes are "transfers targeted to low-income households or specifically to children" (Dodlova et al. 2016, 9). These schemes "range from a basic safety net for those below the poverty line to (universal) child support grants" (Dodlova et al. 2016, 9). Data for unconditional family support schemes are taken from the Noncontributory Social Transfer Database which includes information, on a program-basis, about 186 programs in 101 countries (Dodlova et al. 2016).

In both cases the dependent variable is measured by a binary choice variable coded 0 if a country has not yet introduced a social pension or a family support scheme and 1 in the year when a country introduced the respective program. By now, around 50 LMIC (low- and middle-income countries) have a social pension in place, and a comparable number of countries are provided with a family support scheme. In the BTSCS models the countries are only considered until the event happens. Once a specific program has been introduced, the country is excluded from the analysis of the respective program. I estimate logit equations using a standard maximum likelihood procedure. Ordinary probit or logit rests on the assumption that the observations are temporally independent. However, the probability of introducing social assistance is not equal at any point in time but increases over time. Therefore, ordinary probit or logit would be misleading and the standard errors underestimated. I follow the procedure suggested by Beck et al. (1998) in order to deal with time dependence. Beck et al. (1998) show that binary time-series cross-section data is identical with grouped duration data. They suggest estimating the models including cubic splines, as natural cubic splines capture the time dependence. The estimated coefficients of the cubic splines can be used to trace the path of duration dependence. In comparison to time dummies, cubic splines have the advantage of providing a more parsimonious strategy. I alternatively checked $t$, $t^2$ and $t^3$ as a cubic polynomial approximation in the estimations (Carter and Signorino, 2010). Moreover, robust standard errors clustered by country are used.

In the empirical analyses the influence of the British and French colonial legacy as a central independent variable is captured by including dummies for British or French colonies. Moreover, I include the real GDP per capita (log.) as a control variable (Maddison Project Database 2018) to measure a nation's level of economic development. In line with functionalist theories, it is expected that there is a positive relationship between affluence and the introduction of social protection (Wilensky 1975). Moreover, I include the level of *democracy*, which in many studies is assumed to drive the introduction and emergence of social assistance. I use the polity index which ranges from −10 (autocracy) to 10 (full democracy) (Marshall et al. 2014). A further key variable is the *dependency ratio*, that is, the number of people above 65 and below 15 in relation to the total working-age population (World Bank 2015). A high dependency ratio should be reflected in a strong demand for noncontributory social pensions and family support schemes. Additionally, it can be expected that the colonial legacy diminishes over time after gaining *independence*. Hence the longer a country is independent, the higher is the probability that it is able to follow the recent policy trend. Furthermore, the level of *globalization*, measured as the total of exports and imports in relation to the GDP, might exhibit a negative influence on the introduction of social assistance programs, due to the competitive pressure arising from embeddedness in the international market.[4] As mentioned above, international organizations such as the *ILO* strongly promote the introduction of social assistance programs. I therefore include a dummy capturing whether a country is an ILO member or not. Furthermore, it is checked for *ethnic fractionalization* (Alesina et al. 2003). It is argued that "ethnic diversity has led to social polarization and entrenched interest groups in Africa and thereby should decrease the likelihood that a country introduces a universal noncontributory social protection scheme" (Englebert 2000, 9; Alesina et al. 2003).

In the cross-section analyses, all independent variables are calculated as an average across the ten years prior to the information of the dependent variable. In the BTSCS estimation I additionally check regional diffusion processes by including a spatial lag capturing the number of countries with a respective scheme that share a common border with the focal country. Basic descriptive statistics of the main variables included can be found in the appendix.

---

[4] However, it might also push countries to meet international standards and introduce basic social protection programs.

## Explaining the Existence of Social Assistance in the Global South

Did the spread of social assistance differ by colonial sphere? Table 6.1 shows the empirical results of the logit regressions. In models 1 and 2 the introduction of social pensions is used as a dependent variable, and in

Table 6.1 Introduction of social assistance—cross-section analyses

| Odds ratio | (1) Social pension | (2) Social pension | (3) Family support | (4) Family support |
|---|---|---|---|---|
| **Former British colony** | 6.765*** | | 1.428 | |
| | (4.448) | | (0.748) | |
| **Former French colony** | | 0.108** | | 0.486 |
| | | (0.118) | | (0.282) |
| ILO | 1.029 | 1.024 | 1.020 | 1.019 |
| | (0.0188) | (0.0179) | (0.0154) | (0.0155) |
| Globalization | 1.011 | 1.007 | 0.988 | 0.988 |
| | (0.00769) | (0.00746) | (0.00771) | (0.00756) |
| Ethnic fractionalization | 1.528 | 1.758 | 0.780 | 0.804 |
| | (1.886) | (2.136) | (0.853) | (0.884) |
| Dependency ratio | 0.885** | 0.935 | 0.952 | 0.969 |
| | (0.0525) | (0.0502) | (0.0461) | (0.0475) |
| GDP per capita | 1.000 | 1.000 | 1.000 | 1.000 |
| | (0.000173) | (0.000141) | (0.000146) | (0.000140) |
| Time since independence | 0.971*** | 0.983* | 1.000 | 1.002 |
| | (0.0109) | (0.00988) | (0.00881) | (0.00869) |
| Polity | 1.171*** | 1.146** | 1.006 | 0.997 |
| | (0.0662) | (0.0614) | (0.0439) | (0.0445) |
| **Percentage point change in odds** | | | | |
| Former British colony | 576.5 | | 42.8 | |
| Former French colony | | −89.2 | | −51.4 |
| Polity | 17.1 | 14.6 | 0.6 | −0.3 |
| Corr classified | 80.43% | 77.17% | 66.30% | 65.22% |
| ML Cox Snell | 0.32 | 0.30 | 0.11 | 0.12 |
| Observations | 92 | 92 | 92 | 92 |

Notes: Odds ratio are reported; standard errors in parentheses. The results for the cubic splines are suppressed to conserve space ***$p < 0.01$, **$p < 0.05$, *$p < 0.1$; note that standard errors for odds ratio are calculated as follows: se(OR) = exp(_b[_var])*_se[_var]

models 3 and 4 it is family support schemes. The first and the third model test the influence of the British colonial legacy, and the second and the fourth model test the French colonial influence. Odds ratio are displayed.

The results remarkably confirm the main hypothesis that the likelihood whether a country has a social pension or an unconditional family support program is highly influenced by the colonial legacy. When looking at the results for social pensions, the probability of a former British colony having a social pension is almost 7 times higher than in all other LMIC. On the other hand, being a former French colony decreases the likelihood of having a social pension scheme by 89.2 percentage points. The strong social insurance tradition, especially with regard to retirement schemes, seems to heavily influence the contemporary choices for social policy-making. The situation is slightly different with regard to family support schemes. Even though former French colonies are also less likely to implement these programs, the influence is less hampering than in the case of social pensions. This reflects the importance of family support schemes in the tradition of the French welfare state. In the case of the British colonies, the positive role of the colonial legacy for the introduction of social pensions is not observable with regard to unconditional family support programs. This represents the low British emphasis on family policies and the lacking tradition regarding this scheme.

The results regarding the level of democracy are also interesting. In line with previous research, democratic institutions seem to push the introduction of social pensions. The likelihood of having a social pension increases by about 17 percentage points with a one unit increase in the polity index. However, the positive influence is only observable in the case of social pensions, but not in the case of family support schemes. Interestingly, the effect of democracy differs by colonial sphere. To illustrate the conditional effect of the colonial heritage, I calculated the effect of the regime type on the likelihood of introducing social pensions in dependence of the colonial legacy. Figure 6.2 displays the effect of democratic institutions for former French (right figure) and former British colonies (left figure), each in comparison to the rest of the sample. In the right figure it can be observed that an increase from the lowest possible value for the polity index ($-10$) to the highest one (10) only slightly enhances the likelihood of a former French colony (right figure, solid

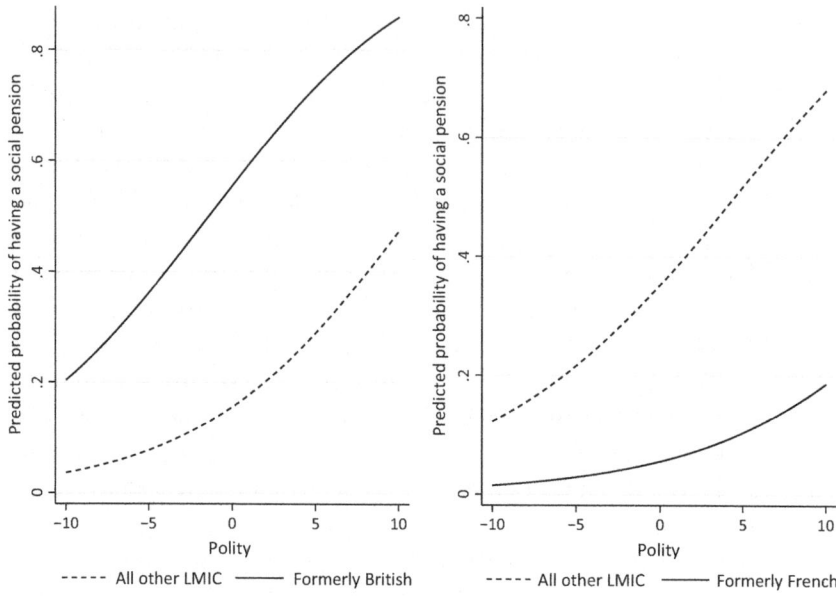

**Fig. 6.2** Effect of democracy by colonial sphere

line) to have a social pension scheme (by around 15 percentage points) in contrast to an estimated increase for all other LMIC by 60 percentage points (right figure, dash line). In the case of former British colonies (left figure, solid line), the marginal effect of democratic institutions on the predicted probability of having a social pension is similar to the non-British colonies (left figure, dash line). However, former British colonies have a higher probability of having a social pension schemes than all other LMIC, independently of the level of democracy.

Table 6.2 shows the results of the binary time-series cross-section analyses.

The results of the BTSCS (binary time-series cross-section) models, which take the time dimension into account, confirm the results of the cross-section analyses. Being a former French colony decreases the likelihood of introducing a social pension by around 90 percentage points. By contrast, ex-colonies of the British Empire introduce social pension schemes very early in comparison to all other LMIC (besides of French ex-colonies). More democratic countries are more likely to adopt social

Table 6.2 Introduction of social assistance—binary time-series cross-section analyses

| Odds ratio | (1) Social pensions | (2) Social pensions | (3) Family support | (4) Family support |
|---|---|---|---|---|
| (Former) British colony | 2.459** | | 1.496 | |
| | (0.938) | | (0.489) | |
| (Former) French colony | | 0.0923** | | 0.117* |
| | | (0.0947) | | (0.130) |
| Neighbors with social pensions | 1.696*** | 1.696*** | 2.233*** | 2.233*** |
| | (0.248) | (0.248) | (0.665) | (0.665) |
| Polity | 1.186*** | 1.159*** | 1.022 | 1.065 |
| | (0.0470) | (0.0445) | (0.0282) | (0.0560) |
| GDP per capita | 1.000* | 1.000 | 1.000** | 1.000* |
| | (8.21e-05) | (7.93e-05) | (0.000105) | (0.000206) |
| Dependency ratio | 0.967 | 0.927 | 0.985 | 0.999 |
| | (0.0561) | (0.0537) | (0.0587) | (0.0626) |
| Observations | 3895 | 3895 | 4157 | 4157 |
| Number of countries | 99 | 99 | 111 | 111 |

Notes: Odds ratio are reported; standard errors in parentheses. The results for the cubic splines are suppressed to conserve space ***$p < 0.01$, **$p < 0.05$, *$p < 0.1$; note that standard errors for odds ratio are calculated as follows: se(OR) = exp(_b[_var])*_se[_var]

pension schemes, while this relationship does not hold in the case of family support schemes. The consideration of the time dimension allows testing for regional diffusion processes. The results strongly corroborate the importance of regional diffusion. The likelihood that a country introduces social assistance increases with the number of surrounding countries with the respective scheme.

## Conclusion

Social assistance is one of the most recent policy trends in the Global South, raising many expectations. Since social assistance is not based on individual contributions, it is assumed to be an effective instrument for reducing poverty and inequality and for expanding social protection to the most vulnerable groups of society. Indeed, there is some evidence of these positive effects of social assistance. This evidence motivates international organizations such as the ILO or the World Bank to promote the introduction of social assistance in developing countries.

When explaining the recent trend of social assistance, studies have particularly emphasized the role of democratic institutions. However, I have argued that this only holds in the case of certain institutional preconditions which depend on the colonial legacy. Colonial empires differed in their imperial strategies and in their notions on the role of the state regarding social protection. These differences have influenced early social protection legislation and institutions but have still consequences for today's social policy-making.

By analyzing the spread of social pensions and unconditional family support programs as two of the most important social assistance schemes in LMIC in a quantitative framework, I can show that former British colonies are more likely to introduce social assistance than all other LMIC. This reflects the British Poor Law tradition and the decentralized imperial strategy of Britain, which have led to a very early diffusion of ideas on social assistance across the Empire. In contrast, in the early days of social protection in the Global South all former French colonies implemented social insurances in line with the strong social insurance tradition that characterizes the French welfare state. A shift from insurance-based social protection to tax-financed noncontributory social assistance would require a complete restructuring of existing institutions and would come along with tremendous costs. As a consequence, former French colonies did not follow the recent trend of introducing social assistance programs. The French colonial legacy even outweighs the positive influence of democratic institutions for which many studies have produced evidence. These findings show that it is very important to take the colonial legacy into account when analyzing early but also contemporary social protection in the Global South. The results also demonstrate that it is not sufficient to simply promote a specific strategy of social protection but rather to consider the historical context to come to a better understanding of the causes and consequences of early and contemporary social protection. However, the results do not imply that national conditions are not important for policy-making but rather that domestic conditions unfold different effects depending on the historical context of a country.

# References

Acemoglu, Daron, Simon Johnson, and James A. Robinson. 2001. The Colonial Origins of Comparative Development: An Empirical Investigation. *American Economic Review* 91: 1369–1401.

Alesina, Alberto, Arnaud Devleeschauwer, William Easterly, Sergio Kurlat, and Romain Wacziarg. 2003. Fractionalization. *Journal of Economic Growth* 8: 155–194.

Barrientos, Armando. 2011. Social Protection and Poverty. *International Journal of Social Welfare* 20: 240–249.

Beck, Nathaniel, Jonathan N. Katz, and Richard Tucker. 1998. Taking Time Seriously: Time-Series-Cross-Section Analysis with a Binary Dependent Variable. *American Journal of Political Science* 42: 1260–1288.

Béland, Daniel, and Randall Hansen. 2000. Reforming the French Welfare State: Solidarity, Social Exclusion and the Three Crises of Citizenship. *West European Politics* 23: 47–64.

Brooks, Sarah M. 2007. When Does Diffusion Matter? Explaining the Spread of Structural Pension Reforms across Nations. *The Journal of Politics* 69: 701–715.

———. 2015. Social Protection for the Poorest: The Adoption of Antipoverty Cash Transfer Programs in the Global South. *Politics and Society* 43: 551–582.

Carter, David B., and Curtis S. Signorino. 2010. Back to the Future: Modeling Time Dependence in Binary Data. *Political Analysis* 18: 271–292.

Cooper, Frederick. 1989. From Free Labor to Family Allowances: Labor and African Society in Colonial Discourse. *American Ethnologist* 16: 745–765.

———. 1996. *Decolonization and African Society. The Labor Question in French and British Africa*. Cambridge: Cambridge University Press.

Dodlova, Marina, and Anna Giolbas. 2015. *Regime Type, Inequality, and Redistributive Transfer in Developing Countries*. GIGA Working Paper Series no. 273, May 2015.

Dodlova, Marina, Anna Giolbas, and Jann Lay. 2016. *Non-Contributory Social Transfer Programmes in Developing Countries: A New Data Set and Research Agenda*. GIGA Working Paper Series no. 290, August 2016.

Echenberg, Myron J. 1975. Paying the Blood Tax: Military Conscription in French West Africa, 1914–1929. *Canadian Journal of Political Science* 9: 171–192.

Eckert, Andreas. 2004. Regulating the Social: Social Security, Social Welfare and the State in Late Colonial Tanzania. *The Journal of African History* 45: 467–489.

Englebert, Pierre. 2000. Pre-Colonial Institutions, Post-Colonial States, and Economic Development in Tropical Africa. *Political Research Quarterly* 53: 7–36.

Fieldhouse, David K. 1967. *The Colonial Empires: A Comparative Survey from the Eighteenth Century*. New York: Delacorte Press.

Grier, Robin M. 1999. Colonial Legacies and Economic Growth. *Public Choice* 98: 317–335.

HelpAge International. 2017. Social Pension Database. http://www.pensionwatch.net/social-pensions-database/social-pensions-database%2D%2D/.

Iliffe, John. 1987. *The African Poor*. Cambridge: Cambridge University Press.

International Labour Organisation. 2017. *World Social Protection Report. Building Economic Recovery, Inclusive Development and Social Justice*. Geneva: ILO.

Kaufmann, Franz-Xaver. 2013. *Variations of the Welfare State: Great Britain, Sweden, France and Germany between Capitalism and Socialism*. Berlin: Springer.

Kott, Sandrine, and Joëlle Droux, eds. 2013. *Globalizing Social Rights. The International Labour Organization and Beyond*. Basingstoke: Palgrave Macmillan.

Kpessa, Michael W., and Daniel Béland. 2013. Mapping Social Policy Development in Sub-Saharan Africa. *Policy Studies* 34: 326–341.

Lange, Matthew K. 2004. British Colonial Legacies and Political Development. *World Development* 32: 905–922.

Leisering, Lutz, and Armando Barrientos. 2013. Social Citizenship for the Global Poor? The Worldwide Spread of Social Assistance. *International Journal of Social Welfare* 22: 50–67.

Lindsay, Lisa A. 1999. Domesticity and Difference: Male Breadwinners, Working Women, and Colonial Citizenship in the 1945 Nigerian General Strike. *The American Historical Review* 104: 783–812.

MacLean, Lauren. 2002. Constructing a Social Safety net in Africa: An Institutionalist Analysis of Colonial Rule and State Social Policies in Ghana and Cote d'Ivoire. *Studies in Comparative International Development* 37: 64–90.

Maddison Project Database. 2018. Bolt, Jutta, Robert Inklaar, Herman de Jong, and Jan Luiten van Zanden. *Rebasing 'Maddison': New Income Comparisons and the Shape of Long-run Economic Development*. Maddison Project Working paper 10.

Mahoney, James. 2010. *Colonialism and Postcolonial Development: Spanish America in Comparative Perspective*. Cambridge: Cambridge University Press.

Marshall, Monti G., Ted R. Gurr, and Keith Jaggers. 2014. *Polity IV Project: Political Regime Characteristics and Transitions, 1800–2012.* Dataset Users' Manual.

Maul, Daniel. 2012. *Human Rights, Development and Decolonization: The International Labour Organization, 1940–1970.* Houndmills: Palgrave Macmillan.

Midgley, James. 1984a. Diffusion and Development of Social Policy: Evidence from the Third World. *Journal of Social Policy* 13: 167–184.

———. 1984b. Poor Law Principles and Social Assistance in the Third World: A Study of the Perpetuation of Colonial Welfare. *International Social Work* 27: 19–29.

Midgley, James, and David Piachaud, eds. 2011. *Colonialism and Welfare. Social Policy and the British Imperial Legacy.* Cheltenham: Edward Elgar.

Orr, Charles A. 1966. Trade Unionism in Colonial Africa. *Journal of Modern African Studies* 4: 65–81.

Overbye, Einar. 2005. Extending Social Security in Developing Countries: A Review of Three Main Strategies. *International Journal of Social Welfare* 14: 305–314.

Palier, Bruno. 2000. "Defrosting" the French Welfare State. *West European Politics* 23: 113–136.

Pedersen, Susan. 1993. *Family, Dependence, and the Origins of the Welfare State.* Cambridge: Cambridge University Press.

Plant, Roger. 1994. *Labour Standards and Structural Adjustment.* Geneva: International Labour Office.

Schmitt, Carina. 2015. Social Security Development and the Colonial Legacy. *World Development* 70: 332–342.

Schmitt, Carina, Hanna Lierse, Herbert Obinger, and Laura Seelkopf. 2015. The Global Emergence of the Welfare State: Explaining Social Policy Legislation, 1820–2013. *Politics and Society* 43: 503–524.

Seekings, Jeremy. 2008. Welfare Regimes and Redistribution in the South. In *Divide and Deal: The Politics of Distribution in Democracies*, ed. Ian Shapiro, Peter A. Swenson, and Daniela Donno. New York: New York University.

———. 2011. British Colonial Policy, Local Politics, and the Origins of the Mauritian Welfare State, 1936–1950. *Journal of African History* 52: 157–177.

———. 2013. Social Policy. In *Routledge Handbook of African Politics*, ed. Nic Cheeseman, David Anderson, and Andrea Scheibler. London: Routledge.

Surender, Rebecca. 2013. The Role of Historical Contexts in Shaping Social Policy in the Global South. In *Social Policy in a Developing World*, ed. Rebecca Surender and Robert Walker. Edward Elgar: Northampton.

Wilensky, Harold L. 1975. *The Welfare State and Equality*. Berkeley: University of California Press.
Williamson, John B., and Fred C. Pampel. 1991. Ethnic Politics, Colonial Legacy, and Old Age Security Policy: The Nigerian Case in Historical and Comparative Perspective. *Journal of Aging Studies* 5: 19–44.
World Bank. 2015. *World Development Indicators*. Washington, DC: World Bank.

**Open Access** This chapter is licensed under the terms of the Creative Commons Attribution 4.0 International License (http://creativecommons.org/licenses/by/4.0/), which permits use, sharing, adaptation, distribution and reproduction in any medium or format, as long as you give appropriate credit to the original author(s) and the source, provide a link to the Creative Commons licence and indicate if changes were made.

The images or other third party material in this chapter are included in the chapter's Creative Commons licence, unless indicated otherwise in a credit line to the material. If material is not included in the chapter's Creative Commons licence and your intended use is not permitted by statutory regulation or exceeds the permitted use, you will need to obtain permission directly from the copyright holder.

# 7

# Colonial Legacies in International Aid: Policy Priorities and Actor Constellations

Bastian Becker

## Introduction

In the past century, international aid has become an essential part of the foreign policy toolkit. It is especially popular among former colonial powers which spend the majority of their aid budgets on countries that once were part of their empires (Alesina and Dollar 2000; Fuchs et al. 2014; Round and Odedokun 2004; Steinwand 2015). However, beyond this general pattern, little more is known about the colonial legacy of international aid. This is unfortunate because recent migration movements have reinvigorated debates about historical responsibilities of European countries. In this chapter I argue that the organization of colonial empires shapes the ways in which former colonial powers provide aid

---

B. Becker (✉)
SOCIUM Research Center on Inequality and Social Policy, University of Bremen, Bremen, Germany
e-mail: Bastian.becker@uni-bremen.de

© The Author(s) 2020
C. Schmitt (ed.), *From Colonialism to International Aid*, Global Dynamics of Social Policy, https://doi.org/10.1007/978-3-030-38200-1_7

today, in particular policy priorities and actors involved in the distribution of aid. This claim is supported by analyses of newly available, highly disaggregated data on aid flows.

In this chapter I focus on the two largest and most recent colonial empires, those of Britain and France.[1] These cases are also interesting as they employed different colonial strategies. Whereas Britain often relied on indirect rule, using existing political structures to project its power, France more commonly used direct rule, imposing new structures with less consideration for local conditions (Gerring et al. 2011; Iyer 2010; Mamdani 1996). Indirect rule also led Britain to more strongly involve other actors, be they local, non-governmental or international. France instead relied on the newly built governmental capacities, and bureaucratic centralization fostered close ties between the metropolitan and colonial governments (Lee and Schultz 2012; Schmitt 2015; Schmitt, Chap. 6, this volume). To facilitate their colonial undertakings (and to decelerate their demise), both powers also promoted social protection policies (see also Schmitt, Chap. 6, this volume). These efforts were especially pronounced in the French empire, due to the application of metropolitan law in colonies and the goal to assimilate subjugated populations (Iliffe 1987; Wesseling 2004). Path dependency, due to lasting economic, political and social ties, suggests that these differences should also be reflected in how Britain and France provide aid today.

Research on colonial legacies of international aid was until recently limited to the analysis of aggregate aid flows. However, newly available, highly disaggregated data makes it possible to analyze aid flows in greater detail (see OECD 2018a). This data allows me to show that colonial legacies are reflected in how former colonial powers distribute aid today. For example, both Britain and France focus aid to their former colonies on social protection, about 9 percentage points more than what they give to other countries. As expected, France strongly relies on governmental actors to channel aid to its former colonies (about 92%), whereas Britain uses governmental channels for a mere 22% of all aid. These differences cannot be accounted for by common explanatory factors, such as economic development, trade openness or democracy. These findings have important

---

[1] Note that in most instances below, country names refer to the respective governments.

implications for our understanding of international aid today. They emphasize that policy priorities and the actor constellations promoted by aid might be harder to change than often expected.

The chapter proceeds as follows. Section "Colonial Legacies in International Aid" introduces literature that informs our understanding of the colonial legacies of international aid, in particular concerning policy priorities and actor constellations. Section "Data" introduces the new aid data and other variables used in the analysis. Section "Analysis" presents the main results, followed by a final discussion in Sect. "Discussion".

## Colonial Legacies in International Aid

It is well established that most donors provide more bilateral aid to former colonies than other recipient countries. This is certainly the case for the two former colonial powers this study focuses on, Britain and France. It is commonly argued that bilateral aid serves for maintaining political influence and economic relationships that developed during colonial times (Alesina and Dollar 2000; Berthélemy and Tichit 2004; Fuchs et al. 2014). However, not all scholars argue that self-interest determines aid disbursements to former colonies. Others point out that colonial powers increasingly assumed responsibility for the well-being of subjugated populations, due to growing cultural similarities (Schraeder et al. 1998) and deliberations among domestic and international political circles (Lewis 2011; Pacquement 2010).

Most comparative work on colonial legacies of international aid focuses on the overall generosity of donors toward former colonies. This chapter seeks to reveal in greater detail how colonial legacies unfold. Therefore, two aspects of contemporary international aid take the center stage. First, the extent to which donors prioritize social protection, promoting activities such as health and education; and second, the actors involved in the distribution of aid, in particular aid directed at social protection. As the review below shows, the existing literature suggests that colonial legacies are likely to become manifest in these regards. Other than that, this choice is arbitrary, and it is likely that colonial legacies affect international aid in many other ways. That said, focusing on policy priorities and aid actors offers a reasonable starting point for advancing knowledge about colonial legacies in international aid.

## Policy Priorities: Social Protection

Colonial empires were first and foremost economic undertakings. Their primary aim was to exploit colonized territories to the benefit of their metropoles. Colonial powers like Britain and France therefore initiated economic structures and re-shaped existing ones to best suit this purpose. This was achieved by aligning policies with the overarching aim of economic exploitation. With regard to social protection, this implied a minimalist approach that focused on attracting Europeans to the overseas territories and on retaining a viable labor force within the colonies. There was little interest in what goods were demanded locally. As a result, colonial economies focused on mining and agriculture, cash crops in particular, and unsurprisingly they were strongly export-oriented.

Social protection was also promoted for non-economic reasons, especially during later years. Colonial administrators were concerned about the well-being and social status of Europeans and, at least to some extent, about the well-being of the subjugated populations (Lewis 2011; Pacquement 2010). Basic social services for the indigenous population were furthermore needed to reduce labor scarcity prevalent in many colonies. Although unintended, migration in both directions led to a growing number of personal ties between metropole and colony, which increased the chances that social needs within the colonies were recognized and addressed (Lahiri and Raimondos-Møller 2000). Furthermore, after World War I international organizations became active in colonial politics and policy-making, urging colonial powers to take more and more responsibility for the situation in territories dependent on them (Pearson 2018).

While the British and the French colonial empires both had the primary aim of economic exploitation, they differed widely when it comes to specific policy areas. Social protection is no exception. British administrations rarely provided benefits to anyone but government workers. Other schemes were initiated only if pre-existing local arrangements would not suffice and, as I discuss further below, if no other external actor, like missions or firms, stepped in. Mirroring social protection policies at home, France provided benefits to a wider set of workers, including many of those in formal employment. More generally, France frequently extended metropolitan laws and rights to colonies, with the ultimate goal of assimilating subjugated populations (Iliffe 1987; Kpessa 2010). At the same time, France's interventionist approach often came at the expense of local practices and institutions, which were rarely promoted and often curtailed instead (Suret-Canale 1971).

Independence had little effect on the economic set-up of (former) colonies, in particular regarding sectoral composition and export orientation. Companies that previously enjoyed quasi-monopolistic positions lobbied for favorable trade agreements with former colonies and, where possible, continued their operations. They were supported by the former colonial powers which continued to shape and influence policy-making in the newly independent territories, for example by providing aid (Alesina and Dollar 2000; Fuchs et al. 2014). In fact, the provision of aid to advance trade interests is not limited to former colonies or the aftermath of independence but continues to be a wide-spread practice (Berthélemy and Tichit 2004; Schraeder et al. 1998). The consequence for former colonies is that many remain dependent on international markets and continue to have strong trade links with their former colonizers (Abernethy 2000; Cardoso and Faletto 1979).

Besides the promotion of trade interests, donors (including former colonial powers) often prioritize aid to countries where social needs go unaddressed. Several studies have shown that most aid goes to countries with high levels of economic poverty (Dollar and Levin 2006; Easterly and Pfutze 2008; Nunnenkamp and Thiele 2006), whereas others have demonstrated a focus on countries with poor health outcomes (Bodenstein and Kemmerling 2015; Boschini and Olofsgård 2007; Schraeder et al. 1998). Although these studies do not explore whether donors prioritize social needs of former colonies over those of other recipients, there are good reasons to suspect that this is the case. Donors might continue to be concerned about the welfare of formerly subjugated populations (Pacquement 2010), personal networks can put former colonies in politically advantageous positions (Lahiri and Raimondos-Møller 2000), and international organizations sustain pressure on donors to assume responsibility for territories they once ruled (Pearson 2018).

Colonial powers promoted social protection for intrinsic and, more commonly, instrumental reasons. However, little is known about whether early investments in social protection of many of today's developing countries affect contemporary patterns of bilateral aid. While independence brought major changes with it, it is also clear that many political, economic and social ties have survived. It can be argued that this is also the reason why many former colonial powers continue to promote social protection. Thus, the first hypothesis I test in this chapter is that donors prioritize social protection when providing aid to former colonies or, to put it differently, that compared to other recipients larger shares of aid to former colonies are directed toward social protection. I have also argued that the French colonial government assumed a more interventionist role in matters of social protection than Britain did in its empire. Thus, the second hypothesis I explore is that the prioritization of social protection is especially pronounced in the case of French aid.

## Actor Constellations

Colonialism is not a unitary phenomenon. Abernethy (2000) explains the rise of European colonial empires with the interplay of three decisive types of actors: governments, firms and missions. While these actors often had competing interests in Europe, their actions overseas proved highly synergetic. It is furthermore important to realize that each type of actor is internally split, consisting of an umbrella organization in the metropole and its representations abroad (Abernethy 2000). Beyond this basic set-up, important differences between colonial empires can be noted. The French empire followed a more centralized approach. This tied administrations in the colonies more closely to the French government and gave them less room to adjust laws and practices to local context (Lee and Schultz 2012; Schmitt 2015). Catholic France also had a more restrictive stance on the activities of Protestant missions. Instead, the British government early succumbed to lobbying by the British East India Company and allowed both Catholic and Protestant missions to operate within its territories (Woodberry 2012).

A common conceptual distinction in scholarship on colonialism is that between direct and indirect rule (Gerring et al. 2011; Iyer 2010; Mamdani 1996). The two kinds of rule mainly distinguish how local political institutions and elites are incorporated into the colonial empire. Direct rule implies the imposition of new administrative structures that overwrite existing ones. Locals that assume positions in the new administration are usually not members of the former elite. To the contrary, indirect rule implies the installation of a new administration at the head of existing structures. While this also imposes a clear hierarchy, power is projected through existing structures and in collaboration with established local elites. Of course, this collaboration was not always voluntary and colonial administrators could, if they deemed it necessary, rely on military force and other more "collaborative" elites.

The French empire applied, with few exceptions, direct rule. The British Empire was mainly characterized by indirect rule. Direct rule in the French empire thus led to the establishment of governmental structures akin to those in mainland France. At the same time existing structures were dwarfed, placing greater relative weight on the new governing bodies. The dwarfing of existing structures was not limited to political institutions but included social and economic ones. This was often justified with ideas about "assimilation", which had the ultimate goal to extent French citizenship to colonial subjects (Wesseling 2004). The British government, instead, accepted local actors and institutions, and if it facilitated economic exploitation, even promoted them (Midgley 2011).

The degree of centralization, type of rule and assimilation strategies also had implications for the provision of social protection in colonies. As regards other local practices and institutions, French administrations ignored, or even worked against, social protection arrangements established before colonization. Local medical practices, which were decried as "witchcraft", are one such example (Suret-Canale 1971). Instead, colonial administrations in the French empire sought to transplant arrangements from the metropole to colonized territories. While social protection spread widely only in the 1950s, after the creation of the French Union, it covered a wide range of social needs, such as illness, maternity or work accidents (Iliffe 1987, 208). Due to the application of French law within colonized territories, social protection provided by the state often extended beyond government workers to also include workers in formal employment (Kpessa 2010).

British administrations were less committed to government-provided social protection. On the one hand, there was a high reliance on pre-existing local arrangements, which were only to be complemented if changes induced by colonization gave rise to new needs, for example due to labor migration (Kpessa 2010; Midgley 2011). On the other hand, British administrations more strongly involved other external actors in the provision of social protection. As such, missions were encouraged to establish schools and hospitals and were called upon to address various social risks through the establishment of provident funds (Dixon 1989). For both empires it must be said that externally initiated initiatives—with the exception of missionary activities—were largely limited to Europeans and only gradually, if at all, extended to local populations. They were extended to local populations; this was usually done to protect the health and well-being of Europeans (Suret-Canale 1971; Wesseling 2004).

In the twentieth century, international organizations entered the field of social protection (Deacon 2007; Pedersen 2015). While their involvement represented an emerging Western-centric consensus on the global stage, colonial powers were frequently opposed to specific initiatives. This is especially true for the French government, which—more often than the British government—regarded the involvement of international organizations to be against its interests. Efforts by the International Labour Organization (ILO) to abolish forced labor are one example. Even a public condemnation of French activities in the Congo at the 12th ILO conference in 1929 had no discernible effect on practices within the empire (Suret-Canale 1971, 244–55). France eventually committed to the abolition of forced labor in its colonies in 1946, a step Britain had taken more than a decade earlier (Daughton 2013; Maul 2007). Similarly, France also perceived the expansion of UN organizations as a threat and opposed the establishment of representations in its colonies (e.g. a regional office of the World Health Organization in Africa). The founding of the French Union itself, which implied the integration of colonies into French territory, can be seen as an attempt to countervail the mounting anticolonial pressures from international bodies (Pearson 2018).

The preceding discussion shows that the two colonial empires, Britain and France, relied on different sets of actors for organizing their colonial empires (see Shriwise, Chap. 2, this volume). Direct rule, a highly centralized bureaucracy and the assimilation strategy in the French empire implied a strong reliance on and promotion of governmental capacities. This also entailed closer institutional ties between the metropolitan government and colonial administrations in the dependent territories than was the case in the British Empire. The government in London not only gave colonial administrations greater leeway, it also collaborated more intensely with other actors. As a result, the British Empire relied relatively less on governmental capacities. Therefore, my third hypothesis concerns the involvement of governmental actors vis-à-vis other actors in the disbursement of bilateral aid: Relative to British aid, more French aid to former colonies is distributed through governmental channels (including the newly independent governments).

These differences between the empires are also found when it comes to social protection. While the French government took charge of activities such as education, health and pensions, the British government eagerly outsourced these activities to other actors, most notably missions, indigenous communities and firms. British authorities were also more likely to nurture ties with international organizations, whereas France often sought to shield itself from their influence. Whether relying on governmental capacities simply mirrors the general approach of the French government or is particularly pronounced with regard to social protection is an open question. To test this, hypothesis four states that the French reliance on governmental channels in distributing aid to former colonies is particularly pronounced with regard to social protection.

## Contribution

Earlier research on aid determinants has shown that colonial legacies lead to greater donor generosity. However, I have argued that colonial legacies should also have an impact on what policy areas donors give aid to and on the actors that donor governments involve in the disbursement of aid. Until recently, these claims could not be tested comparatively, as aid data was only available in highly aggregated form. In the following, I draw on new disaggregated data that allows me to determine the distribution of aid across policy areas and actors. I test the four hypotheses developed above. First, the social protection share is higher with aid to former colonies than with aid to other countries. Second, the social protection share of aid to former colonies is especially pronounced for French aid. Third, a larger share of French aid to former colonies, in comparison to British aid, is disbursed through governmental channels. Fourth, the French reliance on governmental channels is particularly pronounced for aid directed at social protection in former colonies.

## Data

Bilateral aid involves a donor and a recipient and thus constitutes a relational phenomenon. Therefore, the sample I analyze in the following consists of donor-recipient dyads, whereby bilateral aid flows between the two countries constitute the dependent variable. To avoid inducing biases through sample selection, it is important to consider all potential recipients, not only former colonies. Hence, I include all independent nation states, with the exception of high income countries, for which bilateral aid is virtually non-existent, into the sample. Put differently, the sample is composed of all pairs of low and middle income countries (LMICs) with each Britain and France.[2] In the following analyses, donor identity is distinguished by a dummy variable, *Donor: France*, that takes value 1 if the dyad involves France and 0 if it involves Britain.

---

[2] According to the World Bank, whether a country belongs to the groups of LMICs is determined based on its per-capita GDP, and thus changes in the classification are possible over time. In line with the treatment of other variables (see below), I calculate each country's per-capita GDP (2011 US$-PPP) by averaging over the five years preceding the CRS data, that is, 2003–2007. I then use the 2011 cut-off point of US $12,195 (see https://datahelpdesk.worldbank.org/knowledgebase/articles/906519-world-bank-country- and-lending-groups for details) to select the countries to be included in the LMIC sample.

With the founding of the Development Assistance Committee (DAC), which includes most Organisation for Economic Co-operation and Development (OECD) member states, data on bilateral aid has been collected systematically and facilitated the comparative analysis of aid activities. While the data allows research to explore developments from as far back as 1960, only highly aggregated data was available to researchers. It was therefore not possible to distinguish different types of aid flows, leaving many questions unanswered. Is aid provided in the form of grants or loans? What policy areas does it go to? And who is involved in its distribution?

This situation changed with the introduction of the OECD Creditor Reporting System (CRS), which made highly disaggregated aid data publicly available. The CRS is composed of project-level data with information on individual aid agencies, types of finance, sectoral allocations and project descriptions. As such, the CRS allows researchers to address a much wider range of questions about international aid. One disadvantage of the new data is that it covers a much shorter period of time. Although the CRS was initiated in 1973, only data from 2007 onward is considered complete. As such, the CRS data is not as suitable for analyzing temporal developments as the more aggregated data. However, this carries no implications for the present chapter, as I am interested in cross-sectional differences. The CRS data is therefore ideally suited to exploring in how far contemporary bilateral aid reflects colonial legacies.

For the purposes of this chapter, I make use of the sectoral information the CRS provides in order to discern aid flows going toward the social sector, and thus social protection, from aid to other sectors. The three main sectors in the CRS data are "social infrastructure and services" (social sector), "economic infrastructure and services", and "production sectors". Other sectors include "multisector aid", "action relating to debt", and "humanitarian assistance". The OECD defines social sector aid as "efforts to develop the human resource potential and ameliorate living conditions in developing countries. It includes but is not limited to:

- Education: Educational infrastructure, services and investment in all areas. Specialised education in particular fields such as agriculture or energy is reported against the sector concerned.

- Health and population: Assistance to hospitals and clinics, including specialised institutions such as those for tuberculosis, maternal and child care; other medical and dental services, including disease and epidemic control, vaccination programmes, nursing, provision of drugs, health demonstration, etc.; public health administration and medical insurance programmes; reproductive health and family planning.
- Water supply, sanitation and sewerage: All assistance given for water supply, use and sanitation, river development, but excluding irrigation systems for agriculture." (OECD 2018b, 10)

Furthermore, the CRS allows me to discern what actors are involved in the distribution of aid. Actors can be identified by relying on the information provided on delivery channels: "The channel of delivery is the first implementing partner. It is the entity that has implementing responsibility over the funds [...]" (OECD 2010, 8). The CRS distinguishes five delivery channels: "public sector institutions", "non-governmental organizations", "public-private partnerships", "multilateral organizations" and others. Public sector institutions include both donor and recipient governments as well as their agencies. It therefore enables me to distinguish aid that is distributed through governmental channels/actors from aid distributed in cooperation with other actors.

For each donor-recipient dyad, I calculate four indicators to characterize aid flows between them.[3] First, I compute the *total aid* flow by summing over all projects in a given year. Second, I compute the *social aid* flow by summing only over projects aimed at social protection (i.e. social sector). Third and fourth, I compute, for total aid and social aid respectively, the share of aid disbursed through governmental channels. The computation is limited to aid provided as grants, which do not have to be repaid and therefore constitute a clear, unidirectional transfer.[4] To avoid mistaking temporal fluctuations for cross-sectional differences, I compute each indicator for each complete year in the CRS data (2007–2016) and sub-

---

[3] Aid given by country donors to multilateral donors with defined recipient country, so-called bi-multi aid, is included in the calculation.
[4] Aid loans, which have to be repaid, are functionally and strategically distinct and are therefore excluded.

sequently average them. The averages of each indicator are the dependent variables used in the following analyses.

When exploring in how far bilateral aid reflects colonial legacies, it is important to also account for other determinants of aid flows. Becker (2019) provides a comprehensive dataset on the geographic and temporal reach of all major European colonial empires. Based on the dataset, I determine the last colonizer for each country in my sample and create a dummy variable, *colonial legacy*, to indicate whether a given donor-recipient-dyad is characterized by a joint colonial history. As such, colonial legacy is a characteristic of the dyad, not of the recipient country. In addition, the following statistical analyses include a number of control variables. Unless pointed out otherwise, these variables are derived from the World Development Indicators (World Bank 2018). All numeric variables are calculated by averaging data across the five years preceding the bilateral aid data I use (2003–2007). This approach ensures that results are not affected by short-term fluctuations and also takes into account that aid strategies take time to adjust to changing conditions in recipient countries.

Economic interests play an important role in international politics, and when it comes to aid it is often suggested that donors are interested in opening up markets and securing preferential access for their own firms. I therefore include a *trade openness* variable which captures the amount of exports and imports as percentage of the recipient's GDP. Others contend that aid aims at promoting certain values and norms in recipient countries, in particular democracy. To determine whether donors reward democratic practices in recipient countries, I include the Freedom House (2018) political rights score as *democracy* variable into the analysis (original scores inverted for more intuitive interpretation). Most donors focus aid efforts on poor countries. This is commonly referred to as poverty focus. As many former colonies rank among the world's poorest countries, it is also possible that a poverty focus rather than the colonial legacy explains why former colonies receive more or specific types of aid. In line with earlier scholarship, I use *per-capita income* as a proxy for the level of poverty. Although income per capita would preferably be calculated based on gross national incomes, I rely on gross domestic products (US $2011, PPP), due to greater data coverage.

Table 7.1 Descriptives of donor-recipient aid flows

|  | Mean | Median | Min | Max | NA% |
|---|---|---|---|---|---|
| Total aid | 28.30 | 2.14 | 0.00 | 381.26 | 0.00 |
| Social aid | 15.25 | 1.07 | 0.00 | 274.55 | 0.00 |
| Total aid (% Gov.) | 47.82 | 51.73 | 0.00 | 100.00 | 0.00 |
| Social aid (% Gov.) | 47.64 | 43.91 | 0.00 | 100.00 | 0.00 |
| GDP per capita | 4.87 | 3.86 | 0.55 | 12.15 | 0.00 |
| Population size | 39.72 | 7.12 | 0.01 | 1303.42 | 0.00 |
| Trade openness | 84.67 | 80.64 | 0.29 | 244.26 | 3.45 |
| Democracy | −3.91 | −3.80 | −1.00 | −7.00 | 0.86 |
| Colonial legacy | 0.29 | 0.00 | 0.00 | 1.00 | 0.00 |
| Africa | 0.41 | 0.00 | 0.00 | 1.00 | 0.00 |
| Americas | 0.18 | 0.00 | 0.00 | 1.00 | 0.00 |
| Asia | 0.24 | 0.00 | 0.00 | 1.00 | 0.00 |
| Europe | 0.08 | 0.00 | 0.00 | 1.00 | 0.00 |
| Oceania | 0.09 | 0.00 | 0.00 | 1.00 | 0.00 |
| Donor: France | 0.50 | 0.50 | 0.00 | 1.00 | 0.00 |

Note: The sample units constitute donor-recipient dyads (*n* = 232). Income per capita in thousands, Trade openness in percentage of GDP, Population size and poverty headcount in millions. Colonial legacy according to Becker (2019), aid data based on OECD CRS, Democracy derived from Freedom House and all other data based on WDI

Furthermore, I control for *population size* and *geographical region*. Population size accounts for the frequent focus of international aid on large developing countries (McKinlay and Little 1979). Geographical region accounts for unobserved variation across continents, which might otherwise influence results. Table 7.1 displays descriptive statistics for all variables. For five recipient countries, and thus ten dyads, information on trade openness is missing; they are excluded from the following analysis.

## Analysis

As this chapter is interested in the colonial legacies of contemporary international aid, it is informative to take a look at how aid flows to former colonies differ from flows to other countries. Therefore, Fig. 7.1 depicts total aid flows by donor (Britain, France, EU) and recipient (British colony, French colony, other). Information on aid from EU institutions is included as a reference point. However, as it can be observed, the aid patterns

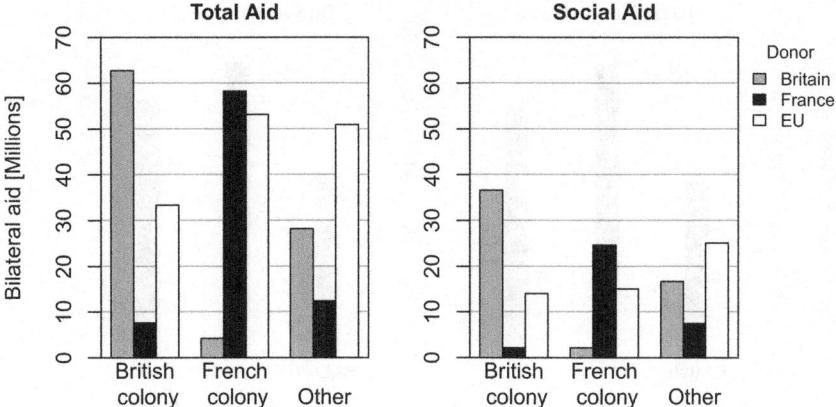

Fig. 7.1 Average annual aid flow by donor and colonial legacy, absolute disbursements (2007–2016)

of both former colonial powers differ sharply from that of EU spending. The left panel reproduces the conventional finding that former colonial powers strongly favor countries that used to be part of their respective empire. Both the 45 British colonies and the 22 French colonies in this sample received an annual average of almost US $60 million aid in grants (between 2007 and 2016). Interestingly, both donors also provide particularly little aid to former colonies of the respectively other donor; they are more generous toward countries not colonized by either of them. The right panel shows how much aid is spent on social protection. For former colonies, a bit more than half of all British aid is spent on social protection, whereas this figure is slightly less than half for French aid.

This chapter further inquires about the extent to which former colonial powers rely on governmental actors for the distribution of aid, be it their own or by including recipient governments. Figure 7.2 shows the share of total aid (left panel) and social aid (right panel) being distributed through governmental channels. While patterns of government reliance are very similar for total and social aid, patterns between British and French aid diverge sharply. For both total and social aid, Britain relies much less on governmental channels, barely reaching 20% within its own former colonies. To the contrary, a majority of French aid is allocated

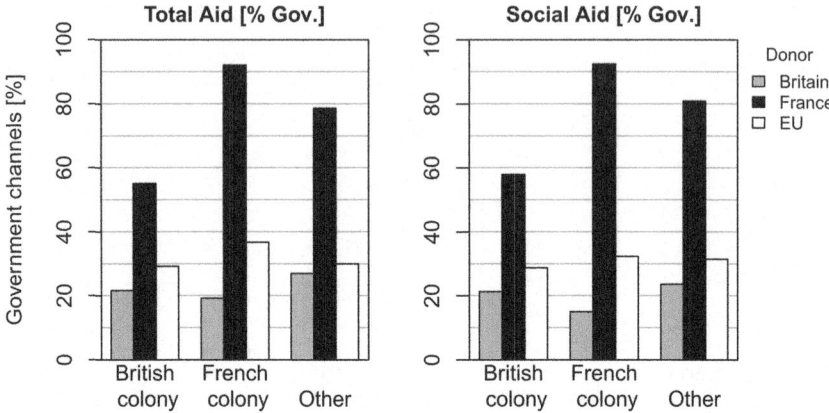

**Fig. 7.2** Average annual aid flow by donor and colonial legacy, share disbursed through government channels (2007–2016)

through governmental channels. In its former colonies, the average government share exceeds 90%, for total as well as social aid.

The descriptive figures lend some support to the above presented hypotheses. French aid to former colonies appears to be more reliant on governmental channels, and both donors provide higher shares of social aid to their own colonies, compared to colonies of the respectively other power (although not compared to other recipients). However, to determine whether these differences are not just coincidental or are confounded by other variables, I now turn to some more systematic tests of the hypotheses about colonial legacies in aid. Therefore, I estimate various linear models with different aid indicators as dependent variables. The main independent variable of interest is the colonial legacy of a dyad as well as its interaction with donor identity. Controls are included to account for potential confounding. The models are estimated by way of using a Bayesian Markov chain Monte Carlo (MCMC) approach, as this is better suited to situations where the sample constitutes the population and it is thus more meaningful to treat the data as fixed and the parameters as random (Western and Jackman 1994).

Bayesian models deviate from the standard frequentist approach in that they do not only provide a point estimate and standard error for each parameter but a complete posterior distribution. The mean of the distribution, here indicated as *b*, corresponds to the point estimate in frequentist statistics. Bayesian estimation usually refrains from strict null hypothesis testing. Instead one can infer the probability that a parameter is within a certain range directly from the posterior distribution. A helpful figure is the probability that the parameter is greater than zero, indicated here by *% > 0*. Values close to 100% indicate a very high probability that the parameter is greater than zero, whereas values close to 0% indicate a very high probability that the parameter is smaller than zero. Values not in the proximity of 0 or 100% indicate little or no evidence that the parameter is different from 0. Analogously to conventional

Table 7.2 Linear model results: Total and social aid to former colonies

| DV | Total aid [US $m] | | | | Social aid [% total] | | | |
|---|---|---|---|---|---|---|---|---|
| Model | (1) | | (2) | | (3) | | (4) | |
|  | b | % > 0 | b | % > 0 | b | % > 0 | b | % > 0 |
| Intercept | 20.38 | 99.50 | 18.68 | 98.80 | 31.96 | 100.00 | 32.40 | 100.00 |
| Donor: France | −6.48 | 17.50 | −2.72 | 36.80 | 10.01 | 99.50 | 9.31 | 97.80 |
| Colonial legacy | 47.55 | 100.00 | 52.83 | 100.00 | 9.23 | 98.40 | 8.08 | 92.30 |
| Donor: Fr.∗Col. Leg. |  |  | −13.70 | 20.00 |  |  | 2.56 | 60.80 |
| GDP per capita | −2.58 | 1.60 | −2.72 | 1.50 | 1.38 | 98.10 | 1.41 | 98.00 |
| Population size | 0.09 | 100.00 | 0.09 | 100.00 | 0.02 | 90.80 | 0.02 | 91.30 |
| Democracy | −1.09 | 30.80 | −1.23 | 28.60 | 0.40 | 62.60 | 0.44 | 64.40 |
| Trade openness | −0.26 | 0.70 | −0.26 | 0.60 | −0.12 | 2.00 | −0.12 | 1.50 |
| Continent |  |  |  |  |  |  |  |  |
| America | −10.02 | 20.30 | −10.30 | 19.10 | −17.66 | 0.30 | −17.74 | 0.40 |
| Asia | 3.54 | 64.60 | 2.70 | 60.40 | 10.05 | 97.00 | 9.97 | 97.10 |
| Europe | 4.26 | 61.40 | 4.58 | 60.60 | 21.45 | 99.30 | 21.28 | 99.20 |
| Oceania | −32.17 | 1.20 | −34.19 | 0.80 | −28.71 | 0.00 | −28.55 | 0.00 |
| $R^2$ | 0.328 | | 0.331 | | 0.254 | | 0.254 | |
| n | 222 | | 222 | | 222 | | 222 | |

Note: Unit of observation is a donor-recipient dyad. *Social aid [% Total]* indicates the share of total aid directed at social protection. *Donor* and *Colonial legacy* refer to the dyad, all other variables to the recipient: *Income* per capita in thousands (2011-US$, PPP), *Population size* in millions, *Trade openness* indicates the trade share of GDP (in %), *Democracy* ranges from −7 to −1, the *Continent* reference category is Africa. All continuous explanatory variables are mean-centered. *b* indicates the mean of posterior distribution, *% > 0* the share of posterior distribution greater than zero. MCMC estimation (Gibbs sampling, chain length = 1 m, burn-in = 1 m, thinning = 100) null hypothesis testing, one might focus on whether % > 0 is within 2.5 percentage points of 0 or 100%.

Table 7.2 presents the first model results. Models 1 and 2 both have the total amount of aid as dependent variable, with the difference that only the second model includes an interaction term between colonial legacy (which indicates the presence of an earlier colonial tie between donor and recipient) and donor identity (which takes the value 1 to indicate France, and 0 for Britain). Both models largely confirm the findings of earlier studies. Donors give more aid to their former colonies (an additional US $47.55 million per year), more economically developed countries receive less aid and countries with larger populations receive more. While the parameter for the effect of democracy is unexpectedly negative, the evidence is very weak (% > 0 close to 0.5). Surprisingly, countries with greater trade openness appear to receive less aid, rather than being rewarded for it. The interaction term in Model 2 indicates that there are no substantial differences in how much aid both donors provide to former colonies.

The dependent variable in Models 3 and 4 is social aid as a share of total aid. In line with the first hypothesis, Model 3 indicates that the social protection share of aid to the respective donor's former colonies is about 9 percentage points higher than aid to other countries. Interestingly, the social protection share is positively related to income per capita, indicating that richer countries receive relatively more international support for investments in social protection. Model 4 further explores whether there are any differences between British and French aid. While the estimate of the interaction term points in the direction expected based on the second hypothesis, the evidence is too weak to be regarded as supporting the hypothesis.

The second set of models concerns the involvement of government actors in the distribution of bilateral aid. The dependent variable in Models 5 and 6 is the share of all aid distributed through governmental channels. Model 5 indicates a positive effect of colonial legacies on the involvement of government actors. However, the interaction effect of Model 6 shows that this effect is entirely driven by France's stronger reliance on governmental channels for disbursing aid to its former colonies. The colonial legacy parameter itself (main effect), which in this model represents the effect on British aid, is effectively reduced to zero. These results strongly support the third hypothesis about the reliance of French aid on governmental ties to former colonies.

Finally, Models 7 and 8 analyze colonial legacies in the share of social aid distributed through governmental channels. The results mirror those of the two previous models. The overall effect of colonial legacies is positive, but this is by and large due to France's higher reliance on governmental

**Table 7.3** Linear model results: Aid disbursement through governmental channels

| DV | Total aid [% Gov.] | | | | Social aid [% Gov.] | | | |
|---|---|---|---|---|---|---|---|---|
| Model | (5) | | (6) | | (7) | | (8) | |
| | b | % > 0 | b | % > 0 | b | % > 0 | b | % > 0 |
| Intercept | 24.96 | 100.00 | 27.89 | 100.00 | 21.17 | 100.00 | 23.28 | 100.00 |
| Donor: France | 50.78 | 100.00 | 45.12 | 100.00 | 55.69 | 100.00 | 51.65 | 100.00 |
| Colonial legacy | 9.94 | 98.50 | 1.51 | 59.80 | 11.54 | 99.50 | 5.49 | 82.80 |
| Donor: Fr.∗Col. Leg. | | | 20.69 | 98.70 | | | 14.76 | 94.60 |
| GDP per capita | 1.07 | 93.20 | 1.27 | 96.20 | 0.95 | 91.10 | 1.09 | 94.00 |
| Population size | 0.01 | 83.50 | 0.01 | 86.30 | 0.02 | 88.30 | 0.02 | 90.00 |
| Democracy | −0.30 | 40.80 | −0.05 | 48.70 | −0.38 | 38.20 | −0.19 | 44.20 |
| Trade openness | −0.18 | 0.20 | −0.18 | 0.20 | −0.17 | 0.20 | −0.18 | 0.20 |
| *Continent* | | | | | | | | |
| America | −23.51 | 0.10 | −23.46 | 0.10 | −21.79 | 0.10 | −21.78 | 0.10 |
| Asia | 5.18 | 81.90 | 5.78 | 85.10 | 5.00 | 81.60 | 5.38 | 83.70 |
| Europe | 12.57 | 91.40 | 11.78 | 89.90 | 15.33 | 95.40 | 14.75 | 94.60 |
| Oceania | −34.04 | 0.00 | −31.61 | 0.00 | −32.40 | 0.00 | −30.71 | 0.00 |
| $R^2$ | 0.509 | | 0.520 | | 0.551 | | 0.557 | |
| n | 222 | | 222 | | 222 | | 222 | |

Note: Unit of observation is a donor-recipient dyad. *Total aid [% Gov.]* and *Social aid [% Gov.]* indicate the share of total respectively social aid disbursed through governmental channels. *Donor* and *Colonial legacy* refer to dyad, all other variables to recipient: *Income* per capita in thousands (2011-US$, PPP), *Population size* in millions, *Trade openness* indicates the trade share of GDP (in %), *Democracy* ranges from −7 to −1, the *Continent* reference category is Africa. All continuous explanatory variables are mean-centered. b indicates the mean of posterior distribution, % > 0 share of posterior distribution greater than zero. MCMC estimation (Gibbs sampling, chain length = 1 m, burn-in = 1 m, thinning = 100) ties to former colonies. That being said, the estimate of the interaction term, about 15 percentage points, indicates a similar, if not smaller, difference between the two empires than that identified for total aid (circa 21 percentage points). As such, this result provides no support for the claim that the reliance on governmental channels diverges especially sharply for social aid to former colonies (fourth hypothesis) (Table 7.3).

## Discussion

Due to the increasing availability of highly disaggregated and standardized data on aid flows, this chapter is able to draw a more nuanced picture of colonial legacies in international aid than earlier scholarship does. The well-established finding that colonial powers provide more bilateral aid to former colonies than to other countries was confirmed. In addition, I have demonstrated that a disproportionately large share of aid to former colonies supports social protection policies, funding activities related to health and education, amongst others. I have also shown that France, as it did during its colonial era, heavily relies on governmental actors to distribute aid. Instead, Britain relies to a much greater extent on non-governmental actors and international organizations when it comes to disbursing aid.

The analysis conducted in this chapter provided no support for two of the hypotheses I presented in the beginning. While both Britain and France provide more aid for social protection in their former colonies, this pattern is not more pronounced in the French case. Compared to other countries, the share of aid supporting social protection is 9 percentage points higher for former colonies. Other than expected, I also found that France's stronger reliance on governmental actors is equally pronounced for aid aimed at social protection and for aid in total. As such, France does not rely particularly much on governmental actors when it comes to promoting social protection in its former colonies.

Although this chapter shows that certain colonial structures are reflected in contemporary patterns of bilateral aid, it does not elucidate the process underlying this continuity. The assumption of path dependencies, resulting from inertia in social, economic and political ties, for example, is certainly a meaningful starting point, but one that needs to be furthered explored. Equally important, one might wonder why bilateral aid carries no resemblance of other colonial structures. What, for example, happened to the unique approach to social protection in the French empire? Did France shed its goal to assimilate populations of (formerly) dependent territories? Does the success of international organizations, charities and civil society actors provide France with leeway to disburse aid through non-governmental channels despite its neglect of these actors during colonial times? Future research should also be concerned with such discontinuities. They constitute the "negative image" of continuities and are therefore just as important for understanding colonial legacies.

Shedding light on the processes underlying colonial legacies in international aid also needs to cope with questions about the motivations of donors to provide aid to former colonies. Earlier scholarship has employed various strategies to explore motivations for aid, mainly focusing on whether aid varied with contextual factors, either cross-sectionally or longitudinally. Some, for example, have analyzed whether aid goes to where it is most needed, for example low-income countries, or whether it complements donors' trade relationships. I have argued above that the social, economic and political ties that emerged under colonialism can affect the motivations of donors to provide aid. This argument finds support in the empirical evidence presented in this chapter, in particular the emphasis on social protection in aid to former colonies. This argument could be further probed by incorporating colonial legacies into existing cross-sectional and longitudinal research strategies.

The emphasis in this chapter was on donors as external actors in LMICs and on how their engagement is defined by colonial legacies. Donors do, however, not operate within a vacuum. Their actions affect the strategies and behavior of other actors, domestic and external. And the actions of these other actors affect donors in turn. I have speculated about one example above, the multiplication of actors concerned with social welfare, which might be one reason why social protection practices by colonial France did not leave a lasting mark. National governments of recipient countries are another highly influential actor when it comes to the distribution of international aid. They assume a decisive role in the negotiation and coordination of aid packages, and just like in the case of donors, their strategies and bargaining positions are likely to carry a colonial imprint. As such, for understanding colonial legacies in international aid it is not sufficient to study only donors, but it is important to consider the constellation of actors and dynamics between them.

A final point refers to the generalizability of the presented findings. The analysis here has focused on the two largest and most recent colonial empires, Britain and France. How do the findings then apply to other colonial empires, such as those of Spain and Portugal, who controlled vast swaths of the world throughout the seventeenth and eighteenth centuries? What policies did they prioritize, what actor constellations did they promote and do colonial legacies prevail until today or have they been eroded over time? Exploring similarities and differences across and within colonial empires, and the duration of colonial legacies in international aid, are another avenue for future research.

# References

Abernethy, David B. 2000. *The Dynamics of Global Dominance: European Overseas Empires, 1415–1980*. New Haven, CT: Yale University Press.

Alesina, Alberto, and David Dollar. 2000. Who Gives Foreign Aid to Whom and Why? *Journal of Economic Growth* 5 (1): 33–63.

Becker, Bastian. 2019. *Introducing COLDAT: The Colonial Dates Dataset*. Working Papers (2), SOCIUM/CRC1342.

Berthélemy, Jean-Claude, and Ariane Tichit. 2004. Bilateral Donors' Aid Allocation Decisions a Three-Dimensional Panel Analysis. *International Review of Economics & Finance* 13 (3): 253–274.

Bodenstein, Thilo, and Achim Kemmerling. 2015. A Paradox of Redistribution in International Aid? The Determinants of Poverty-Oriented Development Assistance. *World Development* 76: 359–369.

Boschini, Anne, and Anders Olofsgård. 2007. Foreign Aid: An Instrument for Fighting Communism? *The Journal of Development Studies* 43 (4): 622–648.

Cardoso, Fernando Henrique, and Enzo Faletto. 1979. *Dependency and Development in Latin America*. Trans. Mattingly Urquidi. Berkeley: University of California Press.

Daughton, J.P. 2013. ILO Expertise and Colonial Violence in the Interwar Years. In *Globalizing Social Rights: The International Labour Organization and Beyond*, ed. Sandrine Kott and Joelle Droux. Palgrave Macmillan: International Labour Office.

Deacon, Bob. 2007. *Global Social Policy and Governance*. Los Angeles and London: Sage Publications Ltd.

Dixon, John. 1989. A Comparative Perspective on Provident Funds: Their Present and Future Explored. *Journal of International and Comparative Social Welfare* 5 (2): 1–28.

Dollar, David, and Victoria Levin. 2006. The Increasing Selectivity of Foreign Aid, 1984–2003. *World Development* 34 (12): 2034–2046.

Easterly, William, and Tobias Pfutze. 2008. Where Does the Money Go? Best and Worst Practices in Foreign Aid. *Journal of Economic Perspectives* 22 (2): 29–52.

Freedom House. 2018. *Freedom in the World 2017: The Annual Survey of Political Rights and Civil Liberties*. Ed. A. Puddington. New York and Washington: Rowman & Littlefield.

Fuchs, Andreas, Axel Dreher, and Peter Nunnenkamp. 2014. Determinants of Donor Generosity: A Survey of the Aid Budget Literature. *World Development* 56: 172–199.

Gerring, John, Daniel Ziblatt, Johan Van Gorp, and Julian Arévalo. 2011. An Institutional Theory of Direct and Indirect Rule. *World Politics* 63 (3): 377–433.

Iliffe, John. 1987. *The African Poor: A History, No. 58*. Cambridge: Cambridge University Press.

Iyer, Lakshmi. 2010. Direct versus Indirect Colonial Rule in India: Long-term Consequences. *The Review of Economics and Statistics* 92 (4): 693–713.

Kpessa, Michael W. 2010. Ideas, Institutions, and Welfare Program Typologies: An Analysis of Pensions and Old Age Income Protection Policies in Sub-Saharan Africa. *Poverty & Public Policy* 2 (1): 37–65.

Lahiri, Sajal, and Pascalis Raimondos-Møller. 2000. Lobbying by Ethnic Groups and Aid Allocation. *The Economic Journal* 110 (462): 62–79.

Lee, Alexander, and Kenneth A. Schultz. 2012. Comparing British and French Colonial Legacies: A Discontinuity Analysis of Cameroon. *Quarterly Journal of Political Science* 7 (4): 365–410.

Lewis, Joanna. 2011. The British Empire and World History: Welfare Imperialism and 'Soft' Power in the Rise and Fall of Colonial Rule. In *Colonialism and Welfare: Social Policy and the British Imperial Legacy*, ed. J. Midgley and D. Piachaud, 17–35. Cheltenham, UK: Edward Elgar.

McKinlay, Robert D., and Richard Little. 1979. The US Aid Relationship: A Test of the Recipient Need and the Donor Interest Models. *Political Studies* 27 (2): 236–250.

Mamdani, Mahmood. 1996. *Citizen and Subject: Contemporary Africa and the Legacy of Late Colonialism*. Princeton, NJ: Princeton University Press.

Maul, Daniel Roger. 2007. The International Labour Organization and the Struggle against Forced Labour from 1919 to the Present. *Labor History* 48 (4): 477–500.

Midgley, James. 2011. Imperialism, Colonialism and Social Welfare. In *Colonialism and Welfare: Social Policy and the British Imperial Legacy*, ed. J. Midgley and D. Piachaud, 36–54. Cheltenham, UK: Edward Elgar.

Nunnenkamp, Peter, and Rainer Thiele. 2006. Targeting Aid to the Needy and Deserving: Nothing But Promises? *The World Economy* 29 (9): 1177–1201.

OECD. 2010. *DAC Statistical Reporting Directives*. Accessed 7 February 2019. http://www.oecd.org/dac/stats/38429349.pdf.

———. 2018a. *Creditor Reporting System: Aid activities*. OECD International Development Statistics. https://doi.org/10.1787/data-00061-en.

———. 2018b. *Geographical Distribution of Financial Flows to Developing Countries 2018: Disbursements, Commitments, Country Indicators*. OECD. https://doi.org/10.1787/fin_flows_dev-2018-en-fr.

Pacquement, Francois. 2010. How Development Assistance from France and the United Kingdom Has Evolved: Fifty Years on from Decolonisation. *International Development Policy | Revue internationale de politique de développement* 1 (1): 51–75.

Pearson, Jessica Lynne. 2018. *The Colonial Politics of Global Health: France and the United Nations in Postwar Africa*. Cambridge, MA: Harvard University Press.

Pedersen, Susan. 2015. *The Guardians: The League of Nations and the Crisis of Empire*. Oxford; New York: Oxford University Press.

Round, Jeffery I., and Matthew Odedokun. 2004. Aid Effort and Its Determinants. *International Review of Economics & Finance* 13 (3): 293–309.

Schmitt, Carina. 2015. Social Security Development and the Colonial Legacy. *World Development* 70: 332–342.

Schraeder, Peter J., Steven W. Hook, and Bruce Taylor. 1998. Clarifying the Foreign Aid Puzzle: A Comparison of American, Japanese, French, and Swedish Aid Flows. *World Politics* 50 (2): 294–323.

Steinwand, Martin C. 2015. Compete or Coordinate? Aid Fragmentation and Lead Donorship. *International Organization* 69 (02): 443–472.

Suret-Canale, Jean. 1971. *French Colonialism in Tropical Africa: 1900–1945*. New York: Pica Press.

Wesseling, H.L. 2004. *The European Colonial Empires, 1815–1919*. Pearson/Longman.

Western, Bruce, and Simon Jackman. 1994. Bayesian Inference for Comparative Research. *The American Political Science Review* 88 (2): 412–423.

Woodberry, Robert D. 2012. The Missionary Roots of Liberal Democracy. *American Political Science Review* 106 (2): 244–274.

World Bank. 2018. *World Development Indicators (WDI)*. Accessed 28 May 2018. https://datacatalog.worldbank.org/dataset/world-development-indicators.

**Open Access** This chapter is licensed under the terms of the Creative Commons Attribution 4.0 International License (http://creativecommons.org/licenses/by/4.0/), which permits use, sharing, adaptation, distribution and reproduction in any medium or format, as long as you give appropriate credit to the original author(s) and the source, provide a link to the Creative Commons licence and indicate if changes were made.

The images or other third party material in this chapter are included in the chapter's Creative Commons licence, unless indicated otherwise in a credit line to the material. If material is not included in the chapter's Creative Commons licence and your intended use is not permitted by statutory regulation or exceeds the permitted use, you will need to obtain permission directly from the copyright holder.

# Part III

The Influence of Donors on Social Protection

# 8

# International Donors and Social Policy Diffusion in the Global South

Marina Dodlova

## Introduction

In the past decades, the bulks of development assistance received by the Global South have been channeled through bilateral aid agencies, multilateral development banks, United Nations (UN) programs and other donor structures and international financial institutions (IFIs). Donor assistance is especially important, as in most cases the national governments' resources are not sufficient to meet specific sectoral targets agreed upon by the international community and ratified by developing countries (Hagen-Zanker and McCord 2013).

This considerable support and the close relationship between the two sides lead to a state in which international donors may exert substantial influence on the pro-poor policies of recipient countries (e.g. Kilby 2006; Khan et al. 2018). Donors often have opportunities to consult on the design and implementation of social policies, provide expertise for

---

M. Dodlova (✉)
Department for Development Economics, University of Passau, CESifo, Passau, Germany

different contexts, impact national policy agendas through external funding and direct their priorities to national policy-makers. Additionally, there is evidence that donor influence might be strong in areas such as health policy (Groves and Hinton 2013), even in the absence of sizable funding. Hence, the IFIs not only provide funds for reducing poverty and vulnerability but also may shape the long-term course of development.

However, while scholars and practitioners acknowledge the contextual differences in poverty alleviation and development outcomes across recipients, the specific role of donors in the formulation and implementation of social policies they finance and support in poor countries remains unclear. Unlike previous research on the effects of the institutions of recipient countries, the systematic policy patterns across donor organizations have been little explored.

This chapter is one of the first attempts to quantitatively investigate systematic patterns of the role of donors in determining the social policy agendas of recipient countries. More specifically, we reveal the impact of IFIs on the types and designs of social assistance programs in developing countries. We argue that international organizations such as the World Bank, European Commission, United Nations International Children's Emergency Fund (UNICEF) and other IFIs can encourage or pressure national governments to adopt specific types of pro-poor policies or even define the components of social transfer programs according to their own agendas. We hypothesize that IFIs increase the adoption of social transfers in total and, in addition, may choose specific types of programs or certain mechanisms of targeting. For example, they may promote conditional social transfers because they imply human capital investments by beneficiaries.[1] The donors can provide substantial technical expertise and other resources for increasing administrative capacity so that national policy-makers can afford to operationalize more complex programs. At the same time, IFIs may also pursue strategic interests in the provision of social assistance, especially in the form of specific policies such as public works programs. We will discuss some of these potential trade-offs in social policy-making.

---

[1] Conditions are behavioral rules that should be compiled by beneficiaries for collecting social transfers. As conditions are typically introduced for education and health care, conditional programs are regarded as poverty alleviation policies with encouraged investments in human capital.

We use two main sources of information. We extract the data from the non-contributory social transfer programs (NSTP, Version 1.1, 2017) and UNU-WIDER Social Assistance, Politics and Institutions (SAPI, Version 1.0, 2018) data sets on social transfers in the developing world. In total, we consider 155 programs in 84 countries, 35% of which have at least one donor involved. The period considered covers the period from 1960 to the year of program adoption, which allows us to focus on the adoption process of social transfer programs and the role of donors in this process. The sample consists of countries with at least one program in operation.

We focus on the types of programs, conditionalities, targeting mechanisms and the details of donor assistance. We classify all programs according to four types: unconditional social pensions, family allowance, conditional cash transfers (CCTs) and employment guarantee schemes. If a program shows elements of two or three types, it is assigned to every applicable type. In addition, we contrast conditional and unconditional transfers in order to trace the extent to which donors care about conditionalities as an instrument for human capital investment. Then we distinguish between six targeting mechanisms: community-based, categorical, geographical, means testing, proxy means testing and self-targeting. We test the hypotheses that IFIs may prefer specific types of social transfer programs, in particular conditional versus unconditional schemes, or certain selection mechanisms that are used to target those among the extreme poor that are most deserving of social benefits. Donors may influence the choice of social transfer programs in order to prioritize their own policy agenda or to facilitate program implementation and operationalization based on their own administrative capacities.

We find that donors have several preferences concerning the choice of both program type and targeting method. In particular, we show that IFIs promote CCTs, family support programs and public works programs, whereas social pensions remain popular in all developing countries, regardless of donor assistance. We also find different preferences among the donors. While the World Bank follows the general pattern and favors all program types except social pensions, UNICEF typically promotes family allowances. This is consistent with the hypothesis that the donors' policies are in line with their own organization's priorities.

Interestingly, conditionalities are promoted only by the World Bank and not by all donors, as might be expected. This might be due to enforcement difficulties and the limited state capacity in recipient countries. Regarding targeting, community-based programs prove to be the most favored ones, as external donors need to rely on the expertise of local community members. We also show that proxy means testing is promoted by the World Bank. This might be explained by the close relationship between the World Bank and recipient countries, or by the large administrative and technical capacity required for implementing proxy means tests, which can be provided by the World Bank. UNICEF and the UK Department for International Development (DFID) more frequently use categorical and geographical targeting, as they primarily favor family support programs. Similarly, the World Food Programme (WFP) more frequently applies geographical targeting and self-selection mechanisms. These findings generally support the hypothesis that international donors exhibit a coercive nature when it comes to social policy diffusion in developing countries.

This chapter is structured as follows. The next two Sections give an overview of the relevant literature and theoretical considerations. We then present the data and the methodology. The following Section reports the impact of donors on the types of social assistance. Then we present our findings on how the donors influence the design of social transfer programs, in particular targeting mechanisms. The last Section discusses policy implications and contains concluding remarks.

## Relevant Literature

Despite broad research on the effectiveness of foreign aid and the reasons behind persistent poverty in developing countries, little is known about the donor-side factors affecting long-term development. Given the donors' power in shaping the goals of social policy, implementation and effectiveness of aid programs, a systematic investigation of their strategic interests, capacities and pursued policy models becomes vital for understanding the failures and inefficiency of aid in developing countries.

It has been shown that the quality of donors may significantly influence both the volumes of development assistance and its effectiveness.

For example, Minasyan et al. (2017) demonstrate that only quality-adjusted aid leads to increasing GDP per capita in recipient countries. The authors base their findings on the donor performance index of the Center for Global Development. However, such overall rankings of aid donors, even across sectors, may be misleading due to measurement errors and construction biases. A more detailed analysis of the components of the donor-recipient relationship helps to gain a better understanding of how donor characteristics and policies influence development outcomes.

Some evidence on the impacts of donor qualities is available from the literature focusing on the political economy of foreign aid. Fuchs and Richert (2018) show that the personalities of ministers in a donor country may affect foreign aid giving. Female ministers with previous experience in development cooperation provide a higher quality of development assistance. Additionally, Hicks et al. (2016) present evidence that female political representation in donor countries increases foreign aid.

Furthermore, political ideology and dominant party platforms in donor countries matter for aid allocation (Dreher et al. 2015; Milner and Tingley 2010; Thérien and Noel 2000; Cashel-Cordo and Craig 1997). Dreher et al. (2015), for example, analyze the shifts in the dominant political orientation of German governments back and forth from conservative to socialist in 1973–2010 and find that the socialist leadership decreases aid commitments. On the other hand, Brech and Potrafke (2014) show that left-leaning governments increase bilateral aid, especially if it is allocated to least developed countries. Milner and Tingley (2010) also demonstrate that the allocation of US aid depends, among other things, upon the left-right ideological predisposition of legislators voting for the distribution of aid. Fuchs et al. (2014) conclude that economic interests, colonial past, terror incidents and aid inertia determine donor generosity. Harrigan et al. (2006) argue that aid allocations to the Middle East and North Africa (MENA) are likely to be influenced by US interests in the region. Donor ideology can also influence aid delivery strategies. In particular, Allen and Flynn (2018) find that more liberal governments tend to channel aid through non-governmental organizations (NGOs), probably with the purpose of inducing a direct effect on poverty alleviation in recipient countries, while more conservative governments prefer government-to-government channels that take economic and geopolitical interests into account.

Many other studies have explored how donors' interests shape the influx of foreign aid into recipient nations, as well as the effectiveness of that aid (Alesina and Dollar 2000; Berthélemy 2006; Dreher et al. 2008; Faye and Niehaus 2012; Hicks et al. 2016; etc.). In particular, Faye and Niehaus (2012) show that countries that are more politically aligned with donors receive more aid during election years, whereas there is no such effect in less aligned recipient countries. Dreher et al. (2008) conclude that the type of aid provided by the US depends on its ability to induce political support by recipients. Several other studies present evidence that "political" aid is allocated to meet political goals or to please political allies. Vreeland and Dreher (2014) demonstrate that United Nations Security Council (UNSC) membership is a critical factor for the distribution of foreign aid. In particular, developed countries may direct financial flows to UNSC members who, in return, provide political support. Dreher et al. (2009) find a positive relationship between temporary UNSC membership and the number of World Bank development projects implemented within a country, although the total aid budget of these projects does not change significantly. Dreher et al. (2018) find that aid to countries temporarily serving on the UNSC is less effective compared to aid received at other times. Moreover, Dreher et al. (2019) present evidence that the amount of development assistance provided by the Chinese government is determined by co-ethnicity and favoritism that is based upon the birth regions of African leaders. It is therefore obvious that the argument regarding the influence of recipient qualities and donor interests in aid allocation has found large support in the literature on foreign aid (Becker, Chap. 7, this volume).

Additionally, the literature further elaborates on the policies pursued by international donors. For example, Bodenstein and Kemmerling (2015) work out in detail that donors face a dilemma when choosing between the total volume of aid and the amount of aid given to individual poor countries. This corresponds to a trade-off between coverage and cost of redistribution in wealthier countries. Efficient targeting becomes critical in such contexts. Fuchs and Öhler (2019) show that private donors follow the same aid allocation pattern of their respective home country.

This result highlights the donor coordination within donor countries. Acht et al. (2015) present evidence that, if faced with high corruption and low quality of governance within recipient countries, international donors may change their strategies and decide to bypass corrupt state actors by delivering social assistance through NGOs and other non-state actors.

These findings, however, are only based on the total volumes and sector components of foreign aid. Only scant evidence exists regarding the impact of donors on the adoption and diffusion of social transfer schemes in developing countries. For example, Maclure (1995) provides an analysis of two health programs in Burkina Faso that induce new bonds of donor dependency. Takala (1998) reveals the consistency between national education sector policy documents in four African countries and the World Bank's educational policy agenda.

These results, though illuminating, are based on qualitative research. Quantitative research on social transfers is much more scarce and generally concerns determinants of social transfers related to politics and governance, such as regime type (Dodlova et al. 2017) or rent seeking (Reinikka and Svensson 2004; Olken 2006; Dodlova et al. 2018b). To our knowledge, there does not yet exist any comparative analysis of the impact of both the characteristics of donors and policy preferences concerning the design of non-contributory social transfer programs.

Nevertheless, the growing diversity in donor strategies and approaches requires a closer look. A thorough comparative analysis of specific social policies, such as non-contributory social transfers, is necessary in order to better understand the contributions by and constraints for donors in terms of their social policy-making strategies in recipient countries. We conduct such an analysis in this chapter.

## Theoretical Considerations

Our main research question aims at the extent to which the adoption and diffusion of social transfer policies in recipient countries are shaped by external donors and IFIs. To achieve this goal, we formulate three main hypotheses based on previous research and theoretical considerations.

It is difficult to a priori disentangle the IFI's incentives and preferences, but it is possible to discover in retrospect which types and design elements of social policies are prioritized by international donors. The research hypotheses are thus formulated so as to reveal empirical patterns of donor interventions in the social policies of developing countries.

First, we argue that the type of social transfer chosen can be partially influenced by the interests of international organizations pursuing their own policy agendas. For example, UNICEF promotes family allowances and child grants, the WFP contributes to the expansion of school feeding programs and United Nations High Commissioner of Refugees (UNHCR) supports refugees and internally displaced people. It has been recognized that international donors target resources according to their own priorities (Eichenauer and Reinsberg 2016).

1. IFIs promote specific types of social transfer programs, which is partly explained by their own policy agenda priorities and/or fields of technical expertise.

Second, international institutions may support human capital development as a part of their long-term development strategies more often than national policy-makers who are more concerned with meeting short-term needs and addressing current vulnerabilities (Browne 2006). Conditional cash transfers would then be more preferred by donors than unconditional cash transfers, as the former are distributed only if certain pre-selected requirements, or the results of these requirements, are met. Often related to education, health or parental support for children below 18, conditions might concern behavioral changes (such as school attendance) or performance (such as graduation). Such conditions entice beneficiaries to invest in human capital accumulation.

This helps to formulate the second hypothesis:

2. International donors more often favor conditional cash transfers in order to support human capital accumulation.

To confirm this prediction, we can check whether international organizations more frequently finance conditional cash transfers (CCTs).

Some scholars have already illustrated this phenomenon, especially in Latin American countries. For example, according to Parker and Todd (2017), Mexico's Prospera, which was introduced in 1997, has influenced the design of CCTs in over 60 countries around the world, primarily with the support of the World Bank.

IFIs may play a key role in supporting certain types of social policies, not only because they provide substantial financial assistance but also because they possess the necessary expertise with poverty alleviation policies (see Devereux and Kapingidza, Chap. 11, this volume). This allows recipients to adopt more complex pro-poor policies that require a higher administrative capacity. This partly confirms Hypothesis 2, as the introduction and enforcement of conditionalities may be costly or socially challenging. For example, Schubert and Slater (2006) argue that contextual differences between Africa and Latin America in public service provision, capacity and the benefit-cost ratio of the conditionalities may have led to the broad expansion of CCTs in Latin America, while their introduction has remained inappropriate in a lower-capacity African context. Consequently, we cannot directly test which channel is more influential with the promotion of CCTs by international donors: prioritizing human capital development or institutional capacity building. We can, however, isolate the effect of capacity and expertise by focusing on one element of the program design, such as beneficiary selection or targeting. This element of the design indeed requires a substantial administrative capacity and operationalization. Thus, the donors' contributions to the implementation of the program lead to the formulation of the next hypothesis about the type of targeting mechanisms used for determining the eligibility of beneficiaries and providing them with transfers:

3. IFI support allows recipient countries to implement more complex targeting mechanisms.

The components of the donor-recipient relationship prove to be relevant for the policy choices of recipient countries. The frequency of communication, usefulness of policy advice, and helpfulness in implementation may serve as proxies for technological expertise and professional support provided by donors in recipient countries.

The next section introduces the data and preliminary descriptive evidence which already highlights some findings that are further confirmed by the quantitative analysis in the following Sections.

## Data

Several recent data sets are used for analyzing the impact of donors on the design of social policy in developing countries. First, we extract the information on social transfers from the non-contributory social transfer programs (NSTP) data set Version 1.1 created by Dodlova, Giolbas and Lay (2017, 2018a). The database contains the main elements of the design of more than 186 social transfer schemes in 101 developing countries from 1960 to 2015. The second source is the UNU-WIDER Social Assistance, Politics and Institutions (SAPI) database. It provides the detailed characteristics, institutionalizations and budgets of 221 social assistance programs in developing countries from 2000 to 2015. More specifically, from both databases we extract information on the types of social transfers and targeting mechanisms used to define the beneficiary base as well as information on the donors or partial assistance provided by the IFIs, which is available for every social transfer program. This allows us to compile a data set which covers the most prominent trends in donor influence on social policy diffusion in developing countries.

We primarily base our results on the NSTP database, as it provides more detailed information on the types of donors participating in the adoption and/or funding of social assistance programs. Based on this information, we determine that about 35% of programs have been initiated or partially funded by at least one donor. Among the most influential donors are the World Bank, UNICEF, EU Commission, WFP and DFID UK. Our empirical analysis investigates the heterogeneity of influence by these donors. The main variables of interest are the dummies specifying that at least one donor participates in financing a social transfer program or a particular donor participates in the funding process. Thus, the coding is based on a donor's financial contribution to a social transfer policy. In total, we have six dummies, one for any donor contribution and one additional dummy for each of the major IFIs: the World Bank, UNICEF,

EU Commission, WFP and DFID UK. If a program is funded by two or more donors, then each dummy for a respective donor equals 1.

We focus on the impact of international actors on three main outcomes:

- type of social policy (CCTs, family support, social pensions, public works);
- conditionalities (conditional vs. unconditional programs);
- targeting method (community-based, categorical, means testing, proxy means testing, geographical, self-targeting).

Following Barrientos (2013), Ellis, Devereux and White (2009), and Coady et al. (2004a, b), we distinguish between four main types of social assistance and six targeting mechanisms. Specifically, we consider social pensions or old-age grants, unconditional family support, CCTs and employment guarantee schemes or public works programs. Based on the NSTP and SAPI databases, we present all types of social transfer programs based on this classification in Table 8.1. If a program shows elements of several types, this is taken into account by coding every type of transfer with a dummy variable. We focus on CCTs which imply that beneficiaries should not only keep edibility rules but also follow certain behavioral rules. In both data sets, the share of CCTs with at least one donor involved is quite high compared with other types of transfers.

Table 8.1 Number of programs with and without donor assistance by type in the year of starting them

| NSTP | | | |
|---|---|---|---|
| | No donor | With donor | Total |
| CCT | 45 | 18 | 63 |
| Pension | 39 | 4 | 43 |
| Family support | 48 | 24 | 72 |
| Public works | 12 | 10 | 22 |
| SAPI | | | |
| | No donor | With donor | Total |
| CCT | 21 | 39 | 60 |
| Pension | 57 | 5 | 62 |
| Family support | 32 | 29 | 61 |
| Public works | 9 | 13 | 22 |

Furthermore, in the SAPI data set the number of CCTs involving donor assistance is even higher than the number of CCTs without any donor assistance. There is consistency between the two data sets in the number of pensions and family allowances with and without donor involvement. IFIs are more active in assisting CCTs, family support programs and public works programs but not social pensions.

Figure 8.1 more clearly illustrates that IFI involvement in the assistance of social transfer schemes is quite heterogeneous. Support by the EU Commission and the WFP includes only two types of programs, namely family allowances and public works. Social pensions are assisted by the World Bank and UNICEF, while CCTs are only promoted by the World Bank, DFID UK and UNICEF.

Six targeting methods were identified. *Categorical* and *geographical* targeting combine all transfers based on a group characteristic such as age, gender, social status or place of residence. For example, social pensions make extensive use of the categorical selection of beneficiaries. Geographical selection is often applied to identify entire regions with the highest poverty rates, lowest consumption measures or extreme food deficits. *Self-targeting* implies that all citizens have an opportunity to receive assistance if they apply, however in principle, only those most in need

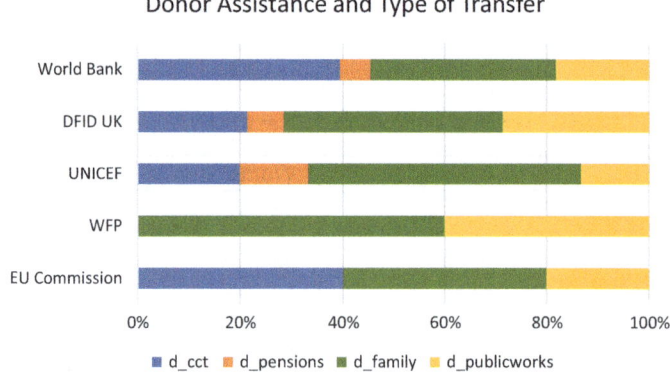

**Fig. 8.1** Donor assistance and type of transfer. (Compiled by the author on the basis of the *NSTP* database. If a program is supported by two or more donors, then a donor with a large share of assistance is considered)

should benefit from the program. Less needy individuals are discouraged from participating in the program by offering beneficiaries an inferior good, such as yellow maize, or by setting the wages for public works below the market level. Other types of targeting are implemented with the purpose of assessing the income level and identifying the potential beneficiaries, based on whether their income falls below a certain cut-off. Under *means testing* the households self-report their incomes or a program official categorizes them into income or poverty groups. The information provided might be verified through tax records or asset ownership, or it might not be verified at all—though this may increase targeting errors. *Proxy means testing* is similar to means testing but is more justified, as it is based on more than one indicator of income and typically makes use of the observable characteristics of the households to construct a wealth or income score. The score is then used to determine the household's eligibility for social assistance. The *community-based* approach is applied if a group of community representatives or head of a community decides on household eligibility for benefits. This method can make targeting more efficient, as it relies on local expertise and better information on poverty within a community at a lower cost. Additionally, the final decisions are generally more supported by the community members, which allows for avoiding potential conflicts among program participants and non-participants.

Targeting methods also differ among the programs with and without donor assistance. Figure 8.2 shows that means testing is practically unused by programs with donor assistance. Donors are typically involved in programs with proxy means testing, community-based, or geographical targeting, and a bit less in categorical and self-targeted schemes. Furthermore, a combination of targeting methods is more often used for programs with donor assistance, which might be due to a higher capacity requirement. Figure 8.3 displays the choice of targeting methods by different donors. The World Bank uses all methods, but proxy means testing dominates and geographical and community-based targeting are used extensively. UNICEF and DFID UK also apply all methods of beneficiary selection, except means testing.

This descriptive evidence already provides some insights into the preferences of international donors in terms of social policies. We are

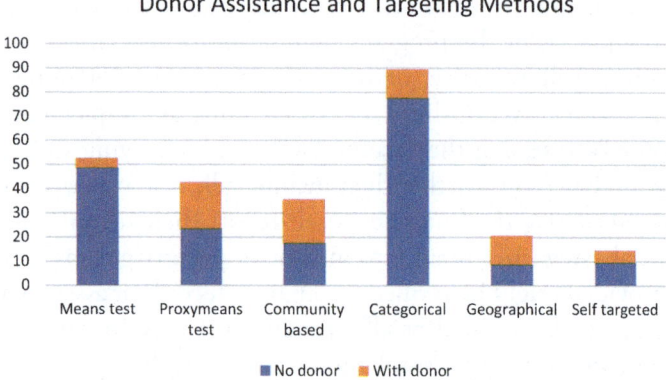

**Fig. 8.2** Donor assistance and targeting methods. (Compiled by the author on the basis of the NSTP database)

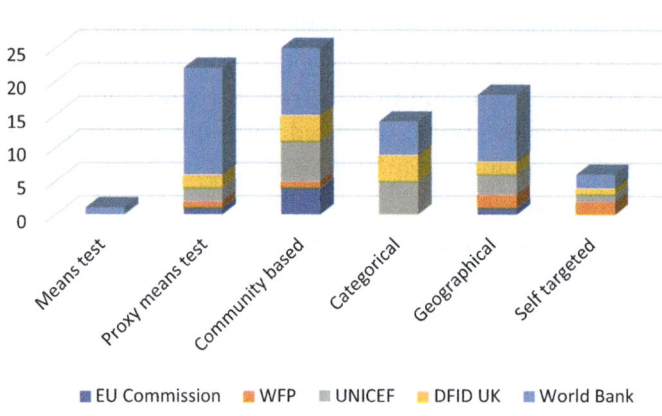

**Fig. 8.3** Targeting methods employed by different donors. (Compiled by the author on the basis of the NSTP database)

now going to empirically test each hypothesis, using the data on non-contributory social transfer schemes in developing countries. The next Section presents the econometric methodology used for checking the hypotheses, and the following Section reports and discusses the main regression results.

## Methodology

To estimate the influence of donors on the types of programs implemented and targeting methods employed we use a duration model focusing on the transfer adoption process. We conduct the empirical analysis at a program level and cut the sample at the starting year of program operation. This approach allows us to mitigate endogeneity and serial correlation problems. Once a transfer program is in place, it is presumably difficult to stop its operation. Moreover, IFIs are typically involved from the year a transfer program begins and continues to support the program, due to long-term relationships between donors and recipient countries. Thus, our approach emphasizes donor assistance at the year of the adoption of a transfer program. We introduce a binary variable that equals 1 if any donor is involved in the year of the adoption of a transfer program and 0 otherwise. All years after the adoption of a program are coded as missing.

This approach is chosen primarily because, during the operation of a program, it is hard for donors to terminate assistance. National governments prove resistant to donor exit after program implementation because of the implied reduction in budget and loss of administrative support. In the NSTP data set, the information on donors remains constant over time. In the SAPI data set, only six programs have 'survived' after the donors' exit.

Our dependent variables are dummies for each of four types of social transfer programs and for each of six types of targeting methods. We assume that specific types of transfers or targeting methods illustrate donor interests in shaping social policies in developing countries. The period considered is from 1960 to the year of the adoption of each program. Hence, we focus on the adoption process of social transfer programs and the role of donors in this process. We include in the sample only those countries where at least one program has been in operation.

Among different controls included in all specifications, there are country-economic and demographic characteristics taken from the World Bank Development Indicators Database. The level of GDP per capita in millions (constant USD) is included to capture the fact that richer countries introduce more social transfer programs. To account for the population structure, three standard demographic controls are used: total population (in mln.), share of the population living in urban areas and age-dependency ratio. A rising age-dependency ratio means that fewer people belong to the labor force and, consequently, that fewer people pay taxes and finance redistributive and pro-poor policies. Dependence on the agricultural sector and natural resources are captured by the value added in GDP that comes from agriculture and by total natural resource rents, respectively. All of these control variables are taken in logarithms and one period lags.

To measure the regime type, we make use of the polity variable of the Center for Systemic Peace's POLITY IV project by Marshall, Gurr and Jaggers (2017). It extends until 2016 and assesses countries on a scale from −10 for a strong autocracy to +10 for a fully consolidated democracy. We take into account a diffusion process by controlling the total number of programs of each respective type or targeting method within a region in a previous year. We also control whether any other programs have previously been introduced in the country by including the number of social transfer schemes in operation in a previous period. We model unobserved heterogeneity by including country and time fixed effects. Our main empirical strategy is a standard linear probability model, because of fixed effects which add a set of dummies with a linear relationship. We also consider a logistic model, but the results do not differ significantly and our findings remain robust to the choice of the functional relationship.[2]

## Do Donors Promote Specific Types of Social Transfer Programs?

Our first hypothesis states that IFIs can contribute to social policy diffusion by promoting specific types of transfer. In Table 8.2 we summarize the results from all regressions where the dependent variable is a dummy for a social transfer of a specific type, and the main control variable of interest is

---

[2] The logistic specification estimations are available upon request.

Table 8.2 Coercion by donor

|  | (1) CCT | (2) Pension | (3) Family support | (4) Public works |
|---|---|---|---|---|
| Any donor | 0.306*** | 0.031 | 0.451*** | 0.208*** |
|  | (0.081) | (0.037) | (0.081) | (0.070) |
| GDP per cap | 0.010 | 0.008 | 0.013 | −0.007 |
|  | (0.013) | (0.011) | (0.014) | (0.009) |
| Population | −0.058 | −0.047 | −0.057* | −0.021 |
|  | (0.037) | (0.033) | (0.036) | (0.021) |
| Urban population | −0.006 | −0.014 | 0.007 | 0.012 |
|  | (0.015) | (0.015) | (0.017) | (0.014) |
| Age dependency | 0.001 | −0.003 | −0.061* | −0.025 |
|  | (0.032) | (0.029) | (0.031) | (0.021) |
| Agriculture VA | −0.006 | −0.010 | −0.006 | −0.003 |
|  | (0.011) | (0.009) | (0.011) | (0.007) |
| Resource rents | −0.002 | −0.002 | −0.007* | 0.004 |
|  | (0.004) | (0.003) | (0.004) | (0.002) |
| Polity dummy | 0.006 | 0.003 | −0.002 | −0.004 |
|  | (0.006) | (0.005) | (0.005) | (0.005) |
| Number of any transfer program | 0.018** | 0.013** | 0.002 | 0.013** |
|  | (0.009) | (0.006) | (0.007) | (0.006) |
| Number of CCTs – region | 0.006*** |  |  |  |
|  | (0.002) |  |  |  |
| Number of pension schemes – region |  | 0.001 |  |  |
|  |  | (0.002) |  |  |
| Number of family support schemes – region |  |  | 0.005** |  |
|  |  |  | (0.002) |  |
| Number of public works programme – region |  |  |  | 0.008* |
|  |  |  |  | (0.004) |
| Observations | 4088 | 4088 | 4088 | 4088 |
| R-squared | 0.175 | 0.047 | 0.220 | 0.150 |
| Number of programs | 155 | 155 | 155 | 155 |

*continued*

Table 8.2 continued

|  | (1) CCT | (2) Pension | (3) Family support | (4) Public works |
|---|---|---|---|---|
| Country FE | Yes | Yes | Yes | Yes |
| Year FE | Yes | Yes | Yes | Yes |

All specifications are duration models with the considered period from 1960 until the year a program starts. The main variable of interest is the dummy for whether at least one donor provides financial or other assistance in order to implement a social transfer program. All specifications include time and country fixed effects as well as control variables such as log GDP per capita, log population, log urban population, log age dependency, log resource rents, log value added from agriculture and a democracy dummy defined by polity2 greater than 5. We also control social policy diffusion by including the number of any transfer programs in operation in a country in a previous year and the number of respective social transfer programs in a region in a previous year. All other variables to the right, with the exception of the donor assistance dummy, are taken in one period lags. Robust standard errors are in parentheses ***$p < 0.01$, **$p < 0.05$, *$p < 0.1$

a dummy for at least one donor participating in financing the social transfer program. All other variables to the right are taken in one period lags.

The results make clear that donors can drive social policy diffusion in developing countries and have some preferences for certain poverty reduction policies. IFIs mostly favor CCTs, family support programs and public works, whereas social pensions are typically adopted without any donor assistance.

The fact that social pensions are primarily initiated by national governments is confirmed by many case studies (e.g. Devereux 2007; Niño-Zarazúa et al. 2012). National governments can adopt social pension not only for poverty alleviation but also for strategic motives. For example, Devereux (2007) argues that in West Africa social pensions were introduced in order to buy opposition and minority support. There is little evidence that IFIs invest extensively in social pensions, with the exception of humanitarian assistance in fragile regions. Therefore, the question of how international donors contribute to the expansion of social pensions remains unclear and probably requires further investigation.

Donor involvement increases the probability of adopting a CCT by 30%, a family support program by 45% and an employment guarantee scheme by 21%. The number of any social transfer programs in operation in a country in a previous period and the number of programs of a respective type within a region in a previous period are quite significant but do not crowd out the significant effect of donor involvement.

McCord (2012) also argues that public works programs, in particular, have been developed through the use of donor funds. She states that IFIs find a way to deal with structural economic transformations by providing additional jobs to stabilize labor markets and ensure subsistence agriculture. These initiatives lead to improvements in infrastructure and means of livelihood for the extreme poor in many developing countries. Along with significant employment and welfare benefits, another reason why public works programs are popular among donors is political stability and the higher degree of social cohesion they may induce (e.g. Buhuwania et al. 2019).[3]

Donors finance pro-poor policy because non-contributory transfers provide not only short-term support that decreases vulnerability but also investments in long-term sustainable development. This is especially applicable to CCTs, which involve investments in human capital accumulation by ensuring school attendance or regular health check-ups. Family allowances are also promoted by donors, as they provide support for pregnant women, young children, orphans, dependent household members and others. Investments in early childhood are extremely important, as they have long-term effects on poor families and thus may contribute to sustainable development from a long-term perspective (see Chinyoka and Ulriksen, Chap. 10, this volume).

Moreover, there is heterogeneity in the policy interests of various donors. Table 8.3 reports the estimation results of the main independent variables serving as dummies for donor types. The findings confirm that donors contribute to pro-poor transfers according to their own policy agenda priorities. While the World Bank promotes all programs except for social pensions, UNICEF assists only family support programs, including cash transfer programs for vulnerable children and pregnant women in Togo, Sierra Leone, Uganda and other African countries. This makes evident that UNICEF prioritizes unconditional transfers in order to meet short-term needs in health and education. The same policy

---

[3] However, there is only limited quantitative evidence on increasing social capital as a result of public work programs. In addition, there are even controversial findings based on the qualitative analysis (see, e.g., Vajja and White 2008). Further research on this issue would be required.

Table 8.3 Coercion by donor type

|  | (1) CCT | (2) Pension | (3) Family support | (4) Public works |
|---|---|---|---|---|
| World bank | 0.410*** | 0.019 | 0.318*** | 0.209** |
|  | (0.103) | (0.034) | (0.094) | (0.088) |
| DFID UK | 0.154 | 0.084 | 0.490*** | 0.420** |
|  | (0.141) | (0.106) | (0.156) | (0.165) |
| UNICEF | 0.160 | 0.069 | 0.700*** | 0.190 |
|  | (0.133) | (0.114) | (0.149) | (0.130) |
| EU Commission | −0.053** | −0.014 | 0.923*** | 0.633** |
|  | (0.024) | (0.015) | (0.030) | (0.272) |
| WFP | −0.033* | −0.040 | 0.221 | 0.651** |
|  | (0.019) | (0.028) | (0.284) | (0.258) |
| Observations | 4088 | 4088 | 4088 | 4088 |
| Number of programs | 155 | 155 | 155 | 155 |
| Country FE | Yes | Yes | Yes | Yes |
| Year FE | Yes | Yes | Yes | Yes |

All specifications are duration models with the considered period from 1960 until the year a program starts. The main variable of interest is the dummy for whether a certain donor or international organization provides financial assistance to implement a social transfer program. All specifications include time and country fixed effects as well as control variables such as log GDP per capita, log population, log urban population, log age dependency, log resource rents, log value added from agriculture and a democracy dummy defined by polity2 greater than 5. We also control for social policy diffusion by including the number of any transfer programs in operation in a country in a previous year and the number of respective social transfer programs in a region in a previous year. All other variables to the right, with the exception of the donor type, are taken in one period lags and their coefficients are not displayed. Robust standard errors are in parentheses. ***$p < 0.01$, **$p < 0.05$, *$p < 0.1$

strategy is pursued by the EU Commission. UNICEF's and EU Commission's support for family allowances increases by 25% and 45% in comparison with any donor assistance.

Interestingly, DFID UK, the EU Commission and the WFP do not favor CCTs and instead prefer direct investments in human capital such as family support and public works programs. In general, conditionalities are promoted only by the World Bank, which might be due to the difficulty of enforcement and lower state capacity in recipient countries. In case of CCTs, the effect is even higher for the involvement of the World Bank than for any donor involvement and makes as much as 40%. Other case studies confirm this finding. According to Pick et al. (2019), the World

Bank is regarded as a key donor and has influenced the expansion of CCTs in developing countries.[4] In particular, because of the World Bank's support for CCTs, Prospera was able to become the model for the design of CCTs in more than 60 countries around the world (Parker and Todd 2017). CCTs also require some behavioral rule compliance and thus might not be optimal under emergency conditions, so most donors do not consider such programs to be among the necessary tools for social protection. CCTs prove to be more effective in promoting long-term, sustainable development, so the involvement of the World Bank can also be explained by its priority for developing infrastructure, communities/cities and strong institutions. These interests are also confirmed through the promotion of public works by the World Bank and the EU Commission, which is also in line with the high priority both place on building infrastructure and developing communities and cities.

These findings confirm our hypotheses that donors differ in their social policy diffusion strategies. They mostly adopt policies according to their own agenda and promote specific policies such as CCTs to expand their technical expertise to developing countries. However, donor funding preferences can be analyzed further, for example, by using their contribution toward achieving the Sustainable Development Goals (SDGs) or qualitative case studies (see Künzler, Chap. 4, this volume; Chinyoka and Ulriksen, Chap. 10, this volume; Devereux and Kapingidza, Chap. 11, this volume).

## Is Donor Involvement Associated with Specific Targeting Methods?

Table 8.4 shows donor influence on the design of social transfer programs, specifically the targeting method used to determine the beneficiary base. Interestingly, the preferences of almost all international organizations are consistent for programs that use community-based targeting. This way of beneficiary selection is strongly favored by all donors except for the WFP. Community-based targeting is considered to be one of the most

---

[4] https://www.oecd.org/dev/inclusivesocietiesanddevelopment/Lessons_learned_social_development_partners_for_social_protection.pdf.

**Table 8.4** Targeting methods promoted by donors

|  | (1) Categorical | (2) Geographical | (3) Means testing | (4) Proxy means testing | (5) Community based | (6) Self-targeted |
|---|---|---|---|---|---|---|
| Any donor | 0.151** | 0.257*** | −0.001 | 0.330*** | 0.382*** | 0.121** |
|  | (0.073) | (0.070) | (0.032) | (0.075) | (0.078) | (0.057) |
| World bank | 0.082 | 0.317*** | 0.013 | 0.436*** | 0.285*** | 0.059 |
|  | (0.083) | (0.093) | (0.049) | (0.098) | (0.090) | (0.055) |
| DFID UK | 0.289* | 0.204 | −0.016 | 0.197 | 0.401** | 0.094 |
|  | (0.159) | (0.138) | (0.012) | (0.144) | (0.161) | (0.104) |
| UNICEF | 0.288* | 0.248** | 0.000 | 0.057 | 0.475*** | 0.092 |
|  | (0.170) | (0.124) | (0.010) | (0.096) | (0.163) | (0.097) |
| EU Commission | −0.046 | 0.319 | −0.026 | 0.311 | 0.957*** | −0.016 |
|  | (0.034) | (0.262) | (0.016) | (0.275) | (0.021) | (0.019) |
| WFP | −0.046 | 0.654** | −0.035 | −0.027 | 0.342 | 0.656** |
|  | (0.044) | (0.274) | (0.039) | (0.031) | (0.275) | (0.272) |
| Observations | 4088 | 4088 | 4088 | 4088 | 4088 | 4088 |
| Number of programs | 155 | 155 | 155 | 155 | 155 | 155 |
| Country FE | Yes | Yes | Yes | Yes | Yes | Yes |
| Year FE | Yes | Yes | Yes | Yes | Yes | Yes |
| Controls | Yes | Yes | Yes | Yes | Yes | Yes |

All specifications are duration models, the period under consideration covering the time from 1960 until the year a program starts. The main variable of interest is the dummy for whether a certain donor or international organization provides financial assistance to implement a social transfer program. All specifications include time and country fixed effects as well as control variables such as log GDP per capita, log population, log urban population, log age dependency, log resource rents, log value added from agriculture and a democracy dummy defined by polity2 greater than 5. We also control for social policy diffusion by including the number of any transfer programs in operation in a country in a previous year and the number of respective social transfer programs in a region in a previous year. All other variables to the right, with the exception of the donor type, are taken in one period lags and their coefficients are not displayed. Robust standard errors are in parentheses ***$p < 0.01$, **$p < 0.05$, *$p < 0.1$

effective methods, as it allows for the use of local information regarding the level of poverty and helps with avoiding social conflicts. On the other hand, as this type of targeting does not always yield an unbiased selection of the most vulnerable individuals, it can also increase local capture (Conning and Kevane 2002).

Any donor participation is an insignificant predictor of means testing targeting, which is typically employed in programs funded by national governments. This result is driven by the fact that very few means testing programs are adopted with any donor involvement (see Fig. 8.2). Thus, our evidence confirms that national governments broadly use this method of beneficiary selection, probably because of its clarity and relatively easy operationalization.

At the same time, proxy means testing is promoted by donor involvement, and especially by the World Bank, which is probably related to the technical expertise and administrative capacity required. Because of its non-transparency, proxy means testing allows for the exclusion of any political manipulations and rent seeking and so might be preferred by the World Bank in order to assure the efficiency and impartiality of social transfers.

DFID UK and UNICEF often use categorical targeting, as they primarily focus on family support programs. More specifically, the involvement of DFID UK and UNICEF increases the probability of using categorical targeting by 30%. Geographical targeting is applied by the World Bank, UNICEF and the WFP to target the poorest and most vulnerable regions. This method might be especially efficient for targeting areas in the aftermath of shocks and crises, which is a priority for both UNICEF and the WFP. For example, the WFP's assistance is associated with the more frequent use of geographical targeting by about 60%. The promotion of self-targeted programs by the WFP might also be related to the offering of inferior quality food in times of crisis. The probability of using this type of beneficiary selection in case of the WFP also makes as much as 60%.

Technical assistance and expertise of international donors might be essential for applying specific targeting methods to social protection policies. Donors can contribute to the development and implementation of the Management Information Systems (MIS), the Harmonized Targeting tools and the Unified Beneficiary Registries (UBR). For example, Malawi's Social Cash Transfer Programme (SCTP) has benefited from UNICEF's support of the pilot project and further from the assistance of the German Institute for International Cooperation (GIZ) and KfW Development Bank in the design and implementation of the targeting system.[5] SCTP uses a mix of categorical, community-based targeting and proxy means testing. Another good example is a Yemen Emergency Crisis Response Project (ECPR) that has provided transfers to the citizens of Yemen during an active conflict using geographical and multi-layered proxy means testing targeting. The project was grounded on the pre-existing national system of social transfers in a close interaction with the Yemen Social Fund for Development (SFD) and the Public works Project (PWP). The operational introduction of a complex system of targeting became possible with the support of the World Bank, UNDP and UNICEF.

Regarding the targeting mechanisms, the basic intuition is that the more influential donors are, the more can they promote more complex systems of beneficiary selection. This might be the case for the World Bank, which has abundant operational capacity and about 180 branches in developing countries. This can also help with explaining its preference for proxy means testing, which can be very effective for detecting the chronically poor (Grosh et al. 2008) but is difficult to realize, as it requires high institutional and statistical capacity. Hence, we can confirm our third hypothesis and therefore emphasize the importance of donor support in the design and implementation of social policies in recipient countries. Community-based targeting is preferred by all donors, probably due to the necessity of involving community agents and local chiefs in targeting and monitoring, but also for controlling their performance in order to avoid potential eligibility manipulation and local capture. Categorical selections are low-capacity measures that are widely used by DFID UK and UNICEF, but this is probably related to their general policy agendas that prioritize support for poor families and children. Geographical targeting is popular among almost all donors, but it is typically applied together with other selection methods like community-based targeting or proxy means testing. These consider-

---

[5] https://www.giz.de/de/downloads/Poverty%20Targeting%20Primer_Full%20Version.pdf.

ations are based on development performance and help with highlighting how certain aspects of donor-recipient interactions shape social policy in developing countries.

## Discussion and Conclusion

The revelation of policy patterns pursued by international donors may help to a better understanding of development policy failures and with improving future development interventions. These findings provide important insights into how donors influence social policies, specifically non-contributory social transfer schemes.

Our findings suggest that IFIs have some preferences concerning which transfer types and targeting mechanisms are adopted. At the same time, their impacts appear to be generally in line with long-term development goals. Donors promote programs which either support families in emergency situations or imply investments in long-term human capital accumulation, such as CCTs or employment guarantee schemes. There is also some heterogeneity among donors. While the World Bank more frequently develops CCTs, UNICEF focuses primarily on family allowances to small children and pregnant women. This is consistent with the general goals and strategies of these financial institutions. It is interesting to note that social pensions, including old-age grants and disability pensions, are not favored by any donor. This reflects the general perspective that these policies are meant for short-term emergency assistance and are therefore not designed to structurally alleviate poverty.

In addition to the type of social transfer program, specific targeting methods are also promoted by different IFIs. Policy effectiveness might be fully undermined if the identification of the extreme poor and the selection of transfer beneficiaries are not correctly carried out. Hence, the choice of targeting method might be strategic, as donors typically finance social policies under the condition that social assistance is adequately distributed. This intuition is partly confirmed by our results, as international donors support either very transparent methods of selection, such as categorical or geographical targeting, or complex identification methods such as proxy means testing in order to avoid eligibility manipulation. Self-selection remains a popular method among donors, which is consistent with the high share of CCTs supported by IFIs. However, the most promoted method, community-based targeting, typically ensures better access to information on poverty status at the local level. Administrative costs and information asymmetries can be reduced by using community agents such as local chiefs or leaders of social or religious groups instead of official agents who are better qualified but less informed. The main threat connected to this type of targeting is that the community agents may pursue their own interests rather than base their analyses on the actual needs of the people (Coady and Skoufias 2004). This is also confirmed by Dodlova et al. (2018b) who show that community-based targeting is quite popular in rent-seeking societies. International donors should take such threats into consideration when supporting social policies in developing countries.

Valuable lessons can be learned from these insights. First, international donors should keep an eye on policy formulation. For example, Khan et al. (2018) find that donors have three different channels of influencing health policies in Cambodia and Pakistan: financial resources, technical expertise and indirect financial and political incentives. Depending on the stage of the policy process, donors may provide financial, technical or evaluation expertise. Second, donors can significantly improve the implementation of any social policy, sometimes at low costs. For example, the WFP was able to build an information database to improve the process of identifying the most vulnerable populations in Colombia in 2004 and 2005. In addition to officially IDPs, the WFP could take into account other vulnerable populations through Church networks and community-based interventions that were designed specifically to identify families affected by conflict and food insecurity. Also, donors can contribute to monitoring and evaluations which appear quite critical in tracking aid allocation. Hence, donors have all of the resources and expertise needed to design innovative, effective social policy interventions in developing countries.

What is most important is that international donors support the policy initiatives of national governments without taking the leading role in their implementation. The keystone of donor interventions should be their complementarity to national initiatives rather than their substitution for them. In particular, donor interventions should not replace the functions of national governments and should allow them to build their own capacities.

Our results confirm that donors contribute particularly to national transfer policies that require a higher level of technical support or operationalization, such as CCTs or proxy means testing targeting. Implicitly, this illustrates that donors are adequately cautious about contributing to social policy assistance. This conclusion is consistent with other literature on social policies. For example, also Holmqvist (2012) stresses that donor policies should not serve as leverage for institutionalizing permanent social protection systems but rather support recipient countries by their initiatives. He also gives an overview of different strategies donors can pursue for their funding while still providing national governments with enough flexibility to design and implement social policies.

We implicitly assume that donors may drive the formulation and implementation of certain policies according to their own interests and priorities. For example, donors may promote specific aid allocation patterns to achieve major Millennium Development Goals (Thiele et al. 2007). However, our findings would be perfectly in line with the view that recipient countries are strategic in their involvement with respective donors. From this perspective, donors behave as benevolent actors and social planners, and national governments appeal to them for help with specific policies. It would be interesting to investigate this hypothesis via case studies and other qualitative research. Our findings may also serve as a starting point for further research, comparing the positive and negative consequences of donor influence on poverty alleviation policies in developing countries. This contribution notably does not focus on how donor involvement influences the efficiency of social transfer programs. For example, Devereux and White (2010) argue that domestic policy-makers are shown to have suggested more efficient initiatives for social policy models than have international development actors. More efficient policies imply nationwide coverage, broad political support and, oftentimes, long-term sustainability. However, the technical expertise and institutional capacity provided by donors might be essential for program implementation. Hence, there should be a balance between national interests and donor influence. Another potentially interesting topic for exploration is donor involvement in countries with different political regimes. According to Dodlova (2018a), in non-democracies almost 40% of programs are co-financed by donors as opposed to 17% in democracies. This suggests that donor influence on social policy in non-democracies is more relevant for a sustainable development, as they are more traditional and less open to policy innovations. Hence, our results can be considered a first step toward investigating many other issues related to donor involvement and influence on social policy in developing countries.

# References

Acht, Martin, Toman Omar Mahmoud, and Rainer Thiele. 2015. Corrupt Governments Do Not Receive More State-to-State Aid: Governance and the Delivery of Foreign Aid Through Non-state Actors. *Journal of Development Economics* 114 (C): 20–33.

Alesina, Alberto, and David Dollar. 2000. Who Gives Foreign Aid to Whom and Why? *Journal of Economic Growth* 5: 33–63.

Allen, Susan Hannah, and Michael Flynn. 2018. Donor Government Ideology and Aid Bypass. *Foreign Policy Analysis* 14 (4): 449–468.

Barrientos, Armando. 2013. *Social Assistance in Developing Countries*. New York: Cambridge University Press.

Berthélemy, Jean-Claude. 2006. Bilateral Donors' Interest vs. Recipients' Development Motives in Aid Allocation: Do All Donors Behave the Same? *Review of Development Economics* 10 (2): 179–194.

Bodenstein, Thilo, and Achim Kemmerling. 2015. A Paradox of Redistribution in International Aid? The Determinants of Poverty-Oriented Development Assistance. *World Development* 76: 359–369.

Brech, Viktor, and Niklas Potrafke. 2014. Donor Ideology and Types of Foreign Aid. *Journal of Comparative Economics* 42 (1): 61–75.

Browne, Stephen. 2006. *Aid and Influence. Do Donors Help or Hinder?* London: Routledge.

Buhuwania, Pragya, J. Hemann, A. Mukherji, A. Nandi, and H. Swaminathan. 2019. *Public Works Programs and Social Capital: An Exploration of MGNREGA in India*. mimeo.

Cashel-Cordo, Peter, and Steven G. Craig. 1997. Donor Preferences and Recipient Fiscal Behavior: A Simultaneous Analysis of Foreign Aid. *Economic Inquiry* 35 (3): 653–671.

Coady, David, and Emmanuel Skoufias. 2004. On the Targeting and Redistributive Efficiencies of Alternative Transfer Instruments. *Review of Income and Wealth* 50 (1): 11–27.

Coady, David, Margaret Grosh, and John Hoddinott. 2004a. *Targeting of Transfers in Developing Countries: Review of Lessons and Experience.* Washington, DC: World Bank.

———. 2004b. Targeting Outcomes, Redux. *The World Bank Research Observer* 19 (1): 61–85.

Conning, Jonathan, and Michael Kevane. 2002. Community-based Targeting Mechanism for Social Safety Nets: A Critical Review. *World Development* 30 (3): 375–394.

Devereux, Stephen. 2007. Social Pensions in Southern Africa in the Twentieth Century. *Journal of Southern African Studies* 33 (3): 539–560.

Devereux, Stephen, and Philip White. 2010. Social Protection in Africa: Evidence, Politics and Rights. *Poverty and Public Policy* 2 (3): 53–77.

Dodlova, Marina, Anna Giolbas, and Jann Lay. 2017. Social Transfers and Conditionalities under Different Regime Types. *European Journal of Political Economy* 50 (C): 141–156.

———. 2018a. Non-Contributory Social Transfer Programmes in Developing Countries: A New Data Set and Research Agenda. *Data in Brief* 16: 51–64.

———. 2018b. *Pro-poor versus Political Targeting: An Analysis of Social Assistance in Developing Countries.* mimeo.

Dreher, Axel, Peter Nunnenkamp, and Rainer Thiele. 2008. Does US Aid Buy UN General Assembly Votes? A Disaggregated Analysis. *Public Choice* 136 (1–2): 139–164.

Dreher, Axel, Jan-Egbert Sturm, and James Raymond Vreeland. 2009. Development Aid and International Politics: Does Membership on the UN Security Council Influence World Bank Decisions? *Journal of Development Economics* 88 (1): 1–18.

Dreher, Axel, Peter Nunnenkamp, and Maya Schmaljohann. 2015. The Allocation of German Aid: Self-interest and Government Ideology. *Economics and Politics* 27 (1): 160–184.

Dreher, Axel, Vera Z. Eichenauer, and Kai Gehring. 2018. Geopolitics, Aid and Growth: The Impact of UN Security Council Membership on the Effectiveness of Aid. *World Bank Economic Review* 32 (2): 268–286.

Dreher, Axel, Andreas Fuchs, Roland Hodler, Bradley C. Parks, Paul A. Raschky, and Michael J. Tierney. 2019. Aid on Demand: African Leaders and the Geography of China's Foreign Assistance. *Journal of Development Economics* 140: 44–71.

Eichenauer, Vera Z., and Bernhard Reinsberg. 2016. *What Determines Earmarked Funding to International Development Organizations? Evidence from the New Multi-bilateral Aid Data*. Center for Comparative and International Studies (CIS), Working Paper No. 88.

Ellis, Frank, Stephen Devereux, and Philip White. 2009. *Social Protection in Africa*. Cheltenham and Northampton, MA: Edward Elgar.

Faye, Michael, and Paul Niehaus. 2012. Political Aid Cycles. *The American Economic Review* 102 (7): 3516–3530.

Fuchs, Andreas, and Hannes Öhler. 2019. *Does Private Aid Follow the Flag? An Empirical Analysis of Humanitarian Assistance*. mimeo.

Fuchs, Andreas, and Katharina Richert. 2018. Development Minister Characteristics and Aid Giving. *European Journal of Political Economy* 53: 186–204.

Fuchs, Andreas, Axel Dreher, and Peter Nunnenkamp. 2014. Determinants of Donor Generosity: A Survey of the Aid Budget Literature. *World Development* 56: 172–199.

Grosh, Margaret, Carlo del Ninno, Emil Tesliuc, and Azedine Ouerghi. 2008. *For Protection and Promotion: The Design and Implementation of Effective Safety Nets*. Washington, DC: World Bank.

Groves, Leslie, and Rachel Hinton, eds. 2013. *Inclusive Aid: Changing Power and Relationships in International Development*. London: Routledge Press.

Hagen-Zanker, Jessica, and Anna McCord. 2013. The Affordability of Social Protection in the Light of International Spending Commitments. *Development Policy Review* 31 (4): 397–418.

Harrigan, Jane, Chengang Wang, and Hamed El-Said. 2006. The Politics of IMF and World Bank Lending: Will it Backfire in the Middle East and North Africa? In *The IMF, World Bank and Policy Reform*, ed. Alberto Paloni and Maurizio Zanardi, 64–99. New York: Routledge.

Hicks, Daniel L., Joan Hamory Hicks, and Beatriz Maldonado. 2016. Women as Policy Makers and Donors: Female Legislators and Foreign Aid. *European Journal of Political Economy* 41: 46–60.

Holmqvist, Göran. 2012. External Financing of Social Protection: Opportunities and Risks. *Development Policy Review* 30 (1): 5–27.

Khan, Mishal S., Ankita Meghani, Marco Liverani, Imara Roychowdhury, and Justin Parkhurst. 2018. How do External Donors Influence National Health Policy Processes? Experiences of Domestic Policy Actors in Cambodia and Pakistan. *Health Policy and Planning* 33 (2): 215–223.

Kilby, Christopher. 2006. Donor Influence in Multilateral Development Banks: The Case of the Asian Development Bank. *The Review of International Organizations* 1 (2): 173–195.

Maclure, Richard. 1995. Primary Health Care and Donor Dependency: A Case Study of Nongovernment Assistance in Burkina Faso. *International Journal of Health Services* 25 (3): 539–558.

Marshall, Monty G., Ted Robert Gurr, and Keith Jaggers. 2017. *POLITY IV Project: Political Regime Characteristics and Transitions, 1800–2016*. Center for Systemic Peace.

McCord, Anna. 2012. *The Politics of Social Protection: Why Are Public Works Programmes So Popular with Governments and Donors?* Overseas Development Institute.

Milner, Helen V., and Dustin H. Tingley. 2010. The Political Economy of U.S. Foreign Aid: American Legislators and the Domestic Politics of Aid. *Economics and Politics* 22 (2): 200–232.

Minasyan, Anna, Peter Nunnenkamp, and Katharina Richert. 2017. Does Aid Effectiveness Depend on the Quality of Donors? *World Development* 100: 16–30.

Niño-Zarazúa, Miguel, Armando Barrientos, Samuel Hickey, and David Hulme. 2012. Social Protection in Sub-Saharan Africa: Getting the Politics Right. *World Development* 40 (1): 163–176.

*Non-Contributory Social Transfer Programmes (NSTP) in Developing Countries Data Set v1.1*. 2017. [Online] Dodlova, Marina, Anna Giolbas and Jann Lay. http://doi.org/10.7802/1530.

Olken, Benjamin A. 2006. Corruption and the Costs of Redistribution: Micro Evidence from Indonesia. *Journal of Public Economics* 90 (4–5): 853–870.

Parker, Susan Wendy, and Petra E. Todd. 2017. Conditional Cash Transfers: The Case of Progresa/Oportunidades. *Journal of Economic Literature* 55 (3): 866–915.

Pick, Alexander, Alexandre Kolev, and Ji-Yeun Rim. 2019. *Optimising the Role of Development Partners for Social Protection*. OECD.

Reinikka, Ritva, and Jakob Svensson. 2004. Local Capture: Evidence from a Central Government Transfer Program in Uganda. *The Quarterly Journal of Economics* 119 (2): 679–705.

Schubert, Bernd, and Rachel Slater. 2006. Social Cash Transfers in Low-Income African Countries: Conditional or Unconditional? *Development Policy Review* 24 (5): 471–478.

Takala, Tuomas. 1998. Making Educational Policy under Influence of External Assistance and National Politics—A Comparative Analysis of the Education Sector Policy Documents of Ethiopia, Mozambique, Namibia and Zambia. *International Journal of Educational Development* 18 (4): 319–335.

Thérien, Jean-Philippe, and Alain Noel. 2000. Political Parties and Foreign Aid. *American Political Science Review* 94 (1): 151–162.

Thiele, Rainer, Peter Nunnekamp, and Axel Dreher. 2007. Do Donors Target Aid in Line with the Millennium Development Goals? A Sector Perspective of Aid Allocation. *Review of World Economics* 143 (4): 596–630.

UNU-WIDER. 2018. *Social Assistance, Politics, and Institutions (SAPI) Database* [Online]. Helsinki: United Nations University World Institute for Development Economics Research (UNU-WIDER). https://www.wider.unu.edu/project/sapi-social-assistance-politics-and-institutions-database.

Vajja, Anju, and Howard White. 2008. Can the World Bank Build Social Capital? The Experience of Social Funds in Malawi and Zambia. *Journal of Development Studies* 44 (8): 1145–1168.

Vreeland, James Raymond, and Axel Dreher. 2014. *The Political Economy of the United Nations Security Council: Money and Influence.* New York: Cambridge University Press.

World Development Indicators. Washington, DC: The World Bank.

**Open Access** This chapter is licensed under the terms of the Creative Commons Attribution 4.0 International License (http://creativecommons.org/licenses/by/4.0/), which permits use, sharing, adaptation, distribution and reproduction in any medium or format, as long as you give appropriate credit to the original author(s) and the source, provide a link to the Creative Commons licence and indicate if changes were made.

The images or other third party material in this chapter are included in the chapter's Creative Commons licence, unless indicated otherwise in a credit line to the material. If material is not included in the chapter's Creative Commons licence and your intended use is not permitted by statutory regulation or exceeds the permitted use, you will need to obtain permission directly from the copyright holder.

# 9

# The World Bank and the Contentious Politics of Global Social Spending

Rahmi Çemen and Erdem Yörük

## Introduction

There has been an aggregate increase in social protection expenditures over the past several decades in most of the Global South and North, despite the expectations of the welfare state retrenchment literature (Korpi and Palme 2003; Scruggs and Allan 2008). Most countries in the Global South, especially the so-called emerging market economies, have opted for creating or expanding innovative welfare programs (i.e. conditional cash transfers, free health care for the poor, food aid and public works programs), while old age pension expenditures, care services and

R. Çemen (✉)
University of Florida, Gainesville, FL, USA
e-mail: rccemen@ufl.edu

E. Yörük
Department of Sociology, Koç University, Istanbul, Turkey

Department of Social Policy and Intervention, University of Oxford, Oxford, UK
e-mail: eryoruk@ku.edu.tr

social assistance programs continue to expand in the Global North. When explaining welfare state expansion, most contemporary studies tend to emphasize *structural* factors, such as aging, previous development strategies, political institutions and the rise of the services sector (Haggard and Kaufman 2008; Pierson 2001; Rudra 2002). Without denying the importance of structuralist explanations, we contend that the contemporary literature has largely under-examined how social expenditures are influenced by the *political* concerns of national and supranational institutions, such as the containment of social unrest. There are a few previous works that tackle similar inquiries; however, they test the opposite direction of the relationship we are interested in: the effect that welfare has on contentious politics (see i.e. Burgoon 2006; Dunning 2008; Pierson 2001; Taydas and Peksen 2012; Weiss 2005). In this chapter, we set out to make a contribution by testing the extent to which social unrest affects public social expenditures.

There are reasons to believe that international financial institutions (IFIs), such as the World Bank, may be playing a mediating role in the relationship between contentious politics and social spending. The World Bank claims that many new social policies (such as social pensions and conditional cash transfers) in borrowing countries are a result of technocratic (read: non-political) imposition (Brooks 2004; Radin 2008). Yet, van Gils and Yörük (2017) show that political objectives have played a critical role in the content of World Bank recommendations, including the prevention and containment of social unrest. In that sense, they show that World Bank social policy recommendations are not solely based on technocratic concerns over poverty alleviation and development but are fueled by the Bank's own political concerns about political stability. Thus, these observations have led us to question whether the social policy recommendations of IFIs, such as the World Bank, are mostly targeted at countries experiencing greater amounts of social unrest. Moreover, we are curious as to whether the World Bank's recommendations are taken into consideration more seriously by borrowing countries if they are challenged by social unrest.

We, therefore, hypothesize that social unrest is a key factor which translates structural effects into actual welfare policies, as part of a benevolent government strategy to contain further unrest. Furthermore, we suspect that this process is facilitated by the intervention of IFIs. The results of our statistical analysis, on a sample of 48 countries from the Global North and South for the years between 1989 and 2015, indicate that social expenditures are, to a significant degree, positively related to social unrest, thus providing evidence of the social containment hypothesis. The results for our second hypothesis are less clear, as there is no evidence of a direct effect of the World Bank on social spending. However, in several models we find that the effect of certain types of social unrest (i.e. general strikes) is significant if interacted with World Bank social policy recommendations (WBSPRs). Thus, there is some evidence of a relationship between World Bank social policy interventions and government decisions to increase social spending as a reaction to social unrest. Taken together, we interpret these results as a sign that social unrest plays a role in how policymakers translate structural forces into actual social policies, as well as providing some insights into the conditions in which policymakers choose to diffuse social policy recommendations from IFIs, such as the World Bank.

## Explaining Welfare State Development

The explanations for modern welfare state development since the nineteenth century can be classified into two main clusters: *structural* and *political* explanations. For the mid-twentieth century development of welfare in the West, *structuralist* theories suggest that the welfare state expanded as a "natural" response to industrialization and urbanization (a.k.a logic of industrialism thesis) (Cowgill 1974; Form 1979; Goldthorpe et al. 1969; Pampel and Weiss 1983) or to resolve the crisis of under-consumption following the Keynesian logic (Garraty 1978; Janowitz 1977; O'Connor 1973; Offe 1984). Scholars oriented toward *political* explanations have argued that demographic and economic exigencies do not automatically lead to changes in welfare policies. Rather, socio-structural factors are translated into social policies through political conflict and struggles. These scholars considered the mid-twentieth-century welfare expansion as part of a strategy to contain political disorder and mobilize popular support (Dawson and Robinson 1963;

Jennings 1979; Olson 1982). For instance, in-depth investigations of the urban riots in the United States during the 1960s provide evidence of the state using welfare programs for controlling, containing and potentially repressing insurgent populations (Gurr 1980; Isaac and Kelly 1981; Offe 1982; Piven and Cloward 1971).

Unlike the previous literature, that delicately fused structural and political perspectives, dominant arguments concerning the contemporary developments of the welfare state have largely focused on how national governments take a number of structural factors into account when formulating social policies, such as globalization, rising poverty, unemployment, deindustrialization, aging and the rise of the services sector (Cerutti et al. 2014; Fernández and Jaime-Castillo 2012; Gough et al. 2004; Hemerijck 2012; Iversen 2001). This structuralist focus has not only characterized the studies on the original Organisation for Economic Co-operation and Development (OECD) countries, but also greatly influenced the scope of questions asked in research on the Global South. For instance, research on the welfare-globalization nexus has often painted a gloomy picture, suggesting that a "race to the bottom" is taking place[1] (Avelino et al. 2005; Kaufman and Segura-Ubiergo 2001; Rudra 2002; Wibbels 2006), the logic being that developing countries lack the domestic mediating factors of globalization found in the original OECD countries (for instance strong democratic institutions) (Haggard and Kaufman 2008; Rudra 2008). The overall evidence has largely contradicted the claims of a "race to the welfare bottom" in the Global South, such as an overall increase in public spending and the proliferation of new social welfare programs (Hulme et al. 2012). Thus, we argue that the globalization-welfare nexus literature provides a good example of the need to take into consideration factors which mediate structural effects into actual social policies, such as *political* effects and their interaction with international/external actors.

With regard to the influence of external actors, a number of studies have begun to place greater emphasis on the political concerns of supranational organizations, such as the World Bank, when explaining the

---

[1] The "race to the bottom" hypothesis can be generally summarized as stating that high universal welfare standards are incompatible with market competition (Mishra 1996; Wibbels 2006).

formulation of social policies in the Global South (Brooks 2015; Simpson 2018). The official discourse of the World Bank is that its objectives are not political, but that it seeks to solve social ills, such as the alleviation of poverty (Litvack 2011; World Bank 2015). However, previous research has demonstrated that these claims do not match up to reality (van Gils and Yörük 2017). A number of studies have found clear references to political concerns in the World Bank's policies (Barnett and Finnemore 2004; Benjamin n.d.; Goldman n.d.; Van de Laar 1976). For instance, van Gils and Yörük (2017) provide systematic evidence of the World Bank making politically motivated social policy recommendations, such as the prevention and containment of social unrest. While it is not surprising to see political rhetoric in the World Bank's policy recommendations, these recommendations are subsumed under the Word Bank's global "equitable growth" strategy. Thus, it appears that the World Bank does not see poverty alleviation as an end in and of itself, but rather as a means to reduce social unrest which could adversely affect the interests of donor governments (see Dodlova, Chap. 8, this volume).

This conclusion fits to the fact that the World Bank is a rationally structured bureaucratic institution with well-defined interests and goals. Furthermore, the Bank has to negotiate with member organizations in order to achieve these goals and maximize bureaucratic interests. This dependency structurally leads the Bank toward a conservative direction and to policy recommendations that are often politically driven. Therefore, when member states have exigencies for the containment of domestic unrest, the Bank is driven to provide blueprints for this course of action. Also, recommending social assistance for political containment is appealing because customers, as political actors, tend to internalize World Bank policy suggestions that would work politically at home. Therefore, recommendations that are politically helpful may find clients easier (Toye 2009).

The World Bank's donor states have a strong influence on the Bank's policymaking (Weaver and Leiteritz 2005), with the US remaining the most influential state (Fleck and Kilby 2006; Morrison 2013). Hence, the Bank acts as an overseer of global political stability, primarily due to the support from donor governments who may have their long-term security interests defended when considering stabilization goals which should, in turn, lead to less migration or terrorism (Keukeleire and Raube 2013, see also Shriwise, Chap. 2, this volume). Donors impose their interests through (1) direct appointment of the leadership cadres of the Bank, (2) donating the majority of funds, and (3) the threat of denying Bank funds access to the national private capital markets in case the Bank declines donors' interests (Weaver 2008).

In sum, we turn to the careful fusion of structural and political factors, common among mid-twentieth-century welfare scholars, to explain recent trends in global welfare provision. According to this literature, the containment of social unrest is a political factor which translates the structural pressures for welfare expansion into actual increases in welfare spending. Furthermore, there are reasons to believe that IFIs, such as the World Bank, play a mediating role in the relationship between contentious politics and social spending by facilitating the containment of social unrest.

## Data and Methods

To answer our research questions, we conduct a panel data analysis on a sample of 48 countries from the Global North and South, across multiple world regions, for the years between 1989 and 2015.[2] Our sample does not include low-income/poor countries which run the risk of introducing a type 2 error to our analysis; as least developed countries have less capacity and resources to increase social protection spending even if policymakers prefer to address unrest through benevolent means. When referring to emerging market economies, we generally refer to countries which show many features of advanced industrialized economies (i.e. high levels of economic growth, open markets, etc.) but at the same time lack many of the common features of these countries (i.e. high GDP per capita, low unemployment and consistent socio-political stability). Although seeking to only include countries which match these characteristics approximates what we are referring to as an emerging market economy, we are nonetheless forced to deal with the difficulty that a commonly

---

[2] For a full list of countries, see Appendix.

accepted definition which would delineate emerging market economies (EMEs) from least developed economies does not yet exist. Thus, to better identify a sample of cases, we include countries as EMEs if they are listed on any one of three popularly applied lists: International Monetary Fund (IMF), Banco Bilbao Vizcaya Argentaria (BBVA) and the Emerging Market Bond Index Global (EMBI Global) by J.P. Morgan.

Table 9.1 provides summary statistics of our data. Our dependent variable is *social protection spending*, measured as a percentage of GDP.[3] Most data for the dependent variable come from the OECD social expenditure database (SOCX). The OECD data are complemented with our own calculations based on national government records and surveys, applying the OECD methodology. We are mainly concerned with the effect of two key independent variables, as well as with their interaction. First, we create an index variable for social unrest[4] composed of the total number of events per year for three major sources of social unrest: general strikes, riots and anti-government demonstrations. All three of these measures come from the cross-national time series (CNTS) domestic conflict event data.[5] The CNTS data currently offers the most reliable cross-national measures for the entire period of interest.

The second independent variable of interest is *IFI influence*. As an indicator of donor diffusion of policy ideas does not currently exist, we create a new measure based on the number of WBSPRs. This measure is based on a survey of a total of 447 World Bank social policy related documents and reports.[6] The core of the WBSPR measure counts the number of

---

[3] Social protection expenditure comprises public cash benefits, direct in-kind provision of goods and services and tax breaks for social purposes. Benefits may be targeted at low-income households, the elderly, disabled, sick, unemployed or young persons. To be considered "social", programs must involve either the redistribution of resources across households or compulsory participation.

[4] The specific weights for the social unrest index are roughly in line with how CNTS scores their own weighted conflict index. The values entered are general strikes (20), riots (35) and anti-government demonstrations (10). We then multiplied the value for each variable by the specific weights; multiplied that sum of products by 100 and divided the result by 3.

[5] Events for these data are recorded through a comprehensive coding of newspaper articles. With regard to sources, the CNTS user's manual notes that "while no bibliographic references are utilized in connection with these data, most are derived from *The New York Times*" (12).

[6] These include Country Focus reports, Economic and Sector work reports, Project Documents and documents from the Publications and Research department, including working papers. These are thus analytical as well as operational reports.

Table 9.1 Summary statistics

| | Count | Mean | SD | Min | Max | Sum |
|---|---|---|---|---|---|---|
| Total public social expenditure (%GDP) | 1002 | 17.20496 | 7.618004 | 0.27 | 34.178 | 17,239.37 |
| Social unrest index | 973 | 993.4909 | 2942.709 | 0 | 33,000 | 966,666.7 |
| General strikes (Total) | 973 | 0.1716341 | 0.6985708 | 0 | 8 | 167 |
| Anti-government demonstrations (Total) | 973 | 1.054471 | 3.488681 | 0 | 50 | 1026 |
| Riots (Total) | 973 | 0.4522097 | 1.549269 | 0 | 17 | 440 |
| WB social policy recommendation (Dummy) | 1002 | 0.507984 | 0.5001859 | 0 | 1 | 509 |
| Multilateral loans (PPG) | 742 | 3.60e+09 | 7.72e+09 | 0 | 4.65e+10 | 2.67e+12 |
| Trade (%GDP) | 1002 | 74.79755 | 38.8536 | 16.0117 | 220.4074 | 74,947.15 |
| Bureaucratic quality | 998 | 3.276453 | 0.7757665 | 1 | 4 | 3269.9 |
| GDP per capita (Constant 2010 US$) (Logged) | 1002 | 9.900857 | 1.012613 | 6.233024 | 11.42537 | 9920.659 |
| GDP per capita growth (Annual %) | 999 | 2.316704 | 3.346165 | −14.55986 | 24.76477 | 2314.387 |
| FH democracy score (Reverse) | 1002 | 12.57186 | 2.369749 | 3 | 14 | 12,597 |
| Old age dependency | 1002 | 19.36657 | 7.027189 | 3.556224 | 39.58342 | 19,405.3 |
| Original OECD country | 1002 | 0.5638723 | 0.4961512 | 0 | 1 | 565 |
| Year | 1002 | 2002.943 | 7.131963 | 1989 | 2015 | 2,006,949 |

World Bank social policy recommendations given to a specific country in a given country-year.[7] This score is then added to the number of relevant regional reports. Finally, the World Bank occasionally publishes several highly influential policy documents which apply to every recipient country for the year in which the document was published. Thus, a single point is also added to every country-year in which an influential multi-country document is published. The equation to calculate the WBSPR variable is as follows:

$$\begin{aligned}\text{WBSPR}(\text{total})_{it} = &\ \Sigma\left(\text{single country social policy recommendations}\right)_{it} \\ &+ \Sigma\left(\text{regional social policy recommendations}\right)_{it} \\ &+ \Sigma\left(\text{influential multi}-\text{country social policy recommendations}\right)_{it}\end{aligned}$$

The issue with measuring WBSPR as an interval variable is that it assumes that a one report increase leads to a single unit increase in the effect on social protection spending. As an extreme example, in the year 2013 we measure a total of 17 WBSPRs for China, up from 6 recommendations the previous year. Thus, as an interval variable, it is assumed that the World Bank impact is 11 times greater in 2013 than in 2012. However, it is unlikely that 17 reports have a much greater influence on social policy than 6 reports. Thus, for all our models we apply WBSPR as a simple dummy variable, (1) if there was a report in a given country-year and (0) if not.

As one of the few studies which cross-nationally analyzes the World Bank's influence on social assistance, Brooks (2015) measures the World Bank leverage as the proportion of loans to country GDP. While this approach may yield general insights concerning the financial leverage of the Bank, financial flows are most likely one out of several mechanisms through which the World Bank exerts influence on policy choices. Other

---

[7] To create this measure, we build on a previous dataset which followed a two-stage keyword search method (van Gils and Yörük 2017). In the first stage, documents on social policies are identified from the World Bank's online archive. In the second stage, these documents are searched for twenty-four specific keywords that are likely to indicate the World Bank's interest in political objectives. NVivo 10 is used to code all relevant documents.

studies have laid the groundwork for cross-national statistical analysis by descriptively measuring the total number of World Bank social policy recommendations across all countries (van Gils and Yörük 2017). This approach moves beyond the World Bank's financial leverage by measuring the diffusion of ideas and best practices. In this sense, measuring policy recommendations serves as a proxy for the extent to which the World Bank serves as a source of information, such as through specific policy reports identifying the changes the Bank would like to see implemented as well as technical support for their implementation. Thus, we use measures of both recommendations and financial flows[8] to measure the influence of the World Bank, although most models apply WBSPR, as this more closely approximates what we are attempting to measure.

Several control variables are included to rule out alternative factors which might affect social protection spending. First, *democracy* is often hypothesized to be positively related to social protection and welfare measures (Rudra and Haggard 2005), although previous studies have also questioned this relationship (Dietrich and Bernhard 2016). Thus, in line with standard best practices, we include the Freedom House democracy scores as our measure of *democracy*. We also control for *bureaucratic quality*, which comes from the International Crisis Risk Group (ICRG), in order to gauge the degree to which a bureaucracy is professional, transparent and effective. The bureaucratic quality measure ranges from 0 to 4, from the lowest levels of bureaucratic quality to the highest. Including this measure is important, as it serves as our proxy of state capacity. States with higher capacity should find it less difficult to translate the preferences of policymakers into actual policies.

Along with political factors, we control for several macro-economic variables. As our measure of wealth, we include *GDP* per capita in constant 2010 dollars[9] (Lequiller and Blades 2014). Including wealth in our

---

[8] The measure of financial flows measures the amount of public and publicly guaranteed multilateral loans (World Bank International Debt Statistics). This measure includes loans and credits from the World Bank, regional development banks and other multilateral and intergovernmental agencies. However, as can be seen in Table 9.1, there is a significant amount of missing values for this data.

[9] World Bank national accounts data, and OECD National Accounts data files.

model should be significantly related to social policy, all else being equal, as a greater share of resources can be allocated to social welfare programs. Additionally, we include *GDP growth*, thus controlling for the possibility that any variation in the dependent variable (which is measured as a percentage of GDP) is caused by differences in growth rates. For reasons discussed previously, we control for *trade* as a proxy for globalization, measured as exports plus imports as a percentage of GDP (IMF Statistics Department 2018). Lastly, we control for the *old age* composition of the population as a factor which should drive up the demand for greater social protection spending (population ages 65 or greater (% of total)) (United Nations 2018).

We use time-series generalized least squares (GLS) regression analysis to test the relationship between social protection spending, social unrest and WBSPR. To increase the robustness of our findings, we apply both random-effects and fixed-effects models. To control for potentially exogenous time trends, which could produce spurious relationships, we include a year-count variable (omitted from output tables). The equation for the model used in the analysis is as follows:

$$sac_{it} = \alpha + \beta 1 su_{it-1,2} + \beta 2 wbspr_{it-1} + \Sigma \left( \beta_k \text{controls} \right)_{it-1} + u + \varepsilon$$

In the above equation, all independent variables are lagged by one year, since we expect their effect to take place after a short period, but not instantly. In alternate model specifications we also test the effects of social unrest using a two-year lag. Adding a two-year lag helps us to assess the interaction between WBSPR and social unrest, as we expect unrest to take place prior to the World Bank making a social policy recommendation. In other words, the logic goes as follows: at time A social unrest occurs → at time B the World Bank recommends increases in social policy → at time C countries react to the unrest and WBSPR by increasing social protection spending. The next section presents our findings.

## Results

The results for our first four models can be found in Table 9.2. As can be seen in all the models, *social unrest* is positively related to *social expenditures*. While the effect of this variable is relatively small, this result is in line with our hypothesis that social containment plays a role in translating structural pressures into actual social policies. Models 2–4 include variables to measure the World Bank effect. In Models 2 and 3, the *WBSPR* variable is included to measure the diffusion of World Bank social policy ideas, whereas the total of *multilateral loans* is included in Model 4, as a measure of World Bank financial leverage. In all three models, the effect of international donors is insignificant. Thus, at first glance, it appears that the World Bank is not related to public *social expenditures*. All other signs of the coefficients in Table 9.2 point in the expected direction, except for *bureaucratic quality*. However, in alternative models, using World Bank Worldwide Governance Indicators (i.e. regulatory quality and government effectiveness) as the proxy of state capacity, the signs point in the expected positive direction. As these measures are strongly correlated with our measures of *GDP* and *democracy*, and thus potentially cause problems of multicollinearity, we keep *bureaucratic quality* as our main measure of state capacity, but with a skeptical eye toward how its inclusion affects our results.

Table 9.3 delves further into the interaction between social unrest and the World Bank. Throughout the models in Table 9.3, we include each component area of social unrest used to calculate the previous index variable and interact it with *WBSPR*. As can be seen in Model 5, including the different areas of social unrest without any interactions yields statistically significant results for *general strikes* and *anti-government demonstrations*. This supports the argument that governments tend to expand social policy as a strategy to contain different types of social unrest. Another key result of Model 6 is the positive significant relationship of the interaction between *general strikes* and *WBSPRs*. One way of interpreting this finding is that high levels of strike activity are related to the diffusion of World Bank social containment practices. While both *general strikes* and *anti-government demonstrations* are positive and significantly related to *social spending*, we do not observe a similar interaction effect between the

Table 9.2 Social expenditure and social unrest

|  | Model 1 | Model 2 | Model 3 | Model 4 |
|---|---|---|---|---|
| Social unrest index | 0.00008*** | 0.00009*** | 0.00008*** | 0.00006* |
|  | (3.55) | (3.66) | (3.43) | (2.18) |
| WB social policy recommendation (Dummy) |  | −0.51014 | −0.28358 |  |
|  |  | (−1.75) | (−0.96) |  |
| Trade (%GDP) | −0.02342*** | −0.02328*** | −0.02094*** | −0.02014** |
|  | (−4.70) | (−4.67) | (−4.19) | (−3.23) |
| GDP per capita, PPP (Logged) | 1.89691*** | 1.80392*** | 1.12940* | 2.70511*** |
|  | (4.32) | (4.08) | (2.36) | (4.05) |
| GDP growth | −13.88796*** | −13.86662*** | −13.56768*** | −14.10258*** |
|  | (−9.54) | (−9.54) | (−9.39) | (−7.73) |
| Bureaucratic quality | −0.81088** | −0.80297** | −1.01979*** | −0.97802** |
|  | (−3.18) | (−3.15) | (−3.91) | (−3.00) |
| FH democracy score (Reverse) | 0.21083* | 0.20110* | 0.16033 | 0.40395*** |
|  | (2.54) | (2.42) | (1.92) | (4.02) |
| Old age dependency | 0.57483*** | 0.57242*** | 0.51949*** | 0.48899*** |
|  | (16.44) | (16.36) | (13.74) | (11.12) |
| Original OECD country |  |  | 4.87736*** | 4.29170* |
|  |  |  | (3.52) | (2.11) |
| Multilateral loans (PPG) |  |  |  | 5.63E-11 |
|  |  |  |  | (1.58) |
| Constant | 124.91549** | 106.24240* | 33.4094 | 126.83635 |
|  | (2.9) | (2.41) | (0.69) | (1.94) |
| Observations | 914 | 914 | 914 | 676 |
| Groups | 48 | 48 | 48 | 36 |
| R2_Within | 0.41 | 0.42 | 0.42 | 0.43 |
| R2_Between | 0.81 | 0.81 | 0.77 | 0.86 |
| R2_Overall | 0.75 | 0.75 | 0.71 | 0.8 |

Note: Random-effects GLS regression, standard errors in parentheses
*$p < 0.05$, **$p < 0.01$, ***$p < 0.001$

*WBSPR* and *anti-government demonstrations* or *riots*. This might suggest that governments in this sample of countries implement World Bank practices only if there is a concrete material challenge emanating from the labor movement.

Table 9.3 Social expenditure, social unrest and the World Bank

| | Model 5 | Model 6 | Model 7 | Model 8 |
|---|---|---|---|---|
| General strikes (Total) | 0.219* | 0.131 | | |
| | (2.30) | (1.01) | | |
| Anti-government demonstrations (Total) | 0.052* | | 0.057* | |
| | (2.19) | | (2.27) | |
| Riots (Total) | 0.001 | | | 0.098 |
| | (0.02) | | | (1.56) |
| General strikes x WBSPR | | 0.382* | | |
| | | (2.05) | | |
| AGD x WBSPR | | | 0.027 | |
| | | | (0.77) | |
| Riots x WBSPR | | | | 0.024 |
| | | | | (0.27) |
| WB social policy recommendation (Dummy) | −0.463 | −0.461 | −0.595* | −0.518 |
| | (−1.58) | (−1.57) | (−1.96) | (−1.68) |
| Trade (%GDP) | −0.024*** | −0.025*** | −0.023*** | −0.024*** |
| | (−4.76) | (−4.95) | (−4.67) | (−4.71) |
| GDP per capita, PPP (Logged) | 1.891*** | 1.862*** | 1.824*** | 1.708*** |
| | (4.25) | (4.19) | (4.15) | (3.87) |
| GDP growth | −13.575*** | −13.334*** | −13.934*** | −13.988*** |
| | (−9.32) | (−9.13) | (−9.58) | (−9.57) |
| Bureaucratic quality | −0.813** | −0.815** | −0.783** | −0.778** |
| | (−3.19) | (−3.19) | (−3.07) | (−3.04) |
| FH democracy score (Reverse) | 0.204* | 0.209* | 0.205* | 0.195* |
| | (2.45) | (2.51) | (2.47) | (2.34) |
| Old age dependency | 0.568*** | 0.566*** | 0.576*** | 0.576*** |
| | (16.21) | (16.1) | (16.5) | (16.39) |
| Constant | 112.545* | 102.328* | 108.274* | 94.665* |
| | (2.53) | (2.32) | (2.46) | (2.15) |
| Observations | 914 | 914 | 914 | 914 |
| Groups | 48 | 48 | 48 | 48 |
| R2_Within | 0.42 | 0.42 | 0.42 | 0.41 |
| R2_Between | 0.81 | 0.81 | 0.81 | 0.81 |
| R2_Overall | 0.75 | 0.74 | 0.75 | 0.75 |

Note: Random-effects GLS regression, standard errors in parentheses
$^*p < 0.05$, $^{**}p < 0.01$, $^{***}p < 0.001$

# 9 The World Bank and the Contentious Politics of Global Social... 235

Given the weak significance of the interaction terms, this raises the possibility that the World Bank is not able to effectively transfer its social policy practices to states which would benefit most from the social containment strategy. This could explain the disconnect between a highly significant social unrest effect and the lack of a World Bank effect, despite the evidence that the Bank forwards a social containment strategy. Nevertheless, we remain optimistic that World Bank social policy interventions are related to government reactions to social unrest through welfare provision. We therefore turn to a marginal effects analysis in order to better understand how social expenditure changes at different levels of change in social unrest.

As can be seen in Figs. 9.1, 9.2, and 9.3, the results of the marginal effects analysis provide some support for the interaction results of *general strikes* and *WBSPRs*, highlighted in Model 6. According to the marginal effects analysis, there is a positive effect for *WBSPRs* in countries with more than five *general strikes* in a given country-year. A similarly positive

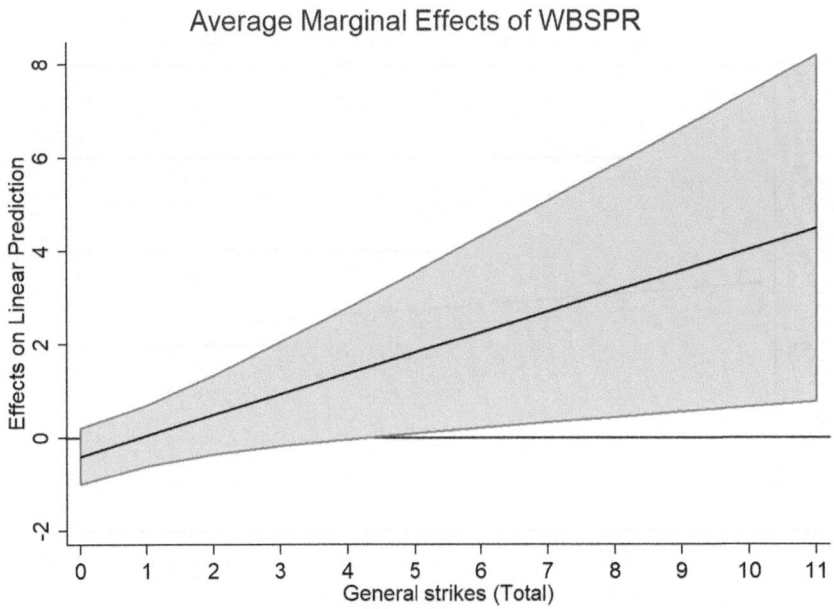

**Fig. 9.1** Average marginal effects of WBSPR I

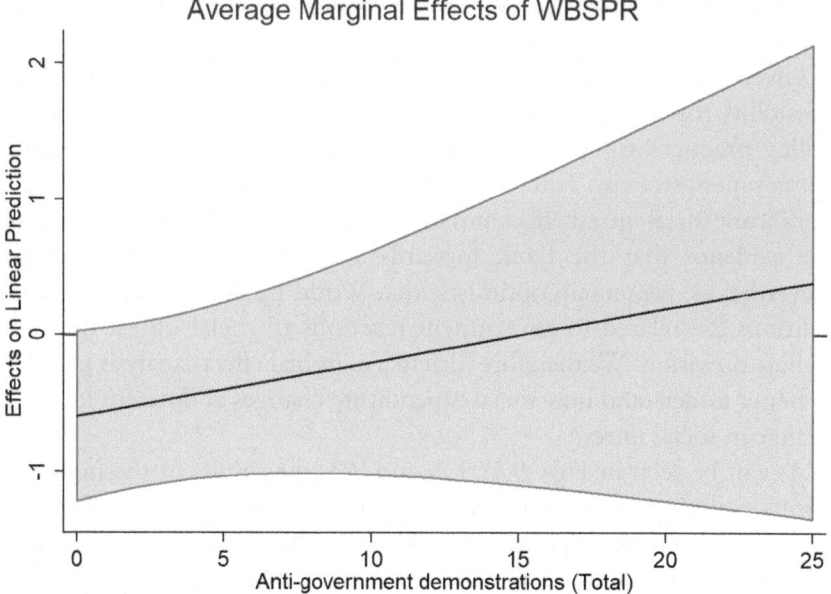

**Fig. 9.2** Average marginal effects of WBSPR II

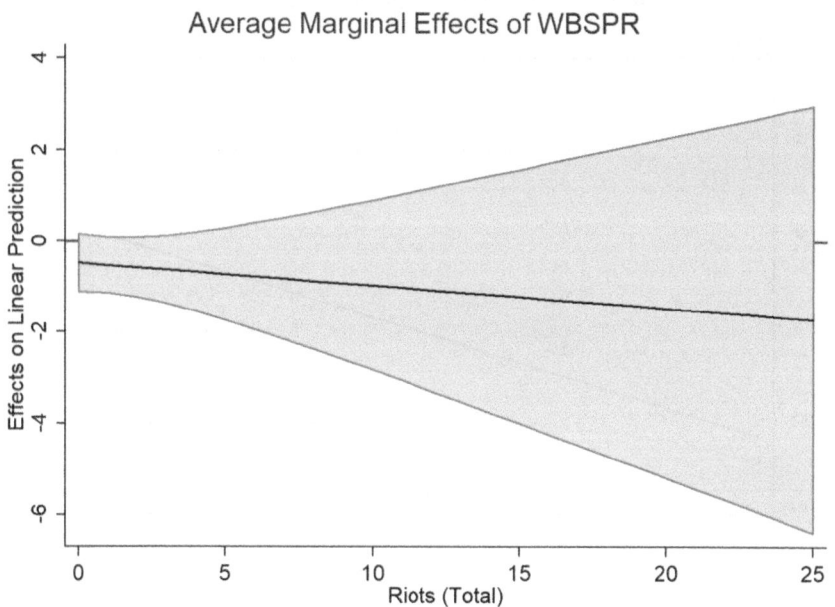

**Fig. 9.3** Average marginal effects of WBSPR III

trend can be seen in the interaction of *anti-government demonstrations* and *WBSPRs*, although this effect remains within the margin of error.

In sum, the results of the analysis indicate that public social spending and social unrest in general, and general strikes and anti-government demonstrations in particular, are significantly and positively related to each other. We also observe that in the case of general strikes this positive effect on social expenditures is heightened if interacted with WBSPRs. We interpret these findings to indicate that social protection spending is extended by policymakers by following the recommendations of the World Bank, as a securitization strategy to contain labor unrest. In general, we suggest that the securitization of social welfare policies depends on an understanding by policymakers that contentious groups may transform grievances into further political activism. Therefore, alleviating these grievances through social spending is seen as an "instrument" rather than an end in itself, to undermine the conditions of this radicalization. Finally, we take these findings to suggest that, at least in the case of general strikes, the World Bank does not solely consider the well-being of people when making social policy recommendations but also as a means of achieving similar political objectives.

## Conclusions

There has recently been a global surge in public social spending. In this chapter we argue that social unrest is a key "political" factor that drives this expansion, translating "structural" pressures into social expenditures. We analyzed a cross-national panel dataset of 48 advanced and developing countries between the years 1989 and 2015. Our results indicate that social unrest, in general, and general strikes and anti-government demonstrations, in particular, have a positive relationship with social expenditures. We also find that when general strikes are interacted with WBSPRs, there is a positive interaction effect. This suggests that governments are more likely to translate WBSPRs into an expansion of social expenditure in countries with a higher number of general strikes. We take these findings to indicate that social policies are adopted and extended by policymakers, at least partially, as a benevolent strategy to contain social unrest. Finally, the results provide some support for the argument that international institutions, such as the World Bank, do not solely consider the well-being of people as an end in itself but also as a means of promoting political stability.

Although we remain optimistic about the World Bank's role in the process outlined above, we are forced to deal with the fact that our results generally indicate a weak or insignificant relationship between WBSPR and social protection spending. As donors such as the World Bank are mainly interested in promoting social policy changes in certain programs, such as poverty relief, it is possible that these ideas are being diffused to policymakers without making a statistically significant short-term impact on overall social spending. Recent regional studies have begun to investigate this and have indeed found a significant relationship between the World Bank's influence and the adoption of specific social welfare programs, such as conditional cash transfers (Simpson 2018). We therefore encourage future works to further investigate the mechanisms underlying the relationship between social spending and the World Bank's influence through more regional and in-depth case study analyses.

## Appendix: Country List

| | |
|---|---|
| Argentina | Japan |
| Australia | Latvia |
| Austria | Malaysia |
| Bangladesh | Mexico |
| Belgium | Netherlands |
| Brazil | New Zealand |
| Bulgaria | Norway |
| Canada | Oman |
| Chile | Pakistan |
| China | Peru |
| Colombia | Philippines |
| Czech Republic | Poland |
| Denmark | Portugal |
| Estonia | Russia |
| Finland | Slovak Republic |
| France | Slovenia |

*(continued)*

(continued)

| | |
|---|---|
| Germany | South Africa |
| Greece | South Korea |
| Hungary | Spain |
| India | Sweden |
| Indonesia | Switzerland |
| Ireland | Turkey |
| Israel | United Kingdom |
| Italy | United States |

# References

Avelino, George, David S. Brown, and Wendy Hunter. 2005. The Effects of Capital Mobility, Trade Openness, and Democracy on Social Spending in Latin America, 1980–1999. *American Journal of Political Science* 49 (3): 625–641.

Barnett, Michael N., and Martha Finnemore. 2004. *Rules for the World: International Organizations in Global Politics*. Ithaca, NY: Cornell University Press.

Benjamin, Bret. n.d. *Invested Interests: Invested Interests: Capital, Culture, and the World Bank*. Accessed 25 July 2019. https://www.upress.umn.edu/book-division/books/invested-interests.

Brooks, Sarah M. 2004. What Was the Role of International Financial Institutions in the Diffusion of Social Security Reform in Latin America? In *Learning from Foreign Models in Latin American Policy Reform*, ed. Kurt Weyland. Washington, DC; Baltimore: Woodrow Wilson Center Press.

———. 2015. Social Protection for the Poorest: The Adoption of Antipoverty Cash Transfer Programs in the Global South. *Politics and Society* 43 (4): 551–582.

Burgoon, Brian. 2006. On Welfare and Terror Social Welfare Policies and Political-Economic Roots of Terrorism. *Journal of Conflict Resolution* 50 (2): 176–203.

Cerutti, Paula, Anna Fruttero, Margaret Grosh, Silvana Kostenbaum, Maria Laura Oliveri, Claudia Rodriguez-Alas, and Victoria Strokova. 2014. *Social Assistance and Labor Market Programs in Latin America: Methodology and Key Findings from the Social Protection Database*. Social Protection & Labor

Discussion Papers No. 1401. Washington, DC: World Bank Group. Accessed 7 November 2015. http://documents.worldbank.org/curated/en/2014/06/19737118/social-assistance-labor-market-programs-latin-america-methodology-key-findings-social-protection-database.

Cowgill, Donald O. 1974. The Aging of Populations and Societies. *The Annals of the American Academy of Political and Social Science* 415 (1): 1–18.

Dawson, Richard E., and James A. Robinson. 1963. Inter-Party Competition, Economic Variables, and Welfare Policies in the American States. *The Journal of Politics* 25 (2): 265–289.

Dietrich, Simone, and Michael Bernhard. 2016. State or Regime? The Impact of Institutions on Welfare Outcomes. *The European Journal of Development Research* 28 (2): 252–269.

Dunning, Thad. 2008. *Crude Democracy: Natural Resource Wealth and Political Regimes.* Cambridge; New York: Cambridge University Press.

Fernández, Juan J., and Antonio M. Jaime-Castillo. 2012. Positive or Negative Policy Feedbacks? Explaining Popular Attitudes Towards Pragmatic Pension Policy Reforms. *European Sociological Review* 29 (4): 803–815.

Fleck, Robert K., and Christopher Kilby. 2006. World Bank Independence: A Model and Statistical Analysis of US Influence. *Review of Development Economics* 10 (2): 224–240.

Form, William. 1979. Comparative Industrial Sociology and the Convergence Hypothesis. *Annual Review of Sociology* 5: 1–25.

Garraty, John A. 1978. *Unemployment in History, Economic Thought and Public Policy.* 1st ed. New York: Joanna Cotler Books.

van Gils, Eske, and Erdem Yörük. 2017. The World Bank's Social Assistance Recommendations for Developing and Transition Countries: Containment of Political Unrest and Mobilization of Political Support. *Current Sociology* 65 (1): 113–132.

Goldman, Michael. n.d. *Imperial Nature: The World Bank and the Struggles for Social Justice in the Age of Globalization.* New Haven and London: Yale University Press. Accessed 25 July 2019. https://yalebooks.yale.edu/book/9780300104080/imperial-nature.

Goldthorpe, John H., David Lockwood, Frank Bechhofer, and Jennifer Platt. 1969. *The Affluent Worker in the Class Structure.* Cambridge: Cambridge University Press.

Gough, Ian, Geoffrey Wood, A. Barrientos, P. Bevan, P. Davis, and Graham Room. 2004. *Insecurity and Welfare Regimes in Asia, Africa, and Latin America: Social Policy in Development Contexts.* Cambridge, UK; New York: Cambridge University Press.

Gurr, Ted R. 1980. *Handbook of Political Conflict: Theory and Research*. New York: "The" Free Press.

Haggard, Stephan, and Robert R. Kaufman. 2008. *Development, Democracy, and Welfare States: Latin America, East Asia, and Eastern Europe*. Princeton: Princeton University Press.

Hemerijck, Anton. 2012. *Changing Welfare States*. Oxford: Oxford University Press.

Hulme, David, Joseph Hanlon, and Armando Barrientos. 2012. *Just Give Money to the Poor: The Development Revolution from the Global South*. Kumarian Press.

IMF Statistics Department. 2018. *Direction of Trade Statistics Yearbook*. http://data.imf.org/?sk=9D6028D4-F14A-464C-A2F2-59B2CD424B85&sId=1488236767350.

Isaac, Larry, and William R. Kelly. 1981. Racial Insurgency, the State, and Welfare Expansion: Local and National Level Evidence from the Postwar United States. *American Journal of Sociology* 86 (6): 1348–1386.

Iversen, Torben. 2001. The Dynamics of Welfare State Expansion: Trade Openness, Deindustrialization and Partisan Politics. In *The New Politics of the Welfare State*, ed. Paul Pierson. Oxford: Oxford University Press.

Janowitz, Morris. 1977. *Social Control of the Welfare State*. Chicago: University Of Chicago Press.

Jennings, Edward T., Jr. 1979. Competition, Constituencies, and Welfare Policies in American States. *The American Political Science Review* 73 (2): 414–429.

Kaufman, Robert R., and Alex Segura-Ubiergo. 2001. Globalization, Domestic Politics, and Social Spending in Latin America: A Time-Series Cross-Section Analysis, 1973–1997. *World Politics* 53 (4): 553–587.

Keukeleire, Stephan, and Kolja Raube. 2013. The Security–Development Nexus and Securitization in the EU's Policies towards Developing Countries. *Cambridge Review of International Affairs* 26 (3): 556–572. Accessed 25 July 2019. https://www.tandfonline.com/doi/abs/10.1080/09557571.2013.822851.

Korpi, Walter, and Joakim Palme. 2003. New Politics and Class Politics in the Context of Austerity and Globalization: Welfare State Regress in 18 Countries, 1975–95. *The American Political Science Review* 97 (3): 425–446.

Lequiller, François, and Derek Blades. 2014. *Understanding National Accounts*. OECD.

Litvack, Jennie I. 2011. *Social Safety Nets: An Evaluation of World Bank Support, 2000–2010*. The World Bank. Accessed 24 July 2019. http://documents.worldbank.org/curated/en/454481468165258565/Social-safety-nets-an-evaluation-of-World-Bank-support-2000-2010.

Mishra, Ramesh. 1996. The Welfare of Nations. In *States Against Markets: The Limits of Globalization*, ed. Robert Boyer and Daniel Drache, 238–251. London, New York: Routledge.

Morrison, Kevin. 2013. Membership No Longer Has Its Privileges: The Declining Informal Influence of Board Members on IDA Lending. *The Review of International Organizations* 8 (2): 291–312.

O'Connor, James. 1973. *The Fiscal Crisis of the State*. New Brunswick, NJ: St. Martin's.

Offe, Claus. 1982. Some Contradictions of the Modern Welfare State. *Critical Social Policy* 2 (5): 7–16.

———. 1984. *Contradictions of the Welfare State*. Cambridge, MA: The MIT Press.

Olson, L. 1982. *The Political Economy of the Welfare State*. New York: Columbia University Press.

Pampel, Fred C., and Jane A. Weiss. 1983. Economic Development, Pension Policies, and the Labor Force Participation of Aged Males: A Cross-National, Longitudinal Approach. *American Journal of Sociology* 89 (2): 350–372.

Pierson, Paul. 2001. *The New Politics of the Welfare State*. Oxford: Oxford University Press.

Piven, Frances Fox, and Richard A. Cloward. 1971. *Regulating the Poor: The Functions of Public Welfare*. New York: Pantheon Books.

Radin, Dagmar. 2008. World Bank Funding and Health Care Sector Performance in Central and Eastern Europe. *International Political Science Review* 29 (3): 325–347.

Rudra, Nita. 2002. Globalization and the Decline of the Welfare State in Less-Developed Countries. *International Organization* 56 (2): 411–445.

———. 2008. *Globalization and the Race to the Bottom in Developing Countries: Who Really Gets Hurt?* Cambridge: Cambridge University Press.

Rudra, Nita, and Stephan Haggard. 2005. Globalization, Democracy, and Effective Welfare Spending in the Developing World. *Comparative Political Studies* 38 (9): 1015–1049.

Scruggs, Lyle A., and James P. Allan. 2008. Social Stratification and Welfare Regimes for the Twenty-First Century: Revisiting the Three Worlds of Welfare Capitalism. *World Politics* 60 (4): 642–664.

Simpson, Joshua. 2018. Do Donors Matter Most? An Analysis of Conditional Cash Transfer Adoption in Sub-Saharan Africa. *Global Social Policy* 18 (2): 143–168.

Taydas, Zeynep, and Dursun Peksen. 2012. Can States Buy Peace? Social Welfare Spending and Civil Conflicts. *Journal of Peace Research* 49 (2): 273–287.

Toye, John. 2009. Social Knowledge and International Policymaking at the World Bank. *Progress in Development Studies* 9 (4): 297–310.
United Nations. 2018. United Nations World Population Prospects.
Van de Laar, Aart J.M. 1976. The World Bank and the World's Poor. *World Development* 4 (10): 837–851.
Weaver, Catherine. 2008. *Hypocrisy Trap: The World Bank and the Poverty of Reform*. Princeton: Princeton University Press. Accessed 25 July 2019. https://press.princeton.edu/titles/8779.html.
Weaver, Catherine, and Ralf J. Leiteritz. 2005. Our Poverty Is a World Full of Dreams: Reforming the World Bank. *Global Governance* 11 (3): 369–388. Accessed 25 July 2019. https://www.researchgate.net/publication/261776065_Our_Poverty_Is_a_World_Full_of_Dreams_Reforming_the_World_Bank.
Weiss, Linda. 2005. The State-Augmenting Effects of Globalisation. *New Political Economy* 10 (3): 345–353.
Wibbels, Erik. 2006. Dependency Revisited: International Markets, Business Cycles, and Social Spending in the Developing World. *International Organization* 60 (2): 433–468.
World Bank. 2015. *The State of Social Safety Nets 2015*. Washington, DC: World Bank. Accessed 7 November 2015. http://elibrary.worldbank.org/doi/book/10.1596/978-1-4648-0543-1.

**Open Access** This chapter is licensed under the terms of the Creative Commons Attribution 4.0 International License (http://creativecommons.org/licenses/by/4.0/), which permits use, sharing, adaptation, distribution and reproduction in any medium or format, as long as you give appropriate credit to the original author(s) and the source, provide a link to the Creative Commons licence and indicate if changes were made.

The images or other third party material in this chapter are included in the chapter's Creative Commons licence, unless indicated otherwise in a credit line to the material. If material is not included in the chapter's Creative Commons licence and your intended use is not permitted by statutory regulation or exceeds the permitted use, you will need to obtain permission directly from the copyright holder.

# 10

# The Limits of the Influence of International Donors: Social Protection in Botswana

Isaac Chinyoka and Marianne S. Ulriksen

## Introduction

Few scholars would question that there has been a "Global Rise of Social Cash Transfers" (Leisering 2019). Since the "quiet revolution" of social protection expansion started in Latin America around the new millennium (Hanlon et al. 2010, 4), social protection programs—be they con-

---

This chapter draws from the in-depth empirical research presented in Chinyoka (2019).

---

I. Chinyoka
Centre for Social Development in Africa, University of Johannesburg, Johannesburg, South Africa
e-mail: isaacc@uj.ac.za

M. S. Ulriksen (✉)
Danish Centre for Welfare Studies, University of Southern Denmark, Odense, Denmark

Centre for Social Development in Africa, University of Johannesburg, Johannesburg, South Africa
e-mail: mu@sam.sdu.dk

ditional or unconditional cash transfers, public works, feeding schemes or combinations of these—have spread across the Global South. In many of these countries, the "primary and most consistent advocates of social protection appear to be global actors" (Rudra 2015, 468). It is the transnational actors—multilateral agencies like the World Bank and the United Nations, as well as bilateral ones such as the Department for International Development (DFID)—who have been most enthusiastic about the poverty-reducing potentials of social protection, and it is largely through their encouragement that national governments have adopted social protection programs (Deacon 2007; McCord 2009; Hickey and Seekings 2017).

In reaction to global social policy research, which emphasizes the role of transnational actors with promoting social policy (e.g. Deacon 2007, 2013; Kaasch 2013), there is increasing attention to the importance of domestic politics in sub-Saharan Africa. External organizations cannot merely impose policy ideas but need to link these ideas to national policy processes and to connect with domestic policymakers (Foli 2016; Ulriksen 2019). Social protection policies are unlikely to take off, let alone be maintained, if they do not fit the developmental ideas of national elites or otherwise appeal to key domestic actors (Niño-Zarazúa et al. 2012; Lavers and Hickey 2016; Hickey and Seekings 2017; Hickey et al. 2019). Even in sub-Saharan African countries committed to the adoption of social protection, many of the national governments have been rather unenthusiastic about programs they perceive to have the potential of creating dependency and of imposing a threat to salient values of self-reliance and family kinship (Ulriksen 2019; Seekings 2019). Consequently, elites in sub-Saharan Africa have often, at least initially, resisted the introduction of social protection programs, and as far as they have been persuaded by donors this has been if the proposed policies fitted the strategies and ideas of national elites.[1]

While the social protection reform processes have been incremental and the expansion of coverage slow (even if the number of programs has increased substantially), most African governments have gone along with

---

[1] For instance, in Ethiopia and Rwanda social protection programs are strongly supported by national governments, as they are seen as being important for maintaining political stability and legitimacy (Lavers and Hickey 2016).

the global social protection agenda although there is also a perception that the "global" agenda is dominated by a "Western preoccupation with the rights of individuals" (Seekings 2019, 7). Not so in Botswana. As we argue in this chapter, the welfare policy regime in Botswana has not *fundamentally* shifted away from its familial focus based on the conservative ideology of the ruling Botswana Democratic Party (BDP), despite various attempts by transnational actors (Seekings, Chap. 5, this volume). As explained elsewhere, welfare policies in Botswana are residual and family-oriented, their main components being workfare for the able-bodied and supplementary feeding schemes for designated vulnerable groups; only selected groups (e.g. orphans) who have ceased to be supported adequately by kin may receive some direct support by the state (in cash and/ or in kind) (Seekings 2016a, c; Ulriksen 2017). Politically, the ruling BDP has been in power since independence in 1966, and although support has declined over time and some political competition has made the BDP introduce broader social protection policies (most noticeably the old age pension of 1996), the party has maintained a strong conservative ethos in policy-making, emphasizing family, self-reliance and hard work (Ulriksen 2012, 2017; Seekings 2016b).

Being today a higher-middle-income country largely independent of international aid, the potential influence of transnational actors may be perceived as being limited. However, there have been pivotal moments when Botswana was extremely reliant on external support, such as during the drought crises of the 1960s (see Seekings, Chap. 5, this volume), during the AIDS pandemic of the 1990s, which hit Botswana particularly hard, as well in the 2010s when transnational actors across sub-Saharan Africa started to promote social cash transfers. In this chapter we focus on the latter two critical moments when one would expect the influence of external actors to be substantial. Furthermore, we concentrate on child welfare policies—the Orphan Care Programme and the non-introduction of a general cash grant—as the well-being of children is an important issue to both the government and transnational actors. Our analysis highlights that although transnational actors have succeeded with persuading the government to change aspects of the Orphan Care Programme, the transnational actors have been unable to fundamentally sway the government to pursue an individual, rights-focused welfare policy paradigm.

Instead, the government maintains a conservative welfare ideology which centers on the family and self-reliance as important virtues of social security. The case studies are based on an in-depth qualitative analysis presented in more detail in Chinyoka (2019). Before we explore the two cases, we first provide an overview of child welfare policies in Botswana.

## Child Welfare Policy in Botswana

In Botswana, the state plays an active role in providing social protection through investment in goods and services including education, housing, water and sanitation (Nthomang 2007, 3). The government funds self-help poverty reduction programs particularly in urban areas. The poor, however, rely on kinship care by the family, albeit with limited family capacity, and work-based social provision such as public works programs.

Botswana is a case of a "familial child welfare regime" where public provision for children reflects a primary commitment to the family: Botswana provides transfers in the form of coupons for orphans but not for non-orphaned children, however poor they are; instead, poor families with children are supported through workfare or other (mostly in-kind) payments to adults, and through feeding schemes. The familial primarily in-kind benefits are generous per household but ungenerous per person relative to the national and international poverty lines. Social protection benefits are not based in statutory provisions.

To elaborate, children in Botswana are supported by several programs (see Table 10.1). The Orphan Care Programme (OCP) provides direct benefits for orphans and vulnerable children, reaching about 5 percent of all children in 2013; the OCP transfers were US $0.90 per person per day (in December 2017), which is ungenerous relative to the international poverty line of US $1.90 per day. Children also benefit directly from government school feeding programs, initiated in the mid-1960s and taken over by the government from the World Food Programme in 1997 (see Seekings, Chap. 5, this volume). These are operated at primary and secondary levels, and in some cases from the registration of children's parents as destitute persons. There are special provisions for the children of remote area dwellers (under the Remote Area Development Programme).

Table 10.1 Programme coverage and spending

| Programme | Budget (Pula millions) 2009/2010 | Budget (Pula millions) 2012/2013 | Share of GDP 2009/2010 | Share of GDP 2012/2013 | No. of beneficiaries (1000s) 2009/2010 | No. of beneficiaries (1000s) 2012/2013 | % of national population 2009/2010 | % of national population 2012/2013 | % of child population 2013 |
|---|---|---|---|---|---|---|---|---|---|
| **Direct coverage** | | | | | | | | | |
| OCP | 47 | 301 | 0.2 | 0.0 | 48,119 | 40,030 | 2.6 | 1.9 | 4.6 |
| Primary SFP | 208 | 275 | 0.2 | | 301,970 | 268,761 | 16.6 | 12.8 | 31.3 |
| Secondary SFP | 172 | 210 | 0.2 | | 165,097 | 161,929 | 9.1 | 7.7 | 18.8 |
| *Total direct coverage*[a] | | | | | | | | | 54.7 |
| **Indirect coverage** | | | | | | | | | |
| Community Home-Based Care | 160 | 38 | | | 3702 | 3434[b] (6868) | 0.2 | 0.2 | – |
| VGFP | 216 | 166 | | 0.1 | 230,985 | 383,392 (192,000) | 12.7 | 18.3 | 30 |
| Destitute Persons | 207 | 241 | | 0.2 | 40,865 | 30,518 (67,000) | 2.2 | 1.5 | 7.8 |
| Old Age Pension | 256 | 279 | | 0.2 | 91,446 | 93,639 (187,278) | 4.8 | 4.5 | 22 |
| World War veterans | 15 | – | | – | 2940 (5880) | – | 0.2 | – | 1 |
| RADP | 49 | – | | – | 43,070 (86,140) | – | 2.4 | – | 10 |
| Ipelegeng[c] | 260 | 409 | | 2.6 | 19,431 | 55,000 (110,000) | 1.1 | 0.3 | 13 |
| *Total indirect coverage*[a] | | | | | | | | | 83 |
| *Total coverage*[a] | | | | | | | | | 85 |

Source: Chinyoka 2019
*OCP* Orphan Care Programme, *SFP* School Feeding Programme, *VGFP* Vulnerable Group Feeding Programme, *RADP* Remote Area Development Programme.
[a]The calculated totals are overestimations due to duplicate counting of children benefitting from more than one program
[b]Direct beneficiaries; numbers in parentheses indicate indirect child beneficiaries
[c]Ipelegeng is a public works program (work for food). Ipelegeng is a Setswana word for "people must carry themselves on their backs"

There are a number of other programs where children are indirect beneficiaries, such as the Community Home-Based Care, Vulnerable Group Feeding, Old Age Pensions, Destitute Persons, and Ipelegeng (a public works program). Generally, these programs offer in-kind benefits that are relatively generous and family-based in that beneficiaries receive a family-based food basket/coupon determined by family size. Notable exceptions are the Old Age and World War Veterans pensions which are cash-based benefits, but there are strong expectations that such benefits are shared among families, not least because—partly due to the AIDS pandemic covered in the next section—many children are still taken care of by their grandparents or other elderly relatives (Dahl 2014). The government's provision of family-based benefits reflects the political elite's ideas about reinventing family bonds and the cultural practice of sharing scarce resources, including food, in times of need. Social policy, hence, is rooted in the cultural attributes of kinship (Durham 2007).

In the following, we focus on the OCP (Orphan Care Programme), as this is the only policy directly targeting children; moreover, it was introduced at a pivotal moment when transnational actors played a critical role in Botswana, due to the HIV/AIDS crisis. The main actors in the policy bargaining processes were political elites in government preferring targeted in-kind transfers and workfare programs, UNICEF pushing for the introduction of cash transfers and universalization to include all children, the World Bank supporting poverty targeting and the introduction of cash transfers and the United States Agency for International Development (USAID) advocating for full government funding of all social cash transfers.

## Case 1: The Orphan Care Programme

Since the diagnosis of HIV in Botswana in 1985, the country has continued to have high prevalence rates. In comparison to its Southern African neighbors—South Africa, Namibia and Zimbabwe—also affected by the advent of HIV and AIDS in the 1990s, Botswana was one of the hardest hit, with high numbers of AIDS-related deaths, triggering an unprecedented increase in "AIDS orphans". A total of 110,000 and 120,000 children lost their parents to AIDS in 2003 and 2005, respectively (UNICEF 2005). An estimated 77 percent of registered orphans and 16 percent of all children in 2007 were AIDS orphans (Central Statistics Office 2009b, 55). Many Batswana children grew up "as double orphans, in single parent families or even in child-headed households" (UNICEF 2012, 17).

Festus Mogae, President of Botswana from 1998 to 2008, viewed HIV/AIDS as "the biggest problem facing post-colonial Botswana", as it became an economic and security threat to the nation (Kaboyakgosi and Mpule 2008, 302). The government, in collaboration with international donors, mounted a strong HIV/AIDS intervention, achieving universal access to HIV treatment by the end of 2011 and halving new HIV infections for infants between 2009 and 2012, thereby making important progress toward achieving an AIDS-free society (GoB and UNDP 2010), although "its capacity to sustain the response [was] being stretched to the limit".[2] Mupedziswa and Ntseane (2012, 60) argue that "the pandemic threatened the socio-economic fabric of Botswana society, with breadwinners succumbing to the virus in large numbers, in the process leaving behind thousands of orphans and vulnerable children requiring assistance".

The concern about AIDS orphans prompted the government to prepare and adopt a National AIDS Policy in 1998 to reduce "the impact of HIV/AIDS on society" through, among other activities, "provisions for orphans", reviewing the Destitute Policy "to make special provision for children orphaned due to AIDS" and "to make provision for distressed children of parents infected with HIV as well as those sick with AIDS" (MLG 2006, 3). The following year, the *Short-Term Plan of Action (STPA) on Care of Orphans in Botswana* was formulated and, based on this, the OCP was initiated to provide orphans with in-kind benefits to cover their immediate basic needs.

The year 1999 was a turning point in the social policy history of Botswana, as the STPA was the first and only policy directly targeting children since independence. The STPA's main objective was "to respond to the immediate needs of orphans, that is, food, clothing, education,

---

[2] UNDP website http://www.bw.undp.org/content/botswana/en/home/countryinfo.html; accessed 30 March 2016.

shelter, protection and care". In keeping with the BDP government's approach of delivering services to the needy, the STPA emphasized that the government will support "community-based responses to the orphan problem" (MLG 1999, 15), suggesting support of the familial and community approaches that existed before the AIDS era (for more details on this see Chinyoka 2019; Seekings 2016a). Although the OCP's ultimate goal was to remove orphans from the poverty trap (Ntseane and Solo 2007, 93), its immediate aim was to "offset the burden of [families/kin] taking on additional mouths to feed" (Dahl 2009, 29). Hence, the OCP promoted kin-based orphan care.

The value of the food basket remained unchanged, with P21,600 per orphan, irrespective of the geographical location of their home from 1999 until 2009. In 2010, the value increased and ranged between P50,000 (US $41) and P65,000 (US $76) depending on geographic location (urban, peri-urban or rural). The amount was supposed to be "adjusted for inflation at the beginning of each financial year but it has not been reviewed since 2010 due to affordability concerns, to allow more children to be enrolled on other programmes, particularly the increasing children in need of care (vulnerable children)" and to "direct more financial resources towards income generating projects for families with children to increase their chances of self-reliance".[3]

Donors were influential in the outreach of the OCP. Although the government-PEPFAR[4] funding partnership was that of a government-supported partnership, the pressure to target orphans was unusual for a higher-/middle-income country. This pressure is attributed to the fact that until 2013 OCP was funded by USAID under the PEPFAR program through the National AIDS Coordinating Agency (NACA). Although the government was committed to the OCP, its willingness to financially support the program was absent until the 2010s, and the government took over only in 2014 when it started funding OCP from the ministerial budget. While donors were heavily involved in funding the

---

[3] Quotes from interviews in Gaborone, cf. Chinyoka 2019.
[4] PEPFAR: The President's Emergency Plan for AIDS Relief is an initiative by the US government to address the global HIV/AIDS pandemic and was launched by President George W. Bush in 2003.

OCP, they did not contradict but rather supported the government's narrow targeting of AIDS orphans, which resonated with the BDP's conservative ideology, as we will explain in the following.

From the outset, the OCP is not means-tested; all families with orphans under 18 years are eligible for the program. An orphan is narrowly defined as "a child below 18 years who has lost one (single parents)[5] or two (married couples, whether married in civil or traditional marriages) biological or adoptive parents". The STPA further defines "social orphans" as "children who are abandoned or dumped or whose parents cannot be traced" (MLG 1999, 9). This definition excluded children living with single parents, such as the mother only but with "absent fathers", who constituted 35 percent and 16 percent of orphans according to a broader definition (see below) in 2001 and 2008, respectively (Central Statistics Office 2001, 2009a).

The orphan definition contrasts with other definitions both within Botswana and internationally. The Botswana Central Statistics Office (now Statistics Botswana) defined orphans as children under 18 years who have lost one or both parents or whose parents' survival status is unknown, while the UNICEF/UNAIDS/USAID (2002, 31) state that "an orphan is a child below the age of 18 years who has lost one or both parents". The latter definition was adopted by Botswana's neighbors, South Africa, Namibia and Zimbabwe. The narrow STPA orphan definition applied by the government excludes children falling under the "orphan" category according to the international definition. Thus, in Botswana, a child born out of wedlock can lose one parent through death and will not be regarded as an orphan. For instance, "single" orphans (either maternal or paternal) are not recognized in Botswana. To compel absent fathers to provide for their children, "[d]eserted children born out of wedlock were excluded from the definition of an eligible orphan, and therefore excluded from benefits under STPA unless there was clear proof that the child's father had indeed died" (MLG 2006, 4). As a result of this disparity, orphan rates were estimated at 7 percent and 17 percent in 2008, applying the Botswana and the international definitions, respec-

---

[5] This definition only refers to children who had a single parent and lost that parent through death and excludes children who had two parents (unmarried) and lost one parent through death.

tively (MLG 2008). By accepting the government's narrow definition of orphans, the example reveals the donors' inability to push the government to agree to international standards; the donors also (inadvertently) consented to many children being excluded from the program.

Furthermore, although the OCP was a programmatic response to AIDS and the associated social and demographic changes, its implementation was residual and conservative. It was residual given the narrow definition of orphans and conservative because orphans were supported within a family, indirectly promoting the extended family (familial). Even though some rich families caring for orphans might have benefitted from the OCP since it was not means-tested, many orphans joined their extended families in the rural areas when their parents died, and most of the caregivers were likely to be elderly and poor (Dahl 2014). The livelihoods of these poor caregivers depended on the food baskets and were, like other beneficiaries of food aid for the poor, BDP loyalists (Ulriksen 2017). Overall, Mogae seems to have intensified his response to AIDS, but the response (introduction of the OCP) also buttressed his election campaign for the 1999 elections. Without specifying the strategies to be taken, Mogae underscored that "[t]he BDP will continue to pursue new strategies to mitigate the effects of HIV/AIDS and arrest the spread of the virus".[6]

The government had spearheaded social transfer provision especially to orphans through the STPA, without a major focus on vulnerable children. The exclusion of vulnerable children during the formulation of STPA was, as a result of the plan, being "largely guided by a rapid assessment of orphans" without considering "the distribution and magnitude of problems facing orphans (not to mention other vulnerable children)" (MLG 2006, 6). A 2005 MLG (Ministry of Local Government)-UNICEF-supported evaluation concluded that "STPA has managed to reach virtually all eligible orphans with food packages" that "helped to protect not only the nutritional status of the orphans, but also other children in orphan caregiving households, and even caregivers" (MLG 2006, 15). The evaluation established that "orphan" food was shared among

---

[6] BDP 1999 Election Manifesto, p1, accessed 16 August 2015, https://sadcblog.files.wordpress.com/2011/07/bdp-1999-manifesto-botswana.pdf.

family members, suggesting that the OCP basket was already a "family basket" although the government did not initially see it as such. While acknowledging that the move from an orphans to an OVCs (orphans and vulnerable children) orientation was already under way, as some vulnerable children in destitute families were supported under the Destitute Persons Programme, the evaluation recommended that the OCP "move from an orphans focus to an OVC focus" (ibid., 17).

Based on these recommendations, the MLG, supported by USAID/PEPFAR, commissioned a National Situation Analysis on OVCs in mid-2007. The OVC situation prompted the MLG through the Social and Community Development departments at council level to start registering "vulnerable children" who were not benefitting from any other social assistance programs under the Destitute Persons Programme. A vulnerable child was defined as a "person below the age of 18 years who is in any situation or circumstance which is or is likely to adversely affect the child's physical, emotional, psychological or general well-being, which prevents the enjoyment of his or her rights, and who is in need of protection". The number of registered vulnerable children benefitting and receiving similar support as orphans has been increasing. The number increased from 25,483 in 2008 to 29,033 in 2009 and to a peak of 34,633 in 2010. By October 2015 the number had decreased to 33,681, as more children exited the program compared to entrants. Entrants were few, due to the shortage of social workers who were overwhelmed by other duties than assessing referred children.[7]

Donors played a significant role in advocating for the expansion of support to vulnerable children other than orphans. The 2006 STPA evaluation and the 2008 Situation Analysis on OVCs were primarily funded by UNICEF Botswana and USAID/PEPFAR, respectively. Through the evaluation UNICEF, as an international United Nations (UN) agency advocating for universal coverage of global child social protection, successfully lobbied for a shift among policy-makers from focusing on orphans to including other vulnerable categories. The government recognized the expansion as a way to strengthen disintegrating family structures struggling to provide for children. While the USAID/PEPFAR would

---

[7] Information received in the course of interviews with key stakeholders.

have preferred a continuation of merely orphan-targeting (which reveals some disagreement among donors as will be discussed in the penultimate section), the USAID went along with the government inclusion of other vulnerable categories, as political and financial buy-in of the expansion was important as a part of its exit strategy. At the time of the expansion, the OCP was principally funded by USAID. USAID's strategy was first to have the government enrol vulnerable children on the tax-funded Destitute Persons Programme and later allow the government to take over OCP. While the government immediately adopted the expansion recommendations, it took over OCP funding only in 2013.

The USAID-funded situation analysis on OVCs (orphans and vulnerable children) became "a precursor to the development of a National Policy on Orphans and Vulnerable Children", still a draft, that would guide the expanded provision of essential services to vulnerable children (GoB 2013). The draft policy is destined to provide an overarching framework to support and guide the delivery of comprehensive, inclusive, "age appropriate, integrated and quality responses to all vulnerable children", contrasting previous OVC responses which tended to separately focus on orphans and other groups of vulnerable children and did not tend to be well guided, coordinated or monitored (GoB 2013). The policy, like Zimbabwe's harmonised social cash transfer, is set to promote a family care approach to the care and support of OVCs. However, the strategic emphasis of the policy on social protection is "targeted interventions and services provided on the basis of assessed needs and vulnerability", presenting both the "government's intention to promote and protect the rights" of Botswana's most vulnerable children and its minimalist approach to social provision for families with children. The proposed policy has gone through two drafts (2009 and 2013) but is—at the time of writing—still awaiting cabinet review, perhaps because the government wants to "discourage dependency" and would rather support OVCs caregivers through employment and self-employment initiatives to strategically limit the number of vulnerable children depending on government support.

The reforms of the OCP to expand the program on vulnerable children indicate a slight but not clear shift to poverty targeting, reflected by the means test (chronically ill or unemployed guardians), but the provision remained familial, in that the program targeted no individual children but families with vulnerable children. Furthermore, despite the augmented wider range of "vulnerable" children, many children continued to be excluded from the category because the government remained anxious about both "dependency" and "affordability". The BDP administration expected that the situation of vulnerable children would improve and that the registered numbers would decrease once their parents or caregivers were empowered through poverty eradication programs such as Ipelegeng and other government-funded income-generating activities. According to that view, against all evidence reported by social workers on the deteriorating situation of vulnerable children, the ongoing increase in the number of vulnerable children was considered temporary and did not warrant a stand-alone, long-term policy intervention.

In sum, transnational actors heavily supported AIDS programs in Botswana and were able to push the government to expand the focus from orphans to vulnerable children. However, the donors did not contradict the government's narrow definition of orphans nor its emphasis on family-oriented food baskets. As we shall see in the following, another push by transnational actors was the idea to introduce a social cash transfer.

## Case 2: Introduction of Cash Grant Versus Rationalization of the Food Basket

Like elsewhere on the African continent (and beyond), transnational actors have sought to promote poverty-targeted cash transfers in Botswana as alternatives to the largely in-kind, family-based benefits. However, to no avail. As we explain in the following, the Botswana government rejected, in turn, the proposals coming forth (first for a child support grant [CSG] and thereafter for a family cash-transfer program) and instead adjusted the existing programs fitting its conservative ideology. These proposals came in the context of a poverty-targeted program that would cover all families in absolute poverty being absent; a program that was favored by international actors, particularly UNICEF and the World Bank.

The first proposal by transnational actors was a child support grant (CSG). The process started in 2009–2010 when the government, through the Department of Social Services in the Ministry of Local Government (MLG), supported by UNICEF and Regional Hunger and Vulnerable Programme (RHVP), commissioned a countrywide situation analysis and development of a framework for social protection led by a team of international and national social protection experts. The international consultants were led by Frank Ellis, a UK-based social protection specialist whose earlier work in Southern Africa and elsewhere had advocated for universal, rights-based cash transfers. The local consultants were Dolly Ntseane, an academic, seasoned researcher and consultant in social policy and social work, based at the University of Botswana, and Tebogo Seleka, the Executive Director of Botswana's leading independent development policy think tank with a history of poverty reduction strategies (the Botswana Institute for Development Policy Analysis [BIDPA]). The team identified emerging social protection needs for children and developed a Social Development Policy Framework for Botswana (see Devereux et al. 2010; Ellis et al. 2010).

The consultants proposed a CSG with the purpose of "curb[ing] the hunger, malnutrition, social exclusion and other forms of deprivation to which many children are vulnerable, especially in poorer families and most seriously in their pre-school years, with potentially lifelong consequences". Like in South Africa, the CSG "would involve payment of a regular monthly cash grant, (adjusted annually for inflation), to the primary caregivers of children" (Turner et al. 2011, 97) and would cost 1.2 percent of GDP (similar to South Africa) in 2010 (but with the anticipated cost dropping to 0.7 percent by 2020, as the GDP grew and poverty declined) (Devereux et al. 2010). Anticipated to make a broader-based assault on poverty and "substantially limit the costs of providing emergency relief in the event of shocks and disasters such as drought" (Turner et al. 2011, 100), the proposed CSG (child support grant) could be introduced incrementally, beginning with the youngest age group (e.g. 0–6 years) and gradually extending it to all those under 18 years. The CSG initial transfer would be set at "P100 per month (with subsequent annual consumer price index linking)" and means-tested "through specifying an appropriate index-linked upper earnings limit for the primary carer and spouse, and/or targeting it to poorer parts of the country, in order to concentrate benefits on the most needy" (Ellis et al. 2010, 13). The rationale for the grant was its potential to combat the "vulnerability and inequality that is offered by the patchwork of existing social assistance measures" (ibid., 11).

Despite support from bureaucrats in the Department of Social Protection, who thought the CSG "would reduce the administrative burden of screening deserving children as well as reduce workload for overburdened social workers",[8] the BDP government rejected the CSG proposal. The cabinet argued against the CSG, as "not every child requires government assistance and universalism will cause dependency and laziness which is against government policy that is encouraging graduation and self-reliance through participation in government funded poverty eradication self-help programmes".[9]

This view was also expressed by the then President, Ian Khama, who had reminded "the nation at large that … we need to rekindle our spirit of self-reliance" in his 2009 inauguration address to the National Assembly (Khama 2009, 5). Makgala (2013) argues that the ethos of self-reliance and self-help has been part of the Batswana tradition but was being eroded and replaced by overdependence on the state. Khama's speech seemed determined to preserve this ethos. Continuing with the current narrowly targeted safety nets would reduce excessive reliance on government support at the expense of *boipelego* (Setswana word for self-reliance). The rejection also reflects the government's view of the poor, that it should only support those that are poor and not able to support themselves and their families through labor. Contrary to evidence from "Mexico's PROGRESA programme and South Africa's CSG", ascertaining that cash transfers "actually reduced dependency by making it possible for recipients to look for and find paid employment" (Devereux et al. 2010, 71; Surender et al. 2010), the Botswana government perceived that introducing the CSG would mean that even the "working poor" families would benefit if their income fell below the established eligibility threshold, which would discourage people from working for their families. UNICEF, RHVP and other partners had sought to provide evidence

---

[8] Interview, cf. Chinyoka 2019.
[9] Interview, cf. Chinyoka 2019.

for the development of "A Social Development Policy Framework for Botswana" to put the CSG on the political agenda but lacked political support from the conservative BDP government that preferred to continue addressing poverty through economic growth rather than introducing a more inclusive child grant.

Perhaps as a strategy to reject the proposed CSG by transnational actors, the government instead pursued a rationalization of the OCP food basket in 2010. Until 2010 each orphan registered under the OCP would receive his or her food ration. A household with three orphans would receive three food baskets. Rationalization implied that a "family" food basket was provided based on the number of household members. In other words, the basket depended on family size rather than eligible individuals, suggesting a further shift from individual to family focus. The food basket per each benefitting household was calculated according to family size and age of household members. Using this formula, one orphan plus two family members were entitled to one food basket, one orphan plus three or four family members would receive one additional food basket and one extra food basket would be allocated for every two additional household members.

This familialist approach was compelled by the government's concern about reported wastage of surplus food especially in houses with many orphans receiving "more than enough", about an increase in the abuse (reselling) of food baskets and about the financial sustainability of the program. There was a need to "rationalise and redistribute" rations from recipient families perceived to be abusing food for other needy groups. The government was aware of the increasing number of OVCs in Botswana (cf. case 1) and realized that many of the households with orphans, who were already receiving a food basket, also included other "vulnerable" children; the government rationalized the food basket to allow both orphans and vulnerable children to benefit from the basket without having to introduce a transfer specific to vulnerable children.

Rationalization also implied a reduction in "destitute" families, as OCP beneficiary households would not qualify for government support under the Destitute Persons Programme. Consequently, it was effective in ensuring that poor families accessed basic needs but created another problem. For, when it came to families that were not considered under the Destitute Persons Programme but had rationalized food baskets (because they had orphans), vulnerable children in such households were at risk of falling into destitution or remaining destitute. While "orphan households" benefitted from the food component, vulnerable children in the same households fell short of school fees and other education-related assistance only available to orphans and needy students or children. This exclusion error was a deliberate mechanism, on the part of the government, to reduce the number of poor families depending on government provision; as a government official explained: the rationalization of the program is "working for us". Rather than introducing an unconditional child grant targeting all children under 18 years living in poor families, the government opted for rationalizing the OCP food basket as, complemented by the already rationalized food basket for destitute persons, more poor people were already receiving government support.

Despite the government's rationalization of the food basket and clear rejection of the proposed child cash transfer, transnational actors continued to make proposals. This time attempts were made to better align policy proposals with the BDP's preferences, but the proposals were still rejected. In 2013 the World Bank collaborated with BIDPA to assess Botswana's social protection system, focusing on social assistance programs to inform the country's "future social protection and labour strategy and help achieve the goals of Vision 2016", which encompasses lifting "84,000 families (336,000 people) from absolute poverty by 2016" (Tesliuc et al. 2013, 3). Even with the existing safety nets, a large number of families were still living in absolute poverty, while the programs, at the same time, drew significantly on the government's budget at a time where "revenues from mining are projected to decline", and hence there was a need to "increase the cost effectiveness of existing programmes" (Tesliuc et al. 2013, 3). This could be achieved through "a better weaving of the safety net through the introduction of a last resort, poverty targeted programme": a Family Support Grant (FSG). Such a program would eradicate poverty in a budget-neutral way, as it would be funded from 0.4–0.6 percent of GDP redirected from sponsorships and scholarships programs that accounted for 1.4 percent of GDP in 2012–2013.

The proposed FSG would offer "a benefit of P85 per capita per month (equivalent to P340 for an average family of four) to cover all families living in absolute poverty that were not reached by the existing programs in 2013". The grant was intended to be implemented gradually, as its design was to be developed in 2013, piloted in 2014 and fully rolled out by end of 2015 (Tesliuc et al. 2013). Three options for the FSG introduction were recommended: the first two options suggested "replacing existing Destitute Persons and Orphan Care programmes with the FSG that would continue to cover poor and lower-middle income families taking care of either orphans or have destitute persons"; the main difference in the two options would be the extent of coverage, the first option being estimated to cover 24 percent of the population and the second option 32 percent of the population. A third option was a "complementary FSG" which entailed offering "P85 per capita per month to all families identified by the proxy-means test as the 24 per cent poorest, but only to family members who are not already covered by other individual, more generous programmes". Beneficiaries of the Destitute Persons, Orphan Care, Old Age Pensions or Ipelegeng programs would be excluded in the third option. Depending on the option taken, the first alternative would be budget-neutral, while options two and three would cost 0.2 or 0.35 percent of the GDP, respectively. The grant was meant to target families in absolute poverty only, and beneficiary households would be selected through a proxy-means test, receive cash benefits and be expected to adhere to conditions, as the government would only provide cash to "poor families contingent on them investing in human capital such as keeping their children in school or regularly taking them to health centres" (Tesliuc et al. 2013, 77).

Although the FSG was to be a family-based poverty-targeted program resonating with the BDP government's preferences for kinship-based benefits, the proposed implementation mechanisms contrasted the BDP's preferred social assistance design. The BDP favored programs that targeted the indigent and provided a safety net as opposed to a poverty-targeted grant. The government mistrusted beneficiaries for their abuse of cash benefits, and consequently the World Bank's proposal of a cash-based benefit was met with resistance. A conditional FSG also did not appeal to the BDP administration as, historically, the government did not impose conditions on social allowances. Moreover, if introduced, the grant was considered more "permanent" than most of the safety nets, safe for the Old Age Pension and was likely to promote rather than discourage dependency, hence contrasting the principle of self-reliance. The BDP found it "politically difficult" to replace existing programs (options 1 and 2) and seemed concerned about the financial sustainability (option 3) of endorsing the FSG. Olebile Gaborone, Permanent Secretary in the Office of President and Head of the Poverty Eradication Unit, distanced himself and the government from the FSG, saying, "They [donors] are just talking about it and courting us [government] to pilot it but I don't see that happening. We are not part of it at the moment."

In sum, despite evidence suggesting that poverty-targeted cash transfers were more likely to reduce child and household poverty, the BDP rejected the CSG and FSG proposals. The BDP administration prioritized market-based poverty reduction (through labor), with the state providing a safety net largely through in-kind assistance to the "very poor and vulnerable groups in society" (Seleka et al. 2007, 2). These policies reflect the norms of the policy-making political elites within the ruling party. The BDP's preference for self-help contradicts the provision of cash-based support to all poor families with children proposed by international agencies and donors. Hence, these proposals were rejected. "The BDP celebrated rural life, self-help and community, weaving these into a conservative ideology of social justice that decried excessive inequality and legitimated targeted interventions" (Seekings 2016b, 13). The political ideology has perpetuated familial in-kind transfers, preferring modest food rations to cash on the assumption that children will be supported by their working parents or caregivers.

## Resistance to Proposals by Transnational Actors

Why did the government of Botswana resist donor-led proposals for improving child welfare, and how were they able to rebuff the transnational actors' advocacy for broader and individual rights-based programs? Although Botswana is a higher-middle-income country, transnational actors are still important partners to the government in many fields, including child welfare policies. Nevertheless, previous research has highlighted how Botswana—together with countries like Ethiopia and Rwanda—has been able to maintain control over its own policy agenda (Whitfield and Fraser 2010). Not only is the political context such that the BDP government experiences relative weak opposition from other political parties and civil society, the bureaucracy is also strong, centralized and professional; the state capacity scores for Botswana ranking among the highest in Africa.[10]

Crucially for our question, Botswana has a tradition of managing aid resources centrally within the Ministry of Finance and of fully integrating them into its own national development plans. The government refused to accept donor-led coordination, such as in the context of Consultative Group meetings, and instead preferred to negotiate with the donors individually (Maipose 2009). Lack of donor coordination is quite common, as donors both compete and cooperate to achieve their goals. However, the centralized domestic management of aid negotiations in Botswana has perhaps further exacerbated the relative weak influence of transnational actors. In our analysis, uncoordinated and competing policy positions were evident in a number of cases. For instance, the transnational actors up to 2013 had conflicting views about the Orphan Care Programme and about whether to continue targeting orphans only or to expand on other vulnerable children, and, with respect to the cash grant, the World Bank showed no support for the otherwise proposed CSG and instead suggested the FSG. Thus, our findings of the limited influence of transnational actors correspond with G. Maipose's conclusion from his study, that "the government has refused aid when it was viewed as not being in the interest of the country, or when it was seen to be incompatible with already identified national priorities" (Maipose 2009, 115).

Having now dealt with the "how" question, we still remain to discuss *why* the government of Botswana has not been persuaded by the arguments of transnational actors which refer to proven poverty-reducing effects as well as intrinsic values such as the rights of the child. One might be

---

[10] Botswana is the second least corrupt country (https://www.transparency.org/cpi2018) and among the top performers on the world governance indicators (http://info.worldbank.org/governance/wgi/index.aspx#reports).

tempted to assume that because countries like Ethiopia and Rwanda (otherwise also relatively strong in their negotiations with donors) have adopted social protection schemes, it is because these governments share the same visions as the transnational actors. However, like Botswana, these two countries have not tended to formulate visions for development just to be in line with donor priorities (Whitfield and Fraser 2010; Furtado and Smith 2009; Hayman 2009), and recent in-depth studies indicate that the introduction of social protection schemes is primarily to secure political legitimacy and that Rwanda and Ethiopia share visions of productive development and self-reliance, which also sits well with the conservative ideology present in Botswana (Lavers 2019a, b).

In fact, there are indications that political elites across many African countries adhere to conservative ideas of family, work and dependency (Seekings 2019). Countries like Uganda and Zambia have adopted social protection programs, but there are also debates on welfare dependency and issues of deservingness (Pruce and Hickey 2019; Bukenya and Hickey 2019). A relatively aid-dependent country like Tanzania has also introduced a poverty-targeted conditional cash-transfer program as promoted by donors. Yet, as in the other cases, current research indicates a strong reluctance by the Tanzanian government to fully take over the funding of the program, which is perceived by many as giving free handouts and encouraging laziness and dependency.[11] Tanzania's founding father, Julius Nyerere, promoted ideas of self-reliance and hard work, and this tradition seems to stick deep (Ulriksen 2019), as does the conservative welfare ideology in Botswana.

## Conclusion and Implication of Findings

This volume focuses on the potential role of external national and transnational actors in driving social policy-making in the Global South, going back as far as to the influence of colonial empires (e.g. Schmitt, Chap. 6, this volume; Künzler, Chap. 4, this volume). The volume also

---

[11] http://ps.au.dk/forskning/forskningsprojekter/political-settlements-and-revenue-bargains-in-africa/; M Ulriksen can be contacted for more details.

emphasizes the *limits* of such external influences, and the case of child welfare policies in Botswana is a good example hereof. Transnational actors had some success with lobbying the government to expand the OCP from being purely orphan-focused to also including vulnerable children but the ultimate goal of introducing a poverty-targeted cash grant was not achieved.

The Botswana government has maintained a conservative welfare ideology even at a time when rights-based cash transfers are promoted globally. Although the government in Botswana has perhaps been more persistent and consistent in following its ideology, and freer to do so, other sub-Saharan African countries also show signs of only reluctant support for the globally appraised social protection floor (Seekings 2019) with a (renewed) interest for values such as self-reliance, hard work and community spirit (Ulriksen 2019; Hickey et al. 2019). This (traditional) emphasis on the collective—the extended family, the community—seems at odds with the rights-based approach entailed in the social protection floors which highlight the rights of individuals toward the state. Consequently, although many African governments have initially accepted social protection programs promoted by transnational actors, the commitment may not stick so deep. The litmus test of the "Global Rise of Social Cash Transfers" lies in its sustainability, based on government funding rather than external support, and some governments—like the one in Botswana—may prefer, and insist on, kinship- rather than rights-based welfare policies in the long run.

# References

Bukenya, Badru, and Sam Hickey. 2019. The Politics of Promoting Social Protection in Uganda: A Comparative Analysis of Social Cash Transfers and Social Health Insurance. In *The Politics of Social Protection in Eastern and Southern Africa*, ed. Sam Hickey, Tom Lavers, Jeremy Seekings, and Miguel Niño-Zarazúa. Chapter 8. Oxford: Oxford University Press.

Central Statistics Office. 2001. *Population and Housing Census*. Gaborone: Government Printers.

———. 2009a. *Botswana AIDS Impact Survey (BAIS) III Statistical Report*. Gaborone: Government Printers.

———. 2009b. *Botswana Family Health Survey IV*. Gaborone: Government Printers.

Chinyoka, Isaac. 2019. *Familial Child Welfare Regimes: The Case of Botswana, 1966–2017*. CSSR Working Paper No. 430, University of Cape Town.

Dahl, Bianca. 2009. The "Failures of Culture": Christianity, Kinship, and Moral Discourses about Orphans During Botswana's AIDS Crisis. *Africa Today* 56 (1): 23–43.

———. 2014. "Too Fat to be an Orphan": The Moral Semiotics of Food Aid in Botswana. *Cultural Anthropology* 29 (4): 626–647.

Deacon, Bob. 2007. *Global Social Policy and Governance*. London: SAGE.

———. 2013. *Global Social Policy in the Making: The Foundations of the Social Protection Floor*. Bristol: Policy Press.

Devereux, Stephen, Frank Ellis, Nicholas Freeland, Dolly Ntseane, Janet Seeley, Tebogo Seleka, Stephen Turner, and Philip White. 2010. *A Social Development Policy Framework for Botswana. Phase II: Framework and Strategy*. Report Commissioned by the Ministry of Local Government of the Republic of Botswana, UNICEF and RHVP. Gaborone: Republic of Botswana.

Durham, D. 2007. Empowering Youth: Making Youth Citizens in Botswana. In *Generations and Globalization: Youth, Age, and Family in the New World Economy*, ed. J. Cole and D. Durham, 102–131. Bloomington: Indiana University Press.

Ellis, Frank, Nicholas Freeland, Dolly Ntseane, Tebogo Seleka, Stephen Turner, and Philip White. 2010. *A Social Development Policy Framework for Botswana. Phase I: Situation Analysis. Report Commissioned by the Ministry of Local Government of the Republic of Botswana, UNICEF and RHVP*. Gaborone: Republic of Botswana.

Foli, Rosina. 2016. Transnational Actors and Policymaking in Ghana: The Case of the Livelihood Empowerment Against Poverty. *Global Social Policy* 16 (3): 268–286.

Furtado, Xavier, and James Smith. 2009. Ethiopia: Retaining Sovereignty in Aid Relations. In *The Politics of Aid: African Strategies for Dealing with Donors*, ed. L. Whitfield, 131–155. Oxford: Oxford University Press.

GoB (Government of Botswana). 2013. *National Policy on Orphans and Vulnerable in Botswana*. Gaborone: Government Printers.

GoB (Government of Botswana) and UNDP (United Nations Development Programme). 2010. *Millennium Development Goals Status Report: Botswana*. Gaborone: Government Printers.

Hanlon, Joseph, Armando Barrientos, and David Hulme. 2010. *Just Give Money to the Poor: The Development Revolution from the Global South*. Sterling, VA: Kumarian Press.

Hayman, Rachel. 2009. Rwanda: Milking the Cow. Creating Policy Space in Spite of Aid Dependence. In *The Politics of Aid: African Strategies for Dealing with Donors*, ed. L. Whitfield, 156–184. Oxford: Oxford University Press.

Hickey, Sam, and Jeremy Seekings. 2017. *The Global Politics of Social Protection*. WIDER Working Paper No. 2017/115.

Hickey, Sam, Tom Lavers, Miguel Niño-Zarazúa, and Jeremy Seekings. 2019. *The Politics of Social Protection in Eastern and Southern Africa*. Oxford: Oxford University Press.

Kaasch, Alexandra. 2013. Contesting Contestation: Global Social Policy Prescriptions on Pensions and Health Systems. *Global Social Policy* 13 (1): 45–65.

Kaboyakgosi, Gape, and Keneilwe P. Mpule. 2008. Beyond Public Administration? HIV/AIDS Policy Networks and the Transformation of Public Administration in Botswana. *Public Administration and Development* 28: 301–310.

Khama, Ian. 2009. *2009 Inauguration Address by H.E. Lieutenant General S.K.I. Khama, President of the Republic of Botswana*. Gaborone: Government Printing and Publishing Services.

Lavers, Tom. 2019a. Distributional Concerns, the 'Developmental State' and the Agrarian Origins of Social Assistance in Ethiopia. In *The Politics of Social Protection in Eastern and Southern Africa*, ed. Sam Hickey, Tom Lavers, Miguel Nino-Zarazua, and Jeremy Seekings. Chapter 3. Oxford: Oxford University Press.

———. 2019b. Understanding Elite Commitment to Social Protection: Rwanda's Vision 2020 Umurenge Programme. In *The Politics of Social Protection in Eastern and Southern Africa*, ed. Sam Hickey, Tom Lavers, Miguel Nino-Zarazua, and Jeremy Seekings. Chapter 4. Oxford: Oxford University Press.

Lavers, Tom, and Sam Hickey. 2016. Conceptualising the Politics of Social Protection Expansion in Low Income Countries: The Intersection of Transnational Ideas and Domestic Politics. *International Journal of Social Welfare* 25 (4): 388–398. https://doi.org/10.1111/ijsw.12210.

Leisering, Lutz. 2019. *The Global Rise of Social Cash Transfers: How States and International Organizations Constructed a New Instrument for Combating Poverty*. Oxford: Oxford University Press.

Maipose, G. 2009. Botswana: The African Success Story. In *The Politics of Aid: African Strategies for Dealing with Donors*, ed. L. Whitfield, 108–130. Oxford: Oxford University Press.

Makgala, Christian John. 2013. Discourses of Poor Work Ethic in Botswana: A Historical Perspective, 1930–2010. *Journal of Southern African Studies* 39 (1): 45–57.

McCord, Anna. 2009. Cash Transfers and Political Economy in Sub-Saharan Africa. Overseas Development Institute, Project Briefing no. 31.

MLG (Ministry of Local Government). 1999. *Short Term of Plan of Action on Care of Orphans in Botswana, 1999–2001*. Gaborone: Ministry of Local Government.

———. 2006. *Final Evaluation Report: Evaluation of the Review of Short Term Plan of Action (STPA) for Orphans in Botswana*. Gaborone: Ministry of Local Government.

———. 2008. *National Situation Analysis on Orphans and Vulnerable Children in Botswana*. Gaborone: Government Printers.

Mupedziswa, Rodreck, and Dolly Ntseane. 2012. Human Security in the Southern African Development Community Region: Learning from Botswana's Social Protection Initiatives. *Regional Development Dialogue* 33 (2): 56–70.

Niño-Zarazúa, Miguel, Armando Barrientos, Samuel Hickey, and David Hulme. 2012. Social Protection in Sub-Saharan Africa: Getting the Politics Right. *World Development* 40 (1): 163–176. https://doi.org/10.1016/j.worlddev.2011.04.004.

Nthomang, Keitseope. 2007. *Provision of Services and Poverty Reduction: The Case of Botswana*. Geneva: UNRISD.

Ntseane, D., and K. Solo. 2007. *Social Security and Social Protection in Botswana*. Gaborone: Bay Publishers.

Pruce, Kate, and Sam Hickey. 2019. The Politics of Promoting Social Cash Transfers in Zambia. In *The Politics of Social Protection in Eastern and Southern Africa*, ed. Sam Hickey, Tom Lavers, Miguel Nino-Zarazua, and Jeremy Seekings. Chapter 7. Oxford: Oxford University Press.

Rudra, Nita. 2015. Social Protection in the Developing World: Challenges, Continuity, and Change. *Politics & Society* 43 (4): 463–470. https://doi.org/10.1177/0032329215602884.

Seekings, Jeremy. 2016a. *Drought Relief and the Origins of a Conservative Welfare State in Botswana, 1965–1980.* CSSR Working Paper No. 378, Cape Town, Centre for Social Science Research, University of Cape Town.

———. 2016b. *"A Lean Cow Cannot Climb Out of the Mud, But a Good Cattleman Does Not Leave It to Perish": The Origins of a Conservative Welfare Doctrine in Botswana under Seretse Khama, 1966–1980.* CSSR Working Paper No. 387, Cape Town, Centre for Social Science Research, University of Cape Town.

———. 2016c. *Building a Conservative Welfare State in Botswana.* CSSR Working Paper No. 388, Cape Town, Centre for Social Science Research, University of Cape Town.

———. 2019. The Limits of the 'Global' Social Policy: The ILO, the Social Protection Floor and the Politics of Welfare in East and Southern Africa. *Global Social Policy.* Online Version. https://journals.sagepub.com/doi/10.1177/1468018119846418.

Seleka, Tebogo B., Happy Siphambe, Dolly Ntseane, Nomtuse Mbere, Charity Kerapeletswe, and Chris Sharp. 2007. *Social Safety Nets in Botswana: Administration, Targeting and Sustainability.* Gaborone: Lightbooks.

Surender, Rebecca, Michael Noble, Gemma Wright, and Phakama Ntshongwana. 2010. Social Assistance and Dependency in South Africa: An Analysis of Attitudes to Paid Work and Social Grants. *Journal of Social Policy* 39 (2): 203–221.

Tesliuc, Cornelia, Jose Silverio Marques, Khaufelo Raymond Lekobane, Lilian Mookodi, Anush Bezhanyan, Jeanine Braithwaite, Anna Mohan, Mimi Otsuka, Elina Scheja, Siddarth Sharma, Dolly Ntseane, Sasun Tsirunyan, and Molly Schmalzbach. 2013. *Botswana Social Protection Assessment.* Pretoria: World Bank & Botswana Institute for Development Policy Analysis.

Turner, Stephen, Philip White, Stephen Devereux, and Nicholas Freeland. 2011. A Child Support Grant for Botswana? In *Thari ya Bana: Reflections on Children in Botswana 2011*, ed. T. Maundeni and M.S. Nnyepi. Gaborone: UNICEF.

Ulriksen, Marianne S. 2012. Welfare Policy Expansion in Botswana and Mauritius: Explaining the Causes of Different Welfare Regime Paths. *Comparative Political Studies* 45 (12): 1483–1509.

———. 2017. Mineral Wealth and Limited Redistribution: Social Transfers and Taxation in Botswana. *Journal of Contemporary African Studies* 35 (1): 73–92.

———. 2019. Pushing for Policy Innovation: The Framing of Social Protection Policies in Tanzania. In *The Politics of Social Protection in Eastern and Southern Africa*, ed. Sam Hickey, Tom Lavers, Miguel Nino-Zarazua, and Jeremy Seekings. Chapter 5. Oxford: Oxford University Press.

UNICEF (United Nations Children's Fund). 2005. *Analysis of Child Focused Indicators*. Gaborone: UNICEF.

———. 2012. *Annual Report 2011*. Gaborone: UNICEF.

UNICEF/UNAIDS/USAID. 2002. *Children on the Brink 2002: A Joint Report on Orphan Estimates and Program Strategies*. Washington, DC: TvT Associates.

Whitfield, Lindsay, and Alastair Fraser. 2010. Negotiating Aid: The Structural Conditions Shaping the Negotiating Strategies of African Governments. *International Negotiation* 15 (2010): 341–366.

**Open Access** This chapter is licensed under the terms of the Creative Commons Attribution 4.0 International License (http://creativecommons.org/licenses/by/4.0/), which permits use, sharing, adaptation, distribution and reproduction in any medium or format, as long as you give appropriate credit to the original author(s) and the source, provide a link to the Creative Commons licence and indicate if changes were made.

The images or other third party material in this chapter are included in the chapter's Creative Commons licence, unless indicated otherwise in a credit line to the material. If material is not included in the chapter's Creative Commons licence and your intended use is not permitted by statutory regulation or exceeds the permitted use, you will need to obtain permission directly from the copyright holder.

# 11

# External Donors and Social Protection in Africa: A Case Study of Zimbabwe

Stephen Devereux and Samuel Kapingidza

## Introduction

More than half the countries in Africa have adopted social protection as a policy instrument since the late 1990s. External actors have been instrumental in this rapid diffusion of social protection policies and programs across the continent. These external actors, also called "transnational actors", "development partners" or the "international development community", include bilateral donors (e.g. the UK Department for International Development [DFID], Irish Aid), multilateral agencies (e.g. the European Union [EU]), United Nations (UN) agencies (e.g. the International Labour Organization [ILO], United Nations Children's Fund [UNICEF]), international financial institutions (IFIs) (e.g. the

---

S. Devereux (✉)
Institute of Development Studies, University of Sussex, Brighton, UK
e-mail: s.devereux@ids.ac.uk

S. Kapingidza
Centre for Social Development in Africa (CSDA), University of Johannesburg, Johannesburg, South Africa

© The Author(s) 2020
C. Schmitt (ed.), *From Colonialism to International Aid*, Global Dynamics of Social Policy, https://doi.org/10.1007/978-3-030-38200-1_11

World Bank) and international non-governmental organizations (INGOs) (e.g. Concern Worldwide, Save the Children).

The success of this policy diffusion process can be observed in the rapidly increasing number of social protection programs implemented and national strategies drafted in numerous African countries. Rather than emerging from the domestic political discourse, however, typically these programs and strategies have been introduced by external actors, using a combination of "carrots" (financial assistance and technical support) and "sticks" (conditionality on loans, or threats to withhold aid). This naturally raises questions about whether a social protection policy process reflects the priorities of domestic (national) or external (transnational) actors.

External actors have greatest potential to dominate a policy process in countries that are politically weak and financially constrained. The promise of free or concessional external funding to boost domestic spending on social programs gives development partners "soft power" to decide how their funds will be spent, often relegating the government to a passive recipient. This power asymmetry explains why many of Africa's poorest countries have implemented almost identical social protection policies and cash transfer programs in recent years. Most of these policies and programs were designed by international consultants and financed by international development agencies, drawing on ideas generated and tested in other countries.

Zimbabwe is a case in point. The evolution of the flagship harmonised social cash transfer (HSCT) program was almost entirely donor-driven, from design to piloting to rolling out and then scaling down. Similarly, the development of the National Social Protection Policy Framework (NSPPF) was pushed by a range of UN agencies and bilateral donors, who disputed among themselves over which direction the policy should take, while the government was little more than a passive observer. Zimbabwe is selected as our case study because it has received less attention in this literature than comparable countries such as Zambia, where the influence of external actors is better documented (Kuss 2015; Pruce and Hickey 2017). Moreover, the case of Zimbabwe is atypical in that external actors managed to influence the social protection policy process despite the international isolation of the government of Zimbabwe.

Sanctions imposed on the Mugabe regime by the EU and USA meant that major bilateral agencies would not fund the government directly, while outstanding arrears to IFIs meant that the government would not be bailed out. Instead, donors funded the social protection policy process through UNICEF. This is contrary to other African countries where donors funded the government directly to introduce or expand social protection. Finally though, Zimbabwe is unusual because, as we will show, the process of introducing social protection seems to have stalled, for reasons that have important lessons for analysts of social policy as well as for other African governments and international agencies.

This chapter first identifies several specific strategies that external actors have deployed to encourage or induce the introduction and expansion of social protection by African governments. Then the application of these strategies in Zimbabwe is reviewed, drawing on the insights and perceptions of external actors and national stakeholders who were directly involved in this policy process. Finally, we conclude by proposing a checklist of indicators that can be monitored to assess the extent to which a social protection policy process is "donor-driven" rather than "nationally owned".

## Strategies of External Actors

In this section we discuss four strategies that are commonly used by external actors to persuade African governments to adopt social protection (see Devereux 2018): (1) *building evidence:* demonstrating the effectiveness of social protection through impact evaluations; (2) *building capacity:* strengthening the human resources and management systems for delivering social protection; (3) *financial support:* contributing toward the development and operational costs of social protection programs and (4) *policy support:* providing technical inputs to the process of developing social protection policies.

## Building Evidence

In the early 2000s donor agencies designed, financed and implemented social cash transfer (SCT) pilot projects at local level in several African countries, either alone or in collaboration with national governments and NGO partners. The primary objective was to improve the well-being of project beneficiaries—cash transfer recipients and their families. However, an equally important secondary objective was to persuade governments to implement cash transfer programs at national level. The implicit theory of change was that demonstrating the positive impacts of cash transfer projects would convince African governments to take over the management and financing of these projects, and scale them up to national coverage.

For this reason, external actors invested heavily in monitoring and evaluation (M&E) of these pilot projects. One of the first was the Kalomo District Pilot Social Cash Transfer Scheme in Zambia, implemented by the Ministry of Community Development and Social Services (MCDSS) from 2003, with technical and financial support from German Technical Cooperation (GTZ). Monitoring of beneficiaries recorded positive changes in household food security, livestock ownership and other indicators after they joined the scheme (MCDSS and GTZ 2007).

In the mid-2000s several more pilot projects were launched by international NGOs with donor funding in southern Africa, usually running for one to two years and experimenting with different modalities—cash versus food, electronic payments, cash transfers in emergencies and so on. Examples include "Food and Cash Transfers" in Malawi, "Emergency Drought Response" in Swaziland and "Cash and Food Transfers Pilot Project" in Lesotho. All these projects were evaluated by independent researchers who were commissioned by the implementing NGO (Concern Worldwide, Save the Children and World Vision, respectively), and paid by the donor agencies who financed each project (Irish Aid, World Food Programme and DFID). Findings were disseminated through research reports, seminars and workshops, and "lesson learning" briefing papers intended to influence policy-makers (cf. Devereux 2008). However, these were not rigorous impact evaluations—not all had control groups, for instance—which made it impossible to attribute any positive changes observed, with confidence, to the project intervention alone.

As the number and scale of social protection programs grew, so did the size and sophistication of the evidence base. Randomized control trial (RCT) evaluations were commissioned that assessed prograe design and implementation features (e.g. targeting options) and impacts (e.g. on poverty reduction), using statistically significant sample sizes and multi-round panel surveys (baseline, midline, endline) of treatment and control households. Donor agencies synthesized the findings of these evaluations in reports and books that were intended to advance thinking and promote best practice on social protection among external actors and especially among policy-makers in African countries. Seminal publications since 2010 include:

1. *Cash Transfers Evidence Paper* (Arnold et al. 2011), written by advisory staff in the Policy Division of the UK Department for International Development (DFID);
2. *The Cash Dividend: The rise of cash transfer programs in Sub-Saharan Africa* (Garcia and Moore 2012), a World Bank book written by an in-house economist and a consultant;
3. *Cash Transfers: What does the evidence say?* (Bastagli et al. 2016), a rigorous review commissioned by DFID from the Overseas Development Institute (ODI);
4. *From Evidence to Action: The story of cash transfers and impact evaluation in sub-Saharan Africa* (Davis et al. 2016), an edited book co-funded by the United Nations Food and Agriculture Organisation (FAO) and UNICEF.

"From Evidence to Action" is an output of the UN-funded Transfer Project, which commissioned evaluations of social cash transfer programs in eight countries: Ethiopia, Ghana, Kenya, Lesotho, Malawi, South Africa, Zambia and Zimbabwe. This was not independent academic research, it served an overt advocacy agenda. In their "Foreword", the Director-General of FAO and the Executive Director of UNICEF write: "These pages also document the ways in which the Transfer Project has influenced the policy debate in each of the eight countries … FAO and

UNICEF have long recognised the critical importance of working as strategic partners to strengthen the case for social protection" (Davis et al. 2016, 6).

## Building Capacity

An important component of the effort to propagate social protection throughout Africa has been investment by external actors in building the capacity of policy-makers and practitioners from governments and agencies in understanding, designing and delivering social protection programs and systems. Capacity-strengthening has taken several forms, from study tours to training workshops to embedding expatriate technical advisors within government ministries. The justification given for this is technical—external actors are filling essential capacity gaps. "Poor country governments typically lack the technical, fiscal, management and logistical capacity to manage complex programmes effectively, hence the need for external support" (Holmes and Lwanga-Ntale 2012, 16).

But social protection is not simply a technocratic issue, it is ideologically inflected and different stakeholders have adopted very different positions, which also influence the direction that capacity building takes. Two of the leading providers of social protection advisory services—the World Bank and ILO—also run their own training courses. Although the training offered by both agencies sounds very similar, the World Bank focuses on the "safety net" component of social protection, while the ILO favors a rights-based approach.

*World Bank*: From the early 2000s the World Bank ran an annual training course in Washington designed around its "social risk management" framework. This evolved into the "Social Safety Nets Core Course", a two-week course that "builds on the latest developments in safety nets as integral part of social protection systems, to provide participants with an in-depth understanding of the conceptual and practical issues involved in the development of social assistance or social safety net programs". The target audience is: "Policymakers and policy analysts from Government agencies, NGOs involved in the implementation of social safety nets, and operational staff from the World Bank and from bilateral and multilateral donor agencies."[1]

*ILO*: The ILO runs a number of social protection training courses at its International Training Centre in Turin, Italy. The "Academy on Social Security" is a two-week course "on the governance, financing, reform and extension of social protection systems". The target audiences are "(1) managers, planners, advisers and professionals working in social security institutions, (2) policy-planners and officials from key ministries responsible for the development and monitoring of social protection systems, (3) representatives of the social partners involved in the governance of social security institutions and (4) practitioners and consultants of UN agencies working on social protection".[2]

An innovative donor-funded initiative that explicitly linked social protection evidence-building and capacity building to policy advocacy was the Regional Hunger and Vulnerability Programme (RHVP), which ran from 2005 to 2011 and was funded by DFID and the Australian Agency for International Development (AusAID). The ultimate indicator of RHVP's success was its impact on policy and practice in six countries: Lesotho, Malawi, Mozambique, Swaziland, Zambia and Zimbabwe. "RHVP wants to change mindsets, practice and policy to ensure that the chronic vulnerability that southern African countries are experiencing year on year is reduced."[3]

RHVP linked evidence-building explicitly to policy advocacy: two of its "overlapping components" were "evidence gathering (the research component), and policy advice and advocacy (feeding new ideas into policy processes in country governments)" (Ellis et al. 2009, 10). Under its Regional Evidence-Building Agenda, RHVP commissioned case studies of 15 social protection programs (cash transfers, public works, school feeding, etc.) in the six countries, which were published in a book titled "Social Protection in Africa" (Ellis et al. 2009). RHVP focused its capacity building efforts on national and regional Vulnerability Assessment Committees (VACs), by strengthening staff capacities in data collection,

---

[1] www.worldbank.org/en/events/2016/04/25/safety-nets-core-course-2016.
[2] www.itcilo.org/en/areas-of-expertise/social-protection/academy-on-social-security.
[3] www.wahenga.net.

analysis and reporting. Unusually, RHVP also engaged directly with parliamentarians, by running policy awareness workshops for the Southern African Development Community (SADC) Parliamentary Forum and sponsoring Members of Parliament to attend social protection training courses.

An assessment of RHVP's policy influence concluded that it had contributed to "significant increases in the level of attention and funding given to social protection by International Development Partners (IDPs), and improvements in the sophistication of their approach" (Jones 2011, 3). However, RHVP failed in two of its objectives: to establish a regional Centre of Excellence on social protection, and to transfer its website (wahenga.net) to a national institution or university. This arguably reflects not only limited technical capacity but also persistently shallow political commitment to social protection within the region. Once the impetus provided by external financing and expatriate technical support ended, so did the structures and activities that RHVP had instigated.

## Financial Support

Many African governments were initially reluctant to introduce social protection programs, arguing that they are too expensive, especially if they involve regular (e.g. monthly) transfers of meaningful amounts of cash to all poor people (or all older persons, etc.) in the country on a long-term or permanent basis. External actors responded to the "unaffordability" argument in two ways.

First, donors and international financial institutions paid for social protection programs themselves, but with the expectation that governments would eventually take over the financing. This can be conceptualized as a "funding seesaw". External actors initially provide 100% of the funding needed for social assistance programs—as is the case with the top seven countries in Fig. 11.1, six of which are low-income economies. Over time a shift is expected to occur, away from external financing toward domestic financing. In the bottom six countries in Fig. 11.1, 100% of social assistance funding comes from the government. Five of these countries are middle-income economies and one (Seychelles) is a

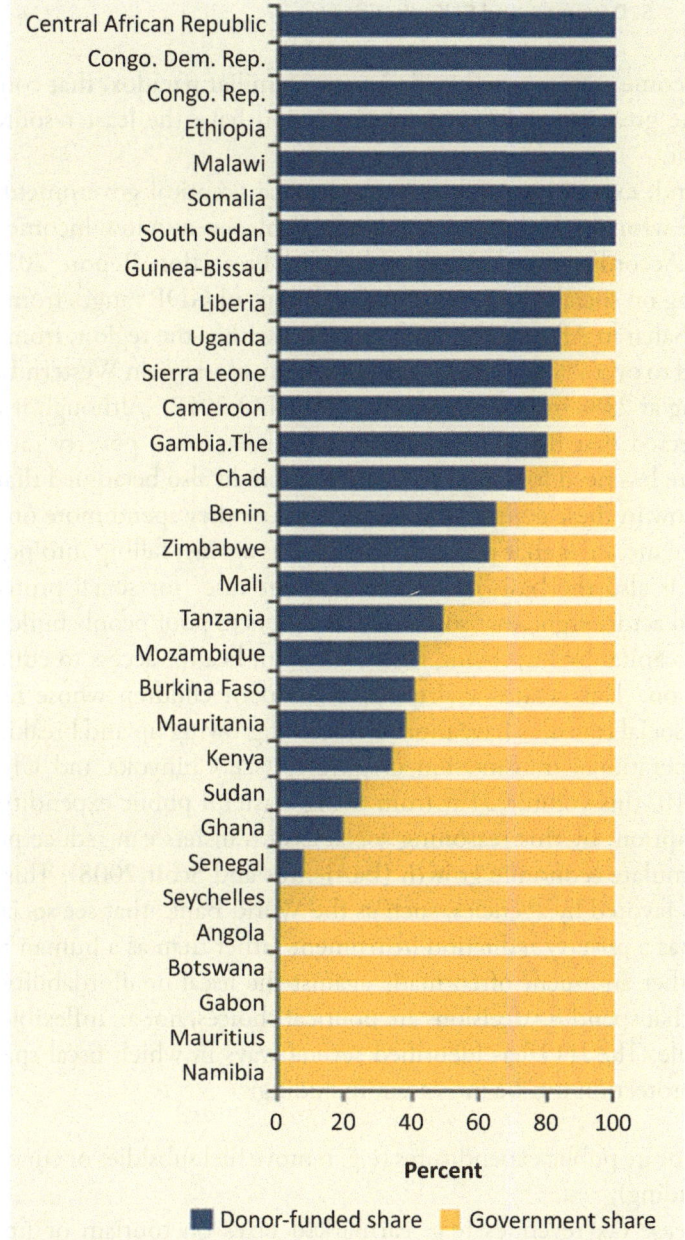

**Fig. 11.1** Share of governments and donors in social assistance funding in Africa. (Source: World Bank 2018, 18. Note: Social assistance programs include "unconditional and conditional cash transfers, noncontributory social pensions, food and in-kind transfers, school feeding programs, public works, and fee waivers" (World Bank 2018, 5))

high-income economy.[4] This illustrates a familiar paradox, that countries with the greatest need for social protection have the least resources to deliver it.

Second, external actors tried to convince skeptical governments that they are wrong: social protection is affordable, even in low-income economies. According to ILO's World Social Protection Report 2017–19, spending on social protection as a percentage of GDP ranges from 4.5% in sub-Saharan Africa (with high variation within the region, from 0.1% in Chad to over 7% in Lesotho and Mauritius) to 18% in Western Europe (peaking at 23% in Finland and France) (ILO 2017). Although it might be expected that high-income economies have lower poverty rates and therefore less need for social protection, it could also be argued that poverty is low in these countries precisely because they spend more on redistributive measures that protect their citizens against falling into poverty.

This is also the basis of the "investment case" for social protection. External actors argue that social cash transfers to poor people builds their human capital by improving their nutrition, health, access to education and so on. This creates a virtuous cycle: poor children whose families receive social transfers have more chances of growing up and breaking the intergenerational transmission of poverty (see Chinyoka and Ulriksen, Chap. 10, this volume). Far from being wasteful public expenditure on consumption, by this reasoning social cash transfers can reduce poverty and stimulate economic growth (Barrientos and Scott 2008). This argument is favored by agencies, such as the World Bank, that see social protection as a poverty reduction instrument rather than as a human right.

Another argument often made against the fiscal unaffordability position is that spending decisions are political choices, not an inflexible technical rule. The ILO has identified several ways in which fiscal space for social protection can be increased, including:

1. reallocate public expenditures (e.g. remove fuel subsidies or cut defense spending);
2. increase tax revenues (e.g. earmarked taxes on tourism or financial transactions);

---

[4] https://datahelpdesk.worldbank.org/knowledgebase/articles/906519-world-bank-country-and-lending-groups.

3. reduce illicit financial flows (which amount to more than ten times official development assistance globally);
4. borrow or restructure existing debt (e.g. renegotiate loans or apply for debt relief);
5. expand contributory social security coverage and revenue (e.g. incentivize participation of self-employed workers in formal social security schemes) (Ortiz et al. 2015).

Although examples can be found where governments have implemented these options—more often in Latin America and Asia than Africa (Ortiz et al. 2015)—donors remain the main source of financing for social protection in most countries where the agenda has been introduced by external actors.

## Policy Support

In the year 2000 not a single African country had a National Social Protection Policy (NSPP) or Strategy (NSPS). As recently as 2010, only five countries had promulgated their NSPP or NSPS. But in 2011, 5 more countries joined this group, doubling the total to 10, and by 2017 this number had trebled to 30, more than half of all African countries. Half of these are in West Africa ($n = 15$), the same as the combined total in Southern Africa ($n = 6$), Central Africa ($n = 5$), East Africa ($n = 4$) and North Africa ($n = 0$) (Devereux 2018). This is intriguing, because West Africa is often perceived as lagging behind East and Southern Africa in terms of social protection programming.

Some of Africa's oldest social protection programs are in Southern Africa—such as social pensions in South Africa (1928) (Seekings, Chap. 5, this volume) and Namibia (1949)—yet neither country has an NSPP or NSPS, nor does Botswana, which introduced a social pension more recently (1996). In West Africa, it appears that social protection policies have generally preceded programs, while in southern Africa, programs have preceded policies. This might be because the introduction of social protection in Southern Africa pre-dates the recent wave of donor-supported social protection, while in West Africa social protection policies were developed with external support as part of a recent push by external actors to accelerate take-up of social protection in these "late adopter" countries. In South Africa, Namibia and Botswana, social protection programs have been well established for several decades, they are tax-financed and they receive very little technical or financial support from development agencies.

At first glance the proliferation of policies within the last decade might appear to endorse the view of social protection as a nationally owned process, but there are at least two reasons to question this interpretation. First, almost every African NSPP or NSPS draws inspiration from four conceptual frameworks, all products of the "Global North" rather than the "Global South". Second, most of these national strategy and policy documents were produced with substantial inputs from international consultants, who were commissioned by development agencies to perform this function on behalf of national governments.

The first conceptual framework for social protection was "Social Risk Management", devised around the turn of the century by the World Bank (Holzmann and Jørgensen 1999). Social Risk Management formalized the World Bank's view of social protection as an extension of "social safety nets"—a term they still prefer—and was extremely influential in the early 2000s, but was later superseded by more holistic approaches and is referenced in only two current African social protection policies.

Another early framework was the "Life-Cycle Approach", which was popularized by UNICEF and ILO (Garcia and Gruat 2003) and remains useful because it disaggregates social protection needs into age cohorts—pre-school, school-age children, youth, working-age adults and older persons—as well as cross-cutting categories such as persons with disability and pregnant and lactating women. The Life-Cycle Approach is the organizing framework for six African social protection policies.

In 2004 the UK Institute of Development Studies (IDS) proposed "Transformative Social Protection", which advocates for taking a social justice perspective (beyond managing livelihood shocks and life-cycle risks) by adding "transformative" measures such as anti-discrimination campaigns to the three foundation pillars of "protection" (social assistance), "prevention" (social insurance) and "promotion" (livelihood support)

(Devereux and Sabates-Wheeler 2004). Transformative Social Protection is referenced by 12 social protection policies or strategies in Africa.

Most recently, the ILO formulated the "Social Protection Floor", a rights-based approach that argues for guaranteed access to essential health care and income security for all, throughout the life-cycle. (Note that the four conceptual frameworks overlap and complement each other, they are not mutually exclusive.) The Social Protection Floor was ratified by all member states of the International Labour Conference in 2012 (ILO 2012). To date the Social Protection Floor has been adopted by five African policies or strategies.

The fact that most African NSPP or NSPS documents favor imported models, instead of building on indigenous concepts of reciprocity and informal social support systems, reflects the reality that the recent wave of social protection policy formulation has been driven primarily by external actors rather than emerging out of context-specific domestic agendas. Many African social protection policy documents are facilitated or even drafted by expatriate experts, who are contracted by and represent the interests of the international development community. The "Acknowledgements" of Ghana's NSPP includes this paragraph:

> The policy process benefited extensively from the technical and financial support of international partners. The Ministry particularly appreciates the collaboration with the United Nations Children's Fund (UNICEF), European Union (EU) and the World Bank in this exercise. Also, the analytical assistance received from the Economic Policy Research Institute (EPRI) from South Africa and the Socieux Team was of considerable benefit. The Ministry's gratitude is extended to United Nations Agencies, Bilateral Partners of Ghana and international and national non-governmental organizations who contributed effective feedback and demonstrated continued interest in the policy. (Government of Ghana 2015, 4)

Some external actors even put their logo on the cover of the social protection policies and strategies they sponsored, alongside the national coat of arms. One example is The Gambia, which displays the logos of United Nations Development Programme (UNDP) and UNICEF on the cover of its National Social Protection Policy (NSPP). Another case is

Liberia, which has the logos of UNICEF, EU, World Food Programme, World Bank, Japan International Cooperation Agency (JICA), African Development Fund and Concern Worldwide on the cover of its NSPP and NSPS.

Despite the impression this gives of unity among development partners, it is important to note that there are deep ideological divisions between them about the purpose and appropriate design of social protection. For example, because of its mandate, UNICEF supports child grants and pro-poor access to essential services such as education and health care. The World Bank promotes conditional cash transfers, which it perceives as an investment in human capital for long-term poverty reduction, and poverty targeting to maximize efficient use of scarce public resources. The ILO believes in a universal human right to social protection, and advocates for a guaranteed "social protection floor" for all. As seen below, some of these differences were played out in Zimbabwe. When external actors are divided about a policy agenda they are proposing to bankroll in a country, this further undermines the government's capacity to lead and own the process.

## External Actors and Social Protection in Zimbabwe[5]

Although a fairly standard set of instruments has been introduced or promoted across Africa under the "new wave" of social protection post-2000, the impetus behind this policy process varied from country to country. In Ethiopia, for instance, large-scale social assistance in the form of the Productive Safety Net Programme (PSNP) was launched in 2005 as an antidote to persistent food insecurity and vulnerability to famine. In Lesotho and Swaziland, social pensions were introduced around the same

---

[5] This section draws on interviews conducted in Zimbabwe between 2016 and 2018 as part of PhD research (Kapingidza 2018). Officials from the government and external agencies were interviewed as key informants and focus group discussions were held with cash transfer beneficiaries. Participation was voluntary and informed consent was obtained. Names of research participants are not revealed, to uphold the principles of confidentiality and anonymity in research.

time in response to HIV and AIDS, motivated by the recognition that older persons were assuming care responsibilities for large numbers of orphaned children. In other countries such as Zambia and Malawi, social cash transfers were piloted and later scaled up as a policy solution to chronic rural poverty. In Mozambique and Ghana, cash transfers are intended to address urban as well as rural poverty.

In Zimbabwe, the main driver for introducing new forms of social protection was the catastrophic economic collapse that peaked in the late 2000s. International development agencies played a leading role in promoting social protection as an instrument to fight rapidly rising levels of poverty and vulnerability. Donor influence was prominent in the establishment of the harmonised social cash transfer (HSCT) in 2011, which overshadowed existing interventions to become the flagship national social protection program, and in developing the National Social Protection Policy Framework (NSPPF) which was passed in 2016. Zimbabwe's development partners used "policy transfer" strategies they had developed elsewhere in Africa to drive the social protection agenda in Zimbabwe, including building evidence and capacity, and providing financial and policy support.

## Building Evidence

A common strategy used by external actors to promote adoption of social protection by African governments was to run a small-scale pilot project, usually delivering cash transfers to poor people in a few rural communities, then commission an impact evaluation to demonstrate the project's effectiveness in improving beneficiaries' well-being, with the intention of persuading the government to implement the project at national scale. The same strategy was pursued in Zimbabwe.[6] Given the fact that social cash transfers were initiated relatively late in Zimbabwe,

---

[6] Significantly, a chapter on Zimbabwe in 'From Evidence to Action' (Davis et al. 2016), the FAO/UNICEF book on cash transfer impact evaluations mentioned earlier, is subtitled 'Using evidence to overcome political and economic challenges to starting a national unconditional cash transfer programme' (Seidenfeld et al. 2016).

learning and evidence generated in other African countries was available. Documentation of experiences, impacts and best practices in Kenya, Zambia and elsewhere was shared with the Ministry of Labour and Social Services (MoLSS).[7]

Apparently convinced by the evidence from other countries that cash transfers "work", the MoLSS requested the donors to commit to funding a full-scale national cash transfer program, but they refused, arguing that they needed to test the model in Zimbabwe first.[8] "Team Consult", led by Bernd Schubert (a German consultant who had earlier led the establishment of similar social cash transfer pilot projects in Mozambique, Zambia and Malawi) was contracted to support the Department of Social Services to "design a national government owned and coordinated cash transfer programme which targeted food poor and labour constrained households" (Schubert 2010, 8). Team Consult was recruited by the MoLSS but paid by UNICEF, which allowed UNICEF to play an oversight role over the process. This had implications for ownership of the process.

Starting with a pilot of just 111 households in Goromonzi district in Mashonaland East province in 2011, cash transfers were rolled out to about 19,000 households in 10 districts in 2012 (MoLSS and UNICEF 2012), extending to 16 districts in 2013 and 20 districts (2 per province) in 2014 (see Table 11.1). A positive initial evaluation of the HSCT led by Bernd Schubert, who was again hired by UNICEF (Schubert 2011), prompted an expansion in coverage and further evaluations. Leading research institutes, the American Institutes of Research and the University of North Carolina at Chapel Hill, in partnership with the University of Zimbabwe's Centre for Applied Social Sciences, were contracted by

Table 11.1 Coverage of the HSCT program in Zimbabwe, 2011–2017

| Year | 2011 | 2012 | 2013 | 2014 | 2015 | 2016 | 2017 |
|---|---|---|---|---|---|---|---|
| Beneficiaries | 111 | 18,940 | 33,200 | 55,509 | 55,509 | 23,000 | 23,000 |
| Districts | 1 | 10 | 16 | 20 | 20 | 8 | 8 |

Source: Kapingidza (2018), compiled from MPSLSW and donor official 2

---

[7] Interview with government official #2.
[8] Interview with government official #3.

UNICEF to evaluate the program. Funding came from United Nations agencies (UNICEF, FAO), a multilateral agency (EU) and European bilateral agencies (DFID, Kingdom of the Netherlands, Swedish International Development Cooperation Agency [SIDA] and Swiss Agency for Development and Cooperation [SDC]). The 2014 and 2017 evaluation reports (AIR 2014; UNC 2017) generally registered positive impacts of the HSCT.

However, despite this evidence of the feasibility and effectiveness of cash transfers, the Government of Zimbabwe has been consistently reluctant to take over full responsibility for funding the HSCT, despite its desire, as expressed in the Zimbabwe Agenda for Sustainable Socio-Economic Transformation (ZimAsset),[9] to reach a target of 100,000 households by 2015 and 200,000 by 2018 (UNCT and GoZ 2014). Coverage actually peaked in 2014 and 2015, when the HSCT paid cash to 55,509 households (Table 11.1), 10% of the national total of 539,000 households, in 20 of Zimbabwe's 59 districts (UNCT and GoZ 2014).

## Building Capacity

In Zimbabwe, as elsewhere, strategic investment in capacity-strengthening became a vehicle for external actors to ensure that they channeled technical assistance toward their preferred programs and policies. Thus, technical support to the Ministry of Public Service, Labour and Social Welfare (MPSLSW)[10] was intended to influence adoption of the HSCT. Capacity building involved the international agencies sponsoring government staff to attend training on social protection, both within the country and abroad. Some MPSLSW officials were funded to participate in courses at the ILO's International Training Centre in Italy (discussed above), to build their theoretical comprehension of social protection and their technical capacity to implement social cash transfers.[11]

---

[9] ZimAsset is the national economic strategy for 2013–2018.
[10] The MoLSS reverted to its former name of MPSLSW after the end of the Government of National Unity (GNU) in 2013.
[11] Interview with government official #3.

Another capacity-strengthening strategy applied by UNICEF and other agencies was to establish a Coordination Unit for the HSCT within the Department of Social Welfare in the Ministry of Labour and Social Services. The Unit was funded through donor resources. It played a secretariat role but it also monitored implementation of the HSCT. "They were actually in charge of running that programme although there were other officers within the ministry who were seconded, overseeing also what was going on for capacity resource transfer, so that when this Unit leaves the programme sails on smoothly."[12]

While donors claim that the ministry now runs the HSCT, since the Coordination Unit was disbanded in 2014, the ministry's role is limited by the fact that approximately 90% of funding still comes from donors and the program has been drastically downscaled due to donor fatigue (see Table 11.1). Given the support it received from the donors, the Unit became envied as it was better resourced than other departments in the ministry. Anderson and Therkildsen (2007, 9) note that "parallel administrative systems to handle the implementation of donor supported activities—such as donor controlled management units—undermine ownership". The Unit did strengthen administrative capacity to deliver the HSCT, but it did not create much government ownership.

## Financial Support

The evolution of the HSCT and the development of the NSPPF reflect how external actors have used their financial leverage to influence the social protection agenda in Zimbabwe. At inception, the HSCT was 100% donor-funded and to date the program is still almost totally dependent on external funding.[13] The setting up of the HSCT does not reflect genuine local ownership and broad participation. The program was initiated and funded by donors and established in parallel to government-run national programs like the Basic Education Assistance Module (BEAM) and Public Assistance. MoLSS only provided implementation structures

---

[12] Interview with a former government official.
[13] Interview with donor official #1.

for the HSCT, while external agencies' funding of the program gave them unprecedented power to play an influencing and oversight role.

Financing decisions provide an unequivocal indication of strategic interests and priorities. As in other African countries, donors in Zimbabwe have consistently shown more interest in supporting social cash transfers than other forms of social protection. Conversely, financial commitment from the government is negligible, violating an agreement with development partners to co-fund the HSCT on a 50:50 basis. "The government never fulfils its mandate to fund 50% of HSCT according to what we agreed."[14] The Child Protection Fund (CPF), administered by UNICEF, is the funding mechanism for the HSCT from the donors' side. DFID is the major donor and contributes 75% of the total cost.[15] In its first phase, DFID, EU, Netherlands, SDC and SIDA co-funded the HSCT. However, the Netherlands and the EU pulled out during the first phase.

Because donors do not fund the government directly, a private security company called Securico collects the money from UNICEF and disburses it to the communities for payment; the ministry only witnesses the payment.[16] Deloitte and Touche initially did auditing until UNICEF persuaded the donors to opt for government auditors,[17] because the use of private security and private auditing firms is expensive and does not build government capacity.

Phase II of the HSCT (June 2016–May 2019) faced a massive decline in external funding that was compounded by the ongoing lack of disbursement of funds from the government. DFID, the largest funder of the HSCT since its inception, halved its funding to £20 million, from £38 million in Phase I. Donor frustration over government's lack of commitment to take over funding of HSCT largely explains this downscaling of donor support. This reflects the dangers of heavy reliance on external funding. No program can be sustained indefinitely by donors, as they are accountable to their own constituencies and their priorities are constantly shifting between programs, sectors and countries.

---

[14] Interview with donor official #1.
[15] Interview with donor official #2.
[16] Interview with government official #3.
[17] Interview with donor official #3.

Phase II of the HSCT therefore has a more limited scale. Only 23,000 households have been reached in the current phase, as compared to 55,000 households targeted in the last years of Phase I. Geographically, the number of districts covered have been reduced from 20 to 8 (see Table 11.1). Beneficiaries in districts that have been dropped from the program were not aware that their benefits were about to be abruptly stopped, because the government did not communicate this to them.[18] Moreover, funding prospects for the HSCT beyond 2019 are uncertain.

Donors also funded the development of the NSPPF from the beginning to its launch, in a process that fell far short of government or national ownership. "Ownership implies that the recipient government's political objectives dominate the development agenda, and that transparent local political decisions are made based on broad involvement and participation of local stakeholders. This requires that government, parliament and other political institutions make decisions about policy and resource allocation serviced and advised by the civil service without distorting donor interference" (Anderson and Therkildsen 2007, 9).

The process of developing the NSPPF was supported by the World Bank, UNICEF, DFID, ILO, FAO, UNDP and all members of the Organisation for Economic Co-operation and Development (OECD) CPF donor group (GoZ 2016). The World Bank funded the first draft and when their funding ended, UNICEF came on board and funded the process until the cabinet approved the policy.[19] The government did not contribute to the costs of policy development. The dominance of development partners in social protection financing is illustrated in Fig. 11.2.

## Policy Support

The idea of developing a national social protection policy framework for Zimbabwe was first mooted by UNDP in 2009, but momentum only accelerated from 2014.[20] There was a realization within government and development partners that the lack of a policy made it difficult to

---

[18] Interview with donor official #2.
[19] Interview with government official #3.
[20] Interview with government official #1.

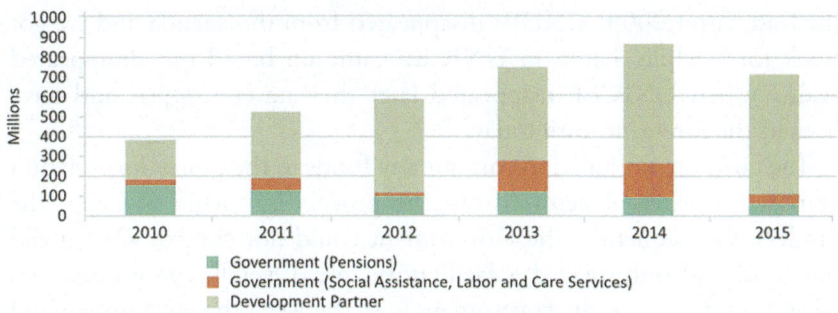

**Fig. 11.2** Sources of financing for social protection in Zimbabwe, 2010 to 2015. (Source: Government of Zimbabwe and World Bank 2016, 15)

coordinate social protection activities. According to a former government official, "In the absence of an overall policy framework, social protection remains ad hoc, piecemeal and of little impact, if any. Harmonisation and coordination are virtually not feasible."[21] National development strategies, including ZimAsset, lamented the lack of a social protection policy.[22] Although a number of relevant policy instruments were in place, notably the Social Transfer Policy Framework, the Basic Education Assistance Module Manual and Public Works Guidelines, those tools and related programs remained isolated and loosely coordinated.[23]

The need for a policy became more urgent after the HSCT program was launched in 2012. "We realised there were other social protection issues that were not covered by the cash transfer programme. So the push for the NSPPF became vocal again as stakeholders desired to finalise the policy document. So UNICEF brought resources to finalise the policy."[24]

The policy framework was eventually approved by the Cabinet in November 2016 and launched in December 2016. However, the process was overly dependent on external funding and for this reason it stopped and started multiple times, whenever an external agency ran out of funds or interest, until another interested external agency stepped up to take

---

[21] Interview with a former government official.
[22] Interview with government official #2.
[23] Interview with government official #3.
[24] Interview with government official #3.

the lead. After 2009, UNDP "disappeared from the agenda and we got stuck for a while. Later on UNICEF came on board but disappeared again. When UNICEF reappeared later they never stopped and have been at the forefront until today."[25]

The government failed to commit any funds to the policy formulation exercise, so external actors drove the process by virtue of being the funders. Consequently, the Government could not control what it did not fund and only played a facilitatory role. Overall, the process was never smooth within the government itself, between the government and external agencies, or between the agencies themselves, as different interests took center stage.

Inter-agency politics also affected the process, as UNICEF tried to advance its own agenda while also needing to incorporate other agencies' interests. A number of bilateral and multilateral agencies were jockeying for influence. While they were generally comfortable with the role played by UNICEF in managing CPF and providing technical assistance to the government, they had different agendas and approaches. For example, the ILO wanted to accelerate the policy process, whereas the UNICEF favored a more consultative and inclusive approach.

> I remember arguing with colleagues in ILO who were pushing the process to be very fast but we said no, we want a national dialogue based process where we try as much as possible to ensure that we involve a wider spectrum of people. At each stage you could get people who would say they were never involved, so we would take time to get their input and assure them that it was never too late. So the process itself was quite long.[26]

There was also tension between UNICEF and the World Bank, which pushed hard for conditional cash transfers, which UNICEF does not believe in, partly because imposing conditionalities violates the human right to social protection.

---

[25] Interview with government official #1.
[26] Interview with donor official #3.

We were quite strategic. When we started to push government we quickly put in resources and brought everyone to the table. I think we played the politics right. We actually requested the World Bank to second a consultant to the team developing the policy just to manage the political dynamics, but it was clear that they were not the drivers of the process. We made sure that the government was in the driving seat, and we provided a lot of backstopping to ensure that they were the ones in charge. We did not get swayed into the World Bank's thinking on social protection. Their thinking on cash transfers has always been conditional.[27]

UNICEF used the "soft power" conferred by its position as the leading funder of the NSPPF to take control of the policy process, and to resist attempts by other stakeholders to pull the policy in different directions. The policy space became a battlefield for external actors led by UNICEF, the World Bank and ILO, as each tried to impose their ideas on how best to program social protection in Zimbabwe. Given this reality, the claim by development partners that the government drove the process is disingenuous.

Due to the leading role of UNICEF and its strategic management of the politics of the policy process, it is hardly surprising that the content of the final NSPPF document reflects UNICEF's influence. The NSPPF adopts three approaches to social protection:

1. *Social protection as a human right*: social protection is an entitlement that the State has an obligation to provide as enshrined in international conventions;
2. *Systems approach to social protection*: poor and vulnerable people are heterogeneous and have different forms of vulnerabilities that require different types of support; and
3. *Multi-sectoral approach to social protection*: a holistic approach is needed that makes cross-sectoral linkages and is anchored in a life-cycle approach, to enhance coordination and harmonisation (Government of Zimbabwe 2016, 24–25).

---

[27] Interview with donor official #3.

These three guiding principles mirror UNICEF's Global Social Protection Strategic Framework, which takes a human rights approach, aims to support the development of nationally owned integrated social protection systems that are grounded in a multi-sectoral approach, and uses the life-cycle approach to disaggregate vulnerabilities and social protection needs (UNICEF 2012).

## External Influence and the National Context

The Zimbabwean case is unusual in the sense that the social protection policy process was introduced by external actors during a period of significant political and socioeconomic uncertainty. The collapse of the Zimbabwean economy, with GDP falling by more than 40% between 2000 and 2008, when inflation reached an unprecedented 500 billion percent (World Bank 2011), resulted in poverty and unemployment rates of 72% and 80% respectively (World Bank 2014). Western governments imposed sanctions against Zimbabwe in the early 2000s over the "fast track land reform" program and, consequently, international bilateral engagements ceased (Seidenfeld et al. 2016). Outstanding arrears to international financial institutions further complicated the crisis, as Zimbabwe could not qualify for a bail-out.

However, after the formation of the Government of National Unity (GNU) in 2009, western governments and development agencies, led by the British, reached a "common consent" with the Government of Zimbabwe to initiate the HSCT program. The international community had a positive perception of GNU, which reflected a compromise between President Mugabe's Zimbabwe African National Union—Patriotic Front (ZANU-PF) and the opposition Movement for Democratic Change (MDC). Significantly, the Minister of Labour and Social Services in the GNU was a member of the MDC, which was more appealing to the international community than ZANU-PF. Upon her appointment to the Ministry of Labour and Social Services (MoLSS) in 2009, "everything had gone down, there was nothing at Pensions and it was difficult to say there was a social protection system in place except a few haphazard interventions".²⁸ She presided over the inception of the HSCT and its implementation until the GNU ended in 2013. Initiatives to develop a national social protection policy also started during the GNU.

Indeed, the recovery in the social sectors during the GNU period is owed to donor support that culminated in multi-donor funding mechanisms like the Child Protection Fund (CPF), Education Transition Fund (ETF) and The Health Transition Fund (HTF). UNICEF managed these three funds as the political context (sanctions and debt arrears) only permitted donors to fund interventions through the United Nations family.

> Why donors are not funding Government directly is a political issue. Relations with the West are frozen and the money is coming from the West. So donors are more comfortable supporting government programmes but not giving government the money. Even when we have the money we have restrictions insofar as what money can be channelled through government systems.²⁹

The political context is unique in the sense that the external actors supported the development of the social protection policy and the HSCT through UNICEF, instead of through budget support to the government. This is contrary to other countries like Zambia and Kenya (see Künzler, Chap. 4, this volume), where direct donor financing of social protection through the government yielded more political buy-in, as evidenced by significant expansion of cash transfers coverage and increasing funding from the government. The attempt to persuade the government of Zimbabwe to adopt the HSCT as the flagship social protection intervention to replace existing safety net programs reflects similar experiences in other African countries, as does the influential role played by UNICEF, DFID, ILO and World Bank—four of the leading global agencies working on social protection in Africa.

---

[28] Interview with a former cabinet minister.
[29] Interview with government official #3.

## Conclusions

The rapid rise of social protection as a development policy agenda in Africa, as reflected in the ever increasing numbers of strategies, programs and poor or vulnerable people reached by social cash transfers and related interventions, can be seen as a success story for African governments who have adopted and implemented these ideas. But it is equally a success story for the external actors who have driven this agenda energetically across Africa, with substantial investments of financial resources and technical expertise, for the past two decades. Using an array of instruments of "soft power", the international development community has cajoled and supported African governments to introduce and scale up cash transfer projects, to formulate and promulgate national social protection policies or strategies and to build increasingly complex social protection systems.

Reflecting on the Zimbabwean experience, which in many respects mirrors that of other African countries, allows us to identify several indicators of the extent to which a social protection policy process can be characterized as "donor-driven" rather than "nationally owned". These indicators include:

1. whether the policy process is conceived, designed and facilitated mainly by external actors through their advisors and consultants, or is truly led by government policy-makers and officials;
2. whether consultation processes are tokenistic and dominated by elites, or wide-ranging and genuinely inclusive of grassroots organizations and poor people (i.e. prospective beneficiaries);
3. whether external actors favor specific instruments (e.g. SCT) rather than other instruments that may be favored by African governments (e.g. agricultural input subsidies);
4. if a donor-supported pilot project becomes a flagship national program, to the detriment of existing national programs that do not receive donor support;

5. whether evaluations of social protection programs are commissioned by external actors and conducted by international research institutes, or commissioned by the government and conducted by local researchers;
6. the proportion of social protection spending that is financed by external actors, versus domestic resource mobilization and government commitment to co-financing that is actually disbursed.

Social protection in Zimbabwe fails the test of national ownership on all six criteria. The Zimbabwean case illustrates the influential role of external actors in the social protection policy transfer process. In particular, it reveals how development partners working in African countries are political actors who use their financial leverage and technical expertise to advance their interests in the social protection agenda, while claiming neutrality and presenting their policy advice as being grounded in technical analysis and empirical evidence. Ultimately, institutionalizing social protection in African countries is not a consensus-building exercise, but a contestation and negotiation among a range of development partners—each of which strives to impose its preferred approach on the policy process—as well as between these external actors and the national government.

The story of social protection in Zimbabwe to date is instructive. Although the international actors deployed the strategies they had applied successfully in several other African countries to induce the adoption of cash transfer programs, these strategies appear to have failed in Zimbabwe, because the process of its introduction was flawed. One clear implication, for Zimbabwe and elsewhere, is that negotiations between national governments and international actors about which policies and processes international actors support in a country must be based on genuine consensus-building about policy priorities, agreed modalities, realistic timelines and division of responsibilities in terms of financing and implementation. Otherwise there is a real risk, as the Zimbabwe case reveals, of social protection programs being introduced and then withdrawn, and the biggest losers from a failed social protection policy process are those who were supposed to benefit—the poor and vulnerable.

# References

American Institutes for Research. 2014. *12-Month Impact Report for Zimbabwe's Harmonised Social Cash Transfer Programmes*. Washington, DC: AIR.

Anderson, Ole, and Ole Therkildsen. 2007. *Harmonisation and Alignment: The Double-Edged Swords of Budgetary Support and Decentralised Aid Administration*. DIIS Working Paper 4, Copenhagen: Danish Institute for International Studies (DIIS).

Arnold, Catherine, Tim Conway, and Matthew Greenslade. 2011. *Cash Transfers Evidence Paper*. London: DFID.

Barrientos, Armando, and James Scott. 2008. *Social Transfers and Growth: A Review*. BWPI Working Paper 52, Manchester: Brooks World Poverty Institute.

Bastagli, Francesca, Jessica Hagen-Zanker, Luke Harman, Valentina Barca, Georgina Sturge, and Tanja Schmidt, with Luca Pellerano. 2016. *Cash Transfers: What Does The Evidence Say? A Rigorous Review of Programme Impact and of the Role of Design and Implementation Features*. London: ODI.

Davis, Benjamin, Sudhanshu Handa, Nicola Hypher, Natalia Winder Wossi, Paul Winters, and Jennifer Yablonski, eds. 2016. *From Evidence to Action: The Story of Cash Transfers and Impact Evaluation in Sub-Saharan Africa*. Oxford: Oxford University Press.

Devereux, Stephen. 2008. *Innovations in the Design and Delivery of Social Transfers: Lessons Learned from Malawi*. Concern Worldwide Policy Paper, London: Concern Worldwide.

———. 2018. *The rise and rise of social protection in Africa*. Keynote speech at the international workshop: Building Social Protection Systems in the Global South: Different Trajectories and the Influence of External Factors. Bremen: University of Bremen.

Devereux, Stephen, and Rachel Sabates-Wheeler. 2004. Transformative Social Protection. In *IDS Working Paper 232*. Brighton: Institute of Development Studies.

Ellis, Frank, Stephen Devereux, and Philip White. 2009. *Social Protection in Africa*. Cheltenham: Edward Elgar.

Garcia, A. Bonilla, and J.V. Gruat. 2003. *Social Protection: A Life-Cycle Continuum Investment for Social Justice, Poverty Reduction and Sustainable Development*. Geneva: International Labour Office.

Garcia, M., and C. Moore. 2012. *The Cash Divided: The Rise of Cash Transfer Programs in Sub-Saharan Africa*. Washington, DC: World Bank.

Government of Ghana. 2015. *Ghana National Social Protection Policy*. Accra: Ministry of Gender, Children and Social Protection.

Government of Zimbabwe. 2016. *National Social Protection Policy Framework for Zimbabwe*. Harare: Government of Zimbabwe.
Government of Zimbabwe and World Bank. 2016. *Zimbabwe Public Expenditure Review: Volume 5 Social Protection*. Harare: Government of Zimbabwe and World Bank.
Holmes, Rebecca, and Charles Lwanga-Ntale. 2012. *Social Protection in Africa: Review of Social Protection Issues in Research*. PASGR Scoping Study, Nairobi: Partnership for African Social and Governance Research (PASGR).
Holzmann, Robert, and Steen Lau Jørgensen. 1999. *Social Risk Management: A New Conceptual Framework for Social Protection and Beyond*. Social Protection Discussion Paper 6. Washington DC: World Bank.
ILO. 2012. *Text of the Recommendation Concerning National Floors of Social Protection*. Geneva: International Labour Conference.
International Labour Office. 2017. *World Social Protection Report 2017–19*. Geneva: ILO.
Jones, Harry. 2011. *Learning Lessons from the Policy Influence of the Regional Hunger and Vulnerability Programme (RHVP)*. London: Overseas Development Institute (ODI).
Kapingidza, Samuel. 2018. The Political Economy of Social Protection in Sub-Saharan Africa: Tracing the Agenda in Zambia and Zimbabwe. PhD Thesis, University of the Western Cape, Cape Town.
Kuss, Maria Klara. 2015. *The Prospects and Politics of Social Protection Reform in Zambia*. IDS Working Paper 453, Brighton: Institute of Development Studies.
Ministry of Community Development and Social Services and German Technical Cooperation. 2007. *Final Evaluation Report: Kalomo Social Cash Transfer Scheme*. Lusaka: MCDSS.
Ministry of Labour and Social Services and UNICEF. 2012. *Manual of Operations for the Zimbabwe Harmonised Social Cash Transfer Programme*. Harare: MoLSS and UNICEF.
Ortiz, Isabel, Matthew Cummins, and Kalaivani Karunanethy. 2015. *Fiscal Space for Social Protection: Options to Expand Social Investments in 187 Countries*. Extension of Social Security (ESS). Working Paper 48. Geneva: International Labour Office.
Pruce, Kate, and Sam Hickey. 2017. *The Politics of Promoting Social Protection in Zambia*. Effective States and Inclusive Development (ESID). Working Paper 75. Manchester: University of Manchester.
Schubert, Bernd. 2010. *Child-Sensitive Social Protection in Zimbabwe*. Harare: UNICEF.
———. 2011. *Lessons Learned from Ongoing Social Cash Transfer Programmes in Zimbabwe*. Harare: UNICEF.

Seidenfeld, David, Lovemore Dumba, Sudhanshu Handa, Leon Muwoni, Hannah Reeves, and Elayn Sammon. 2016. Zimbabwe: Using Evidence to Overcome Political and Economic Challenges to Starting a National Unconditional Cash Transfer Programme. In *From Evidence to Action: The Story of Cash Transfers and Impact Evaluation in Sub-Saharan Africa*, ed. Benjamin Davis, Sudhanshu Handa, Nicola Hypher, Natalia Winder Rossi, Paul Winters, and Jennifer Yablonski. Oxford: FAO, UNICEF and Oxford University Press.

UNICEF. 2012. *Integrated Social Protection Systems: Enhancing Equity for Children. UNICEF Social Protection Strategic Framework*. New York: UNICEF.

United Nations Country Team and Government of Zimbabwe. 2014. *Country Analysis Report*. Harare: UNCT and GoZ.

University of North Carolina at Chapel Hill. 2017. *Zimbabwe's Harmonised Social Cash Transfer Programme: Endline Impact Evaluation Report*. North Carolina: UNC.

World Bank. 2011. *Challenges in Financing Education, Health, and Social Protection Expenditures in Zimbabwe. Zimbabwe – Public Expenditure Notes (Vol. 3)*. Washington, DC: World Bank.

———. 2014. *Republic of Zimbabwe Economic Policy Dialogue: Policy Notes for the New Government – 2013*. Report No: ACS13915. Washington, DC: World Bank.

———. 2018. *The State of Social Safety Nets 2018*. Washington, DC: World Bank.

**Open Access**  This chapter is licensed under the terms of the Creative Commons Attribution 4.0 International License (http://creativecommons.org/licenses/by/4.0/), which permits use, sharing, adaptation, distribution and reproduction in any medium or format, as long as you give appropriate credit to the original author(s) and the source, provide a link to the Creative Commons licence and indicate if changes were made.

The images or other third party material in this chapter are included in the chapter's Creative Commons licence, unless indicated otherwise in a credit line to the material. If material is not included in the chapter's Creative Commons licence and your intended use is not permitted by statutory regulation or exceeds the permitted use, you will need to obtain permission directly from the copyright holder.

# Part IV

## Critical Reflections and Conclusion

# 12

# Transnational Actors and the Diffusion of Social Policies: An Ideational Approach

Privilege Haang'andu and Daniel Béland

## Introduction

Political scientists have established compelling scholarly evidence that transnational actors (TNAs) such as international organizations (e.g. the World Bank, International Monetary Fund [IMF] and United Nations Educational, Scientific and Cultural Organization [UNESCO]), advocacy networks and epistemic communities can have a significant effect on state policies, on the creation of international norms and on the subsequent diffusion of these norms into domestic practices (Boli and Thomas 1999; Checkel 1997, 2005; Evangelista 1995; Finger and Princen 2013). Predominantly, the transnational policy diffusion literature focuses on

P. Haang'andu
Johnson-Shoyama Graduate School of Public Policy, University of Saskatchewan, Saskatoon, SK, Canada

D. Béland (✉)
McGill Institute for the Study of Canada, McGill University, Montreal, QC, Canada
e-mail: daniel.beland@mcgill.ca

the institutionalist approach which holds that political institutions "mediate, filter, and refract the efforts by transnational actors and alliances to influence policies in the various issue-areas" (Risse 2007, 269). According to this hypothesis, political institutions are necessary and sufficient gateways toward successful policy diffusion (for a discussion see Orenstein 2008). The main task of TNAs, therefore, is to seek strategic engagement with domestic, institutionalized political actors and to create among them winning coalitions for the acceptance of new policies and norms. In this chapter, using the example of disability and gender-based policies in Sub-Saharan Africa (SSA), we suggest that key actors involved in transnational social policy diffusion have overemphasized the role of political institutions. This is the case because TNAs focus their mobilization on the engagement with powerful institutionalized domestic actors to foster successful policy diffusion. However, while institutional factors are important and might be enough to foster success in some policy domains, they fail to explain why some transnational networks operating in the same institutional context succeed, while others fail (Keck and Sikkink 1998). As Risse (2007, 270) argues, the political-institutional approach to transnational mobilization stresses "formal aspects of political and social institutions rather than the substantive content of ideas and norms embedded in them". We selected disability and gender policy domains because of two reasons: first, because the study is about the success and failure of policy diffusion, we needed two policy areas with contrasting success rates. Disability and gender policies, despite facing significantly similar social barriers, show contrasting policy diffusion success rates in southern Africa. Moreover, we aimed at comparing two policy areas whose appearance on the transnational scene is not punctuated by large temporal gaps. International issues of advocacy, disability, and gender became central at about the same time (2000 for Millennium Development Goals [MDGs] with MDG 8 specifying gender equality and 2006 for the Convention on the Rights of Persons with Disabilities [CRPD]). This situation makes it easier to compare the simultaneous fate of disability and gender policies in SSA. Second, both policy areas face similar ideational challenges (e.g. cultural-cognitive biases, stereotypes and marginalization).

In this chapter, therefore, we develop an alternative approach to transnational mobilization built on ideational factors (e.g. cultural contexts, identities, norms, symbols and language) to explain the variation of TNA success with policy diffusion. Simultaneously, we lay out ideational factors shaping social policy diffusion in SSA and demonstrate the necessity of an ideational approach.

Our theoretical approach, contrary to the predominantly supply-driven institutionalist approach, is driven by symmetrical interactions between the supply of policy ideas and the demand for these ideas in the policy diffusion process. Our approach, anchored in the role of ideas in policy diffusion, claims that policy diffusion is significantly impacted by local ideational factors beyond the reach of formal political institutions. As both supply and demand matter for policy diffusion, we argue that the bricolage and translation of ideas are important for achieving successful policy diffusion. While translation is about adapting foreign ideas to a particular normative or institutional setting, so that they can blend (Clarke et al. 2015), bricolage is about combining different pre-existing ideas and institutional components to create something new (Campbell 2004).

## An Ideational Framework

### Bricolage, Translation and Policy Transfer

To conceptualize a policy diffusion approach that goes beyond the dominant political-institutional perspective discussed above, we propose an ideational approach (Parsons 2007) that finds expression by way of bricolage and translation (Campbell 2004). This new framework stresses the importance of ideational persuasion (see Fig. 12.1) for transnational actors seeking to bring about domestic policy change while minimizing the risk of resistance on the part of domestic actors (elected officials and the electorate).

To understand ideational processes, we can turn to Parsons (2007) who couches a typology for explaining political behavior according to two logics: the logic of position (structural and institutional) and the logic of interpretation (psychological and ideational). The logic of

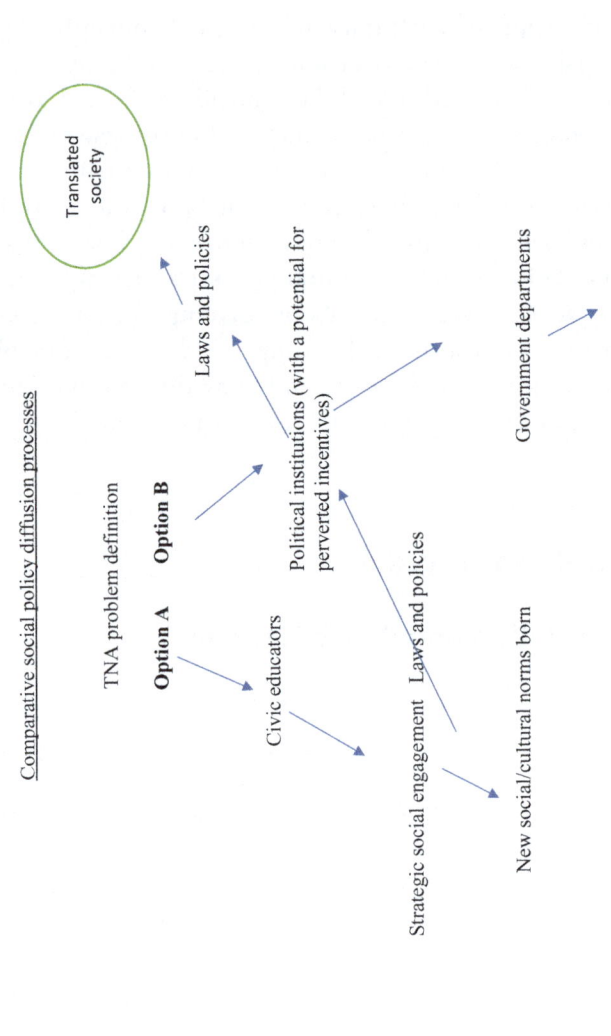

**Fig. 12.1** Ideational negotiation vs. reductionist political-institutional policy diffusion. (Notes: **Option A**: Bricolage and translation (through socialization, rationalization and institutionalization); **Option B**: Political instututional approach)

position "explains by detailing the landscape around someone to show how an obstacle course of material or man-made constraints and incentives channels her to certain actions" (Parsons 2007, 13). On the other hand, the logic of interpretation "explains by showing that someone arrives at an action only through one interpretation of what is possible and/or desirable" (Parsons 2007, 13). According to Parsons, therefore, explanations of political behavior can be classified as one out of four types contained in the two logics above: structural, institutional, psychological and ideational. According to the logic of interpretation, the difference between ideational and psychological forces is stark: the former are historically constructed and the latter are about hard-wired cognitive processes. What we abstract from Parsons is the concept of ideational explanations. For Parsons (2002, 48), ideas—which give ideational explanations of their name—are "claims about descriptions of the world, causal relationships, or the normative legitimacy of certain actions". Ideas are constructive interpretative lenses through which actors make sense of their material, social and political environment.

Parsons argues that ideational claims are particularistic in that they rely on the consequences of prior contingent actions, and that they trace the causes of action to some historically constructed practices, norms and ideas through which individuals interpret the world. However, as Parsons (2007, 97–98) notes, "people may invent a stunning range of beliefs and practices, but they do not quite do so in infinitely flexible ways". Ideational foundations, though amenable to alternative persuasion through framing, foster stable sociological identities. As Trebilcock (2014, 39) argues, because societies' ideational positions are relatively stable over time, they "serve as an important foundation to which policy proposals must generally be tied, in one form or another, in order to gain popular acceptance". The fact that these beliefs are to some extent flexible makes it important to consider translating policy proposals for local appeal to a sense of normative fairness and appropriateness (see Trebilcock 2014). It is this need for framing in policy diffusion that necessitates the next part of our ideational framework.

The concepts of bricolage and translation at the core of our ideational framework are derived from Campbell's work on institutional change. In his analysis of how various ideas can shape institutional change, Campbell

(2004) discusses translation and bricolage, two mechanisms according to which different ideas and institutional elements are combined and reframed in particular institutional contexts. On the one hand, Campbell argues that when new ideas are introduced into a new cultural and institutional context through diffusion processes, these ideas are typically translated into local practice to varying degrees. From this perspective, translation is about adapting foreign ideas to a particular normative or institutional setting so that they can blend in (Clarke et al. 2015). Bricolage, on the other hand, is about combining different pre-existing ideas and institutional components to create something new (Campbell 2004). In other words, bricolage relates to the capacity of actors to create something new out of the ideational and institutional legacies that already exist in their environment (Campbell 2004; Carstensen 2011).

Bricolage and translation in policy diffusion in SSA are necessary to enhance policy diffusion. Empirically, because of its unique historical, cultural, economic, religious and political experiences that collectively shape social and political existence in a unique way, the SSA social context does not render itself adequately amenable to the Western-centric legislative approach without addressing preliminary contextual and cultural factors. As illustrated, existing models of concentrating on legislative procedures and targeting political institutions for envisioned transformation have proved futile and even counterproductive, demanding alternative approaches. In practice, social norms cannot change overnight through the prescription of legislation. Unfortunately, as Grech (2011, 93) argues, the Global South has since colonial times been "construed as a blank slate, waiting for outside intervention". Social norms, likable or not, constitute identities and meanings that cannot be supplanted through legislation alone. As Scott (2005) argues, cultural knowledge is an essential component of policy design and meaning.

Contrary to the institutional approach, the translation and bricolage of ideas offer a more viable and tenacious promise as a mechanism for cultural and ideological policy change in the Global South. This change works both through strategic social agents at the societal level and, although later, through political institutions. While political institutions are often susceptible to political and economic manipulation by the powerful, they are socially ill-positioned to drive such bottom-up ideational innovation. Figure 12.1 illustrates the difference between the two diffusion approaches. In the words of Miljan (2012, 5), "a program, law, or regulation hardly ever 'solves' a problem in the sense of eliminating the conditions that inspired demands for action. When a problem does disappear, the reason often has less to do with government action than with changing societal conditions—including the emergence of new problems that push old ones below the surface of public consciousness".

Without any ideational fix, therefore, law enforcement is powerless. Political actors, often perceived as elitists, are ineffective with engendering changes of norms embedded in existing cultural and religious identities. In their place, we propose the deployment of strategic social actors whom we call civic educators as translators and bricoleurs (i.e. ideational entrepreneurs): traditional leaders, religious leaders, teachers, issue-based advocates, journalists and other social entrepreneurs. It is among communities, families, social groups and associations that ideological frames are constituted and sustained. In her argument about when a subject ripens for public attention, Miljan (2012) demonstrates how, in industrialized democracies, a change of cultural attitudes preceded the political agenda to address unequal social conditions of males and females, for example equal pay for equal work. It was cultural change, not legislation per se, that necessitated the revolution for gender equality. Subsequent legislative efforts supported the ideational transformation that was a result of a policy discourse.

Civic educators are strategically positioned to reinforce or alter social beliefs, to challenge epistemological positions and to help re-align norms, values and "truths". Simply put, they are well-positioned to actively promote ideational transformation. For example, in the Global South transnational actors can work through community players such as community leaders and heads of religious organizations incorporating endogenous norms, values and ideas. This is more impactful in reversing trends such as child marriage and domestic violence.

A potential entry point for championing ideational and policy influence in the Global South is an appeal to the pre-existing communitarian sense of solidarity, family care and social cohesion. For instance, Grech (2011) acknowledges the importance of family ties for offering solidarity and social support in the Global South. Communal solidarity provides a profound opportunity for social policy development in the region.

## Supply and Demand in Policy Diffusion

While some scholars believe that political institutions are necessary and sufficient gateways toward successful policy diffusion (Risse 2007), others see a stronger symbiosis between formal rules/laws that constrain and shape social action and the embedded informal norms that legitimate those formal rules (Campbell 2004; North 1994; Scott 2005). The latter ideational approach stresses that institutional change does not simply mean a change of policy instruments, but, most profoundly, a change of norms that underpin the objectives of these instruments and provide them with legitimacy.

We argue that this constructivist and ideational approach, which has two implications for policy diffusion, suggests a two-faceted policy diffusion process: supply and demand. Before explaining this in greater detail, we are going to deal with the implications of our constructivist and ideational approach. First, because policies—as formal rules and precepts—are institutional realities, their change must seek to alter not just the instrumental aspects represented by formal rules but also the normative aspects including social expectations, customs and belief systems. These social factors, which Parsons (2007) calls ideational factors, matter significantly for policy diffusion because every society is defined by its own sets of persistent cultural ideas. These ideas define societies, and they create and establish social interests that societies live by and would not willingly sacrifice because policy instruments have changed.

Without ideational strategies that socialize and rationalize the new precepts, no punitive law would easily engender any change of core social norms. This, therefore, raises an important issue about framing in policy processes. As Baumgartner and Jones (1991, 1046) demonstrate in what they call "policy imaging", the framing of policy ideas is crucial not only for the justification of new policies but also for the legitimation of alternative world views.

Second, the degree of policy change is only as profound as the policy proposers' scope of engagement with diverse social actors who legitimate a given political idea. If Hall's (1993) third level of policy change (paradigm shift) is desired, context-specific ideas that determine social objectives and goals according to which institutions and policies are designed must be taken into account. To do this, any meaningful activism should be based on a coherent and contextual understanding of institutions, their rules and operations. The assumption that institutions have a universal character often leads to the pitfall that they could resolve all social problems regardless of cultural and normative circumstances (Haang'andu 2018). In this case, social scientists have shown that the logic according to which the change of formal rules (or policy instruments) is sufficient for changing human behavior is flawed. Douglas North (1994), for example, argues that while it is easy to change formal rules overnight, informal norms, which are the anchor for belief, identity, knowledge and behavior, usually change only gradually. The logic here is that institutions are birthed through social interactions and that they are often a representation of the people's cultural-cognitive values and informal beliefs (see also Campbell 2004, 1–9). Institutions and their enforcement build on and reinforce informal norms and beliefs. They create reciprocal expectations and standards because of repeated human behavior and in response to them. In other words, they create a culture.

The preceding discussion leads to the conclusion that transnational policy diffusion should be mindful of two important components of diffusion: the supply and the demand components (see Fig. 12.2). These two components have implications for understanding power relations in policy diffusion and for determining the success and failure of policy diffusion. The supply side simply means that a policy entrepreneur identifies a situation (problematic or not) requiring a policy response and proposes a solution. For example, the observation that socio-economic and political benefits are unequally distributed among men and women has led to the emergence of feminist solutions.

However, supplying policy ideas should be balanced with the demand side. The demand side has two components: inactive demand and active demand. The inactive demand side is primarily guided by what Campbell (2004, 94) refers to as "public sentiments". It means that if an outsider

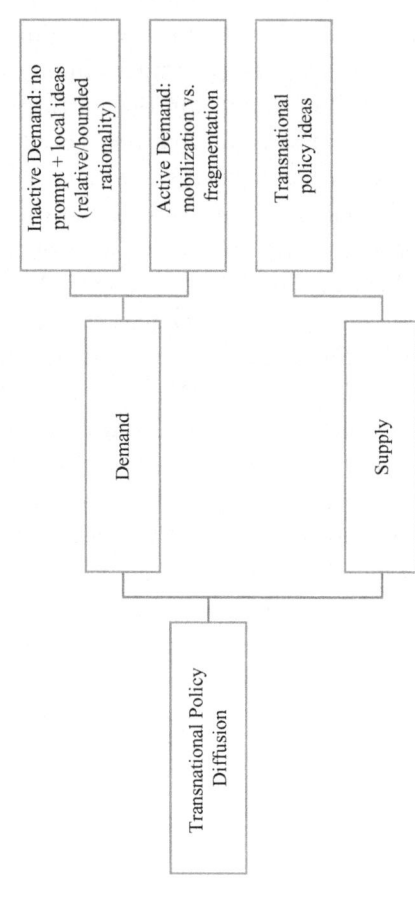

**Fig. 12.2** Demand and supply sides of policy diffusion

attempts to change them, public normative resistance is imminent, potentially seeing such attempts as ideological and cultural intrusion. From this perspective, the inactive demand is where a given society does not actively seek change to its status quo, but an outside policy proposer seeks to initiate change based on perceptions of a situation the outside actor sees as problematic. The policy proposer must prove through a compelling indicator that there is need for a change of the status quo. As Kingdon (2003, 93) argues, "constructing an indicator and getting others to agree to its worth become major preoccupations of those pressing for policy change". For instance, society A could have traditional gender relations it does not see as problematic, although actor B (a TNA) considers them a problem. On the whole, transnational actors and policy proposers see problems beyond their jurisdictions and promote solutions, assuming or believing that a perceived problem borders on a universal principle or that their proposed solution is responsive to their diagnostic (see Shriwise, Chap. 2, this volume, but also Chinyoka and Ulriksen, Chap. 10, this volume).

The demand side also has an active component where a given policy community actively seeks policy solutions for a perceived problem. Still, this demand for policy solutions could be either endogenously or exogenously created. Moreover, the interactions of the supply and demand sides of policy diffusion inherently entail power relations, whether symmetrical or asymmetrical. For policy diffusion to be legitimate, policy entrepreneurs must be aware of the potential for ideational domination. The next section specifies why and how power matters in policy diffusion and how, if not properly managed, it could result in ideational asymmetries and policy impositions.

## Power and Policy Diffusion: Implications for Political and Ideational Asymmetries

Although international organizations often present transnational policy ideas and norms as being neutral, universal and disinterested, political scientists have demonstrated that transnational policy diffusion is characterized by power contestations (Waltz 2000; Shriwise, Chap. 2, this volume). A perspective on the idea of power that has sparked academic controversy is the one by Steven Lukes (2004). Lukes holds a neo-Marxist view according to which power is relational and asymmetrical. It is power over others. According to him, power is the ideological capacity to misleadingly shape the preferences of other actors, in order of reinforcing their domination (Béland 2010). Contrary to Lukes' conception of power as "power over", Morriss (2006, 126) argues that "our primary understanding of power is as 'power-to'" and that "it follows from this that 'power' is best thought of as the ability to effect outcomes, not the ability to affect others". Understanding the conceptual distinction between Lukes' "power over" and "power to", which refers to the capacity to shape outcomes (Morriss 2006), is crucial for our understanding of transnational policy diffusion.

While transnational players are autonomous actors, their policy ideas are seldom those without the backing of powerful countries that finance their operations (see Shriwise, Chap. 2, this volume; Mioni and Petersen, Chap. 3, this volume). While many times TNAs have openly used their control over these institutions to manipulate global political outcomes (which Lukes suggests as "power over"), transnational policy is almost always characterized by power asymmetries. Although transnational policy diffusion, as Hall (1993) puts it, is always about "powering" and "puzzling", achieving policy outcomes through the manipulation of formal political institutions, particularly on matters socially and culturally entrenched, is seldom a viable way of diffusing policy. In the case of disability policy, the failure has more to do with assumptions of Western-centric norms that overshadow the predominance of local cultural ideas in influencing collective identities that could stifle policy diffusion. As Campbell (2004) suggests, policy change should address not only cognitive but also normative ideas, bearing in mind the background and foreground variables affecting the acceptability of policy change.

## Case Study: Transnational Policy Diffusion in SSA

A couple of key points emerge from the preceding discussion that point to the inadequacy of the political-institutional framework and stress the need for our alternative ideational approach. To illustrate the usefulness of this approach, we apply it to transnational disability policy diffusion in SSA, which we then compare with diffusion in the field of gender equality. By way of these factors outlined below as part of our general framework, we demonstrate how the policy diffusion process could be enhanced.

The reason why we selected disability policy to illustrate the benefit of our approach is twofold. First, it is a field in which the limits of the traditional-institutionalist approach to social policy diffusion are easy to identify (Haang'andu 2019). Second, it is a field where the supply side to social policy diffusion has been overemphasized without paying attention to the demand factors. Disability literature is dominated by a strong Western-centric institutionalist approach that has effectively marginalized the role of local ideas in building strong social policy responses to disability. As some scholars have acknowledged (e.g. Devlieger 1999; Grech 2011; Meekosha 2011; Soldatic and Grech 2014), despite accounting for over 80% of persons with disabilities worldwide, the Global South remains at the periphery of "development policy, research and programs, and virtually excluded from the Western-centric disability studies" (Grech 2011, 87). In addition, they argue that the "universalization" of Western-founded disability paradigms, which in our model is denoted by the supply component, has negative impacts, especially on the Global South where experiences of disability are profoundly different.

What we see in SSA in the two policy domains under consideration is a contrast between how gender policy entrepreneurs designed a very well-orchestrated diffusion approach addressing both the demand and the supply sides, while the disability policy entrepreneurs stagnated at the supply side, weakly addressing the demand side. Where the supply side is emphasized, especially if policy ideas border on power relations, policy change evokes ideational asymmetries, something Grech (2015) calls epistemic violence. Often, this leads to ideational acquiescence and conquest. In Haang'andu's (2019) study, disability policy participants agreed that cultural barriers such as beliefs in ancestral curses, myths about the causes of disability and religious beliefs were strong, but also that organizations of persons with disability (PDOs) are fragmented. This means that the two demand components (active and inactive) of the disability policy framework are unviable. While the inactive component of the demand side of gender policy was equally non-viable (by being ideationally guarded), its active demand component facilitated dynamic changes to the two demand ends (active and inactive) to increase cultural receptiveness at the supply end. This process is key to the legitimation of policy change.

Moreover, in SSA, disability policy diffusion is an understudied topic that requires a more systematic approach, something we offer in the following sub-sections. In these sections, where useful, we compare policy diffusion in the field of disability with the situation prevailing in the area of gender equality. We do so because gender equality as an issue provides a revealing contrast with disability policy as far as the study of diffusion patterns is concerned. First, because the chapter is about the success and failure of policy diffusion, we needed two policy areas with contrasting success rates. Moreover, we selected two policy areas whose appearance on the transnational scene is not separated by a large time difference. These two became prominent on the transnational scene at about the same time, the year 2000 for gender, as one of the eight United Nations' MDGs, and the year 2006 for the CRPD. The fact that they have had fairly an equal time for implementation legitimates a comparison. Second, both policy areas face similar ideational challenges (e.g. cultural-cognitive biases, stereotypes and marginalization). Our interest here is not why gender equality and not disability has made it among the core MDGs. Instead, our goal is to compare policy processes that transnational actors and their domestic allies have undertaken to reverse women's marginalization and those that transnational actors and their allies have deployed the past two decades in disability advocacy. How did transnational actors transcend the political processes to attend to sociological causes such as child marriages, gender-based spousal violence, sexual cleansing/HIV and female genital mutilation? These are entrenched social/cultural issues that formal political processes alone could not resolve. Considering that transnational disability actors face similar ideational challenges, how could gender policy diffusion processes shed light on disability policy diffusion?

## Individual Rights, Communitarianism and Policy Diffusion: Contesting Universality

In a statement disputing the assumed universality of a Eurocentric disability discourse, Grech (2015, 11) writes:

> Despite the attempts by a handful of materialist disability theorists to engage with the so-called 'majority world' [...], it becomes immediately clear that these efforts appear to be limited to writing in, or making the Global South fit into their dominant perspectives as opposed to learning about this complex and hybrid space in its own right [...]. For some, the objective may well be the transfer and exportation of discourse, in this case the strong social model of disability to everyone, everywhere, with the objective of reinforcing its universality as a global narrative and perhaps reasserting the power of those generating and selling it.

Indeed, the current transnational disability discourse is imbued in Western knowledge and ideological, theoretical, cultural and historical assumptions (Grech 2015), with little sensitivity to different ideational local contexts. One such method is the rights-based approach to disability that seeks to valorize the individual against the collective. One of the biggest challenges with transnational human rights-oriented policy diffusion in Africa is the overlooking of historically entrenched collective identities which are essentially non-individualistic. Many African scholars have written on the *Bantu* philosophy of *Ubuntu* (e.g. Christians 2004; Mji et al. 2011; Wiredu 2008) that so profoundly characterizes the *Bantu* people of SSA. The term *ubuntu* is common among many *Bantu* languages across the continent and it translates as "humanity for others" (Christians 2004, 241). In the Zulu language, for example, *ubuntu* derives from a maxim *umuntu ngumuntu ngabantu*, which translates as "a person is a person through other persons" (Christians 2004, 241; see also

Mji et al. 2011) or *I am because we are*. As Christians (2004, 241) explains, *ubuntu* "means that a person depends on personal relations with others to exercise, develop and fulfil those capacities that make one a person [...]. Personhood comes as a gift from other persons". Central to the concept of *ubuntu* is the understanding that human beings are intrinsically social beings and that their dignity is integrated in rationality and morality (Christians 2004).

Contrary to this approach by disability advocates, in his comparative study on disability and gender policy advocates in Malawi and Zambia, Haang'andu (2019) finds that while the promotion of gender equality was central to the objectives of feminist TNAs, persuading endogenous ideational factors was equally important. The most notable intermediary TNAs and local organizations engaged with transforming social norms were traditional leaders, teachers, religious leaders and husbands. Haang'andu (2019) shows that TNAs and their partners used framing techniques to persuade ideational, cultural and knowledge leaders toward alternative frames of gender relations. This helped, prior to the attainment of effective institutional frameworks, with altering entrenched societal ideas maintained in the context of belief systems and practices that placed women at the periphery.

The comparison demonstrates that cultural identity, unlike Western individualism, is more of involuntary acquiescence. People are born into a culture they can individually hardly control. Individuality versus communitarian comparatives has serious implications for the applicability of legal and judicial frameworks that stress individual rights against common values. In entrenched Western democratic societies, where individual liberties and freedoms are central to civilization, court systems and litigation are effective. In these societies, judicial processes through institutionalized courts are strong and binding for all parties involved. The institutional court system as we know it today, as a pinnacle of individual emancipation, is an abstraction of the Western civilization. The judiciary, as an arm of government, is a colonial inheritance. Like other colonial institutions of governance in Africa, the concept of the Western-centric judiciary is still struggling to entrench itself in African political cultures.

This has created two problems. First, the sense of communal solidarity, collective responsibility and shame is more binding than the doctrine of individual exoneration through judicial victories (Haang'andu 2018). Second, judicial impartiality in Africa remains a significant problem. Some scholars have argued that judicial systems in developing countries are generally weak (Besley and Persson 2014). In a robust study on the adjudication of electoral disputes in SSA, O'Brien Kaaba (2015) documents the challenges of judicial neutrality throughout Sub-Saharan Africa. In all SSA countries, constitutions allow presidents to appoint judges, often without tenure of office, leaving the judges' security of office to the caprices of politicians: the result has been that judges are often politically pliable. In the rare cases when judges exhibit independence and rule against government officials, their verdicts are ignored, publicly ridiculed and sometimes judges are removed (Haang'andu and Béland 2019).

The foregoing two points have far-reaching implications for policy diffusion in SSA, when we bring the example of gender equality to the fore as a comparative device. First, women and persons with disabilities, like everybody else, hold collective purposes more than individual "rights", contrasting the experience of Western civilizations (see also Grech 2011). These social ties shape the experience of gender relations and the disability experience in a way that creates unique opportunities and challenges for policy intervention. Our experience of research in Malawi and Zambia shows that women are overly reticent about gender-based abuses because of this cultural-blanket. In many cases when reports are filed, they are often withdrawn, and cases can be withdrawn to preserve collective "integrity". Second, although courts have mostly acted efficiently in case of gender-related violations where they have been allowed to, the implication of weak judicial systems for the transnationalization of disability norms is that there is no predictability as to whether court systems would act as credible remediation for disability causes. In SSA, where government executives frequently influence the judiciary or defy judicial rulings, it is difficult to imagine that courts would—contrary to Vanhala's (2010) arguments for the relevance of courts in Canada and in the United Kingdom—be credible means to champion disability "rights", especially when judicial outcomes have punitive financial implications on arms of government (Haang'andu 2018).[1]

## Ethnolinguistic Fractionalization and Policy Diffusion

One of the conspicuous characteristics of many SSA societies is cultural heterogeneity. Political scientists have theorized about the implications of ethnolinguistic fractionalization when it comes to the building of institutions. One of the arguments brought forward is that ethnolinguistic fractionalization complicates institution-building and policy change (Besley and Persson 2014; Mauro 1998). In an ethnolinguistically fractionalized society, the diversity of cultural ideas makes it difficult to impose a homogenous policy across the country. The assumption that gender equality norms, disability knowledge and policy ideologies founded in one part of the world would seamlessly localize in ethnolinguistically fractionalized SSA is problematic (Haang'andu 2018).

Because of their ethnolinguistic fractionalization, many SSA societies are ideationally and culturally fragmented and require more complex strategies of disability and gender policy response than the Western universalistic agenda. The existential realities of persons with disabilities in SSA are, in terms of both challenges and opportunities, uniquely shaped by local ideational factors that might not be amenable to a universal policy prescription. Building universal disability regimes that command voluntary multi-ethnic acceptance is much more complex than the transnationalization of unquestioned Western-based ideologies (Haang'andu 2018).

In his study on Malawi and Zambia, Haang'andu (2019) finds that an important obstacle to disability policy diffusion in SSA is the lack of TNAs and their partners' strategic engagement with grassroots actors to initiate a critical ideational shift that both backs the change in formal laws and rules and, at the same time, puts pressure on social factors sustaining existing frames about disability. Gender activists and their TNA

---

[1] This is a good project for future investigation. There is the need to study how effective courts have been in adjudication disability and gender cases in SSA. It is not the priority of this research to delve into such details.

partners have applied this model. While fighting for legislative reform (laws, budget inclusiveness, increased electoral participation, more representation in appointed senior government positions, etc.), they took to the grassroots to sell and rationalize alternative ideational images and frames about male-female relations. Gender activists and disability activists in SSA face similar social obstacles: inhibitive social and religious belief systems, stereotypes, contested status and so on. Like gender TNAs and advocates acknowledged in Haang'andu (2019), framing requires skillful engagement with oppositional and often-entrenched cultural images that people could be defensive about. It also requires persuasion rather than conquest.

As Grech (2011, 89) aptly observes, when disability knowledge and policy is grounded on Western-centric ideologies and experiences, "it implies that it is theoretically ill-equipped to deal with majority world views and the nuances of majority world contexts (historical, social, economic and political)". Given the cultural-cognitive embeddedness of both gender relations and disability in SSA countries, it is important to understand that whatever policy interventions are made, they must confront the harsh reality of the deep ideational understanding of gender relations and disability (Haang'andu 2018). As such, activist efforts in these contexts need to employ effective discursive (or rationalization) frames toward the public through carefully selected strategic intermediaries (i.e. civic educators) to convince them that reform is necessary (Kingdon 2003). Like any other societies, SSA societies have unique cultural idiosyncrasies that are difficult to change overnight. Many countries in SSA have a strong adherence to social collectivism and family ties (for disability in the Global South in general, see Clare Barker and Stuart Murray 2010; Grech 2011).

In his research on Zambia, Haang'andu (2019) found that over 90% of domestic child sexual defilement cases were perpetrated by close relatives and not by unknown strangers. He found that the greatest obstacle to fighting sexual violence and rape of women and young girls is not the lack of punitive laws but that families decide to protect violators to prevent "family shame". In this example, despite the existence of punitive legislative provisions, social norms, beliefs and practices (which Elinor Ostrom (2014) refers to as evolutionary and cultural social norms that create reciprocal expectations) stifle the prosecutorial prospects. While most of the cases remain unreported due to these social justifications, in some instances victims report violations but withdraw complaints yielding to family and societal pressure, to avoid "family shame". Often, families prefer secret domestic dispute settlement to judicial proceedings that could potentially result in the arrest and persecution of one of their kith and kin, sometimes the family breadwinner. Haang'andu (2019) found that familial protectionist tendencies exacerbate the sexual abuse of girls and women. Women with disabilities, whom some African societies believe to possess spiritual powers to cure sexually transmitted diseases, are at a higher risk.

How should activists confront such socially entrenched barriers? Any gender or disability activism that insists on the supremacy of individual rights is not only incongruent to the experience of gender relations or of persons with disabilities in this context, but it is counterproductive. Given all the historically created and sustained social expectations, it is unlikely that women or individuals with disabilities—so embedded within this social fabric—would seek litigious measures against their immediate family, community or ethnic group for perceived violations.

Where powerful policy proposers use their economic incentives to manipulate and obtain compliance, 'power over' could secure a change of policy instruments but not of social identities, norms and practices. With transnational actors playing dominant roles in financing development policies in both gender and disability in SSA, these countries are faced with the challenge of "puzzling and powering". Presented with treaties at the international level, disregarding their capacity and desire to implement the provisions, these countries' dispositions to accept policy proposals are constantly determined by the "powering" dynamics of appeasement and the fear of retributions. For example, in September 2018, the British Government, along with the Swedish, Irish and Finnish governments, suspended donor aid to Zambia after the Zambian government had misappropriated over $4 million meant for social cash transfer programs for poor people and people with disabilities. Therefore, the split of control between transnational actors who wield financial power and state actors who organize their local systems threatens the viability of real paradigmatic change in policy diffusion in general. Although there are no absolute solutions to this problem, aligning both actors' goals through ideational bricolage and translation provides a strong remedy. Bricolage and translation offer an ideational approach that both presents legitimacy for locals and satisfies the universalistic aspirations of the TNAs.

## Bricolage and Translation of Ideas

At first, to make disability policy pathways that might break up the sociological and cultural foundations of African societies, disability activism in SSA should be informed by the endogenous understanding and experience of society. In other words, both translation and bricolage should be cognizant of endogeneity. Using bricolage and translation, we can begin to build an Afrocentric disability activist paradigm whose foundations derive from African cultures themselves. To start off the bricolage process, we acknowledge that typically African societies are characterized by a culture of reciprocity, dignity, humanity and mutuality in the interest of building and maintaining communities with justice and communal caring (Gyekye 1997). Bricolage entails the incorporation of these pre-existing endogenous attributes into policy responses. For example, the institutionalist introduction of designated homes for persons with disabilities, such as mental health clinics and hospices, negates the entrenched community predisposition of caring for "disadvantaged" members of society. A welfare system created through bricolage that seeks to address the needs of persons with disabilities in such a context would be responsive to pre-existing societal attributions and combine them with other policy elements. The abovementioned African philosophies present profound opportunities for the reconceptualization of a context-responsive model of disability activism within the SSA context. Because it is among communities, families and sociological groups and associations that disability frames are constituted and sustained, it is also from among them that ideational spinners for conceptual shifts should emerge. The preoccupation of transnational activists with political processes of disability policy change and rights promotion misses this point.

Unlike bricolage that maximizes pre-existing attributes for anchoring policy change, translation is predominantly supply-driven. Because the supply aspect of policy ideas could easily be perceived as an imposition or as the supplanting of a status quo and, therefore, trigger oppositional public sentiments, it requires a careful framing and translation of ideas. While political institutions play a significant role in the policy process, they are ill-positioned to mediate the framing and translation of supply-driven ideas to how to reconcile them with entrenched non-formal cultural-cognitive beliefs and attitudes. Instead, it is civic educators (traditional leaders, religious leaders, community leaders, teachers, etc.) that are best placed to be ideational entrepreneurs. Civic educators, particularly in the African context, are strategically positioned to reinforce or alter social beliefs, to challenge epistemological positions and to help re-align norms and values. The pitfall of the Western-centric disability activism is both its assumed universalistic disability knowledge paradigm and its methodological approach that, despite ideational variation, seeks an institutional expansion of individual rights in a deeply communitarian society.

To amplify the mechanisms of policy translation, let us consider a concrete gender-related example that enriches our comparative analysis of the two policy domains under consideration. In the early 2000s, transnational activists sponsored and supported a vibrant gender activism in Africa that resulted in a plethora of women-led activist organizations (Haang'andu 2018). At inception, there was a strong focus on criminalizing certain social ills; for example, spouse inheritance, sexual cleansing, gender-based violence, the marriage of underage girls and so on. Certain male-female interactions that are commonly taken for granted in African societies came under scrutiny, and many were deemed violations of women's rights. Although these efforts were obviously important for trying to deter the abuse of women and for enhancing women's rights, transnational and domestic organizations that worked to reverse these trends in many African countries eventually realized, after decades of working through legislative avenues of government with little success, that working through community leaders such as chiefs and heads of religious organizations, incorporating endogenous norms, values and ideas, was more impactful for reversing the trends. In fact, in some cases, simply enforcing the law was counterproductive because societies became more reticent about the occurrences of some of these ills. For example, the

Zambia National Women's Lobby, the largest women's movement in Zambia with a wide regional range in southern Africa, acknowledged during an interview that they had learned that they needed to desist from framing their messages as "promoting women's rights" during their campaigns to make an impact on the heavily patriarchal Zambian society (Haang'andu 2019). The justification for using alternative frames was that the patriarchal Zambian society would be aversive to such language and, therefore, resistant to transformation. Yet, the result of its advocacy was the attainment of communities that developed a new sense of respect for women and their contribution to society and the condemnation of the physical and emotional abuse of women in marriage as well as the increased appreciation of education for girls. The organization also reiterated the importance of working through informal structures as opposed to concentrating on legislation. This point was reiterated by a senior Zambian government official during an interview: "we do not want to be a police state. We need transformation of attitudes and not mere forced compliance to legislation".

This illustration serves to stress a couple of points. First, understanding ideational and cultural contexts is fundamental for activism on sociologically entrenched phenomena like gender and disability. Assumptions of universal categories only serve for stifling progress in ideational transformations. To maximize their impact, transnational activists therefore need to avoid assuming that a knowledge paradigm generated in one cultural-cognitive context meets universal resonance and, instead, seek niches for bricolage and identify effective intermediaries for translation.

Second, while the strengthening of institutions is important and in fact essential for a sustained policy, political institutions are not always the best entry points for socially effective policy change. The above illustration shows that informal community structures could be more impactful with proliferating alternative worldviews and with reversing historical frames about taken-for-granted social experiences. In African settings, elected leaders, frequently construed as "seasonal visitors" who show up near election time, are often less trusted than community and religious leaders when it comes to norms-related issues. Traditional ethnic leaders and religious leaders wield both political and ideational authority over communities. They are influential normative spinners and can function as strategic ideational entrepreneurs for new knowledge shifts. They are better placed socially to be carriers of new disability frames and to be agents of ideational change than conventional political institutions.

## Conclusion

The contribution our ideational approach makes to transnational policy diffusion is threefold. First, using the examples of disability and gender social policies, it strives to explain the limitations of the institutionalist approach to transnational policy. More broadly, focusing on both, the supply and the demand sides, the framework strives to determe the circumstances under which TNAs succeed and/or fail to diffuse transnational norms in an ideationally charged socio-political environment. Second, the framework abstracts the implications of underlying power factors in policy diffusion. Here we propound the ideational and policy implications of a policy exchange situation that is characterized by power asymmetries. Third, our framework bridges complex public policy concepts to devise an explanatory framework for social policy diffusion that could be applied to many policy situations. Through Parsons' (2007) notion of ideational explanations, we have abstracted ideational components of SSA societies and how they define these societies' identities. Using Campbell's (2004) concepts of bricolage and translation, we devise a comprehensive and inclusive approach to policy diffusion that institutions could adopt to strengthen their own chances of success in diffusing social policies.

This constructivist argument we advance for disability policy diffusion based on ideational considerations, and against a purely positivist political-institutional approach, adds a novel approach both to disability literature and to transnational policy diffusion thought. The approach stands in contrast to the dominant and often-unquestioned political-institutional paradigm of the transnationalization of the disability discourse which, if anything, overlooks context-specific cultural and ideational factors by assuming the universality of Western geopolitical ideologies, norms and interests. Through a strong emphasis on the importance of ideas, social meanings, as well as historical and cultural identities in disability policy design and implementation, this study contributes to constructivist theory-building in public policy research.

While this chapter, to a large extent, breaks new ground in social policy diffusion, the framework could benefit from further research work. First, future research could focus on concrete comparative cases drawn from SSA countries while representing internal political and cultural variations (e.g. colonial legacies), to find out: (1) if political historicity has any influence on policy diffusion behavior by TNA; and (2) if colonial legacies have significance for local societies' disposition to exogenous influence. Second, future research could compare what the dynamics of policy diffusion are between more ethnically heterogeneous societies and those less ethnolinguistically fractionalized. Here, it would be useful to investigate whether less fractionalized societies are more or less cohered to social identities such as culture, belief systems and norms. It would also be useful to know whether such societies are ideologically more amenable to political-institutional influence than the more heterogeneous ones.

Further research could also examine differences in the progression of disability policy design and implementation among various SSA countries, ascertaining sets of key players and their respective influence both in policy advancements and sociological ideational reforms at the local level.

# References

Barker, Clare, and Stuart Murray. 2010. Disabling Postcolonialism: Global Disability Cultures and Democratic Criticism. *Journal of Literary & Cultural Disability Studies* 4 (3): 219–236.

Baumgartner, Frank R., and Bryan D. Jones. 1991. Agenda Dynamics and Policy Subsystems. *The Journal of Politics* 53 (4): 1044–1074.

Béland, Daniel. 2010. The Idea of Power and the Role of Ideas. *Political Studies Review* 8 (2): 145–154.

Besley, Timothy, and Torsten Persson. 2014. Why Do Developing Countries Tax So Little? *Journal of Economic Perspectives* 28 (4): 99–120.

Boli, John, and George M. Thomas, eds. 1999. *Constructing World Culture: International Nongovernmental Organizations Since 1875*. Stanford: Stanford University Press.

Campbell, John L. 2004. *Institutional Change and Globalization*. Princeton: Princeton University Press.

Carstensen, Martin B. 2011. Paradigm Man vs. the Bricoleur: Bricolage as an Alternative Vision of Agency in Ideational Change. *European Political Science Review* 3 (1): 147–167.

Checkel, Jeffrey T. 1997. International Norms and Domestic Politics: Bridging the Rationalist – Constructivist Divide. *European Journal of International Relations* 3 (4): 473–495.

———. 2005. International Institutions and Socialization in Europe: Introduction and Framework. *International Organization* 59 (4): 801–826.

Christians, Clifford G. 2004. Ubuntu and Communitarianism in Media Ethics. *Ecquid Novi: African Journalism Studies* 25 (2): 235–256.

Clarke, John, Dave Bainton, Noémi Lendvai, and Paul Stubbs. 2015. *Making Policy Move: Towards a Politics of Translation and Assemblage*. Bristol: Policy Press.

Devlieger, P.J. 1999. From Handicap to Disability: Language Use and Cultural Meaning in the United States. *Disability and Rehabilitation* 21 (7): 346–354.

Evangelista, Matthew. 1995. The Paradox of State Strength: Transnational Relations, Domestic Structures, and Security Policy in Russia and the Soviet Union. *International Organization* 49 (1): 1–38. http://www.jstor.org/stable/2706865.

Finger, Matthias, and Thomas Princen. 2013. *Environmental NGOs in World Politics: Linking the Local and the Global*. London: Routledge.

Grech, Shaun. 2011. Recolonising Debates or Perpetuated Coloniality? Decentring the Spaces of Disability, Development and Community in the Global South. *International Journal of Inclusive Education* 15 (1): 87–100.

———. 2015. *Disability and Poverty in the Global South: Renegotiating Development in Guatemala*. Basingstoke: Palgrave Macmillan.

Gyekye, Kwame. 1997. *Tradition and Modernity: Philosophical Reflections on the African Experience*. Oxford: Oxford University Press.

Haang'andu, Privilege. 2018. Transnationalizing Disability Policy in Embedded Cultural-Cognitive Worldviews: The Case of Sub-Saharan Africa. *Disability and the Global South* 5 (1): 1292–1314.

———. 2019. *Transnational Actors and Policy Diffusion: Ideational Pathways Towards Successful Disability Policy Diffusion in Southern Africa*. Saskatoon: University of Saskatchewan (PhD Dissertation in Public Policy).

Haang'andu, Privilege, and Daniel Béland. 2019. Democratization Without Westernisation? Embedding Democracy in Local African Cultures. *Politikon* 46 (2): 219–239. https://doi.org/10.1080/02589346.2019.1612179.

Hall, Peter A. 1993. Policy Paradigms, Social Learning and the State: The Case of Economic Policymaking in Britain. *Comparative Politics* 25 (3): 275–296.

Kaaba, O'Brien. 2015. *The Challenges of Adjudicating Presidential Election Disputes in Africa: Exploring the Viability of Establishing an African Supranational Elections Tribunal*. PhD diss., University of South Africa.

Keck, Margaret E., and Kathryn Sikkink. 1998. Historical Precursors to Modern Transnational Advocacy Networks. In *Activists Beyond Borders: Advocacy Networks in International Politics*, ed. Margaret E. Keck and Kathryn Sikkink, 59–66. Ithaca and London: Cornell University Press.

Kingdon, John W. 2003. *Agendas, Alternatives, and Public Policies*. New York: Longman.

Lukes, Steven. 2004. *Power: A Radical View*. 2nd ed. Basingstoke: Palgrave Macmillan.

Mauro, Paolo. 1998. Corruption and the Composition of Government Expenditure. *Journal of Public Economics* 69 (2): 263–279.

Meekosha, Helen. 2011. Decolonizing Disability: Thinking and Acting Globally. *Disability & Society* 26 (6): 667–682.

Miljan, Lydia. 2012. *Public Policy in Canada: An Introduction*. Oxford: Oxford University Press.

Mji, Gubela, Siphokazi Gcaza, Leslie Swartz, Malcolm MacLachlan, and Barbara Hutton. 2011. An African Way of Networking Around Disability. *Disability & Society* 26 (3): 365–368.

Morriss, Peter. 2006. Steven Lukes on the Concept of Power. *Political Studies Review* 4 (2): 124–135.

North, Douglass C. 1994. Economic Performance Through Time. *The American Economic Review* 84 (3): 359–368.

Orenstein, Mitchell A. 2008. *Privatizing Pensions: The Transnational Campaign for Social Security Reform*. Princeton: Princeton University Press.

Ostrom, Elinor. 2014. Collective Action and the Evolution of Social Norms. *Journal of Natural Resources Policy Research* 6 (4): 235–252.

Parsons, Craig. 2002. Showing Ideas as Causes: The Origins of the European Union. *International Organization* 56 (1): 47–84.

———. 2007. *How to Map Arguments in Political Science*. Oxford: Oxford University Press.

Risse, Thomas. 2007. Transnational Actors and World Politics. In *Corporate Ethics and Corporate Governance*, ed. Walther Ch. Zimmerli, Markus Holzinger, and Klaus Richter, 251–286. Berlin: Springer.

Scott, Richard W. 2005. Institutional Theory: Contributing to a Theoretical Research Program. In *Great Minds in Management: The Process of Theory Development*, ed. Ken G. Smith and Michael A. Hill, 460–485. Oxford: Oxford University Press.

Soldatic, Karen, and Shaun Grech. 2014. Transnationalising Disability Studies: Rights, Justice and Impairment. *Disability Studies Quarterly* 34 (2). https://dsq-sds.org/article/view/4249.

Trebilcock, Michael J. 2014. *Dealing with Losers: The Political Economy of Policy Transitions*. Oxford: Oxford University Press.

Vanhala, Lisa. 2010. *Making Rights a Reality? Disability Rights Activists and Legal Mobilization*. Cambridge: Cambridge University Press.

Waltz, Kenneth N. 2000. Structural Realism After the Cold War. *International Security* 25 (1): 5–41.

Wiredu, Kwasi, ed. 2008. *A Companion to African Philosophy*. Oxford: John Wiley & Sons.

**Open Access** This chapter is licensed under the terms of the Creative Commons Attribution 4.0 International License (http://creativecommons.org/licenses/by/4.0/), which permits use, sharing, adaptation, distribution and reproduction in any medium or format, as long as you give appropriate credit to the original author(s) and the source, provide a link to the Creative Commons licence and indicate if changes were made.

The images or other third party material in this chapter are included in the chapter's Creative Commons licence, unless indicated otherwise in a credit line to the material. If material is not included in the chapter's Creative Commons licence and your intended use is not permitted by statutory regulation or exceeds the permitted use, you will need to obtain permission directly from the copyright holder.

# 13

# Transnational Actors and Institutionalization of Social Protection in the Global South

Armando Barrientos

## Introduction

Low- and middle-income countries are engaged in a large expansion of social protection institutions, but especially social assistance. Some comparative research on the growth of social assistance has attributed this expansion to the influence of transnational actors, particularly multilaterals (Peck and Theodore 2015; Yeates 2018).[1] This chapter challenges this widely held view, for which a review of the findings and approaches of the

---

The chapter benefitted from detailed comments by Carina Schmitt and participants in the workshop on "Building social protection systems in the Global South: different trajectories and the influence of external factors", at SOCIUM Research Centre on Inequality and Social Policy, Bremen University, 7–8 June 2018. Any remaining error is mine alone.

[1] This is an abridged list; see the text for further references.

---

A. Barrientos (✉)
Global Development Institute, University of Manchester, Manchester, UK
e-mail: Armando.Barrientos@manchester.ac.uk

current comparative literature fails to find strong support. Addressing this issue is important because it raises fundamental questions about the focus, scope and methods of comparative research on emerging welfare institutions in low- and middle-income countries. Interdependencies, transnational actors included, are likely to have a stronger influence on the shape of welfare institutions in low- and middle-income countries than they did in the development of welfare states in long-standing industrialized countries. The chapter argues that a focus on institutions as opposed to policies, better data and quantitative methods as well as a clearer conceptualization of the role of transnational actors will take us further toward theorizing emerging welfare institutions in low- and middle-income countries.

In low- and middle-income countries, social assistance consists of programs and policies providing budget-financed and rules-based transfers to households and individuals, with the aim of facilitating sustained exit from poverty.[2] Based on data from the World Bank's ASPIRE database (The Atlas of Social Protection Indicators of Resilience and Equity), the 2015 State of Safety Nets Report stated that social assistance reached 2 billion people in low- and middle-income countries (World Bank 2015).[3] A regional breakdown from the same data confirms that social assistance is the predominant component of social protection in low- and middle-income countries when measured in terms of range.

This expansion of social assistance has far-reaching implications for emerging welfare institutions. One of these is the likely balance between social insurance and social assistance components within social protection. Expectations that social insurance institutions would come to dominate social protection in low- and middle-income countries, based on the development of similar institutions in Europe and on long-standing International Labour Organization (ILO) advocacy, would need to be heavily discounted. The scope and scale of social assistance institutions in

---

[2] Social assistance is heterogeneous across, and within, national and sub-national contexts (Barrientos 2013).

[3] A global count using the Social Assistance in Low and Middle Income Countries database SALMIC (Barrientos 2018) puts the range of social assistance at below 1 billion. The World Bank measures safety nets, which combine social assistance and emergency and humanitarian assistance. In sub-Saharan Africa and perhaps elsewhere, short-term public works and school feeding programs, arguably emergency assistance, bulk up the World Bank estimates.

low- and middle-income countries belies the residual and compensatory role of social assistance in European countries. A strong focus on social investment, innovations in information tracking of vulnerable population groups, impact evaluations and the emergence of dedicated Ministries of Social Development, all these indicate a distinctive institutional development in low- and middle-income countries.

The expansion of social assistance has coincided with an increased interest in growing interdependencies in policy-making, including social policy (Obinger et al. 2013). It is a fact that economic liberalization, migration and global value chains, among others, work to limit the explanatory power of research focusing exclusively on domestic social protection policy. Comparative research, paying attention to interdependencies, stands a better chance to understand emerging welfare institutions everywhere, but especially in low- and middle-income countries.

Disproportionate attention given to the role of transnational actors in current comparative research on emerging welfare institutions in low- and middle-income countries might turn out to be counterproductive. First, it biases the focus of comparative research toward short-term policies as opposed to long-term institutions, and overwhelmingly on the processes of policy adoption and diffusion. The research question implicit in this approach is "what makes policies move transnationally?" This is in contrast to "what explains the shape of emerging welfare institutions in low- and middle-income countries?" Whereas the former can be answered with little or no engagement with domestic conditions, the latter requires a deeper engagement with domestic politics. Second, distance has encouraged a focus on ideational factors in social policy adoption, especially the ideational flows associated with international organizations (Béland 2016; Béland and Orenstein 2013; Jenson 2010). Third, an excessive focus on the agency of transnational actors diverts attention from discussing appropriate comparative methods, both qualitative and quantitative.[4]

---

[4] Peck and Theodore eloquently describe the problem: "[T]he persistent challenge was to avoid slipping into a form of sampling, as it were, on the dependent variable, and merely affirming some anticipated account of policy hypermobility, as articulated by the most powerful players (many of whom had interests in promoting such narratives). We had to avoid becoming dupes of the policy networks themselves" (Peck and Theodore 2015, Loc254). From my reading, they were not entirely successful.

Some of these shortcomings are acknowledged in the literature. Yeates (2018) discusses current gaps in appropriate tools and approaches. Obinger et al. (2013) undertake a balanced assessment of qualitative and quantitative methods applied to the studying of social policy diffusion and transfers. They note the scarcity of "empirical analysis of the exact conditions and mechanisms of diffusion and transfer" (Obinger et al. 2013, 122).

This chapter argues that disproportionate attention paid to ideational flows from international organizations imposes a reductive perspective which moves us away from theorizing emergent welfare institutions in low- and middle-income countries. This is partly due to deficiencies in the conceptualization of transnational actors and their influences and partly to the challenges faced by comparative methods, data included. In this chapter, alternative conceptualizations of the role of transnational influences are sketched. It makes a case for refocusing comparative research on explaining the shape of emerging institutions in low- and middle-income countries, paying greater attention to the influence of interdependencies on domestic factors and encouraging quantitative comparative methods.

The chapter is organized around three further sections and a conclusion. Section "Comparative Research on Social Assistance" provides a brief review of methods and findings in the scarce comparative literature on the expansion of social assistance in low- and middle-income countries. Section "Social Policy Adoption and Emerging Institutions" discusses two "canonical" examples of transnationally driven social policy diffusion: provident funds and individual retirement accounts. They demonstrate that a focus on transnationally driven policy transfers might not tell us very much about the emerging welfare institutions in low- and middle-income countries. Section "Conceptualizing Transnational Actors" sketches a conceptualization of the role of transnational influences and actors in social policy, distinguishing phenomenological from realist perspectives. A final section presents conclusions.

## Comparative Research on Social Assistance

This section aims at providing a very brief review of available comparative research on emerging social assistance in low- and middle-income countries. The section focuses solely on multi-country studies and on their methods and key findings.[5] This literature is scarce and predominantly based on qualitative methods. Its bulk focuses on policy diffusion and policy transfers. To my knowledge, few comparative studies seek to explain emerging social assistance institutions (Leisering 2019; Schmitt et al. 2015; Schmitt 2019; Dodlova et al. 2018; see Schmitt, Chap. 6, this volume).[6]

Quantitative studies are scarce, which is largely due to the paucity of reliable data. Díaz-Cayeros and Magaloni (2009) are interested in factors explaining the timing of the adoption of conditional income transfers in Latin America and the Caribbean. Relying on a survival model and on data for 21 countries in the region, they find that inequality, the level of development, state capacity and the durability of the political regime all contribute to earlier adoption, but economic growth is identified as a potentially delaying factor. Their key finding is that, after controlling for these factors, the ideology of the executive plays no significant role, suggesting that "the convergence we see when it comes to poverty-fighting strategies may have to do with dilemmas that all Latin American governments must face, whatever their own or their supporters' ideologies and policy preferences" (Díaz-Cayeros and Magaloni 2009, 47). By contrast,

---

[5] Single country studies on the expansion of social assistance contribute significantly to our understanding of the processes involved but are not reviewed here. In Latin America, single country studies focus on identifying preferences of social assistance programs and potential electoral implications. These studies rely on standard regression techniques, using attitudinal or experimental household survey data. More recently, Zucco has collected and analyzed experimental data (Zucco et al. 2019). In sub-Saharan Africa, two research programs on the politics of social protection (led by Jeremy Seekings at the University of Cape Town and by Sam Hickey and Tom Lavers at Manchester) have produced scores of single country studies (Hickey et al. 2020).

[6] Haggard and Kaufman (2008) and Huber and Stephens (2012) develop theoretical accounts of social policies and institutions in middle-income countries and Latin America, respectively, but do not focus on the recent growth of social assistance. Two studies provide information on the emergent institutions themselves in Latin America (Székely 2015; CEPAL 2015).

Borges (2018) finds that left ideology has contributed to the diffusion of conditional income transfers in Latin America.

Borges Sugiyama (2011) discusses the spread of conditional income transfer programs in Latin America, applying a Cox event history model to data from Latin American countries, combined with a qualitative study of the role of transnational actors. The quantitative component finds that a variable capturing neighborhood effects is the only significant independent variable. The model finds no support for variables capturing "policy bargaining" explanations (needs, capacity and governing coalition ideology). The qualitative component finds that international organizations display multiple and overlapping effects on diffusion: "They help shape international norms and then reinforce them through funding arrangements" (Borges Sugiyama 2011, 264).

Brooks (2015) applies a logistic regression-weighted lag-dependent variable model to a cross-section sample of social assistance programs, with the objective of identifying correlates of conditional income transfer program adoption. Her findings are summarized as follows: "the recent shift toward cash transfers for the poorest citizens in the developing world has emerged through a deepening of democracy, macroeconomic conditions, and horizontal channels of communications across nations that enable governments to discern whether such design is a reasonable investment of financial and institutional resources for their country" (Brooks 2015, 575). Regarding the role of the World Bank (captured by a variable indicating the total bank funding flowing to the specific country), she finds no statistically significant correlation with conditional income transfer adoption but a significant correlation if all types of cash transfers are included. Brooks' findings are challenged by Simpson (2018) who relies on non-parametric measures of association and an updated cross-section sample of programs. If anything, this study demonstrates that findings are highly dependent on particular samples and analytical methods.

The absence of comprehensive comparative data on social assistance was a major challenge, but several new datasets now available should facilitate comparative research. They include the World Bank's ASPIRE database (World Bank 2016), the non-contributory social transfer program dataset NSTP (Dodlova et al. 2018), the Floor-Cash dataset

(Weible et al. 2015) and Social Assistance in Low and Middle Income Countries (SALMIC) (Barrientos 2018).

Qualitative studies rely almost exclusively on expert interviews and documentation. The sample of countries is largely ad hoc, and expert interviews are heavily weighted toward transnational actors and agency officials. Process tracing and network analysis are sometimes employed, but counterfactuals are seldom discussed.

The findings from qualitative studies on Latin American conditional income transfers and those focusing on sub-Saharan Africa show some subtle differences. Fenwick (2013) examines Brazil and Argentina and finds that transnational actors played a secondary role with conditional income transfer adoption. As she puts it, "what matters most is what type of feedback effect intersects with transnational policy ideas" (Fenwick 2013, 162). Martínez Franzoni and Voorend (2011) compare the adoption of conditional income transfers in Chile, Costa Rica and El Salvador. They stress the role of the *inter*national epistemic community and the consensus on how best to deploy antipoverty programs; "[h]owever, differences in each program's design hint at cross-national differences and the role of domestic factors in adapting policy recommendations to national environments" (Martínez Franzoni and Voorend 2011, 285). Garay (2016) provides a detailed and comprehensive analysis of the growth of social assistance in four Latin American countries (Mexico, Argentina, Brazil and Chile). She finds no evidence in support of the view that transnational actors have played a significant role in the expansion of social assistance in these countries. In sum, qualitative studies on Latin America acknowledge transnational actors but discount their influence on the growth of social assistance.

Hickey and Seekings (2020) and Hickey et al. (2020) provide a perspective on the adoption and diffusion of social assistance in sub-Saharan Africa. Their research relies on qualitative methods, complemented by process tracing and the analysis of documentation. Hickey and Seekings (2020) focus specifically on the role of donors with the expansion of social assistance. Their approach to policy diffusion is in line with the global social policy perspective, including an emphasis on ideational factors. In their view, "the global SCT [Social Cash Transfer] agenda has been created by international organizations" (Hickey and Seekings 2020,

17). Hickey et al. (2020) extend their analysis to including domestic policy factors in the adoption of social assistance.[7] They find that transnational influences have been important in some countries, but not everywhere. Their process tracing analysis failed to "uncover evidence that these external agreements did more than legitimate—to some extent—the possibility of social protection" (Hickey et al. 2020, 11). They conclude that "whether or not national governments introduce or expand social assistance programmes depends primarily on politics within each country" (Hickey et al. 2020, 10).

The brief review of the comparative literature on the emergence of social assistance in low- and middle-income countries suggests the following points: (1) the bulk of available research focuses on policy adoption; (2) quantitative methods are scarce, perhaps due to the paucity of reliable data; (3) qualitative methods rely on key informant interviews and documentary analysis, sometimes complemented by process tracing; (4) apart from a subset of aid-dependent countries in sub-Saharan Africa, the literature does not find strong support for the view that the influence of multilaterals can explain the expansion of social assistance programs in low- and middle-income countries.

## Social Policy Adoption and Emerging Institutions

A focus on transnationally driven social policy diffusion might not contribute significantly to our understanding of emerging institutions in low- and middle-income countries. Policy adoption and policy transfers emphasize short-term, perhaps fleeting, government decision-making. Instead, the study of institutions focuses attention on longer-term redistributive patterns and commitments embedded in norms and practices and consistent with economic, social and political conditions. In the con-

---

[7] "Foreign donors operate as a distinct faction (or factions) within political settlements, whose power and influence do not simply flow from the importance of the resources they provide but, vitally, depend on the evolution of aid relations over years and the strategies African governments have devised to manage these donors" (Hickey et al. 2020, 7).

text of the recent expansion of social assistance, a focus on policy adoption reflects the short-term focus of transnational actors and international assistance. A brief review of two past examples of transnationally driven social policy transfers—provident funds and individual retirement accounts—will help clarify this point.

Colonial administrators were central to the adoption of provident funds in several British colonies in the 1950s and 1960s. Provident funds are compulsory saving schemes in which workers and employers make payroll contributions to a fund attracting uniform rates of interest. Workers can withdraw their savings and interests accrued for specified purposes: retirement, medical expenses, education expenses and housing. Colonial administrators "pushed" provident funds as a scaled-down version of social insurance, in the belief that the colonies lacked the capacity to support the latter (McKinnon et al. 1997). Provident funds were also appropriate to conditions in which labor moved between colonial territories as it enabled savings portability (Parrott 1968).

Provident funds were first adopted in Asia (Indonesia and Malaysia in 1951, India in 1952, Singapore in 1953, Sri Lanka in 1958); the Middle East (Egypt in 1955, Iraq in 1956) and later Africa (Nigeria in 1961, Tanzania in 1964, Zambia, Ghana and Kenya in 1965, Uganda in 1967) and finally in the Caribbean and Pacific Islands in the early 1970s.

The adoption of provident funds matches a "canonical" model of transnationally driven policy diffusion and transfer. Yet, with few exceptions, provident fund diffusion sheds very little light on existing welfare institutions in the countries concerned. Most of the colonies replaced provident funds by social insurance soon after independence. In Africa, provident funds collapsed under spiraling debt and public deficits in the 1980s. Singapore and Malaysia represent a handful of examples of countries maintaining provident funds as their core welfare institution.

Pension reform in 12 countries in Latin America in the 1990s led to the replacement of defined benefit pay-as-you-go pension schemes with individual retirement accounts (Mesa-Lago 2007). Later, pension reform spread to ten countries in Central and Eastern Europe. Policy transfers associated with individual retirement accounts have been studied closely (Orenstein 2011; Weyland 2008). Strong support and advocacy from the

World Bank appeared to provide another "canonical" case of transnationally driven policy diffusion (Béland and Orenstein 2013).

In Latin America, individual retirement accounts remain in place in only nine countries. They are largely residual institutions in terms of the share of contributors in the labor force, except for Chile and Costa Rica (Kritzer et al. 2011). In Central and Eastern Europe, individual retirement accounts introduced in the late 1990s and 2000s differed in important respects from the Latin American reforms, as they did not replace public pension systems but served as a complementary second pillar. The 2007 global financial crisis led to pension reform reversals (Whitehouse 2012). Hungary renationalized individual retirement accounts, and parametric reforms in most of the other countries have rebalanced public and private pension system components, strengthening the former.

These examples show that a focus on transnationally driven social policy adoption, whilst valuable in their own domain, might not take us very far with developing theories capable of explaining the shape of emerging welfare institutions in low- and middle-income countries.

## Conceptualizing Transnational Actors

Theories seeking to explain the development of welfare institutions in long-standing industrialized countries have focused attention on underlying economic and political conditions. Welfare institutions are studied as the outcome of processes of social stratification and coalition politics (Castles et al. 2012). For example, the influential work by Esping-Andersen and the power resources school (Esping-Andersen 1990, 1999; Korpi 1980) distinguished three main types of welfare regimes: a social democratic regime in the Nordic countries, a conservative regime in Central Europe and a liberal regime in the Anglo-Saxon countries. The distinctiveness of these welfare regimes is explained as the outcome of alternative class coalitions between workers and the middle class, leading to distinct institutional patterns. The nature of participation of the middle classes in redistributive coalitions emerges as key to the distinctive pattern of welfare states (van Kersbergen and Vis 2014). Theories of the development of welfare institutions in long-standing industrialized countries did not pay significant attention to external factors, but more recent research on welfare state retrenchment takes account of globalization and regional integration (Manow 2001).

## Integrating Transnational Actors

Theories of emerging institutions in low- and middle-income countries will need to address the specific forms of stratification and coalition politics present in low- and middle-income countries. In addition, they will need to pay particular attention to cross-national interdependencies and transnational actors. This section focuses on the latter.

The Introduction advanced the view that comparative literature on the expansion of social assistance has overstated the role of transnational actors, particularly multilaterals (see Chinyoka and Ulriksen, Chap. 10, this volume). The discussion in earlier sections argued that this bias has implications for the formulation of core research questions and for the effectiveness of qualitative methods. Uncritical assessments of the influence of transnational actors in the expansion of social assistance are reinforced by deficits in the conceptualization of the role of transnational actors in social policy. Theories of welfare institutions in long-standing industrialized countries have taken great care to conceptualize the role of key actors: trade unions, left parties, middle classes and employers. Yet transnational actors, especially multilaterals, are seldom the subject of serious scrutiny in discussions on welfare institutions and social policy in low- and middle-income countries. In literature, transnational actors appear either as binary variables in quantitative studies or as exogenous agents or stakeholders in qualitative studies. Which interests do they represent? What is the source of their power or influence? What is their ideology? Are they an economic class? These prior methodological questions, helping to conceptualize transnational actors, are seldom considered systematically. This section discusses two alternative perspectives.

A good starting point is Meyer's (2010) distinction between phenomenological approaches on the one hand and realist approaches on the other. Realist approaches explain welfare institutions in terms of power and interests. Policy models are "constructed to their advantage by powerful and interested actors" (Meyer 2010, 11). Instead, phenomenological approaches emphasize the role of cultural processes of the dissemination of world norms and values, in the context of which actors implement highly standardized and scripted narratives. We will return to realist accounts below, but it will be helpful to review how Meyers's *world society* perspective would explain the role and influence of transnational actors.

## Phenomenological Accounts of Transnational Actors

In Meyer's world society, national and supranational bureaucracies and policy networks disseminate, design and implement world norms. These norms "are universalistic, but also provide a universal orderly control system" (Meyer 2010, 11). In this phenomenological perspective, "institutionalised systems construct the actors as well as their activities" (2010, 2) where "the actor on the social stage is a scripted identity and enacts scripted action … [whilst] the institutional system—the organizations and cultural meanings that write and rewrite the scripts—become central" (Meyer 2010, 11).[8] The primacy of universalistic norms entails that models "of the modern actor stress cooperation in a global or universal order and good global citizenship" (Meyer 2010, 11).

Meyer explains the growth of professional and organizational structures as a means of combining constructed universalistic actor scripts by a context in which "no state-like authority can arise to organize perceived interdependencies and moderate conflict … And their social authority derives from their disinterested reflection of transcending purposes, not from their own interests" (Meyer 2010, 6). Professional and expert individuals and their bodies are "disinterested Others". "They represent such collective and putatively universal goods as the environment, generalized human rights, or principle of rationality and progress" (Meyer 2010, 7).

The disjunction between these universalistic models and actual practice reinforces supranational interventions. "Everywhere there are injus-

---

[8] Although not directly relevant for the focus of this chapter, Usui (1994) tests the word society perspective by way of using data on social security legislation and attendance to ILO Conferences. The findings "suggest that the world institutional environment is a strong force in the universalisation of social welfare policies" (Usui 1994, 271).

tices and inconsistencies made visible through forms of scrutiny including scientific measurement and investigation. The injustices in a stateless world, call for further expansion in the imagined capacities and responsibilities of human and organizational actors" (Meyer 2010, 13).

This perspective is reflected in the global social assistance models developed in von Gliszczynski and Leisering (2016) and Leisering (2019). They understand global social policy models as models originating from, and associated with, international organizations. Their legitimacy rests on their claim to represent universal world cultural values and ideas rather than vested interests, they are "disinterested others". According to Meyer, they focus on "cognitive and normative models of SCT devised by *international organisations* rather than actual social cash transfer programmes" (von Gliszczynski and Leisering 2016, 326). They find that "in the 2000s international organizations established a new field of global social policy, SCT, defined by way of four models—social pensions, family allowances, conditional cash transfers and general household assistance" (von Gliszczynski and Leisering 2016, 337).

*Global social policy* also assigns a central role to transnational actors in the formation of social policy in low- and middle-income countries (Deacon 1997). While acknowledging the influence of domestic factors on social policy, its core aim is to "restate the importance of a focus on the specific social policy recommendations which certain global players make to countries concerning their national social policies" (Deacon and Stubbs 2013, 6). Its main focus is "on the one hand, the ideas, discourses and programmes of social policy developed by international (multilateral) organizations, and on the other hand the influence of transnational policy actors on domestic policy change" (Yeates 2018, 28). The justification of this central focus on transnational actors rests on the view that they "shape policy agendas globally, and can change the course of institutional pathways by exercising coercive and persuasive resources that initiate and progress policy initiatives" (Yeates 2018, 29).

Global social policy shares with world society a globalist approach, but it places a stronger emphasis on the agency of transnational policy actors, whereas they are simply scripted others in world society. Global social policy and world society also emphasize a primary role for discourse in the construction of policy models (Tag 2013).[9] This connects directly to a series of recent papers discussing ideational dimensions of social policy (Béland 2016; Béland and Orenstein 2013; Jenson 2010). Ideational accounts of social policy reforms are well in line with the emphasis on discourse in world society and global social policy perspectives. Ideational processes "help construct the social and economic problems most public policies are designed to address… [and] help actors define their interests, which are shaped not only by material conditions but through interpretations of these conditions" (Béland and Orenstein 2013, 127). The main premise justifying the interest in ideational processes in social policy reform is that they influence domestic policy, especially ideational processes among multilaterals.[10] Ideas matter because they result in policy change.

Applying ideational perspectives to international organizations, Béland and Orenstein (2013) provide an interesting characterization. First, international organizations are "open systems" in the sense that they interact freely with their environment, without the restrictions of a worldview or core interests and preferences.[11] Second, international organizations have a measure of autonomy with respect to the countries they serve. Third, their lack of "hard" power gives a prominent role to ideational processes in defining their influence on domestic policy.[12] This characterization of the "power" of international organizations is a close relative of the "disinterested Other" in Meyer's world society, however with an added emphasis on the role of contestation and learning in global social policy.

---

[9] Deacon and Stubbs refer to discourse as the "most slippery of concepts". They define it as "the inter-subjective production of meaning" and as "order of ideas and practices which frame the context within which specific policy debates are situated" (Deacon and Stubbs 2013, 15).

[10] "Examining changing ideational and discursive processes within international organizations matters because studies have shown that these processes can have a direct influence on domestic policy. This makes the analysis of how ideas and discourse evolve within international organizations one of the most important frontiers of global policy theory" (Béland and Orenstein 2013, 127).

[11] "In contrast to advocacy think tanks, which identify with relatively stable ideological creeds and policy paradigms, international organizations can and do change" (Béland and Orenstein 2013, 137).

[12] Taking on board international organizations' "lack of veto power … and the limits of financial conditionalities, ideational processes are the most central means through which they attempt to shape domestic policy" (Béland and Orenstein 2013, 127).

This characterization resonates with the international organizations' own reflective view of their place in the world—one they miss few opportunities to project.

## Realist Accounts of Transnational Actors and Influence

Realist accounts of transnational actors and influences in social policy in low- and middle-income countries depart from the basic proposition that social policy reflects the "distribution of preferences and their political organizations" in their respective polities (Haggard and Kaufman 2008, 359). External factors are important because they influence the political and economic conditioning of domestic preferences, and in some cases directly through exercising power over jurisdictions (e.g. structural adjustment in Latin America, the Soviet Bloc).[13] Transnational influences are one of the factors capable of influencing domestic social policy.

What explains the particular preferences and interests of transnational actors? In realist perspectives, international organizations are primarily theorized as reflecting the preferences of hegemonic countries or groups of countries. When discussing pension reform in Latin America, for example, Huber and Stephens (2012) underline the crucial role of international financial institutions (IFIs). The spread of pension is explained by the fact that "neoliberal ideology penetrated the policy-making circles in many Latin American and (European) countries ... There is clearly a material basis to the hegemony of neoliberalism in the form of control by advanced countries of the IFIs" (Huber and Stephens 2012, 252). This is disputed by Haggard and Kaufman (2008) in their study on social policy reforms in middle-income countries in Latin America, East Asia and Eastern Europe. They argue that the hegemonic influence of the USA has largely subsided compared to the earlier Cold War period. While acknowledging that social policy shows some convergence in a neoliberal direction,

---

[13] "There is a plethora of ways in which 'the international' operates on states: war and security calculations; cleavages over economic openness; the influence of international organizations; and the diffusion of policy ideas" (Haggard and Kaufman 2008, 348).

they see "very little evidence that international political forces ... are leading to a homogenization of social policy" (Haggard and Kaufman 2008, 350).

Some studies on the influence of international organizations on the recent expansion of social assistance in low- and middle-income countries echo Huber and Stephens' description of the dominance of neoliberalism in pension reform. Teichman (2007), for example, finds a consistent thread from neoliberal ideas to the IFIs' endorsement of conditional income transfers. Conditional income transfers, and more generally tax-financed social assistance, are assessed as being consistent with a residual view of social and public policy present in neoliberalism.

Discussing social policy in Latin America, Huber and Stephens (2012) find a shift in the position of international organizations as regards social spending. They suggest "the IFIs, particularly the World Bank, have abandoned their Washington Consensus position and now advocate investments in human capital and reductions in poverty and inequality" (Huber and Stephens 2012, 261). Arguably, this is consistent with the IFIs' advocacy of safety nets and especially conditional income transfers.[14]

In the context of a realist perspective on the role of transnational actors in the expansion of social assistance in low- and middle-income countries, a key question is whether the IFIs' potential shift in preferences reflects a shift in the domestic preferences of long-standing industrialized countries or a shift in the latter's preferences regarding social policy in low- and middle-income countries. The former follows from proposals for reforming welfare states in a social investment direction (Hemerijck 2013). The latter would be consistent with long-standing industrialized countries' concerns with conflict (e.g. "fragile" states) or transnational migration. A shift in the preferences of transnational actors for social policy in low- and middle-income countries might also be explained by potential contestation among international organizations, perhaps reflecting differences across long-standing industrialized countries, leading to a

---

[14] I say arguably because it is not clear that, in the context of social policy, the World Bank has a preference for investment in human development (conditional cash transfers). If anything, the safety net operational work of the Bank is a mixed bag.

paradigm shift.[15] An alternative reading is that the change in the social policy preferences of international organizations reflects changes in domestic social policy among emerging economies.[16] It is worth restating the fact that the World Bank built on experiences about conditional cash transfers made in Brazil, Mexico and Bangladesh.

## Transnational Actors and Social Assistance Expansion

This brief review was meant to shed light on alternative conceptualizations of the role of transnational actors in domestic policy. Can they help us understand the recent expansion of social assistance in low- and middle-income countries?

*World society* phenomenological accounts would suggest, as von Gliszczynski and Leisering (2016) do, that transnational actors are best conceptualized as "disinterested Others" devising and implementing a universalistic script. The evolution of *global social policy* suggests a certain degree of convergence with *world society*. Earlier versions of global social policy (Deacon 1997) show multiple references to the hegemony of the Washington Consensus advanced by realist perspectives, but growing reliance on ideational approaches in later versions (Deacon and Stubbs 2013) moves it closer toward the universalistic script in *world society* (Tag 2013).

The findings from the review of comparative studies in section "Comparative Research on Social Assistance" and the broader literature on the growth of social assistance challenge phenomenological perspectives in important ways. The multiplicity of scripts (e.g. policy instruments), the indeterminacy of transnational advice and influence (e.g. contrasting assessment of conditional income transfers) and the lack of

---

[15] See Jenson (2010) for a comparison of the diffusion of social investment policies in the OECD and Latin America, the latter emphasizing the growth of conditional income transfers. Pritchett (2002) provides a perspective on the role of contestation within the World Bank to explain the incidence of impact evaluations and, generally, evidence gathering.

[16] Researchers have suggested that conditional income transfers could in principle appeal to both neoliberal and progressively oriented policy-makers (González de la Rocha and Escobar 2012; Brooks 2015). In fact, conditional income transfers have been supported by left-of-center and right-of-center coalitions in Latin America.

evidence concerning the very influence of multilaterals—all work to challenge phenomenological accounts. This is significant because phenomenological perspectives provide, albeit implicitly, much of the grounding for ideational studies on social assistance diffusion in low- and middle-income countries.

Realist perspectives on the influence of transnational actors conceptualize international organizations in terms of the preferences and power of hegemonic early industrializers.[17] The influence of transnational actors on domestic policy flows from the global power of long-standing industrialized countries. Realist accounts have interpreted the growth of social assistance as an extension of neoliberal policies pushed by hegemonic long-standing industrialized countries. Again, comparing this perspective with the main findings from the review of comparative studies in section "Comparative Research on Social Assistance" suggests that they are significant. Chief among them is the fact that conditional income transfers did not emerge from the prescriptions of IFIs in indebted or aid-dependent countries, but instead they emerged from domestic policy innovations in Brazil and Mexico.

An alternative realist approach is to suggest that there has been a shift in the preferences of hegemonic actors toward social investment, consistent with the view put forward by Huber and Stephens (2012). It is perhaps too early to assess this hypothesis. There is growing interest and discussion around social investment in European countries (Hemerijck 2013) but, aside from long-standing social policy in the Nordic countries, it would be difficult to describe these developments as a paradigm shift at this point in time. Social investment is hardly a priority in the USA.

Perhaps the main conclusion that can be drawn from this section is that further research is needed to construct a persuasive account of the

---

[17] From a realist perspective, the view of multilaterals as "ideas brokers" does not take us very far with theorizing their role. Whatever explanatory power multilaterals could offer in theorizing emerging welfare institutions in low- and middle-income countries could be captured more directly by the core interests and preferences they intermediate. This would also apply to contestation among transnational actors. Contestation reflecting the preferences of grouping (factions) among long-standing industrialized countries in the context of social assistance in Africa is discussed in Hickey et al. (2020).

role of transnational actors in the expansion of social assistance in low- and middle-income countries (see Shriwise, Chap. 2, this volume).

## Conclusions

The rapid growth of social assistance in low- and middle-income countries has highlighted the need to develop theories capable of explaining emergent welfare institutions in these countries. Comparative research is essential to this project. It is urgent to identify with precision the forms of stratification explaining the shape of emerging institutions. It is also important to pay attention to interdependencies, especially as these are likely to have stronger influence on the shape of the emerging welfare institutions in low- and middle-income countries than they did in the expansion of welfare states in long-standing industrialized countries.

To date, the scarce comparative literature has paid considerable attention to the role of transnational actors. Prominent studies attribute the expansion of social assistance, conditional income transfers in particular, to the influence of transnational actors, especially multilaterals. This contribution has challenged this widely held view. Transnational actors are highly visible in international policy debates and in some cases in domestic debates in low- and middle-income countries, especially in aid-dependent countries. However, the view that the expansion of social assistance is explained by the influence of multilaterals finds limited support in the literature reviewed in this contribution.

It is important to address this issue because it carries implications for the focus, scope and methods of comparative research. A disproportionate focus on transnational actors biases comparative research in ways that might turn out to be counterproductive. Its implicit research question—what makes policies travel?—crowds out more fundamental questions about the causal factors giving shape to emerging welfare institutions in low- and middle-income countries (Schmitt et al., Chap. 14, this volume). A brief review of two "canonical" transnationally driven social policy reforms, provident funds and individual retirement accounts, has demonstrated the need to look beyond short-term transnationally driven policy diffusion processes in order to explain the shape of medium- and longer-term institutions in low- and middle-income countries.

The discussion in the contribution has questioned the, at best partial, conceptualization of transnational actors in the comparative literature. Transnational actors often appear as binary variables in quantitative research or as exogenous actors in qualitative studies. The contribution has sketched alternative phenomenological and realist perspectives on transnational actors and assessed their potential contribution to understanding the role of transnational actors in the emergence of welfare institutions in low- and middle-income countries. Further research is needed to refine these perspectives before they can shed light on the role of transnational actors in shaping emergent welfare institutions.

The way forward for comparative research on emerging welfare institutions in low- and middle-income countries involves more of the following: study of institutions, study of domestic factors in the context of political and economic interdependencies, quantitative comparative analysis, attention to counterfactuals and better data.

# References

Barrientos, Armando. 2013. *Social Assistance in Developing Countries*. Cambridge: Cambridge University Press.

———. 2018. *Social Assistance in Low and Middle Income Countries Dataset (SALMIC)*. Manchester: Global Development Institute, University of Manchester. www.social-assistance.manchester.ac.uk.

Béland, Daniel. 2016. Ideas and Institutions in Social Policy Research. *Social Policy and Administration* 50 (6): 734–730.

Béland, Daniel, and Mitchell A. Orenstein. 2013. International Organizations as Policy Actors: An Ideational Approach. *Global Social Policy* 13 (2): 125–143.

Borges, Fabián A. 2018. Neoliberalism with a Human Face. *Comparative Politics* 50 (2): 147–167.

Borges Sugiyama, Natasha. 2011. The Diffusion of Conditional Cash Transfer Programs in the Americas. *Global Social Policy* 11 (2–3): 250–278.

Brooks, Sarah. 2015. Social Protection for the Poorest: The Adoption of Antipoverty Cash Transfer Programs in the Global South. *Politics and Society* 43 (4): 551–582.

Castles, Francis G., Jane Lewis Stephan Leibfried, Herbert Obinger, and Christopher Pierson. 2012. *The Oxford Handbook of the Welfare State.* Oxford: Oxford University Press.

CEPAL. 2015. *Desarrollo Social Inclusivo. Una Nueva Generación de Políticas Para Superar La Pobreza y Reducir La Desigualdad En América Latina y El Caribe.* Report LC.L/4056 (CDS.1/3). Santiago, Chile: CEPAL, División Desarrollo Social.

Deacon, Bob. 1997. *Global Social Policy. International Organizations and the Future of Welfare.* London: Sage.

Deacon, Bob, and Paul Stubbs. 2013. Global Social Policy Studies: Conceptual and Analytical Reflections. *Global Social Policy* 13 (1): 5–23.

Díaz-Cayeros, Alberto, and Beatriz Magaloni. 2009. Aiding Latin America's Poor. *Journal of Democracy* 20 (4): 36–49.

Dodlova, Marina, Anna Giolbas, and Jann Lay. 2018. Non-Contributory Social Transfer Programmes in Developing Countries: A New Dataset and Research Agenda. *Data in Brief* 16: 51–64.

Esping-Andersen, Gosta. 1990. *The Three Worlds of Welfare Capitalism.* Cambridge: Polity Press.

———. 1999. *Social Foundations of Postindustrial Economies.* Oxford: Oxford University Press.

Fenwick, Tracy Beck. 2013. Stuck Between the Past and the Future: Conditional Cash Transfer Programme Development and Policy Feedbacks in Brazil and Argentina. *Global Social Policy* 13 (2): 144–167.

Garay, Candelaria. 2016. *Social Policy Expansion in Latin America.* New York: Cambridge University Press.

von Gliszczynski, Moritz, and Lutz Leisering. 2016. Constructing New Global Models of Social Security: How International Organizations Defined the Field of Social Cash Transfers in the 2000s. *Journal of Social Policy* 45 (2): 325–343.

González de la Rocha, Mercedes, and Agustín Lapatí Escobar. 2012. *Pobreza, Transferencias Condicionadas y Sociedad.* Mexico City: CIESAS.

Haggard, Stephan, and Robert R. Kaufman. 2008. *Development, Democracy and Welfare States. Latin America, Asia and Eastern Europe.* Princeton: Princeton University Press.

Hemerijck, Anton. 2013. *Changing Welfare States.* Oxford: Oxford University Press.

Hickey, Sam, and Jeremy Seekings. 2020. Who Should Get What, How and Why? DfID and the Transnational Politics of Social Protection. In *The Politics of Social Protection in Eastern and Southern Africa*, ed. Sam Hickey, Tom Lavers, Miguel Niño-Zarazúa, and Jeremy Seekings, 249–276. Oxford: Oxford University Press.

Hickey, Sam, Tom Lavers, Miguel Niño-Zarazúa, and Jeremy Seekings. 2020. The Negotiated Politics of Social Protection in Sub-Saharan Africa. In *The Politics of Social Protection in Eastern and Southern Africa*, ed. Sam Hickey, Tom Lavers, Miguel Niño-Zarazúa, and Jeremy Seekings, 249–276. Oxford: Oxford University Press.

Huber, Evelyne, and John D. Stephens. 2012. *Democracy and the Left in Latin America. Social Policy and Inequality in Latin America*. Chicago: University of Chicago Press.

Jenson, Jane. 2010. Diffusing Ideas for After Neoliberalism: The Social Investment Perspective in Europe and Latin America. *Global Social Policy* 10 (1): 59–84.

van Kersbergen, Kees, and Barbara Vis. 2014. *Comparative Welfare State Politics: Development, Opportunities, and Reform*. Cambridge: Cambridge University Press.

Korpi, Walter. 1980. Social Policy and the Distributional Conflict in the Capitalist Democracies: A Preliminary Comparative Framework. *West European Politics* 3: 296–316.

Kritzer, Barbara E., Stephen J. Kay, and Tapen Sinha. 2011. Next Generation of Individual Account Pension Reforms in Latin America. *Social Security Bulletin* 71 (1): 35–76.

Leisering, Lutz. 2019. *The Global Rise of Social Cash Transfers. How States and International Organizations Constructed a New Instrument for Combating Poverty*. Oxford: Oxford University Press.

Manow, Philip. 2001. Comparative Institutional Advantages of Welfare State Regimes and New Coalitions in Welfare State Reforms. In *The New Politics of the Welfare State*, ed. Paul Pierson. Oxford: Oxford University Press.

Martínez Franzoni, Juliana, and Koen Voorend. 2011. Actors and Ideas Behind CCTs in Chile, Costa Rica and El Salvador. *Global Social Policy* 11 (2–3): 279–298.

McKinnon, Roddy, Roger Charlton, and Harry T. Munro. 1997. The National Provident Fund Model: An Analytical and Evaluative Reassessment. *International Social Security Review* 50 (2): 43–61.

Mesa-Lago, Carmelo. 2007. *Reassembling Social Security. A Survey of Pensions and Healthcare Reforms in Latin America*. Oxford: Oxford University Press.

Meyer, John W. 2010. World Society, Institutional Theories, and the Actor. *Annual Review of Sociology* 36: 1–20.

Obinger, Herbert, Carina Schmitt, and Peter Starke. 2013. Policy Diffusion and Policy Transfer in Comparative Welfare State Research. *Social Policy and Administration* 47 (1): 111–129.

Orenstein, Mitchell A. 2011. Pension Privatization in Crisis: Death or Rebirth of a Global Policy Trend? *International Social Security Review* 64 (3): 65–80.

Parrott, A.L. 1968. Problems Arising from the Transition from Provident Funds to Pension Schemes. *International Social Security Review* 21 (4): 530–557.

Peck, Jamie, and Nick Theodore. 2015. *Fast Policy. Experimental Statecraft at the Thresholds of Neoliberalism*. Minneapolis: University of Minnesota Press.

Pritchett, Lant. 2002. It Pays to Be Ignorant: A Simple Political Economy of Rigorous Program Evaluation. *The Journal of Policy Reform* 5 (4): 251–269.

Schmitt, Carina. 2019. The Coverage of Social Protection in the Global South. *International Journal of Social Welfare*. Online first.

Schmitt, Carina, Hanna Lierse, Herbert Obinger, and Laura Seelkopf. 2015. The Global Emergence of Social Protection: Explaining Social Security Legislation. *Politics and Society* 43 (4): 503–524.

Simpson, Joshua. 2018. Do Donors Matter? An Analysis of Conditional Cash Transfer Adoption in Sub-Saharan Africa. *Global Social Policy* 18 (2): 143–168.

Székely, Miguel. 2015. *Cambios En La Institucionalidad de La Política de Protección Social En América Latina y El Caribe: Avances y Nuevos Desafíos*. Nota Técnica 810, Washington, DC: Inter-American Development Bank.

Tag, Miriam. 2013. The Cultural Construction of Global Social Policy: Theorizing Formations and Transformations. *Global Social Policy* 13 (1): 24–44.

Teichman, Judith. 2007. Redistributive Conflict and Social Policy in Latin America. *World Development* 36 (3): 446–460.

Usui, Chikako. 1994. Welfare State Development in a World System Context: Event History Analysis of First Social Insurance Legislation among 60 Countries, 1880–1960. In *The Comparative Political Economy of the Welfare State*, ed. Thomas Janoski and Alexander M. Hicks, 254–277. Cambridge: Cambridge University Press.

Weible, Karen, Tobias Böger, John Berten, Moritz von Gliszczynski, and Lutz Leisering. 2015. FLOORCASH. Bielefeld: Bielefeld University. www.floorcash.org.

Weyland, Kurt. 2008. *Bounded Rationality and Policy Diffusion. Social Sector Reform in Latin America*. Princeton: Princeton University Press.

Whitehouse, Edward. 2012. *Reversals of Systemic Pension Reforms in Central and Eastern Europe, OECD Pensions Outlook*. Paris: OECE Social Policy Division.

World Bank. 2015. *The State of Social Safety Nets 2015: Report.* Washington, DC: The World Bank.

———. 2016. *Atlas of Social Protection – Indicators of Resilience and Equity.* Database ASPIRE. http://datatopics.worldbank.org/aspire/home.

Yeates, Nicola. 2018. *Global Approaches to Social Policy, 2018–2.* UNRISD Working Paper, Geneva: UNRISD.

Zucco, Cesar, Juan Pablo Luna, and Gokce Ozgen Baykal. 2019. Do Conditionalities Increase Support for Government Transfers? *Journal of Development Studies*, online.

**Open Access** This chapter is licensed under the terms of the Creative Commons Attribution 4.0 International License (http://creativecommons.org/licenses/by/4.0/), which permits use, sharing, adaptation, distribution and reproduction in any medium or format, as long as you give appropriate credit to the original author(s) and the source, provide a link to the Creative Commons licence and indicate if changes were made.

The images or other third party material in this chapter are included in the chapter's Creative Commons licence, unless indicated otherwise in a credit line to the material. If material is not included in the chapter's Creative Commons licence and your intended use is not permitted by statutory regulation or exceeds the permitted use, you will need to obtain permission directly from the copyright holder.

# 14

## Critical Assessment and Outlook

Carina Schmitt, Bastian Becker, Judith M. Ebeling, and Amanda Shriwise

This volume has traced the role played by external actors in social protection in the Global South, from colonialism to international aid. The authors aimed at elucidating whether and how external actors and transnational relationships have influenced the formation, development and transformation of social protection arrangements. In this critical assessment and outlook, we first summarize the main findings of the book volume in a synthesized way (see section "Synthesized Summary"). Subsequently we discuss and critically evaluate our findings (see section "Discussion and Critical Evaluation"). A final section provides an outlook on potential future avenues for research (see section "Outlook").

---

C. Schmitt (✉) • B. Becker • J. M. Ebeling • A. Shriwise
SOCIUM Research Center on Inequality and Social Policy,
University of Bremen, Bremen, Germany
e-mail: carina.schmitt@uni-bremen.de; Bastian.becker@uni-bremen.de; judith.ebeling@uni-bremen.de; shriwise@uni-bremen.de

© The Author(s) 2020
C. Schmitt (ed.), *From Colonialism to International Aid*, Global Dynamics of Social Policy, https://doi.org/10.1007/978-3-030-38200-1_14

## Synthesized Summary

This book volume focuses on the role of external actors and transnational relationships from a more theoretical perspective in Parts I and IV, while Parts II and III present more empirically oriented chapters. The chapters of this book have contributed to studies on social protection in the Global South by ascertaining the types of external actors involved, how they exert their influence over time (see section "External Actors and Their Strategies from Colonialism to International Aid"), what their main objectives and preferences with regard to social protection look like (see section "External Actors' Objectives and Preferences Regarding Social Protection") and how they interact with domestic actors and in what ways their influence is conditioned, limited or translated by national factors (see section "Interaction with Domestic Factors").

## External Actors and Their Strategies from Colonialism to International Aid

External actors have played a major role in policy-making from the very outset. Those contributions which focused on colonial times highlighted the role of European colonial actors, either comparing the British and the French colonial empires (Schmitt, Chap. 6, this volume; Becker, Chap. 7, this volume) or comparing cases within one of the empires (Mioni and Petersen, Chap. 3, this volume; Künzler, Chap. 4, this volume; Seekings, Chap. 5, this volume). *Across* empires, distinct imperial strategies led to differing approaches to social protection, despite the shared objective to decelerate the demise of the respective colonial empire (Becker, Chap. 7, this volume). Whereas the French focused on income maintenance of waged labor and the social insurance principle in their colonies (as reflected by the *Code du Travail* of 1952), the British Poor Law tradition led to an early diffusion of social assistance concepts (Schmitt, Chap. 6, this volume). Moreover, while the British typically used indirect rule, involving also non-state actors, the French employed more direct rule during colonial times. This is reflected by France's strong reliance on governmental actors for the distribution of aid to former colonies still today (Becker, Chap. 7, this volume).

Strategies also differed *within* empires. For example, the British incorporated their territories into the colonial economy in different ways. Kenya's incorporation as a "labor reserve economy" and Tanganyika's as a "cash crop economy" led to higher taxation (and later more extensive tax-financed social protection) in the former than in the latter (Künzler, Chap. 4, this volume). Moreover, colonial actors were not homogeneous, such that colonial officials in the colony at times also acted in disagreement with those in the metropole for instance (Künzler, Chap. 4, this volume). In South Africa, the colonial-era design was retained *despite* the ruling elite's strong reservations about it, and as a result, the system of combining social assistance with 'semi-social insurance' was transferred from the pre- to the post-independence period. In addition to direct influence by colonial actors, Seekings (see Chap. 5, this volume) stressed the role of more indirect external influence through the diffusion of ideas. In the case of South Africa, these ideas came from Britain, Australia and New Zealand through white elites "embedded in imperial networks" (117).

International organizations started to become more significant external actors after the period of colonial rule. For instance, Mioni and Petersen (see Chap. 3, this volume) found that the International Labour Organization (ILO) played a more important role in social reforms in newly independent Burma than in colonial Malaysia. In both countries, it was the Cold War context—rather than the common British colonial heritage—that determined the timing of early social welfare reforms (Mioni and Petersen, Chap. 3, this volume). Other international organizations that became increasingly active in social protection in the Global South include multilateral agencies, like United Nations (UN) agencies (e.g. the World Food Programme in Botswana), or the international financial institutions of the World Bank and the International Monetary Fund (IMF) and bilateral ones, such as the UK's Department for International Development (DFID). Moreover, additional external actors like international non-governmental organizations (INGOs), advocacy networks and epistemic communities have become more and more involved. On the African continent, the four leading global agencies working in social protection today are United Nations International Children's Emergency Fund (UNICEF), DFID, ILO and the World Bank (Devereux and Kapingidza, Chap. 11, this volume).

Often times, these international organizations employ a combination of financial leverage (i.e. providing or withholding aid) with technical support, expertise and policy recommendations (Dodlova, Chap. 8, this volume; Çemen and Yörük, Chap. 9, this volume; Devereux and Kapingidza, Chap. 11, this volume). Furthermore, strategies followed by contemporary external actors include, for example, setting norms and standards and building evidence (Devereux and Kapingidza, Chap. 11, this volume). However, the instruments at their disposal are at least at the surface those of "soft" rather than "hard" power, such that their influence may also be transmitted more indirectly and through ideational processes (Seekings, Chap. 5, this volume; Devereux and Kapingidza, Chap. 11, this volume; Haang'andu and Béland, Chap. 12, this volume; Barrientos, Chap. 13, this volume). Problematically, the policy ideas and norms disseminated by (contemporary) external actors are often presented as being neutral and universally applicable, despite being rooted in Western ideologies and likely to be shaped by Western political interests (Haang'andu and Béland, Chap. 12, this volume).

Moving from colonialism to international aid, certain changes and continuities among external actors involved in social protection-making can be observed. In Malaysia, for example, the British-run colonial government acted as a 'gatekeeper' against interference by international organizations in its territory, yet in newly independent Burma, not part of the British Commonwealth, the ILO was able to play a greater role. Here also national governments, other than those of the colonial metropole such as the US, began to play a part in social protection-making, in particular during the Cold War (Mioni and Petersen, Chap. 3, this volume). Nonetheless, the British maintained their post-independence influence through other channels, such as concentrating the work of their DFID in former British colonies (Seekings, Chap. 5, this volume). In fact, Becker was able to show that the colonial past affects the ways in which former colonial powers distribute aid still today, that is, to which sectors and through which actors international aid is distributed. Thus, aid is one way through which former colonial powers continue to exert their influence, particularly in the field of social protection (Becker, Chap. 7, this volume).

## External Actors' Objectives and Preferences Regarding Social Protection

There are various reasons for external actors to get involved in the field of social protection in countries of the Global South. They may be motivated by political objectives, like seeking to promote political stability as an anti-revolutionary/anti-protest strategy. In Burma and Malaysia during the Cold War period, social reforms constituted part of anti-communism strategies. While the US, the UK and the ILO initially pursued differing agendas—the US being focused on its geo-strategic concerns; the UK on upholding the British Empire (later the Commonwealth); and the ILO on its more technical agenda—their interests eventually converged,[1] allowing for high levels of coordination among them (Mioni and Petersen, Chap. 3, this volume). Containing social unrest was found to also be motivating social protection recommendations by the World Bank nowadays (Çemen and Yörük, Chap. 9, this volume). Haang'andu and Béland, but also Barrientos, stressed that the objectives of international organizations may in fact reflect the preferences of hegemonic countries that contribute to their resources (Chaps. 12 and 13, this volume). The ILO's activities in Burma and Malaysia, for instance, were also largely influenced by prevailing Western ideological concerns (Mioni and Petersen, Chap. 3, this volume).

However, international organizations may also differ with regard to their objectives. Künzler, for example, found that in both Kenya and Tanzania there was disagreement among the donor community on models for both pensions and health in the early 2000s. As a result, domestic politics appear to have played a more significant role, particularly in the case of the latter. In areas where there is less disagreement than in the field of education, donor influence tends to be greater (Künzler, Chap. 4, this volume). In Zimbabwe, on the other hand, inter-agency disagreements on how to best implement social protection turned the political arena into a "battlefield for external actors", namely the World Bank, UNICEF and the ILO (Devereux and Kapingidza, Chap. 11, this volume, 295). Part of the reason for this is that different international organizations may prefer dif-

---

[1] Not least due to the intertwined nature of communist uprisings and decolonization as well as the ILO's proximity to Western ideologies.

ferent types of social protection. The World Bank, for instance, is the most prominent supporter of conditional cash transfers (CCTs), while UNICEF and DFID typically prefer unconditional family support schemes, and the ILO pursues a rights-based approach to social protection (Seekings, Chap. 5, this volume; Dodlova, Chap. 8, this volume; Devereux and Kapingidza, Chap. 11, this volume). Social pensions, on the other hand, are pushed to a lesser extent by external actors (Dodlova, Chap. 8, this volume). International organizations were also found to differ with respect to other program design questions. Whereas DFID and UNICEF are more likely to promote categorical targeting, the World Bank favors proxy means testing, among others (Dodlova, Chap. 8, this volume).

In the past, French colonial rulers supported family allowances to strengthen the core family, whereas social pensions are more likely to be found in (former) British colonies (Schmitt, Chap. 6, this volume). What is more, the early decision of the French to implement insurance-based social protection in its territories continues to decrease the likelihood of tax-financed, non-contributory social assistance being introduced in former French colonies today, as restructuring existing institutions would involve great costs. Conversely, the greater incidence of social assistance programs in former British colonies (in contrast to French ones) is linked to the Poor Law tradition guiding British colonial social policy (Schmitt, Chap. 6, this volume).

Despite external actors engaging in a broad range of social protection, including famine relief, pensions, health, disability policy and education, there has been an increasing focus on non-contributory social protection schemes, i.e. social assistance (or social cash transfers). This has significantly affected the balance between social assistance and social insurance in countries of the Global South (Barrientos, Chap. 13, this volume). Moreover, donor-financed social cash transfers have been criticized for their short-term focus as opposed to aiming for long-term social protection institutions—a dissonance that is also reflected by research on social protection in the Global South. Building sustainable, long-term institutions for social protection "requires deeper engagement with domestic politics" (Barrientos, Chap. 13, this volume, PAGE). Consequently, it is crucial to pay close attention to their interplay with domestic factors when examining the role of external actors.

## Interaction with Domestic Factors

On the one hand, there are instances in which the sway of the external actors supersedes that of domestic factors. In other instances, domestic factors considerably constrain and/or shape the scope of external influences. The legacy of French colonial rule, for instance, with its emphasis on the social insurance-based model appears to outweigh the positive influence of democratic institutions for the adoption of social assistance schemes (Schmitt, Chap. 6, this volume). In present times, external actors exert greater influence in countries that are dependent on aid and/or politically weak. The introduction of social protection reforms through external actors in Zimbabwe, for example, coincided with the country's economic collapse and significant domestic political uncertainty in the late 2000s (Devereux and Kapingidza, Chap. 11, this volume). Despite being largely independent of international aid, also Botswana was more susceptible to external support at key moments in its history, such as the drought in the 1960s or the AIDS crisis in the 1990s, when external actors were able to promote their agendas more efficaciously (Chinyoka and Ulriksen, Chap. 10, this volume). Similarly, UNICEF took advantage of the intensified political competition during the run-up to Kenya's national elections in 2002 to garner political support for its proposed child grant (Künzler, Chap. 4, this volume).

Moreover, social protection recommendations by the World Bank alone do not appear to have a strong direct effect on social protection spending in emerging economies. Yet, if preceded by certain cases of social unrest, general strikes in particular, policy recommendations by the World Bank are found to reinforce the positive relationship between social unrest and social protection spending (Çemen and Yörük, Chap. 9, this volume). In other words, domestic "social unrest plays a key role in how policy-makers translate structural forces into social policies and whether they choose to diffuse recommendations from IFIs" (PAGE). Furthermore, the influence of external actors appears to lessen when their agendas run contrary to domestic priorities. While having successfully lobbied for an unconditional cash transfer aimed at children in Kenya, external actors faced resistance from the Tanzanian government, whose affordability and long-term sustainability concerns led it to prefer productivist elements and conditions (Künzler, Chap. 4, this volume). In fact, in many sub-Saharan African countries indigenous concepts of informal social support and reciprocity do not combine easily with the emphasis on the individual inherent in the rights-based approaches of many Western external actors (Chinyoka and Ulriksen, Chap. 10, this volume; Devereux and Kapingidza, Chap. 11, this volume; Haang'andu and Béland, Chap. 12, this volume). The government of Botswana, for instance, has resisted the introduction of a poverty targeted cash grant, instead of emphasizing family/community, self-reliance and hard work (Chinyoka and Ulriksen, Chap. 10, this volume). Across the sub-Saharan region, the transnational disability movement has also failed to take into account context-specific norms and experiences of disability by falsely assuming the universality of Western paradigms (Haang'andu and Béland, Chap. 12, this volume).

Preceding the more recent wave of donor-supported social protection, the pre- and post-independence social protection models in Southern Africa were also not merely imposed by external actors but rather resulted from combinations of external ideas and predominant norms among local elites, adapted to local conditions (Seekings, Chap. 5, this volume). In the Cold War context in South East Asia, Western ideas on social reform were also adapted to local conditions, such as pronounced nationalism in independent Burma, and the quest for legitimizing the state during transition from colonial rule to independence in Malaysia (Mioni and Petersen, Chap. 3, this volume). Accordingly, Burma's development plan in the 1950s was formulated in a way as to appeal to both foreign donors and potential nationalist critics. More generally, Haang'andu and Béland (Chap. 12, this volume) conclude that foreign external ideas can be adapted or translated to fit domestic conditions (ideational translation) or they can be combined with local norms to create new ones (ideational bricolage). The way in which external actors interact with domestic (f)actors has important implications for social policy-making and its longevity in the Global South.

## Discussion and Critical Evaluation

### Learning from Quantitative and Qualitative Approaches

Following recent developments in the discipline, we approached the influence of external actors by way of quantitative and qualitative methods. Quantitative methods provide a bird's eye perspective, while qualitative methods delve into the intricacies of specific cases. Several well-known differences between the two methodological camps became also manifest in this volume. Where quantitative analyses often make strong assumptions about external actors and mechanisms, qualitative analyses shed light on how actors shape preferences and make specific choices. For example, Dodlova (Chap. 8, this volume) uses a quantitative approach that finds a correlation between specific social protection programs and the involvement of specific donors. However, on the basis of quantitative studies it is not possible to empirically assess whether this is a result of different donor preferences or whether recipient countries are strategic in the involvement of respective donors. As a consequence, the author points out that "it would be interesting to investigate this hypothesis on the basis of case studies and other qualitative research" (p. XX). Chapter 10 by Chinyoka and Ulriksen offers exactly such a qualitative study, attesting to the important role of domestic governments, especially their ideological stances. Similarly, Haang'andu and Béland (Chap. 12, this volume) argue that local demand for (external) social policy ideas is decisive for them to be implemented sustainably.

Similar comparisons, although with regard to colonial legacies, can be made regarding the quantitative chapters by Becker (Chap. 7, this volume) and Schmitt (Chap. 6, this volume), and the two qualitative chapters by Künzler (Chap. 4, this volume) and Seekings (Chap. 5, this volume). Both Becker and Schmitt sketch a broad picture, highlighting divergent preferences and institutions across colonial powers, in particular Britain and France. In contrast, the two qualitative chapters both compare social protection trends within the British Empire, each comparing two former colonies. This allows the authors not only to show how legacies of the British Empire become manifest in specific cases, but also to shed light on differences within the British empire, the importance of contextual factors and how these factors can condition colonial legacies.

While the attention to detail of qualitative studies facilitates the exploration of the agencies of different actors, quantitative studies more commonly aim at testing the generalizability of specific claims. As such, they capture average effects across a variety of geographic regions or determine statistical relationships over long timeframes. Case-specific insights such as those uncovered in the chapters by Chinyoka and Ulriksen (Chap. 10, this volume), Künzler (Chap. 4, this volume) or Seekings (Chap. 5, this volume) can inform quantitative studies that test their applicability more broadly. Whether such testing is possible depends much on data availability and on how easily concepts unveiled by qualitative research can be operationalized for quantitative measurement. The latter challenge is especially pronounced in relation to qualitative research in the constructivist tradition (e.g. Haang'andu and Béland, Chap. 12, this volume).

With regard to most aspects, the chapters within this book volume, even though applying different methodological approaches, succeed with speaking to each other. They sometimes reinforced each other's findings, at other times prompting further debate. While such debates often originate at the divide between quantitative and qualitative research, it is important to note that such debates can also be evidenced within each camp. For example, the qualitative studies by Künzler (Chap. 4, this volume) and Seekings (Chap. 5, this volume) attest to the importance of colonialism for the formation of social protection-making, but Mioni and Petersen (Chap. 3, this volume) find that this effect can be eclipsed by other factors, in particular Cold War politics. However, these debates are necessary to identify the national and international conditions for the influence of external actors on social protection pathways.

## Taking Scope and Context into Account

In this book volume, the more quantitatively oriented chapters look at a broad set of countries, each covering the majority of the Global South. The qualitative chapters, with the exception of Mioni and Petersen

(Chap. 3, this volume) who compare two South East Asian countries (Burma and Malaysia), zoom in on different African countries or regions. These qualitative chapters provide a close look at actors' motivations, strategies and relationships that cannot be achieved by macro-quantitative approaches. Even though most qualitative chapters have focused on African countries, some expectations regarding the transferability of insights from these African case studies can be formulated. On the one hand, bilateral donors and international organizations are involved in the design of social protection and a wide range of other policies, all across the Global South, even if to varying degrees. While the role of contextual factors should not be underestimated, the centralized character of these actors provides some reason to believe that corresponding insights from African case studies might apply more broadly. On the other hand, there are colonialism and Cold War dynamics and the long-term legacies of actors involved in both. While almost all countries in the Global South were affected by colonialism at some point, the intensity it reached in Africa was not as common in other world regions. This is especially true for Latin America, which the Portuguese and Spanish colonized well before the 'Scramble for Africa'.

Second, the influence of colonialism and Cold War on social protection in dependent territories and the succeeding nation states is far from being uniform. Quantitative chapters point out to broad differences between colonial empires, especially the British and French. Qualitative chapters emphasize complex interactions with pre-existing conditions and how external influence is translated into local ideas and action. At the same time, there can be other important influences, such as the Cold War, that drown out or moderate the effect of colonial dependencies. As such, even if colonialism and colonial legacies are a unique feature of social protection-making in the Global South, it necessitates further research into interrelationships with other influences.

Such interrelationships between external actors and domestic factors are not limited to the pre-independence period. On the one hand, many colonial effects are likely to carry on, as, for example, Becker (Chap. 7, this volume) has shown for international aid provided by former colonial powers. On the other hand, contemporary actors have their own goals and interests and similarly adjust their behavior to domestic conditions.

The chapter by Çemen and Yörük (Chap. 9, this volume) on World Bank activities provides one such example. In addition to a new set of actors, there are other important differences between pre- and post-independence periods. For example, the sovereign control of external governments over territories in the Global South has largely vanished. Even though often these external governments still play a dominant role in countries that used to be under their control, they now have to compete for influence. How this new competition has altered these actors' responses to domestic conditions is an open question. While it goes beyond the scope of the present volume, research in this direction would provide further valuable insights.

## External Actors in the Global South and Global North

This volume, with its focus on the role of external actors for social protection in the Global South, also aimed at counterbalancing comparative social policy research that is heavily tilted toward industrialized economies in the Global North. This leads to the question of whether social protection-making in the Global South underlies rules and processes which are fundamentally different from what we know from the Global North in the light of the findings in this book volume.

When summarizing the chapters of this book volume, we do confirm that social protection-making is different in some respects. Those chapters focusing on the long-lasting influence of colonial and Cold War superpowers show that for decades foreign governments tried to interfere in political, social and economic affairs of dependent territories or countries in the Global South. This included past but also contemporary social protection-making. At least colonial influence is not so heavily present in much of the Global North. Other chapters in this volume point out the importance of international organizations and donors in social protection-making in the Global South today. These actors provide ideational and financial resources to promote a variety of policies, including social protection. While some of these actors also influence policy-making in the Global North, they tend to be most involved and effective in the Global South.

Moreover, most chapters in this volume have focused on external governmental and intergovernmental actors. While these actors play a central role on the international stage, be it historically within colonial empires or currently in the field of international development, they are not the only relevant ones. Research on welfare state development in the Global North emphasizes labor market questions and thus the role of firms. Economic actors such as companies should also play a decisive role in the Global South, where national governments compete for international investments and, more historically, where, for example, the large trading companies used to put strong demands on colonial governments.

Furthermore, it is worth reiterating and developing Barrientos' (Chap. 12, this volume) earlier warning that external actors, especially international organizations, have strongly invested in advising and guiding policy-making and implementation. Therefore, they should also have an interest in research on their role in the Global South.

Additionally, there is the risk of researchers overemphasizing the role of external actors. Many international organizations provide data sources that greatly facilitate research but also focus on topics these organizations are interested in.[2] As the impact of many external actors is considered to be global, or at least to affect a set of countries, it is also often easier for researchers to focus on the actions of external actors rather than to explore the actions of local actors who reside at multiple sites. As some chapters did in this volume, case studies—qualitative and quantitative—are a strategy that should be more frequently pursued. While they are time-consuming, costly and data is less available, they are important for shedding more light on domestic processes and on how local actors adjusted to independence and work with external actors today.

While social protection-making in the Global South is different from that in rich democracies, it is important to be cautious about overstating its uniqueness. A search for similarities with the Global North might be also fruitful and provide explanatory power (Kpessa and Béland 2013). In this volume, an example of such work is the chapter by Çemen and

---

[2] At the same time other external actors, presumably fearing law suits or economic losses, might be eager not to provide any data for research purposes.

Yörük (Chap. 9, this volume) who include countries from the Global South as well as the Global North in their analysis. Their findings suggest that the relationship between social unrest, World Bank involvement and social spending is comparably similar in both world regions.

# Outlook

The chapters in this volume suggest several avenues for future research that may help to further specify changes and continuities with regard to the role of external actors in social protection arrangements in the Global South amid the shift from colonialism to international aid. This section discusses the future outlook in relation to transnational approaches to research design and methodology, geographic scope of research on social protection in the Global South, and transnational dynamics and actor constellations that shape, and are shaped by, social protection.

## Transnational Approaches to Research Design and Methodology

From a conceptual standpoint, taking a transnational approach to research designs makes it possible to see how external actors and transnational relationships interact with domestic circumstances in ways that affect social protection arrangements in the Global South. From an analytical standpoint, while context is important to consider when analyzing social policy-making processes, greater emphasis needs to be placed on the identification of causal mechanisms, with attention to policy instruments, institutions and ideas in ways that are generalizable in order to contribute to theory-building. As illustrated by both Becker (Chap. 7, this volume) and Dodlova (Chap. 8, this volume), the presence of a policy instrument promoted or pushed by external actors such as development assistance/foreign aid provides a clear entry point through which to examine transnational processes affecting social protection in the Global South. Furthermore, the critical reflections by Haang'andu and Béland (Chap. 12, this volume) and Barrientos (Chap. 13, this volume) highlight the importance of viewing ideational and institutional mechanisms with a transnational lens first from the perspective of countries and peoples in the Global South, which draws attention to those aspects of social protection that are more deeply embedded rather than superficially imposed on countries.

Moreover, quantitative methods have distinct advantages in generalizability. However, generalizability is not only about sample size and average effects but also about the extent to which a finding in one context is applicable to another. The use of comparative methods of both the quantitative and qualitative varieties has the potential to make substantial theoretical contributions if thoughtfully designed. While it is important to keep pushing for higher quality comparable data on social protection systems throughout the Global South, strategically employing equivalencies in research designs also offers a way in which to extend the number of cases as well as a means of supporting pattern identification across different contexts in qualitative work. Together this could lead to theoretical advances in both quantitative and qualitative work that were previously unattainable.

Finally, this volume presents a clear call for more historical research in the social sciences. The findings by Schmitt (Chap. 6, this volume) suggest that colonial legacies play a key role in explaining differences in social protection arrangements in the Global South today, in ways that the shift to an international order has occluded. This is a critical methodological point. Transnational approaches to historical research help to ensure that external actors and transnational relationships influencing social protection arrangements during colonial times are not omitted from consideration, mistaken for being "new", or considered to be strictly domestic in nature. For instance, while the growth and role of non-governmental organizations have been increasingly recognized in recent literature on development and social protection, less attention has been paid to the way in which this growth is part of a broader shift away from religious missions and toward the secularization of third sector organizations, which began during colonialism and continued in the course of the twentieth century (Woodberry 2012; Dromi 2016). In sum, understanding how, in what ways and to what extent historical legacies affect current social protection arrangements requires an awareness of the ways in which transnational actors and relationships have impacted social protection arrangements over time.

## Geographic Scope

While many of the chapters have focused on Africa specifically, there is a need to expand understandings of the transition from colonialism to international aid to other regions, including Latin America, Asia and the Middle East. Moreover, international organizations but also colonial empires were often organized according to region. However, little is known about how regional geographies and organizations address cross-border challenges and affect social protection arrangements (Riggirozzi and Yeates 2015; Yeates 2014). For example, the foreign offices of colonial powers were often organized according to region, but also UN agencies are internally organized geographically. The effect of this on policy implementation remains largely unknown. Also, a growing number of regional organizations, ranging from the African Union to the League of Arab States to the South American Common Market, have all played a role in social policy-making throughout their member states. Additionally, there are countries and regions such as the Middle East or specific African and Asian states that are simply lesser examined in the literature, due to a lack of available data, language barriers, among other non-random factors.

Also, while this volume has focused predominantly on transnational relationships between the Global North and Global South, South-South cooperation and an increase in the number of middle-income countries (Surender and Urbina-Ferretjans 2015), transitioning from being recipients to donors, such as China, serves as a reminder that the future of transnational asymmetries may run from East to West as much as from North to South (Urbina-Ferretjans and Surender 2013). New lines of global conflict and contestation are likely to continue to shape the emergence of social protection; regional and sub-regional pockets of differentiation related to social protection, also referred to as "micro-paradigms" (von Gliszczynski and Leisering 2016), may emerge in line with current global trends and norms of social protection.

## Transnational Dynamics and Actor Constellations

This volume identified a shift in the transnational dynamics of social protection when moving from colonialism to the post-independence era. Current evidence suggests that the transformation of dependent territories into sovereign national states across the Global South might have empowered transnational actors. As territories throughout the Global South became sovereign nation states, former colonial powers were unable to utilize hard power instruments within these territories to achieve their aims. As a result, transnational actors, particularly intergovernmental organizations and international non-governmental organizations (Boli and Thomas 1997), were incentivized to exercise influence through soft power mechanisms.

Moreover, transnational actors such as intergovernmental organizations are not the only external actors that matter. As demonstrated particularly clearly in the case of Mioni and Petersen (Chap. 3, this volume), external influential national states might also behave transnationally. Superpowers such as the US and the former Soviet Union shaped the emergence of social protection arrangements in the Global South during the Cold War in line with their foreign policy interests and objectives. Considering how key states in the Global North view social protection within their foreign policy context may help to better understand the policy positions of international governmental organizations on social protection in the Global South. This is partly due to the fact that transnational actors appear to be of a dualistic nature. On the one hand, they are autonomous actors in their own right that may behave according to their own interests. On the other hand, they were largely created by, continue to receive financial support from, and may at times operate as instruments of powerful countries in the Global North. A better understanding of the interrelationships between influential nation states and international organizations, which also draw attention to the critical role of ideas and discourse in framing social protection in policy debates, would greatly enrich the state of the art.

Moreover, in line with Barrientos (Chap. 13, this volume), who emphasizes the importance of considering the drivers behind the emergence of domestic welfare institutions supporting social protection in the Global South, it may be important to re-examine the role of employers in the formation of social protection arrangements. From an historical standpoint, this requires considering the role and interests of concessional companies, as highlighted by Künzler (Chap. 4, this volume), in the formation of social protection arrangements during colonial times. The construction of labor markets and social protection in the Global South has clearly been impacted not only by colonialism but also by capitalism. While we know that social protection has been introduced in the Global South in a way that has been less clearly coordinated with domestic industrialization, we need to know more about the mechanisms through which employers exert influence on the structure of labor markets and social protection policies in the Global South as well as why, how and in what ways this legacy persists to date.

Considering transnational actor constellations and the ideas and institutions that influence their dynamics helps to address several gaps in the literature on social protection in the Global South by way of (1) specifying the linkages and asymmetries between external and domestic actors, factors and influences; (2) understanding how these relationships affect domestic policy-making environments in the Global South and (3) clarifying the mechanisms behind the introduction and reproduction of social protection arrangements. The emphasis placed on the need for transnational approaches (Shriwise, Chap. 2, this volume) should not be reduced to a focus on transnational actors alone (Barrientos, Chap. 13, this volume) nor should it exclude the examination of domestic/national actors and factors. The study of transnational actor constellations and their dynamics could help us to fill critical gaps in the literature. In so doing, we can gain a better understanding of the role of external actors for social protection-making in the Global South.

Finally, this work has critical implications for policy-making in the present. Careful research designs that are highly generalizable and the appropriate amalgamation and integration of findings across time and space can improve the quality of policy advice generated by academics, transnational actors and epistemic communities. For instance, the checklist generated by Devereux and Kapingidza (Chap. 11, this volume) serves as one example of a policy tool that can be iteratively refined in light of additional findings across a number of cases and contexts over time.

Theoretically situating case studies is critical to ensure coherent and pluralistic theoretical development on the emergence of social protection in the Global South in ways that help policy-makers to move beyond the simple recognition that context matters. In so doing, it becomes possible to produce better guidance that supports evidence-informed policy-making and supports more sophisticated approaches to advancing human and social rights in complex policy-making environments.

# References

Boli, John, and George M. Thomas. 1997. World Culture in the World Polity: A Century of International Non-Governmental Organization. *American Sociological Review* 62 (2): 171–190.

Dromi, Shai M. 2016. For Good and Country: Nationalism and the Diffusion of Humanitarianism in the Late Nineteenth Century. *The Sociological Review Monographs* 64 (2): 79–97.

Kpessa, Michael, and Daniel Béland. 2013. Mapping Social Policy Development in Sub-Saharan Africa. *Policy Studies* 34 (3): 326–341.

Riggirozzi, Pia, and Nicola Yeates. 2015. Locating Regional Health Policy: Institutions, Politics, and Practices. *Global Social Policy* 15 (3): 212–228.

Surender, Rebecca, and Marian Urbina-Ferretjans. 2015. 'New Kids on the Block?': The Implications of the BRICS Alliance for Global Social Governance. In *Actors and Agency in Global Social Governance*, ed. Alexandra Kaasch and Kerstin Martens, 130–152. Oxford: Oxford University Press.

Urbina-Ferretjans, Marian, and Rebecca Surender. 2013. Social Policy in the Context of New Global Actors: How Far Is China's Developmental Model in Africa Impacting Traditional Donors? *Global Social Policy* 13 (3): 261–279.

von Gliszczynski, Moritz, and L. Leisering. 2016. Constructing New Global Models of Social Security: How International Organizations Defined the Field of Social Cash Transfers in the 2000s. *Journal of Social Policy* 45 (2): 325–343.

Woodberry, Robert D. 2012. The Missionary Roots of Liberal Democracy. *American Political Science Review* 106 (2): 244–274.

Yeates, Nicola. 2014. The Socialization of Regionalism and the Regionalization of Social Policy: Contexts, Imperatives, and Challenges. In *Transformations in Global and Regional Social Policies*, ed. Alexandra Kaasch and Paul Stubbs, 17–43. Basingstoke: Palgrave Macmillan.

**Open Access** This chapter is licensed under the terms of the Creative Commons Attribution 4.0 International License (http://creativecommons.org/licenses/by/4.0/), which permits use, sharing, adaptation, distribution and reproduction in any medium or format, as long as you give appropriate credit to the original author(s) and the source, provide a link to the Creative Commons licence and indicate if changes were made.

The images or other third party material in this chapter are included in the chapter's Creative Commons licence, unless indicated otherwise in a credit line to the material. If material is not included in the chapter's Creative Commons licence and your intended use is not permitted by statutory regulation or exceeds the permitted use, you will need to obtain permission directly from the copyright holder.

# Index[1]

### A

Actor constellation, 7, 21, 31–35, 161–182, 370, 373–375
African National Congress (ANC), 113, 120–122
Agenda for Sustainable Development, 20
Agricultural workers, 61
AIDS, 247, 250–254, 252n4, 257, 287, 363
Anti-Communism, 11, 47, 57, 361
Anti-Fascist People's Freedom League (AFPFL), 51, 53, 65, 72
Anti-government demonstration, 227, 227n4, 232, 233, 237
Apartheid, 113, 114, 118, 119, 131
ASPIRE, 338

### B

*Bantu*, 319
Bechuanaland (later Botswana) Democratic Party (BDP), 124–126, 128, 129, 247, 252–254, 257, 259–264
Bayesian models, 176
Bilateral aid, 163, 166, 169–171, 173, 178, 180, 181, 189, 193
Binary time-series cross-section (BTSCS), 139, 149–151, 154, 155
Bismarckian, 117
Botswana, 12–14, 109–131, 143, 245–266, 283, 284, 359, 363, 364
Brazzaville Conference 1944, 49

---

[1] Note: Page numbers followed by 'n' refer to notes.

Bricolage, 307–312, 325–328
British colonial heritage, 47, 359
British colonial legacy, 79, 153
British colony, 12, 13, 48n1, 49–54, 85, 87n8, 102, 110, 111, 122, 127, 140, 143–145, 149, 153, 154, 156, 174, 175, 341, 360, 362
British Empire, 51, 58, 109, 112, 115, 123, 140, 143–145, 154, 167, 169, 361, 365, 366
British government, 59, 69, 166–169, 324
British Poor Laws, 143, 144, 156, 358
Burma, 12, 45–73, 359–361, 364, 367

C

Case studies, 6, 33–35, 72, 109, 112, 206, 208, 209, 215, 238, 248, 273–299, 317–328, 365, 367, 369, 375
Cash crop economy, 12, 82, 82n4, 98, 359
Cash transfers, 27, 30, 80, 90, 93–98, 100, 101n13, 127, 128, 149, 196, 207, 246, 247, 250, 257–259, 261, 263, 266, 274, 276, 277, 279, 286n5, 287–289, 287n6, 293, 295, 297–299, 338, 363
Child welfare policies, 13, 247–250, 264, 266
China, 4, 45, 52, 53, 60, 229, 372
*Code de la Famille*, 146
*Code de L'Indigénat*, 146, 147
Code du Travail, 11, 110, 147, 358

Cold War, 4, 9–12, 45–73, 347, 359–361, 364, 366, 367, 373
Cold War superpowers, 6, 11, 12, 368
*Colonial Development and Welfare Act*, 58
Colonial empires, 4, 139, 145, 156, 161, 162, 164, 166, 167, 169, 173, 182, 265, 358, 367, 369, 372
Colonial Office, 54, 84, 98, 99, 101, 102, 122–124, 143
Colonial officers, 84, 98, 99, 101, 102
Colonial subjects, 123, 146, 167
Commonwealth, 50–52, 57–59, 64, 67, 361
Communism, 6, 46, 47, 49, 52, 53, 55, 57–60, 63–72
Communist regimes, 4
Community leaders, 311, 326
Conditional cash transfer programmes, 94, 100, 265
Constructivist, 8, 312, 328, 329, 366
Consultants, 25, 127, 258, 274, 277, 279, 284, 288, 295, 298
Contentious politics, 221–238
Corruption, 97, 195

D

De-coupling, 88
Demand, 4, 85, 89, 112, 120, 142, 151, 231, 307, 311–315, 317, 318, 328, 365, 369
Democracy, 4, 53, 55, 57, 114, 141, 151, 153, 154, 162, 173, 174,

177–179, 204, 206, 208, 210, 216, 230, 232, 311, 338, 369
Democratic institutions, 63, 139, 141, 142, 153, 154, 156, 224, 363
Department for International Development (DFID), 90, 92, 94, 95, 97, 111, 127, 192, 198–201, 208, 211, 212, 246, 273, 276, 277, 279, 289, 291, 292, 297, 359, 360, 362
Dependent territories, 4, 10, 11, 28, 48, 140n3, 142–144, 169, 181, 367, 368, 373
Developing countries, 9, 12, 14, 23, 30, 63, 137, 139, 156, 166, 171, 174, 189–192, 195, 196, 198, 202, 203, 206, 207, 209, 212–216, 224, 237, 321
Developmental state, 120
Disability policies, 316–319, 322, 325, 328, 329, 362
Donor-driven, 14, 274, 275, 298
Drought relief, 113, 122–126, 128–131

E

Economic exploitation, 164, 167
Economic liberalization, 335
Education, 5, 30, 62, 64, 65, 69, 72, 80–87, 89–92, 92n10, 95, 100, 111–113, 115, 117, 120, 123, 126, 140n2, 163, 169, 171, 180, 190n1, 195, 196, 207, 248, 251, 282, 286, 327, 341, 361, 362
Education policies, 5

Emerging market economies (EMEs), 221, 226, 227
*Employer's Liability Scheme*, 69, 70
Employment guarantee scheme, 191, 199, 206, 213
Employment injury, 62, 69, 84
Endogeneity, 203, 325

F

Family allowances, 85, 99, 102, 110, 145–148, 191, 196, 200, 207, 208, 213, 345, 362
Family-based benefits, 250, 257
Family cash-transfers, 257
Family policies, 146, 147, 149, 153
Famine relief, 5, 86, 88, 99, 102, 362
Feeding schemes, 124, 125, 246–248
Food security programmes, 5
Foreign aid, 48, 51, 56, 66, 120, 192–195, 370
Formal employment, 82, 115, 116, 118, 165, 168
Formal labor market, 84, 138, 147
Framing, 21, 114, 309, 312, 320, 323, 326, 327, 373
French colonies, 13, 48n1, 110–112, 140, 147, 148, 150, 153, 154, 156, 174, 175, 362
French Union, 167, 168

G

Gender policies, 306, 317, 318, 320, 322
German Institute for International Cooperation (GIZ), 212

Global institutions, 21, 28–31, 33, 35
Global social policy, 8, 9, 24, 27, 32, 33, 35, 246, 339, 345, 346, 349
Governance, 8, 20, 22–24, 26, 28, 36, 195, 264n10, 279, 320
Great Britain, 114, 143, 145, 148

### H

Hard power, 10, 346, 360, 373
Health care, 80, 84, 87–92, 100, 117, 118, 120, 121, 123, 137, 190n1, 221, 285, 286
Health policies, 64, 190, 214
Hearts and minds, 45, 48, 59, 65, 72
HelpAge International, 127, 149
HIV, 82, 250, 251, 252n4, 254, 287, 318
Human capital, 149, 190, 190n1, 191, 196, 197, 207, 208, 213, 262, 282, 286, 348
Human rights, 63, 142, 282, 286, 294–296, 344

### I

Ideational approach, 14, 305–329, 349
Ideational framework, 307–319
Independence, 47, 48, 50–53, 58–60, 69, 70, 72, 79n1, 85, 87, 87n8, 96, 101, 110, 111, 119, 122–124, 139, 147, 148, 151, 165, 166, 247, 251, 321, 341, 364, 369
Indigenous population, 164

Individual retirement accounts, 336, 341, 342, 351
Industrialization, 8, 49, 55, 61, 72, 130, 131, 143, 223, 374
Institutionalist approach, 306, 307, 317, 328
Interdependencies, 8, 33, 334–336, 343, 344, 351, 352
Intergovernmental organizations, 8, 10, 23, 25, 27, 30, 33, 373
International aid, 13, 161–182, 247, 357–360, 363, 367, 370, 372
International development agencies, 274
International Labour Organization (ILO), 4, 20, 93, 116, 138, 168, 273, 334, 359
International Monetary Fund (IMF), 27, 87, 227, 305, 359
International relations (IR), 21–26, 28–30, 36

### K

Kenya, 12, 79–103, 277, 288, 297, 341, 359, 361, 363

### L

Labor movements, 47, 85, 85n7, 142, 233
Labor reserve economy, 81, 82, 112, 359
Left parties, 343

Logic of interpretation, 307, 309
Logic of position, 307–309
Low- and middle-income countries (LMIC), 3n1, 14, 137–141, 150, 153, 154, 156, 170, 170n2, 181, 333–337, 340, 342, 343, 345, 347–352

M

Malawi, 97, 212, 276, 277, 279, 287, 288, 320–322
Malaysia, 12, 45–73, 341, 359–361, 364, 367
Middle East and North Africa (MENA), 193
Migration, 22–24, 36, 86, 161, 164, 168, 226, 335, 348
Millennium Development Goals (MDGs), 90–92, 306, 318
Ministry of Overseas Territories, 147
Mugabe, Robert, 275, 296
Multilaterals, 4, 172n3, 189, 230n8, 246, 273, 279, 294, 333, 340, 343, 345, 346, 350, 350n17, 351, 359
Muslim, 79

N

Nationally owned, 14, 275, 284, 296, 298
Noncontributory social protection, 138, 139n1, 141, 149, 151, 362
Non-contributory social transfer programmes (NSTP), 13, 191, 195, 198–200, 202, 203, 338

Non-governmental organizations (NGOs), 4, 8, 10, 19, 23–25, 27, 33, 61, 95, 103, 172, 193, 195, 274, 276, 278, 285, 371, 373

O

Old age, 11, 62, 83–85, 103, 110, 117, 118, 123, 128, 129, 144, 145, 149, 199, 213, 221, 231, 247
Orphan, 94, 128, 207, 247, 248, 251–257, 260–262, 264
Orphan Care Programme (OCP), 247, 248, 250–257, 260–262, 264, 266

P

Paradigm shift, 313, 349, 350
Pension funds, 85, 116, 121
Pension policy, 93
Phenomenological approaches, 343, 344
Philadelphia Declaration, 62
Policy adoption, 335, 340–342
Policy change, 26, 30, 85, 89, 91, 100, 238, 307, 310, 313, 315–318, 322, 325, 327, 345, 346
Policy diffusion, 189–216, 274, 305–310, 312–329, 336, 337, 339–342, 352
Policy implementation, 25, 26, 30, 192, 372
Policy transfer, 121, 130, 287, 299, 307–312, 336, 337, 340, 341

Post-colonial, 12, 48, 72, 80, 82, 83n5, 102, 110, 111, 251
Post-independence, 131, 359, 360, 368, 373
Poverty, 59, 62, 68, 70, 80, 80n2, 91, 120, 121, 123, 126–128, 130, 138, 148, 149, 155, 165, 173, 190, 190n1, 192, 193, 197, 200, 201, 206, 211, 213–215, 222, 224, 225, 238, 248, 250, 252, 256–263, 277, 282, 286, 287, 296, 334, 348, 364
Power asymmetries, 10, 28, 328
Process tracing, 33–35, 339, 340
Prospera, 197, 209
Provident funds, 85, 120, 121, 143, 168, 336, 341, 351
Public education, 113, 115, 117
Public health, 67, 112, 172
Pyidawtha Plan, 65–67, 71

R

Realist approaches, 343
Recipient countries, 163, 173, 174, 181, 189, 190, 192–195, 197, 203, 208, 212, 215, 365
Rights-based approach, 11, 266, 278, 285, 319, 362, 364

S

School feeding programme (SFP), 248, 249
Second World War, 4, 11, 28, 49, 51, 55, 61, 83–85, 115, 122, 140, 142, 144
Social assistance, 7, 11, 13, 14, 56, 101, 101n13, 110, 112–117, 119–121, 127, 129–131, 137–156, 190, 192, 195, 198, 199, 201, 213, 222, 225, 229, 255, 259, 261, 262, 278, 280, 281, 284, 286, 333–341, 334n3, 343, 345, 348–351
Social containment hypothesis, 223
Social insurance, 7, 11, 54, 60, 62, 64, 85, 93, 110, 112, 115, 116, 118, 120, 130, 137–141, 145–148, 153, 156, 284, 334, 341, 358, 362
Social investment, 335, 348, 349n15, 350
Social pensions, 93, 97, 115–117, 119, 127, 131, 138, 140, 145, 148–156, 191, 199, 200, 206, 207, 213, 222, 281, 283, 286, 345, 362
Social protection floor, 11, 20, 24, 127, 266, 285, 286
Social unrest, 13, 46, 71, 222, 223, 225–227, 227n4, 231–235, 237, 361, 363, 370
Soft power, 48, 274, 295, 298, 373
South Africa, 12, 13, 83, 98, 109–131, 144, 145, 149, 250, 253, 258, 277, 283–285, 359
South East Asia (SEA), 45–49, 54–64, 71, 72, 364
Strikes, 85, 142, 147, 223, 227, 227n4, 232, 235, 237, 363
Sub-Saharan Africa (SSA), 87, 93, 246, 247, 277, 282, 306, 307, 310, 317–329, 334n3, 337n5, 339, 340, 364

Supply, 57, 62, 67, 83, 172, 307, 312–315, 317, 318, 326, 328
Sustainable Development Goals (SDGs), 209

T

Tanganyika, 79n1, 80–87, 82n4, 98, 99, 101–103, 359
Tanzania, 12, 79–103, 143, 265, 341, 361
Targeting mechanism
  categorical, 191, 199–201, 211–213, 362
  community-based, 191, 192, 199, 201, 209, 212, 214
  geographical, 191, 199–201, 213
  means testing, 191, 199, 201, 362
  proxy means testing, 191, 192, 199, 201, 212, 213
  self-targeting, 191, 199, 201
Tax, 79–83, 95, 99, 137, 201, 227n3, 282
Tax-financed social policies, 101
Technical assistance, 63, 211, 289, 294
Trade unions, 19, 25, 54, 68, 120, 121, 343
Translation, 307–312, 325–328, 364
Transnational actors, 4, 9, 13, 14, 19–22, 25–36, 246, 247, 250, 257, 260, 261, 263–266, 273, 274, 305–329, 333–352, 371, 373, 374
Transnational law, 23, 24

U

*Ubuntu*, 319, 320
Uhuru Kenyatta, 91, 95
Unconditional cash transfer programmes, 94, 287n6
Unconditional family support programmes, 138, 140, 141, 149, 153, 156, 362
United Nations International Children's Emergency Fund (UNICEF), 92, 94, 95, 127, 129, 190–192, 196, 198, 200, 201, 207, 208, 211–213, 250, 251, 253–255, 257–259, 273, 275, 277, 278, 284–286, 287n6, 288–297, 361–363
United States (US), 4, 45, 46, 48–51, 53–57, 57n11, 59–61, 63, 65–67, 71, 72, 80, 101n14, 175, 178, 193, 194, 224, 225, 248, 252, 252n4, 360, 361, 373
UNU-WIDER, 191, 198

V

Vulnerable children, 94, 96n11, 207, 252, 254–257, 260, 261, 264, 266

W

Wage earners, 70
Washington Consensus, 348, 349
Welfare institutions, 3, 5, 14, 29, 334–336, 341–343, 350n17, 351, 352, 374

Welfare state, 3, 46–48, 48n1, 50, 55, 64, 66, 67, 73, 113–122, 126, 129, 130, 140, 141, 146–149, 153, 156, 221–226, 334, 348, 351, 369
Welfare state regimes, 29
White settlers, 82–84, 98, 99n12, 102, 123
World Bank, 3n1, 4, 8, 11, 13, 26, 87, 90–97, 100, 101n13, 101n14, 127, 129, 138, 156, 170n2, 173, 190–192, 194, 195, 197, 198, 200, 201, 203, 207–209, 211–213, 221–238, 274, 277, 278, 281, 282, 284–286, 292–297, 305, 334, 334n3, 338, 342, 348, 348n14, 349, 349n15, 359, 361–363, 368, 370
World Bank social policy recommendations (WBSPRs), 222, 223, 227, 229–232, 235, 237, 238
World Food Programme (WFP), 114, 124–127, 129, 131, 192, 196, 198–200, 208, 209, 211, 214, 248, 276, 286, 359
World Polity Theory, 88
World society, 344–346, 349

Z

Zambia, 123, 143, 265, 274, 276, 277, 287, 288, 320–324, 327, 341
Zimbabwe, 14, 250, 253, 256, 273–299, 361, 363

The manufacturer's authorised representative in the EU is Springer Nature Customer Service Centre GmbH, Europaplatz 3, 69115 Heidelberg, Germany. If you have any concerns regarding our products, please contact ProductSafety@springernature.com

Printed and bound by CPI Group (UK) Ltd, Croydon, CR0 4YY
25/03/2026
02078175-0009